Public Lives, Private Secrets

Public Lives, Private Secrets

GENDER, HONOR, SEXUALITY,
AND ILLEGITIMACY IN
COLONIAL SPANISH AMERICA

Ann Twinam

STANFORD UNIVERSITY PRESS
STANFORD, CALIFORNIA

Stanford University Press
Stanford, California

© 1999 by the Board of Trustees of the Leland Stanford Junior University

Published with the assistance of the Charles Phelps Taft Memorial Fund,
University of Cincinnati

Printed in the United States of America
CIP data appear at the end of the book

To the 244, the 13, and Andy

Acknowledgments

This project has taken many years, and in the process has been helped along by many people whose support I gratefully acknowledge. My first thank-you must go to those unknown persons, whose names I do not know, who spent untold thousands of hours over the past two hundred years in archives throughout Spain and Latin America. Without their catalogues and indexes this work would not exist.

Special thanks to those professionals who guard these archival treasures today. These include the staffs of the following institutions: the Archivo General de Indias (Seville); the Archivo Histórico Nacional (Madrid); the Archivo General de Simancas; the Archivo Histórico de Guanajuato; the Archivo General de la Nación (Mexico City); the Archivo Histórico Nacional (Bogotá); the Archivo Histórico de Antioquia (Medellín); the Archivo del Consejo de Medellín; the Archivo Nacional Histórico (Quito); the Archivo General de la Nación (Lima); the Archivo Departamental de La Libertad (Trujillo); the Archivo Departamental de Arequipa; the Archivo Nacional de Bolivia (Sucre); the Archivo General de la Nación (Buenos Aires); the Archivo General de la Nación (Caracas); the Archivo Arzobispal (Havana); the Archivo del Consejo Municipal (Havana); the Biblioteca Nacional (Havana); the Biblioteca Nacional (Madrid); and the Newberry Library (Chicago). I am especially grateful to the staff of the Archivo Nacional (Santiago), who not only anticipated my arrival but also let me into the archives even though the building was closed because of a water shortage!

I particularly recognize the assistance of Maria Antonia Colomar Albajar, Pilar Fájaro de la Escosura, Manuel Romero Fallafigo, and Rosario Parra in Seville; Isabel Aguirre in Simancas; Julio Le Riverend, Luis Hartley-Campbell, and Leandro Romero Estébanez in Havana; Grecia Vasco de Escudero and P. Zambrano in Quito; Alicia Pérez Luque, Irma Leticia Arellano

Bustos, and Marina Rodríguez in Guanajuato; Lydia Sada de González in
Monterrey; Herlinda del Aguila Bartra and Nora Romero Sánchez in Lima;
Gunnar Mendoza and Hernán Rodríguez in Sucre; and Regina Solís Jara
Graciela Swiderski, Rosana Zavagilia, and Liliana Crespi in Buenos Aires.
My days in Colombian archives became warm homecomings thanks to Pa-
tricia Londoño, Beatriz Patiño Millán, Roberto Luis Jaramillo, Victor Al-
varez (who generously shared archival notes), Cecília Inés Restrepo, Juan
Manuel Ospina, Pablo Rodríguez, and everyone at FAES (Fundación Antio-
queño para los Estudios Sociales).

A number of colleagues provided intellectual support and helpful criticism along the way. My special thank-you to Asunción Lavrin, who suggested additional readings, sent pithy e-mails, read the final manuscript with
a critical eye, and became a cheerleader and a friend. A brilliant reader's report by Linda Lewin pinpointed flaws, helping me to improve the manuscript greatly. Judith Daniels dissected the manuscript word by word, combating wordiness, enhancing logic, and fixing grammar—and we are still
speaking! John TePaske helped me grapple with monetary issues; Mark
Burkholder guided me through the intricacies of Bourbon administration;
and Robert McCaa quelled my anxieties about the demographic analysis.

Others who offered their knowledge and support include Susan Socolow,
Solita Villalón, Lynn Stoner, Ken Andrien, Francie Chassen-López, Lyman
Johnson, William Taylor, Frank Safford, and Ramón Gutiérrez. Fritz Schwal-
ler and Gaston Gabriel Doucet made sure that microfilm orders arrived from
Lima and Buenos Aires. Richard Morse, my dissertation advisor, encouraged
me at the very start; Natalie Zemon Davis and John Lombardi helped secure
funding in the middle. At the University of Cincinnati, Zane Miller, Roger
Daniels, and Barbara Ramusack cheered me on, and the gang at interlibrary
loan deserve medals. And yes, I promised the students in my "Gender and
Latin American History" class (fall 1996) that I would remember their helpful comments on key chapters.

I must thank the American Philosophical Society, which funded me at
the start when I was not sure the documents could be found; the Spanish
Fulbright Commission, which supported my research in Seville; and the
Tinker Foundation, which provided me with a year off so that I could master computer techniques and consult South American archives. Resources
from the University of Cincinnati were fundamental: The University Research Council supported microfilm expenses and research trips to Cuba

and Mexico; the Charles Phelps Taft Foundation helped with microfilm expenses and research in Spanish archives, and also provided key support during a sabbatical; and the Institute for Policy Research guided me through the intricacies of computer codes and SAS.

The final efforts that turn a manuscript into a published work can often be traumatic. Thanks to the professionals at Stanford University Press (Norris Pope, editor; Stacey Lynn, associate editor; Martin Hanft, copyeditor), the last months have been a pleasure.

And then there is my husband. In our household, When The Book Is Done became a mantra that explained postponed vacations, delayed house repairs, hasty meals, deferred entertainments, and much, much more. Andy maintained his usual grace, understanding, and sense of humor. He proved to be an invaluable research partner and note-taker throughout Spain, Mexico, Bolivia, Chile, and Argentina—and he also listened over and over as I worked it out. He remains my bulwark and soulmate everywhere and always.

A.T.

Contents

Maps and Tables

Public Lives, Private Secrets

PART ONE

Introduction

ONE

Antecedents

It is not often that an author knows where the idea for a book was born, but the incident that precipitated this work occurred on a street in Medellín, Colombia, more than two hundred years ago. In 1787, Don Pedro Elefalde, a new royal official in town, exchanged greetings with Gabriel Muñoz, a local merchant. It is impossible to know precisely what Don Pedro said; it might well have been "Buenos dias, Gabriel," but it was clearly not "Buenos dias, *Don* Gabriel."[1] The encounter became historic precisely because Don Pedro did not use the prefix "Don," an honorific invariably invoked whenever elite peers encountered each other within the town.[2] Gabriel Muñoz was so incensed by this omission that he engaged in an expensive and protracted lawsuit, the sole purpose of which was to force the royal official to call him "Don" and to show him the proper respect.

I would like to think that I did not smile too much when, as a graduate student, I first ran across the documents chronicling his lengthy lawsuit. As a novice, however, and deeply engaged in research on such "hard" data as mining records and merchant registers, I was certainly amused that such an insignificant incident could produce such an avalanche of papers. By the end of my archival stay, I was—I think—somewhat wiser, and certainly more trusting of the intelligence and the common sense of those whose lives I had been privileged to study. As the years passed, and I learned more concerning Gabriel Muñoz's world, I reread his lawsuit with serious interest and growing understanding.

My first insight was that his complaint provided a fascinating glimpse into that usually hidden process through which local notables recognized each other as peers. Don Pedro Elefalde, a royal official, testified that he had omitted the honorific "not because I wanted to injure him, but because I had examples of others who did not do so."[3] His remarks instantly illuminated how a newcomer might use the visual and verbal cues provided by other members of the local elite to decide who did, and who did not, belong. Embedded in a simple hello could be underlying codes that precisely located an individual's rank within the social hierarchy.

It was only later that I realized that, while Don Pedro Elefalde's remarks were insightful, the even greater puzzle rested with the merchant's arguments. Gabriel Muñoz did not base his lawsuit on whether he was entitled to the title of "Don," the basis for which was legitimate descent from parents of high status. Instead of producing his genealogy or his baptismal certificate, he rested his plea on the more oblique reasoning that he was treated as a "Don," that he had done things that only "Dons" could do, and that therefore he must certainly be a "Don." He argued that only "Dons" had ever been voted by the local elite to host the annual town fiesta or to hold public office, and he pointed out that he had done both of those.[4] He plaintively noted that he would never have questioned whether Don Pedro Elefalde should be called "Don," since as an office holder he surely merited the title. Gabriel Muñoz simply insisted that he deserved the same consideration, for his civic service proved that he also was a "Don."

What is going on here? Why did Don Pedro Elefalde get a cue, as he must have done from at least some members of Medellín's elite, that Gabriel Muñoz was not to be called Don? Why did the merchant not prove that he was a Don, but rather argue that it was his engagement in, so to speak, Don-like activities that made him a "Don"? What can be learned from the unspoken but underlying meanings of this confrontation over a proper hello?

On one level the answer is simple, for by the traditional standards of Medellín's elite—or, indeed, by those of most colonial Spanish-American elites—Gabriel Muñoz was not a Don. Although he was white, a relatively

well-off merchant, and the son of one of the most powerful men in town—
he was also illegitimate. Elite Medellinenses were generally scrupulous in
denying the honorific of Don to those of "defective" birth.[5] Although Gabriel Muñoz's connections and wealth had apparently motivated many to
make an informal exception in his case, his acceptance was not universal.
Some local notables still refused to recognize him as a peer. Don Pedro Elefalde had but copied their example when he omitted the coveted address.
This was why Gabriel Muñoz felt that he had to sue, for he rightfully perceived that this omission threatened his precarious social position. Fundamental perceptions regarding how status might be accorded were at the heart
of this simple clash over a hello: One standard awarded or withheld honorific titles according to ascriptive criteria such as birth; another permitted a
modicum of social mobility when the subject was rich or well connected.

But this insight suggests an even greater mystery. Since Gabriel Muñoz
was so personally vulnerable, given his illegitimacy, why did he press the issue? Wasn't he clearly destined to lose, inasmuch as illegitimates were not
customarily addressed with the honorific of Don? The merchant apparently
believed that he could make a case by arguing that his civic service reflected
an alternative and publicly established reality. Totally bypassing the issue of
illegitimacy, he argued that his reputation as a "Don" should be accepted on
his public merits, and he more or less begged the question of whether his
public persona need be the same as his private reality. The royal official who
heard Muñoz's case recognized such duality, for he ordered Don Pedro Elefalde to address the merchant as Don. His ruling effectively sanctioned the
disparity between the private reality of illegitimacy and the public persona
as "Don." The resolution of this seemingly simple conflict illuminated a
profound duality in Hispanic culture that permitted individuals to have different status in their private and their public spheres.

Although Don Gabriel Muñoz won his lawsuit, he remained anxious
about the security of his position. He applied to the Cámara, a subcouncil of
the Council of the Indies, to purchase an official decree of legitimation
known as a *cédula de gracias al sacar*.[6] This document literally permitted him
to change his birth status, confirming that he was officially legitimate, honorable, and worthy of the title of Don. The Medellín elite responded even
more enthusiastically to this royal confirmation of his standing, for he was
promptly elected to one of the most prestigious positions on the city council, a post never held by those who were illegitimate.[7]

My attention was initially caught by Don Gabriel Muñoz's problem, and by the legitimation decree that had confirmed his social mobility and that had changed his life. His quest for a proper hello had led him far beyond his mountain-locked Andean valley, to seek redress from officials in Spain. His search revealed tantalizing hints of those usually hidden processes through which colonial elites ordered their social relationships and constructed their worlds. I wondered if there might not be other Don Gabriel Muñozes with similar problems, who had sought equivalent resolutions, and whose life stories might provide further insight into colonial ways.

It turned out that Don Gabriel Muñoz was not alone in his quest, for his petition joined 243 others that streamed into Spain from all corners of the Spanish-American empire, as illegitimates from Florida and Louisiana, the Caribbean, Mexico, and Central and South America sought relief. Their detailed depositions revealed that their decisions to appeal were not made lightly; sometimes years passed between the first gathering of testimony and the submission of the application.

The price of legitimation proved to be much higher than the fees paid for the *gracias al sacar*. The preparation of a detailed deposition could be a personally painful process that rekindled forgotten anguish and shame. Unwed mothers testified about their broken engagements, their pregnancies, and sometimes even included love letters from their now-estranged lovers. Fathers recalled past affairs, admitted their rejection of pregnant fiancées, or relived the death in childbirth of prospective spouses. Illegitimates vividly described the embarrassments and frustrations that marked their lives, and they sometimes provided specific references to those humiliating incidents that had finally motivated them to seek a decree. The testimony could span several generations as witnesses not only commented on the plight of the lovers but also on that of their illegitimate children, and even their grandchildren.

Anyone with relevant knowledge might become a participant in the legitimation process. When parents proved unavailable, illegitimates called upon town elders to dredge up their memories of past gossip and scandals. Members of older generations became oral historians as their remembrances were woven into a record that preserved the secret and intimate histories of their communities. When such testimonies arrived in Spain royal officials debated which situations merited redress, and in the process they forged policies that became part of that collective of measures known as the Bourbon Reforms (1759–1808).

Such testimonies revise and enhance our understanding of gender relationships, sexual mores, and illegitimacy in Spanish America. They provide insight into those processes that sometimes abetted and sometimes hindered social and racial mobility as the colonial era drew to a close. Since the personal quest of Don Gabriel Muñoz to be legitimated intersects with many such matters, let us begin with him.

ILLEGITIMACY AND THE EIGHTEENTH CENTURY: CONTINENTS COMPARED

For more than twenty years demographers and historians have designated the eighteenth century as the century of illegitimacy. Edward Shorter was among those who observed that "in every city in England and the continent for which data are available, the upsurge in illegitimacy commenced around 1750 or before."[8] Continuing research in England (Newman; Rogers), Scotland (Mitchison and Leneman), France (Depauw; Meyer; Segalen), Germany (Knodel and Hochstadt; Lee; Watt), Italy (Kertzer), and the United States (Rothman; Smith; Wells) has substantiated a rise in illegitimacy rates between the 1740s and 1780s, with only central Europe (Gieysztor [Poland]; Palli [Estonia]) as an exception.[9] Demographers and historians have not been shy in assigning significance to this trend. John D. Post concluded that it marked "the modern rise of European population," while Peter Laslett described it as "one of the outstanding discoveries of sociological history."[10]

To what extent was the illegitimacy of Don Gabriel Muñoz, or the 244 applications for *gracias al sacar*, or eighteenth-century rates of illegitimacy in Spanish America any part of this trend? Comparative exploration of demographic patterns in Europe and the United States, as well as the debate over their significance, is critical, for—at least on the surface—there appears to be a striking correlation between the rise of illegitimacy in the West and increased Spanish-American applications for legitimation. More than half of *cédula* petitioners appealed after the demographic benchmark at the middle of the eighteenth century (see Table 1). Does this post-1760 flood of applications reflect real increases in the pool of illegitimates in colonial Spanish America? Does this pattern parallel the findings for Europe and for the United States, or had other historical processes been at work?

Such questions take on an additional importance, given the ongoing de-

TABLE I

Frequency and Percentages of 'Cédula' Petitions by 'Audiencia' and Decade

Audiencia	before 1720	1720	1730	1740	1750	1760	1770	1780	1790	1800	1810	1820	Total	Percent
Buenos Aires	—	—	—	—	—	1	3	3	9	2	—	—	18	7.4
Caracas	—	—	—	1	—	—	1	5	1	1	—	—	9	3.7
Charcas	—	—	—	—	—	—	1	—	6	4	—	—	11	4.5
Chile	—	—	—	—	—	—	—	1	4	—	—	—	5	2.0
Guadalajara	—	—	—	—	—	2	1	2	—	—	—	—	5	2.0
Guatemala	1	—	—	—	—	1	—	5	5	1	1	—	14	5.7
Lima	1	—	—	—	—	—	1	10	9	6	2	—	29	11.9
Mexico City	3	1	1	4	4	3	1	9	5	3	2	1	37	15.2
Panama	—	—	—	—	—	1	—	1	2	—	—	—	4	1.6
Quito	2	—	—	—	—	—	—	—	3	3	—	—	8	3.3
Santo Domingo	—	6	1	5	1	5	3	20	23	4	21	—	89	36.5
Santa Fe	2	—	—	—	—	1	—	3	4	3	2	—	15	6.2
Total	9	7	2	10	5	14	11	59	71	27	28	1	244	100.0
Percent	3.7	2.9	.8	4.1	2.0	5.7	4.5	24.2	29.1	11.1	11.5	.4	100.0	

SOURCE: DB 1-244. See Appendix 1.

bate among historians over the question of why European and U.S. illegitimacy was on the rise in the first place. Edward Shorter presented one side of the issue when he proposed his classic iceberg metaphor. He suggested that "sexuality in traditional society may be thought of as a great iceberg, frozen by the command of custom, by the need . . . for stability at the cost of individuality and by the dismal grind of daily life."[11] Shorter postulated that an eighteenth-century meltdown produced real changes in sexual expression that led to greater individual choice for lovers and a transformation from a "manipulative" to an "expressive" sexuality, in which couples engaged in sexual intercourse more often prior to marriage and more often for their own enjoyment.

Faced with criticism that his theory outpaced his proof, Shorter later backtracked, but he still insisted that the rise in illegitimacy signified a substantive change in mentality: a "sudden rejection by a whole generation of young people of their parents' values towards premarital intercourse."[12] Lawrence Stone furthered the debate when he wondered "why so few girls in the seventeenth century in English and New England rural communities allowed themselves to be impregnated by their swains before marriage in church, and why so many did so in the eighteenth century."[13] Stone's assumption, that the critical change was a shift from the resistance to premarital sexual intercourse by seventeenth-century women to the more liberal attitudes of their eighteenth-century counterparts, has also proved controversial.

A logical alternative might be that women of both centuries engaged in premarital intercourse at more or less the same rate, but that eighteenth-century liaisons were less likely to end in marriage. An influential article by Louise A. Tilly et al. presented another side of the debate, proposing that most women who produced illegitimate children "expected to get married." The structural changes that accompanied nascent industrialization and urbanization—"propertylessness, poverty, large scale geographic mobility, occupational instability"—created social dislocations that made it more difficult for lovers to marry.[14] Couples began sexual relationships with "established expectations" but failed to fulfill them because of "changing contexts."[15] In addition, as Rosalind Mitchison and Leah Leneman later pointed out, historians could not necessarily assume that women's attitudes were solely responsible for change: "Conception, within or without wedlock, is not parthenogenetic. . . . Unless we are to see the entire male sex as invariably set on seduction we must enquire into the motives and deliberations of both parents."[16]

Subsequent historiography has supported a range of positions that substantiate variants of both the changed mentality and the thwarted expectations hypotheses. Those who favor the mentality side of the equation have explored alterations in courtship rules, including increasing potential for personal choice in spouses, a search for greater compatibility, the proclivity for earlier sexual intimacy, increased pressure for premarital sexual intercourse, and lessened moral condemnation of out-of-wedlock sexuality and illegitimacy. Supporters of the failed courtship equation reveal how alterations in material circumstances, including unemployment, war, poverty, and deteriorating social and economic circumstances, could make it difficult to marry. Others suggest that legal reforms might have expanded the technical definition of illegitimacy and thereby increased the statistical count, although not necessarily the actual rate.[17] Most scholars agree that the geographical mobility of one or both partners—no matter the underlying reason—enhanced the potential for illegitimate offspring.[18]

To what extent might this debate over demographic trends and causation be relevant to eighteenth-century Spanish America? The state and focus of demographic research in the European and Anglo-American worlds are different enough from those of Hispanic America as to render direct comparisons difficult. While European and U.S. demographers have produced volumes of research on municipal, regional, and national rates of illegitimacy, and on differentials between urban and rural populations, they seldom distinguish between social groups.[19]

In contrast, with the exception of Mexico, analyses of eighteenth-century demographic trends in Hispanic America are sparse, but the existing documentation often permits the breaking down of illegitimacy rates not only by rural and urban populations but also by race and, inferentially, by status. Although comparison of such disparate materials must necessarily be tentative, even preliminary analysis suggests that the Hispanic world marched to the beat of a very different demographic drummer. As in Europe and the United States, illegitimacy still served as a provocative marker of change, but in Spanish America it occupied a significantly different mental and material landscape.

Seen from a grand perspective this should not be terribly surprising, since one of the greatest demographic disasters and colonization efforts known to human history occurred in Spanish America. Native populations in the Spanish conquest zones declined by millions between the time of the first contact and their nadir in the middle of the seventeenth century, only after which did they begin to recover. By the eighteenth century unknown thousands of Spaniards had emigrated, and their American descendants had multiplied and flourished. In addition, hundreds of thousands of Africans had arrived as slaves, and unknown thousands of those had become free.

Natives, Spaniards, and Africans all maintained their group distinctiveness yet also intermingled, forming complex racial and social combinations. Sexual encounters that spanned racial boundaries—whether they reflected unequal liaisons between conquerors and conquered, masters and slaves, or white elites and everyone else, or whether products of the more socially equal relationships between the various racial categories or castes—typically occurred outside of matrimony. At least in the first colonial centuries, to be racially mixed in colonial Spanish America was virtually synonymous with being illegitimate.[20] Yet illegitimacy was not solely confined to the racially mixed, for the white population also produced its own significant portion of offspring stigmatized by their birth.[21]

Comparisons of general levels of illegitimacy in eighteenth-century Europe and Anglo America with those of Spanish America reveal the enduring legacy of centuries of conquest and colonialism. Even when the mid-eighteenth-century increase is factored into the equation, the rates of illegitimacy in Europe and the United States are remarkably below those of Spanish America. For example, Edward Shorter's compilation of illegitimacy rates between 1700 and 1800 in thirty-three villages, towns, and cities in France, Germany, Switzerland, Belgium, and Sweden reveals that illegitimacy rates still remained below 10 percent in 85 percent of the localities, even after the mid-century increase. Only in Frankfort and Leipzig did illegitimacies reach 10 and 20 percent, while Paris, Bordeaux, and Normandy saw somewhat greater numbers.[22]

Although the English colonies shared a heritage of conquest and colonization with Hispanic America, the absence of a high-density indigenous population combined with an Anglo anti-assimilationist mentality to maintain mostly white and homogeneous societies, with some notable exceptions in frontier or slave zones. When Robert V. Wells reviewed existing studies of the colonies from Massachusetts south to Virginia, he not only noted the typical mid-eighteenth-century rise in illegitimacy but also observed that such rates still remained well under 5 percent. He concluded that "illegitimacy . . . did not have a profound demographic impact."[23]

In contrast, in Spanish America total rates of illegitimacy were commonly double, triple, or even quadruple their European or Anglo-American counterparts. Rather than a predominant pattern of increase in the mid-eighteenth century, illegitimacy rates fluctuated erratically; the tendency was toward stability or even downward. In a field in which much is yet to be done, the most suggestive data still come from Mexico (see Table 2). Demographers show that while total illegitimacy rates varied between 7 and almost 50 percent in the seventeenth century, they were on a general decline in the eighteenth century, at which time they ranged between 7 and 35 percent. These contradictory directions provide the first hint of a provocative divergence between Europe, the United States, and Spanish America. In Europe and Anglo America, increased illegitimacy rates signaled the dislocation of traditional norms caused by changes in mentality and socioeconomic conditions. In Spanish America, stable and decreased illegitimacy rates suggested a social and racial consolidation as the colony passed through a third century.

The decline of illegitimacy rates in eighteenth-century Mexico takes on special significance when caste and class are factored into the equation, for

TABLE 2

Mexican Illegitimacy Percentages

	Year	Total	Españoles	Mestizos	Mulattos	Indians	Non-Indians
Guadalajara	1692	—	—	—	—	—	—
	1698–1702	48.0	39.0	42.8	60.5	50.0	—
Zacatelco	1721–26	—	—	—	—	4.0	24.1
	1785–91	—	—	—	—	2.7	12.6
Azcatzingo	1650–1712	—	—	—	—	10.8	14.5
	1720–1802	—	—	—	—	4.1	12.5
Mexico City	1724	36.4	36.9	29.6	44.4	34.8	—
(Sagrario)	1753	31.0	27.7	30.5	34.2	31.6	—
	1762	27.0	17.3	29.0	30.3	31.6	—
	1782	36.2	23.7	35.7	53.0	32.6	—
San Luis de la Paz	1645–64	6.8	6.8	43.4	43.7	3.9	—
Guanajuato	1700–19	14.5	9.2	21.1	33.3	12.6	—
	1750–69	10.5	10.3	12.5	14.4	9.6	—
	1790–1809	6.9	10.5	11.5	6.6	5.7	—
Parral	1770	22.0	6.0	30.0	—	—	—
Chilapa	1772–82	11.0	—	—	—	—	—

SOURCES: (Guadalajara) Calvo, "Concubinato," p. 211; (Zacatelco, Azcatzingo) Rabell, *La población*, p. 21; (Mexico City) Pescador, p. 139; (Guanajuato) Rabell, *La población*, p. 23; (Parral) McCaa, "Gustos," p. 583; (Chilapa) Chena, p. 187.

there were dramatic differences among racial groups. *Españoles*, which included not only the elite population but other less well-to-do whites as well, had rates of illegitimacy closer to the European levels, both in large cities (Mexico City, over 30 percent) and smaller towns (Guanajuato, 9–10 percent, Parral, 6 percent). The century-long Mexican trend was for white illegitimacy to be stable or on the decline. The predominant change in overall illegitimacy rates derived from stunning decreases in the proportion of illegitimate births among mestizo (Indian-white) and mulatto (white-black) populations (Zacatelco, Axcatzingo, Guanajuato), although Mexico City remained an exception.

Yet Mexico does not a Spanish empire make. Other regions have contradictory trends, a fact that should not be surprising given that demographers have long noted that illegitimacy rates varied widely by microlocalities.[24] Susan Socolow has documented increases in white illegitimacy in the 1770s and 1780s in central Buenos Aires. Guiomar Dueñas-Vargas has found the rates of Spanish illegitimacy in one Bogotá parish went up, while those in another went down.[25] At the same time as illegitimacy rates among mestizo populations were decreasing in Mexico, they rose in Colombia.[26] The trees should still not obscure the forest, for mid- to late-eighteenth-century commentary as well as statistics suggest that a new demographic cohort was in the process of formation. A significant group of mestizos and mulattos were almost white, and many no longer fit the colonial stereotype that linked racial mixture with illegitimacy.[27]

Such selected drops in illegitimacy and widespread racial blurring are just part of a much larger trend that historians have recognized for some time: that the closing decades of the eighteenth century marked rising tension between white and racially mixed populations.[28] It was, as Magnus Mörner noted, "the advance and expansion of the intermediate groups that essentially motivated the increased exclusivism displayed by the criollo elite."[29] In a colonial society in which elites traditionally justified their status in the hierarchy by their legitimacy as well as by their whiteness, the presence of such upwardly mobile groups—some who participated in the economic boom, some who were now legitimate, and some who could pass as white—posed a particular challenge to the established order. Both royal bureaucrats and local elites responded with even more vigorous enforcement of traditional and new discriminatory barriers to forestall such upward mobility. It is within this context of demographic and economic change, and what Daisy Rípodas Ardanaz has styled as "socio-chromatic tensions," that another possible motivation for the late-century flood of *gracias al sacar* petitions comes into focus.[30]

The simplest questions are often the most difficult to answer. Did the dramatic sixfold increase in *gracias al sacar* petitions in the last quarter of the eighteenth century result because there were more whites who were illegitimate, or simply because there was more discrimination (see Table 1)? Which was changing? Was it, as in Europe and Anglo America, transformations in mentality and material conditions that expanded the pool of illegitimates? Or was this a different kind of turning point—did a rising number of illegitimates purchase *gracias al sacar* to blunt an increased prejudice against them?

Consideration of the variables that had to coalesce before someone such as Don Gabriel Muñoz appealed to the Cámara of the Indies reveals the unpredictable relationship between the pool of illegitimates and those few who might apply for legitimation. In his case, his mother, Doña Catalina Casafus, had to become engaged to a prominent Medellín merchant (Don Francisco Muñoz), consent to sexual intercourse, become pregnant, and carry to term; and the baby had to survive the dangerous early years. The couple had to choose not to marry, for even a delayed ceremony would have provided automatic legitimation. Gabriel had to grow up and achieve sufficient success so that he was at the edge of acceptance by the Medellín elite—neither so fully established that an official legitimation proved unnecessary, nor so totally ostracized that it would have been ineffective had he received it. Gabriel had to be white, to possess sufficient wealth, and, equally important, he had to care enough to make a formal application for legitimation after encountering discrimination on that Medellín street. The large majority of applicants were the white offspring of local elites, blood kin deprived of equal status only because of their birth.[31] Yet personal, familial, and local factors importantly affected why these 244 applied and others did not.

So which is more important, the date of Don Gabriel Muñoz's birth, or the date that he applied for *gracias al sacar*? If it were the first, and his birth were part of a pattern whereby white illegitimacy was on the increase, we might expect to find—as do researchers of European and U.S. illegitimacy— that there were notable changes in mentality or in material conditions that altered customary arrangements or that changed the outcome of sexual relationships, so as to result in greater illegitimacy. Succeeding chapters will suggest that while the biographies of both mothers and fathers of illegitimates provide rich information on prevailing customs, they demonstrate—contrary to the findings of other scholars—fewer substantive changes in mentality than might be expected throughout the century.

Nor did material circumstances much affect the potential of these local elites to marry, since lovers rarely cited economic reasons for their failure to wed. Instead, the life stories of illegitimates document real and widespread increases in discrimination against them as the eighteenth century drew to a close. Putting this complex picture together suggests that more than half of the petitioners applied in the last two decades of the eighteenth century not because there had been increased rates of illegitimacy, but because elites were increasingly inclined to discriminate.

To this point, this introduction has concentrated as much on historical silence as on historical sound, because the only way to understand what the *gracias al sacar* documents can tell us is first to understand what they cannot. Illegitimates in colonial Spanish America occupied a radically different social and racial matrix from that of their European and U.S. contemporaries. The striking midcentury increase in legitimation petitions cannot be directly correlated either to rising rates of illegitimacy, as in Europe and the United

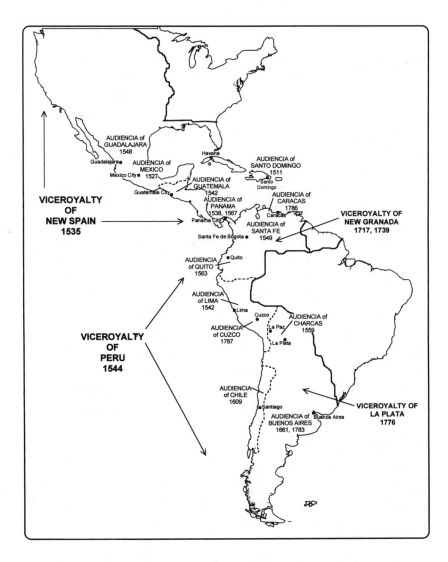

MAP I. Founding dates of Spanish-American viceroyalties and *audiencias*

States, or to demographic trends in colonial Spanish America. Instead, at the end of the eighteenth century a challenged colonial elite threw up the barricades to protect itself against mobility from below. Yet even though discrimination intensified, it was not totally exclusionary, for, as the tales of Don Gabriel Muñoz and the other *gracias al sacar* applicants will prove, potential for upward mobility at both local and imperial levels remained.

THE EIGHTEENTH CENTURY, THE BOURBONS, AND THE REFORMS

While colonial elites proved to be particularly vigorous defenders of their honor as the eighteenth century progressed, the degree to which the Spanish state supported their efforts is much more ambiguous. This century marked change on the peninsula and in the Americas as a new dynasty assumed the throne. The Spanish Bourbons had to confront both international and domestic crises, inasmuch as the integrity of their empire was threatened not only by European aggressors but also suffered internal debility caused by governmental incompetence and economic weakness. The response was a century of wide-ranging reforms. While an introduction to the Bourbons, and an enumeration of their principal reform measures, can be fairly straightforward, any serious evaluation of the era of Bourbon Reform (1759–1808) treads on devilishly complicated ground. It seems appropriate to provide some of the accepted views here, and to reserve revisionist conclusions for the relevant chapters.[32]

French Bourbon King Louis XIV put his grandson, Philip of Anjou, on the throne in 1700 because the Spanish branch of the Hapsburgs had died out with the death of Charles II (1664–1700). Charles had been best known as "The Bewitched" but was also, and probably more aptly, called "*El Impotente.*" The Spanish Hapsburgs had started on a high note with the reign of Charles V (1516–1556). A series of strategic dynastic marriages and fortunate deaths had left Charles the heir to a magnificent empire that included the Spanish kingdoms of Aragón (from Ferdinand [1479–1516]), Castile and the Americas (from Isabella, [1474–1504]), Burgundy and the Low Countries (from Mary of Burgundy [1457–1482]), and Austrian possessions (from Maximilian [1459–1519]). While the Spanish Hapsburgs remained a pre-eminent European power with the succession of Philip II (1556–1598), the later monarchs Philip III (1598–1621) and Philip IV (1621–1665) became associated with decline on the continent and in the Americas, manifesting the more negative effects of generations of inbreeding. They ceded imperial power to favorites and failed to confront fundamental crises, such as the wide-ranging inflation that devastated the Spanish economy or the demographic disaster and economic collapse that transformed the Americas.

Even though the French Bourbons succeeded in obtaining the Spanish throne in 1700, they had to fight to win it, because the rival Austrian Hapsburgs contested the accession and European powers took sides in the War of Spanish Succession (1702–1713). The Peace of Utrecht (1713) confirmed the Spanish Bourbons, but not without the loss of territories in the Low Countries, Italy, and Gibraltar. Four monarchs dominated the next century: Philip V (1700–1746), Ferdinand VI (1746–1759), Charles III (1759–1788), and Charles IV (1788–1808), during which time French models of state absolutism were integrated into Spanish programs for reform.

The conventional wisdom is that the Bourbon need to defend Spanish territory on the continent and in the Americas engendered a complicated chain of responses. The heart of the reforms was national security, for the first priority was the improvement and strengthening of the military. Yet this required money, which necessitated further reform, for the government had to transform itself by improving its efficiency to raise this money. That led to additional reforms, siphoning finances from already existing sources, and engendered yet other reforms to develop new financial resources. The Bourbons saw the reviving populations and economies of their American possessions as one engine of Spanish revival, and thus it is no accident that the colonies—especially during the reigns of Charles III and Charles IV—were a particular focus of the Bourbon reformers.

Although this causative chain is far too simplistic, it explains why Bourbon reforms in the Americas concentrated on the development of colonial militias; the stationing of professional troops in strategic locations; governmental reorganization (the establishment of two new viceroyalties [New Granada, Río de la Plata] and the intendant system of professional and paid government officials); the more efficient collection of existing taxes; the establishment of revenue-producing tobacco and *aguardiente* monopolies; the encouragement of peninsular-colonial trade through "free commerce"; the promotion of silver and gold mining; and the development of cacao, sugar, and other new exports. Because only a strong state could undertake such a program, another component of Bourbon reforms was promotion of royal absolutism, which in the eighteenth century still faced competition from papal and ecclesiastical authority. The Bourbon expulsion of the Jesuits from Spain and the Americas in 1767 proved to be the most obvious in a series of moves that attempted to establish royal authority over issues previously reserved to the Catholic Church.

This simple description of the principal Bourbon measures obscures the complexities occasioned by the differences among the Bourbon monarchs and their reforming ministers, the dissimilarities between reform in Spain and in the Americas, as well as striking variations within the American viceroyalties. Sometimes Bourbon reformers introduced change; in other instances they responded to phenomena such as increases in population or in gold mining production that were already in progress. Monographs have been written, and more are needed, to analyze the variability and evaluate the long- and short-term influences of these reforms.

While historians have written much on the military, political, administrative, and economic aspects of reform, they have paid less attention to the Bourbon social agenda and have not incorporated it into any comprehensive evaluation of the whole. Four key Bourbon measures affected the contested questions of birth and race. While three of them can at least be superficially linked to larger agendas, given their money-making potential or anticlerical bent, in other respects the social reforms ostensibly had contradictory goals.

The Royal Pragmatic on Marriages, issued in 1776 in Spain and 1778 in the Americas, aimed to maintain social and racial equality by giving fathers more control over their children.[33] If a potential spouse had "defects," such as of race or as a result of illegitimacy, a father could appeal to royal officials to prevent clerics from sanctifying such "unequal" marriages and punish defiant offspring with disinheritance. This interposition of the state in what had customarily been an ecclesiastical tradition of free spousal choice was consistent with the Bourbon inroads against papal authority, and aligned the state with local elites who were challenged by the upwardly mobile.

The other Bourbon social measures seemed to promote contradictory goals, for they encouraged the mobility of the illegitimate and racially mixed, who were among the targets of the 1778 Pragmatic Sanction. Civil legitimations figured in Bourbon legislation, for even though such state redress was traditional, the crown issued a 1795 price list, or *arancel*, for the American *gracias al sacar*.[34] This decree supported the Bourbon financial

MAP 2. Home cities of *gracias al sacar* petitioners

agenda by raising the prices charged for legitimations while it additionally publicized the procedure. The *arancel* also established a process whereby mulattos and *pardos* (those with dark skin) might purchase whiteness and become persons of honor.

An even more radical degree in 1794 had neither anticlerical nor money-making potential. It declared that those baptized as *expósitos*, or of "unknown parentage," were entitled to many of the privileges of legitimates, imposing a monetary fine on anyone who called an *expósito* "illegitimate, bastard, sacrilegious, incestuous, or adulterous."[35] The *cédula* concluded that if there were a question concerning the "quality"—including the race—of the *expósito*, "the doubt would be for the best part." Given the tension over racial ambiguity in the Americas, the explosive potential of this decree cannot be underestimated.

While historians have studied individual Bourbon social reforms, there has been little effort to reconcile these striking differences. Magnus Mörner's classic discussion of racial mixture presents the Bourbon measures that legitimated and whitened as examples of liberal or even radical social policies. He posits that an activist Bourbon state intervened against the wishes of the Creole elite. Royal officials attempted to vent the social pressures of oppressed castes and classes by promoting the selected upward mobility of some illegitimates and mulattos. In the process the state not only won their loyalty but also benefited from their contributions. Yet others, such as Daisy Rípodas Ardanaz and Susan Socolow, emphasize the other side of the Bourbon social reforms. They portray the Pragmatic Sanction on Marriages as a conservative attempt to defend the colonial hierarchy, for it buttressed the power of the white elite to maintain endogamy by preventing the marriage of unequals. One of the themes that will necessarily be addressed in succeeding chapters is the consistency of the Bourbon social reforms, whether they promoted change or were conservative, and where they fit within the comprehensive agenda of reform.

METHODOLOGICAL CONSIDERATIONS

Introductions customarily provide overviews of principal themes, as well as acknowledging the processes that have guided the analysis and conclusions reached in the text. Inasmuch as the *gracias al sacar* depositions number in the hundreds, span a century, and provide varying testimony, a computer was essential for calculating thirty-three variables in seven data bases and for providing cross-tabulations by gender, chronology, and geography.[36] A multilevel analysis—with a novel imperial focus—probed beyond the legitimation petitions to locate additional information on mothers, fathers, and illegitimates in their local, provincial, and national archives. The techniques forged by anthropologists and family historians—collective biography, life-course analysis, exemplification, emic and etic analytical approaches—guided subsequent analysis.

Statistics can be the Scylla and Charybdis of any investigation, for the author must necessarily steer between a numbing overabundance and a confusing scarcity. Equally important is the mandate to explain clearly where the numbers come from, how they might or might not be linked to any historical actuality, and how they might be interpreted. Such scrupulosity is particularly essential here, because the statistics generated by *gracias al sacar* data prove to be intrinsically meaningless. In only one arena do such statistics measure substance rather than reflect the shadow of reality: The raw numbers of petitions sent from the Americas to Spain throughout the eighteenth century, and the responses of the royal officials who approved or rejected them, constitute a set of data complete in itself.

In most cases there can be no direct linkage between the statistical patterns generated by the *gracias al sacar* pool of petitioners and any demographic reality. To cite an example, when testimonies reveal that at least a quarter of unwed mothers were betrothed when they became pregnant, that number bears no direct relationship to any actual percentage of eighteenth-century elite women who might have given birth during their engagements. Yet even if legitimation statistics cannot measure demographic reality, they can signal trends worthy of additional research. It would be useful to know whether the percentage of pregnant fiancées changed much during the century. Numbers also complement anecdotal material. For example, sixty-seven, or more than 30 percent, of the mothers of illegitimates fall into a distinctive pattern defined as "private pregnancy." Although the details are not relevant here, the numbers do matter, so that the reader knows how many case studies suggested such a model—even if only a few examples are provided in the text.

A final use of *gracias al sacar* statistics involves judgment, because numbers help to keep any author honest. But there are also limits to the weight of statistics that readers need be asked to endure. Since my idea of "few" or "many" may not be universally shared, and inasmuch as a detailed decade-by-decade analysis of a topic may become tedious, although supportive of a point, statistics will be presented in three formats. Absolutely essential numbers appear in the text or in nearby tables within the chapter. Verifying numbers that can be simply presented are located in footnotes. Confirmatory statistics that are too complex for footnotes appear as tables in Appendix 2 and are noted in parentheses in the text.

Inasmuch as *gracias al sacar* petitions originated throughout the Spanish

Americas, they provide a rare imperial focus: an opportunity to assess continuities and contrasts on a continental scale. This coverage encouraged a fairly novel research strategy, for limited topics could be investigated at a multitude of archival sites throughout the empire. The initial research strategy involved the collection of the legitimation cases scattered throughout the Archive of the Indies in Seville—a mystery quest in its own right (see Appendix 1). However it quickly became clear that the mothers, fathers, and illegitimates who appeared in legitimation depositions were local notables who had likely generated archival documents in the Americas that might provide further insight into their lives.

The professionalism and extraordinary efforts of the last generations of Latin American archivists have made it possible to undertake research that would have been impossible years ago, for the growing compilations of indexes to Latin American city, regional, and national archives permit the reasonably rapid collection of information. Research in Spanish archives (Seville, Madrid, Simancas) was supplemented by archival investigations in Mexico (Guanajuato, Mexico City), Cuba (Havana), Venezuela (Caracas), Colombia (Medellín, Bogotá), Ecuador (Quito), Peru (Lima, Trujillo, Arequipa), Bolivia (Sucre), Chile (Santiago), and Argentina (Buenos Aires). The results permitted in-depth analysis of some of the lives of the *gracias al sacar* principals, and proved invaluable in evaluating the subsequent effects of civil legitimations.

Such a multilevel imperial focus adds an additional dimension. By contrast, most historians who have explored issues of gender, sexuality, or illegitimacy in Latin America have necessarily limited their geographical scope to a city or a region, although they have expanded their social and racial coverage to include most elements of the population. Recent studies by Asuncíon Lavrin, Richard Boyer, Robert McCaa, Steve Stern, Patricia Seed, Susan Socolow, Ramón Gutiérrez, María Emma Mannarelli, Guiomar Dueñas-Vargas, Pablo Rodríquez, Beatriz Patiño Millán, Linda Lewin, María Beatriz Nizza da Silva, and Muriel Nazzari—to name just a few—focus on discrete areas, be they Mexico, Oaxaca, Morelos, Mexico City, Buenos Aires, New Mexico, Lima, Bogotá, Medellín, Antioquia, or Brazil. They generally analyze the social and racial spectrum ranging from elites to castes to indigenous populations.[37] The *gracias al sacar* documents permit a contradictory if complementary analysis: They provide empirewide coverage, although they limit the social focus to colonial elites.

Both approaches have their merits and their weaknesses. The first permits in-depth regional coverage, but the result can sometimes be idiosyncratic and frustrate systematic comparisons.[38] Methodological difficulties emerge in data generated from criminal, ecclesiastical, or demographic records in which all ranges of the social spectrum are present, and where contextual information is frequently not sufficient to separate castes and classes or to distinguish discrete norms and mentalities. On the other hand, legitimation petitions provide imperial coverage and unquestionably reveal the distinctive mentality of colonial elites, although they are limited to this group and even then prove less-than-reliable statistical indicators. Whenever possible, the observations of these historians and others are woven into the text and notes to assess the uniqueness of the patterns revealed in legitimation depositions.

Since those who testified told different tales about similar topics, their recollections concerning the circumstances of mothers, fathers, and illegitimates lent themselves naturally to the analysis and organization of chapters as prosopographies, or collective biographies. These involve, as Louise Tilly suggests, the "assembly of standardized descriptions of individual units—persons, household, firms, places, events . . . into portraits of the entire sets and into means for studying variation among the individual units."[39] Charles Tilly has pointed out the advantages of such an approach, especially for social history, given that "the method makes it possible to look simultaneously at the individual and the collective without sacrificing the connection between the two."[40]

Certainly the frequent appearances of Don Gabriel Muñoz at various stages of this introduction demonstrate the power of the detailed personal experience to illustrate the broader process. Elizabeth and Thomas Cohen have termed this approach "exemplification," whereby "the event recounted becomes a cameo, finely, densely wrought, on which we may trace the lineaments of grosser grander sculpture. The microcosm of a moment thus reflects the larger social macrocosm."[41] Along with Don Gabriel Muñoz there will be many others who surface in succeeding pages, including "Doña X," of Buenos Aires, Don Diego Alarcón of Havana, and the "Leoncitos" from Arequipa. Their stories take on additional historical heft when used to illustrate the collective.

Prosopography and exemplification become yet more powerful approaches when linked with life-course analysis, a perspective promoted by family historians who study, as Tamara K. Hareven puts it, the "complexity of individual and family change in the context of historical time."[42] A life-course analysis of Don Gabriel Muñoz might first encounter him as a babe in his mother's womb, or trace his later circumstances as an infant, a child, and at various stages in his maturation as an adult. Characteristic life course patterns associated with sexuality and illegitimacy can be followed in chapters that explore the collective biographies of mothers and fathers, infants, children, and illegitimate and legitimated adults. Internally, chapters explore changes in life course to consider what happened to men and women who produced illegitimate children—not only in their teens, twenties, or thirties but also in their later lives. Issues surrounding sexuality and illegitimacy necessarily affected the individual in different ways at different points in the life cycle: Matters that might be critical to a woman of twenty might not be as key when she was forty; concerns of a boy of twelve might impact the man of fifty differently. At its best, life-course analysis meets Charles Tilly's prescription to measure "exigencies that become more or less likely, more or less pressing at different points in life . . . choices that entail further exigencies, prescriptions, and choices."[43]

Anthropologists have justly chastised historians for borrowing those parts of their methodologies that seem most interesting but not adhering with the rigor of social science to the rest. In defense, historians have seldom aspired to be scientists but have always been intellectual omnivores, borrowing inspiring ideas wherever they may be found. And anthropologists seem to understand, in a way that historians sometimes have not, that any exploration of Spanish America's past must travel back not only in time but also in culture. For that reason, I have found the anthropological distinction between emic and etic methodological approaches to be fundamental in the analysis of the *gracias al sacar* depositions. It has produced the unifying themes that most deeply link this work together.

At its most simplistic, the difference between emic and etic is that the first analyzes from the inside out, while the second from the outside in. The emic approach, as Tamara K. Hareven aptly notes, "reconstructs the processes inherent in the society studied and develops the analytical categories from the inside," while the etic "applies social scientist definitions of categories to the population patterns studied."[44] In an emic approach, the sources themselves shape the topics to be studied; in an etic approach, topics defined by social scientists or historians become the research agenda.

For example, an emic approach could (and will) use the *gracias al sacar* depositions to study the issue of honor from what witnesses testified about honor, how they defined it, as well as how these statements contrasted with their actual behavior. In contrast, an etic analysis might start with variables generated by previous studies of honor in Spain, the Mediterranean, or Spanish America—"honor in literature," or "honor and sexuality," or "honor and violence"—and then compare those paradigms with existing sources. Both approaches have validity and can be used concurrently. Yet if the goal is to discover, as Clifford Geertz challenges, the "webs of meaning" in which people live, it is essential first to listen to them before we ourselves speak.[45]

PERVASIVE THEMES

Studying legitimation depositions from the "inside out" reveals fundamental patterns in a colonial mental matrix in which issues involving sexuality and illegitimacy were but a constituent part. Four organizing fulcrums of colonial life are essential to any understanding of what follows: First, race and illegitimate birth were not necessarily ascriptive characteristics assigned permanently at birth but could be changed, or even achieved. Second, elites consciously defined and manipulated disparities between their private and public worlds. Third, personalism not only precisely measured interpersonal relationships but also rationalized violations of traditional norms through informal and formal "passing." The fourth is the concept of honor that coded the eighteenth-century expression of all of the above. Although subsequent chapters will explore permutations and combinations of these four in detail, some comments can pave the way for what follows.

Unlike English America, where a person's race and birth tended to be sharply defined and permanently fixed, in Hispanic America both variables had in-between categories, and an individual might have more than one racial or birth status at the same time.[46] It has often been noted that the Hispanic concept of race, although racist in its attachment of highest status to whites, also recognized and developed vocabulary and law that differentiated many in-between categories. In Anglo America the idea of racial mixing was so taboo that, with the exception of compound words like half-breed, the words for racial mixture had to be borrowed from other languages (octoroon, mulatto); in Hispanic America a rich vocabulary signaled popular consciousness of intermediary positions, such as *pardo, moreno,* mulatto, *quarteron, puchuelo,* mestizo, and a multitude of others.[47] In Anglo America the racially mixed could never be white; in Hispanic America those with less than one-eighth mixture might become so.[48]

In matters of birth as well, the stark Anglo dichotomy between legitimacy and bastardy was softened in the Hispanic world. As early as 1236 the English Statute of Merton had decreed that "once a bastard, always a bastard," and that rigid distinction remained in effect until the twentieth century.[49] Even if unwed English parents eventually married, any children born before the ceremony maintained their status as "bastards," although they might be designated as "special bastards."[50] In contrast, the Hispanic terms "illegitimate" and "bastard" were not synonymous. Both common law and popular custom established various intermediary categories, including *hijos naturales,* or children born to single parents who would be automatically and totally legitimated by a subsequent marriage ceremony. Neither in canon law nor in popular custom were these children ever referred to as bastards. That term was solely reserved for those of adulterous, sacrilegious, or incestuous birth. Furthermore, between the extremes of the *hijo natural* and the bastard were mitigating opaque categories such as "orphan" (*expósito*) and child of "unknown parentage" (*padres no conocidos*), which could be used to hide every variety of illegitimacy.[51] The recognition of intermediary positions between the extremes of black and white, or legitimate and bastard, not only revealed the presence of but also created the potential for significant racial and social flexibility.[52]

Colonists who were illegitimate or racially mixed did not need to look solely to their descendants to erase the "defect" of their birth or to "better" their race. Individuals could immediately enhance their position and enjoy more than one birth status or more than one racial status at the same time. In effect, that is what happened to Don Gabriel Muñoz when he was treated as legitimate and worthy of the title of "Don" on the streets of Medellín, even though he actually was illegitimate. To understand how colonists rationalized such dual persona it is necessary to explore the difference between their private and public worlds.

An extensive historiography has explored the dichotomy between private and public, providing a useful overview, even though it should not set the primary agenda for discussion of dual spheres in the Hispanic world.[53] In a recent article, Leonore Davidoff reviewed the contributions of previous scholarship and suggested some useful research guidelines.[54] She noted that the public-private dichotomy has a "long history," becoming a particularly powerful analytical construct when feminists and anthropologists suggested that the history of women revealed an "apparent universal sexual asymmetry" that circumscribed women to the private, while men moved in the public, arena. The "separate spheres" dichotomy encompassed the nineteenth-century cult of domesticity, which confined women to the private spaces of the home, centered on reproduction and consumption. Men dominated the public world of economic productivity and civil authority.

Leonore Davidoff also notes that some scholars have challenged these "conceptual absolutes" of private-public, female-male dualities and charged that such interpretations are class-based, imprecise, and culture bound. Research that emphasizes "gender distinctions . . . particularly within the sexual division of labour" inevitably reaches the dead end of "biological constants," since the "body . . . becomes too much the bearer of the timeless and static." She suggests that future investigation focus on "institutions of family, kinship, marriage and parenthood," for these "have been neglected or taken for granted." Noting that some cultures do not even make the private and public distinction, she concludes that for others it can be a "basic part of the way . . . social and psychic worlds are ordered." She cautions historians to be aware that definitions of public and private are not static but rather "constantly shifting, being made and remade."

The construction of the Hispanic version of the private-public dichotomy from inside out reveals that it was an integral constituent of colonial mentality, but that it differed substantially from more familiar English, U.S., or German counterparts.[55] Language provides the first indication that colonial Spanish-American elites divided their world into private and public spheres. Elites constantly evoked this division in multiple contexts, using the Spanish words *privado* ("private") and *público* ("public") to convey their meanings. Sometimes witnesses spoke of the "secret" to refer to private matters, or to note that something was "notorious" when it was publicly known. Often they linked these concepts together and referred to "private and public." Anyone who has read colonial documents knows that the oft-used phrase "public and notorious" is meant to confirm that information was known to all. What has been less understood is what this phrase leaves unspoken, that there also could be information that was "private and secret."

The inescapable presence of this bifurcated view is compelling, and it has not gone unnoticed by colonial historians. Richard Cicerchia suggested that late-colonial Buenos Aires families be studied as a "mixture of public and private relations."[56] María Emma Mannarelli's superb study of illegitimacy in seventeenth-century Lima both produced testimonies that specifically referred to the private and the public and led her to conclude that historians need to distinguish between an "appropriately public culture" and an "interior world."[57]

Yet, as Leonore Davidoff also reminds us, confirmation of a private-public dichotomy is just the first step, for it is equally mandatory to test the nature of the divide. It is here that the Hispanic version of private-public veers from more familiar versions, for elite women had public persona, and happenings considered private could occur in public space.[58] Although the Hispanic version of private and public included components of gender and geography, it was sociology—family, kinship, friendship—that set the decisive parameters.

The significance of personal linkages not only within the family and related kin but also beyond has been particularly noted by historians who research issues concerning sexuality and the family. They have begun to recognize, as Diana O'Hara has pointed out in her work on sixteenth-century Canterbury, that "kinship is variously articulated and is not to be defined simply in genealogical or biological terms."[59] Instead, the "vocabulary of kinship" can be "extended to biological non-kin, to affines, and to neighbours, in order to express either the existing quality of relationships, or to create obligations." The Hispanic inclusion of others beyond immediate family into the private circle provides an eighteenth-century example of the dynamics of such a process.

Colonial elites divided their private and public worlds by degrees of personal intimacy. The private world included family, kin, and intimate friends; the public world was everybody else—although other elite peers counted far more than the rest. Evidence of this division is readily apparent in legitimation depositions in which witnesses usually first signaled their relationship to the person or event they were testifying about. Since family and blood kin were automatically considered to be included within the private circle, it was usually friends who justified their intimate knowledge. They might comment that they were "treated familiarly" (*"trato familiarmente"*) or that they had "intimate friendship" (*"estrecha amistad," "intima amistad"*), or "very special friendship and abundant confidence" (*"muy particular amistad y sobrada confianza"*), or many other variants of the above.[60] In contrast, those who were not members of the private circle could testify only to issues that were "public" or "notorious," because they were not privy to the confidences held by the private circle.[61]

Colonial elites lived in two spheres. The first was a private world of family, kin, and intimate friends who shared confidences and trust, provided mutual support, and promoted each other's status in the outside world.[62] The second was the public world inhabited by everyone else, where maintenance, enhancement, or loss of reputation (*honor*) was determined by imperial and local elites. Such bifurcation was sufficiently distinct that individuals could have different status in their private and public worlds, a potential that went far beyond the usual mobility expressed in Anglo-American conceptualizations of "passing."

Again, vocabulary can provide some first clues as to mentality. There are rare examples, especially relating to race, where colonists use the Spanish word for passing (*pasar*) to describe dual status.[63] It was far more common, however, to employ circumlocutions to justify a superior status in the public world than traditional norms might accord, given private reality. In those cases, colonists argued, much like Don Gabriel Muñoz, that they had essentially achieved an alternative public status, not because of what they really were but because they "were treated as if they were"—and here one could append a number of desired variables: "white," "legitimate," "honorable," "Don," "Doña."[64] Such ability to pass made it possible for some individuals to achieve racial, natal, and many other kinds of status in the public sphere that differed from their private reality.

Each attempt to pass balanced private and public interests. The private circle provided group solidarity and functioned to forward the interests of its members, often including racially mixed or illegitimate kin who sought to pass. Contraposed to the private sphere was the public world, where imperial as well as local elites enforced written and unwritten discriminatory practices, defended their status, and thereby maintained the exclusivity of the existing hierarchy. Each attempt to pass was a negotiation between historical norms of discrimination and the decisions by elites as to whether that prejudice would be carried out.

While private and public interests naturally conflicted, evidence of such personal decisions rarely appears in the historic record. A hypothetical elite male might be expected to use his influence so that a member of his private circle, perhaps an illegitimate nephew, might hold a political position normally impossible given the "defect" of his birth. Yet that same elite male, in his public persona as defender of the hierarchy, would not be hypocritical if he opposed the appointment of someone else's illegitimate nephew to the same post. This elite male had yet another option, however, for he might accept such passing, making a personal choice to treat someone else's illegitimate nephew "as if" he were legitimate. His concession would be effective only to the extent that it was supported by other members of the elite, who also validated such passing.

This process created the potential for enhancement or maintenance of individual reputation without any challenge to traditional norms. If illegitimates could not be Dons, then Don Gabriel Muñoz had to become legitimate—or at least to be considered legitimate in the public sphere—if he were to be called "Don"; if a mulatto could not hold office because of his race, he could still become an official if he could project a public persona in which he were accepted and treated as white. Rather than having individuals succeed in spite of their birth or their race, individuals changed their birth or race to conform at least in public to traditional norms.[65]

Peter Laslett once commented that observers "can only get to know about the effectiveness or often even the existence of a rule from the records of what happened when this rule was breached."[66] The very breaking of custom, he suggested, produced a social "paradox," given that "breaches of social rules do not necessarily weaken those rules, and under certain circumstances can even serve to strengthen them."[67] Passing fits Laslett's description, for it proved a popularly accepted way to bypass traditional norms although not ultimately to challenge them. Passing permitted social and racial mobility in a society that was hierarchical and racist.

Although Don Gabriel Muñoz might possibly have recognized the cultural patterns discussed up to this point—flexible attitudes toward the construction of natal and racial categories, the division between the private and the public, the individual exceptions characteristic of informal or official passing—it is equally likely that he might suggest that all of these topics were variants of just one: who had honor and who did not. To eighteenth-century elites, the word "honor" embodied a complex of characteristics, attitudes, and conduct that rationalized their social and racial hierarchy and that determined the parameters of discrimination against everyone else. Since honor has been a topic much written about, and even more confused, a consideration of earlier approaches follows.

The extensive and valuable historiography on the issue of honor must be approached with caution.[68] Assumptions derived from research concerning honor in one time and place have too often become assimilated into generalizations concerning honor in other centuries or other cultures. For example, analyses of medieval law and literature have promoted influential stereotypes as to how honor shaped the lives of Hispanic women. Statements such as "No wife could be permitted to commit adultery," or "No daughter [is] to have sexual relations out of wedlock," have been followed by extreme conclusions, including that sexual misconduct led to "total collapse of social esteem and personal pride," or to severe reactions by males who "avenged the deed, usually by violent means."[69] Sixteenth-century Spanish literature has frequently been used to promote images of swashbuckling Don Juans or other protagonists obsessed by issues of honor.

More recent anthropological studies of the Mediterranean discuss how the concept of honor has affected gender relations in twentieth-century Greece, Italy, and Spain. There is no question that an understanding of the honor codes of medieval Spanish matrons, sixteenth-century Don Juans, or twentieth-century Greek peasants might provide insight into the uses of the concept of honor by colonial Spanish Americans. Such comparisons, however, should be made only after the fact.

Unfortunately, some Latin American historians have used these interpretations of honor as a priori assumptions. One legal scholar concluded that "among the families of the distinguished classes, offenses [against] honor [were] only erased with the death of the guilty, and the religious profession of the injured."[70] Patricia Seed's more recent analysis of honor in colonial Mexico provides a typically etic (outside-looking-in) mode of analysis. Relying on generalizations derived from sixteenth-century Spanish playwrights such as Lope de Vega and Calderón de la Barca to develop a concept of honor as "virtue," she found this view characteristic of seventeenth-century Mexico. She then referred to modern anthropological research on honor to formulate the category of honor as "status," which she argued became dominant in the late colony.[71] The methodological question is whether sixteenth-century playwrights or twentieth-century anthropologists should set any fundamental agenda by which to analyze the concepts of honor of eighteenth-century elite Mexicans.[72]

Recent research on honor has been alive to such methodological flaws.[73] Elizabeth S. Cohen's investigations of early-modern Rome provide one of the more useful correctives. She insists that honor be viewed as a "complex of values and behavior" that varies widely in its meaning and practice.[74] Even cultures that share somewhat similar theoretical conceptions of honor may act in different ways. Cohen's work provides both a warning and a challenge:

> To understand honor, it is important to distinguish region from region, urban from rural, elite from popular, male from female and one era from the next. Furthermore, despite its rhetoric, honor is seldom absolute, but rather subject to negotiation. However clear honor culture may appear in the scholar's theoretical construction, its application in social practice is riddled with ambiguity.

Subsequent chapters will explore how honor was expressed in Spanish history and legislation, as well as how the presence or absence of honor affected the lives of Spanish American mothers, fathers, and illegitimates throughout their life courses. Embedded within these different manifestations are two pervasive and continuing themes. The first is that eighteenth-century elites used the word "honor" without any qualifiers. The second is that honor was constantly "subject to negotiation."[75]

Honor had no qualifiers. Unlike scholars who have industriously chopped it up into a myriad of subtopics—honor as status, honor as virtue, sexual honor—colonial elites never divided it. They used the single word to encompass a multitude of shifting meanings that were intrinsically linked.[76] To understand honor is to discard preconceived notions and to try to listen to the voices of colonial Spanish Americans, who explained what it was and how its absence or presence affected their lives. What first becomes clear is that even though honor was not a physical entity, colonial elites conceived of it as tangible—perhaps more like intelligence than eye color—but nonetheless something that under proper circumstances they might unmistakably pass on to their children.

Honor was profoundly important because it rationalized hierarchy, the division of Hispanic society between a privileged few and a deprived majority. It established a distinctive agenda of discrimination, because those who possessed it were privileged with special access to political, economic, and social power, and they maintained their superior rank by discriminating against everyone else. Those with honor recognized it in others and accorded those peers an attention and respect they denied the rest of society. Issues of honor were involved in courtship, sexual intercourse, pregnancy, and marriage, as well as in race, birth, access to political office, and employment. Honor determined who was considered trustworthy, who did favors for whom, who were one's friends, who were invited to parties, who was "in," and who received greetings on the street.[77] Even though colonial Spanish Americans from all castes and classes might have their own versions of honor—which are equally important for us to understand—it cannot be overstated that only colonial elites reserved it exclusively to themselves.[78] To understand the elite version of honor is to probe the hierarchical ethos at the core of colonial society.

The second component of honor was its variability, for its presence or absence was constantly subject to negotiation. Within their communities, elites constantly evaluated each other to determine who did, and who did not, possess honor; within the empire, royal officials decided who should receive the *gracias al sacar*, which officially confirmed honor. In either case, honor was never absolute: It could be challenged, threatened, lost, gained, and even regained. Such variability could occur because honor was not an internalized prescription for proper ethical action—it was not primarily synonymous with integrity, or honesty, or virtue—although proper action might be necessary to conserve or to pass on honor.[79] Instead, honor was located in the public sphere, where an individual's reputation was malleable and ultimately defined by other peers.

The private-public mentality combined with the public nature of honor to create the potential for colonists to "pass" to be considered persons of honor. We have already discussed how the racially mixed and illegitimate might construct alternative persona in the public sphere. What needs to be added is that such mobility permitted the upwardly mobile not only to bypass their racial and natal "defects" but also to acquire honorable status. Eighteenth-century colonists who passed were far more likely to describe their mobility in such positive terms—that they were now accepted as persons of honor—than to explain the negative—that they had erased "defects" in race or birth. The dynamic of such a transformation was also recognized in the phraseology of *gracias al sacar*, for, when petitioners asked to be legitimated, they specifically did so for reasons of "honor."

Passing not only empowered the racially mixed and illegitimate to construct public reputations as persons of honor; it also permitted elites whose actions might deprive them of honor to retain it. Subsequent chapters will demonstrate the variety of ways in which colonial elites consciously manipulated the private-public duality to construct public reputations superior to private realities. The lives of those who follow reveal a colonial Spanish America that was far more flexible, and infinitely more complex, than ever imagined. Yet behind that eighteenth-century world lay centuries of Hispanic traditions, laws, and customs that influenced colonial attitudes toward discrimination, sexuality, illegitimacy, and civil legitimation. It is to these precedents that we now turn.

Precedents: Sexuality and Illegitimacy, Discrimination, Civil Legitimation

In 1453 the Castilian count of Castañeda approached his king, John II, and asked a personal favor—that the monarch use his royal dispensing power to override existing law and grant the privileges given only to legitimate offspring to his illegitimate son, García.[1] It is no accident that the wording of this legitimation decree was paralleled by the language that Charles IV would use in 1793 to provide a similar favor for Don Gabriel Muñoz. The bonds that linked a medieval lord and his vassal, and that prompted King John's personal favor to the count in the fifteenth century, had, by the eighteenth century, been transformed into a bureaucratic process through which the king and his ministers granted legitimations in the Americas. The echoes of this original feudal exchange resonated in late colonial petitions when a minor bureaucrat in Caracas or a matron in Havana also styled themselves as a loyal "vassal" of the imperial state.[2] Whether in medieval or Bourbon times, legitimation decrees endured as a vital manifestation of the royal power to dispense with the universal effects of law and to make individual exceptions for favored subjects.

Without question, a great divide separated the worlds of the newly legitimated son of a late-medieval count and an eighteenth-century Medellín merchant. Don García became legitimate before the marriage of Ferdinand and Isabella (1469) and the eventual union of their Castilian and Aragonese kingdoms into the Spanish nation, and before the voyages of Columbus. Don Gabriel lived in a late-eighteenth-century America characterized by internal renewal, stimulated by the external measures of Bourbon reforms, and soon to move beyond Spanish control. Yet answers to three fundamental questions surrounding issues of illegitimacy—how it is created, how to discriminate against it, and how to remedy it—provide links between their discrete epochs.

This chapter traces historical Hispanic attitudes and practices concerning three issues—sexuality, discrimination, and civil legitimation—to explore their influence on eighteenth-century Spanish-American mentality and practice. Between the worlds of Don García and Don Gabriel stood the major watershed of the sixteenth-century Council of Trent, which defined ecclesiastical authority to regulate customs surrounding sexuality, courtship, marriage, and illegitimacy. The late fifteenth and early sixteenth centuries crystallized distinctive Hispanic modes of discrimination that were echoed in law and in popular custom in eighteenth-century America. The legitimations of Don García and Don Gabriel equally suggest that there was a three-hundred-year tradition of redress, for the king or his ministers might intervene to erase illegitimacy and to remove prejudice. Exploration of these precedents provides insight into the continuities as well as the alterations that shaped the world of illegitimates in eighteenth-century Spanish America.

SEXUALITY, COURTSHIP, ILLEGITIMACY, AND THE COUNCIL OF TRENT: CHANGES AND CONTINUITIES

The time has come to lay the myth of the virgin bride to rest for once and for all. What Peter Laslett proclaimed for Europe and Anglo America was equally true for Spain and the Spanish colonies: "An agreement to marry meant freedom to copulate."[3] This is not to deny that sexual encounters could exact a social price for couples who were intimate—especially for elite women, who might risk their honor if they became pregnant and marriage did not eventually occur. Yet historical practice and popular attitudes permitted alternative paths, and couples might be sexually intimate, and parents, for months, years, or even decades before a final marriage ceremony.[4] To understand why this was so is to explore continuities in attitudes and practices before and after the historic Council of Trent (1545–1563).

Before the Council of Trent was a European, a Spanish, and a Hispanic-American divide in which marriage was not the sole formal commitment that might be recognized between sexual partners, and in which the couple rather than the priest were the agents of matrimony. After the Council of Trent, only marriages performed by a cleric legitimized sexual liaisons. The implications of Trent radically changed the accepted guidelines concerning mating, procreating, and the legitimacy of offspring. The potential consequences were so culturally profound that two centuries later those canons had still been neither popularly accepted nor uniformly implemented.[5]

Even the Catholic Church could not begin to eliminate the human propensity for arranging sexual liaisons outside of sanctified unions. During the Spanish Middle Ages some nonmarital arrangements had enjoyed a legal basis. Single men and women commonly entered into contracts of *barraganía*, or quasi-marriages. In these contracts the parties had to be single, unrelated by prohibited decrees of kinship, and faithful to each other.[6] But, unlike the case of an agreement to marry, the pair did not exchange any promise to wed, and the relationship could be terminated by a notary. Such temporary liaisons were still common in the fifteenth century, and they prevailed to a lesser degree into the sixteenth.[7] The Council of Trent delegitimized such arrangements, for it recognized only permanent marriages.

A second turning point promulgated by Trent was the council's insistence that it was the cleric, rather than the couple, that actuated the matrimony. Before Trent the stages of the marriage process could be prolonged and ambiguously defined. The medieval Spanish *Siete Partidas* (1256–1265) reflected civil and canonical procedures whereby a couple might effectively marry with the immediate exchange of vows (*esponsales de presente*), or whereby they might promise to do so in the future (*esponsales de futuro*).[8] In the second instance, couples might initiate sexual relationships and live together as man and wife. Such extended betrothals were serious affairs, tantamount to marriage itself. Often sealed with solemn oaths and exchanges of goods, they provided few opportunities for one or the other party to renege.[9]

The Council of Trent not only rejected the supposition that couples might marry without the aid of clergy but also devalued the intermediary process whereby lovers might live together under the future promise of matrimony.

One of the church's goals was to compress the time between the initiation of sexual intercourse, the procreation of children, and an eventual religious ceremony. As one historian put it, the Council of Trent "wage[d] a struggle against the cohabitation of the engaged."[10] Trent erected a distinctive barrier between the status of those sexually active couples who had been married by a priest and who could produce legitimate offspring, and everyone else. This distinction created a new world of illegitimates.

Even though the Catholic Church might proclaim doctrine, there were limits to the extent to which this might immediately, or even eventually, alter deeply held beliefs.[11] Popular acceptance of a preliminary stage of sexual relations prior to marriage continued. Nor could Trent affect existing laws that recognized the special nature of the offspring produced by such premarital liaisons. It was not uncommon in eighteenth-century Spain and Spanish America for couples to pledge matrimony (*palabra de casamiento*) and become sexually intimate before they wed; some lived together openly and produced children before they finally tied the knot. Spanish law still maintained its pre-Trent recognition of the special nature of such sexual arrangements: The offspring of unmarried lovers belonged to the most favored category of illegitimates, known as *hijos naturales*, and enjoyed a superior potential for inheritance and subsequent legitimation.[12]

Yet Trent had not been totally ineffective, for by the eighteenth century the *palabra de casamiento* had evolved into a pale version of its preconciliar counterpart.[13] The promise of matrimony could range from a hasty pledge in secret between young lovers that the virginity lost that night would be eventually redeemed by matrimony, to informal ceremonies in which the couple exchanged token gifts in front of friends and family, to the more unusual execution of written contracts.[14] But, in comparison with earlier centuries, the force of the promise of matrimony was weakened, since it was no longer bound by oaths which if broken would be a sacrilege; nor did it usually involve exchanges of significant property that might be forfeited. Nor was the state eventually as willing to use punishments such as exile or prison to force recalcitrant men, the usual renegers on vows, to marry.[15] By 1803 royal officials had refused to accept the word of the engaged, ordering instead that betrothals be considered valid only when the eligibility and intentions of the contracting parties were confirmed in writing before a notary.[16]

Yet even though weakened, the promise of matrimony still maintained some validity in eighteenth-century sexual politics.[17] The church supported verbal pledges, and priests considered such vows to preclude those involved from making similar promises or contracting marriage with anyone else. The *palabra de casamiento* still gave the benefit of the doubt to couples who became sexually intimate. Explicit in *gracias al sacar* testimony is the continuation of the belief that marriage was a process, and that sexual intimacy did not damage a woman's honor if there were promise of an eventual ceremony.[18]

A conscious delineation of such eighteenth-century courtship rules appears in an intimate letter written by Querétaro Regidor Don Joseph Martin de la Rocha to his spinster sister, Doña Elvira, who lived in Vera Cruz, Mexico.[19] Don Joseph broached a most delicate subject as he admitted that he had fathered an illegitimate child, and he begged his sister to assume responsibility for her baby niece. Don Joseph confessed:

> I tell you in all confidence, and confident in the love you have for me, that this baby is my daughter, and I recognize her as such, and that her mother was a lady, that nothing takes away from my circumstances that I knew her as a virgin, and that she died in childbirth, and for that reason all my plans have been frustrated.

The manner in which this eighteenth-century elite Mexican man chose to describe his courtship to his unmarried sister is telling. Don Joseph justifies his affair, saying that his lover was a social peer, a "lady," and a woman of honor, for she was a "virgin." Nor had Don Joseph seduced her with unworthy motives, as the couple had exchanged the promise of matrimony ("all my plans have been frustrated"). In another case, Peruvian Don Antonio Bedoya similarly confessed that he had a sexual relationship with Doña Francia de la Fuena, "a girl who was a virgin and of all honor and with whom he thought to marry."[20] Even after these men had taken the virginity of their fiancées, they still considered them to be women of honor.

Thus, if a couple were social equals and exchanged the promise of matrimony, an elite woman might lose her virginity and engage in a sexual relationship without immediate loss of her honor. Although a courting man customarily demanded virginity of an intended wife, he expected her to prove her virtue at the time of first sexual intercourse, which might significantly precede any wedding ceremony. Such a custom explains the seeming paradox of a society dominated by worship of the Virgin and promotion of female virginity, while at the same time a significant number of women, including elite women, engaged in premarital sexual relationships. The Spanish-American propensity to engage in sexual intercourse prior to matrimony has been noted by a number of historians and places Hispanic-American courtship customs firmly within the parameters of their eighteenth-century European and Anglo-American counterparts.[21]

Just as the Council of Trent failed to curtail the popular belief that marriage was a process that might include sexual intimacy between unmarried lovers, Spanish law continued to favor the illegitimate offspring created by such unions. Such treatment had precedents, including the edicts of Constantine, early canon law, and medieval Spanish codes such as the *Fuero Real*, the *Fuero de Soria*, and the *Siete Partidas*.[22] The legal tradition persisted that if the lovers were unmarried and not related by prohibited degrees of kinship, any subsequent marriage between them would both regularize their relationship and automatically and fully legitimate their *hijos naturales*.[23]

These Hispanic attitudes and the concomitant potential for total legitimation contrasted sharply with Anglo-Saxon traditions. Even prior to Trent, the English Statute of Merton (1236) had differed from the original Roman and Catholic tradition, decreeing that the eventual marriage of unwed parents did not legitimate offspring born prior to the ceremony.[24] It hardened the distinction between those who were legitimate and those who were not, since the latter had few possibilities of changing their status.[25] In contrast, in Catholic societies or Protestant localities such as Scotland, where post hoc legitimations were customary, the boundaries between legitimacy and illegitimacy remained permeable.[26] Premarital sexuality and resulting illegitimacy might be forgiven, not only in church but also in law. Marriage ceremonies could change mistresses into wives and natural children into legitimate heirs.[27]

Evidence of after-the-fact legitimations abounds in baptismal registers throughout the Spanish empire. These parish books not only recorded an illegitimate infant's reception of the sacrament but might also later add notes, to the side of the entry, recording subsequent parental marriage and resulting legitimation.[28] Don Juan Cavallero, a Spaniard resident in Mexico City, followed such a process in 1722. He explained that he and his lover, Doña Teresa Maldonado y Zapata, had been "unwed and able to marry" when they produced a son named Don Andrés, who had been baptized as an *hijo natural*.[29] Since that time the couple had married, "as the certificate proves," and so they requested that the registry recognize their child as "a legitimate son of a legitimate marriage." Yet another Mexican father sent similar proof of matrimony to the priest in Tlacopán with the request that he "change the relative section, putting in place of '*hijo natural*' [that the baby was] legitimate from the marriage of Don José María Bernal and Doña María Loreta de la Portilla."[30]

In Hispanic societies it was not uncommon for engaged women and men to be sexually active, and for their *hijos naturales* to become legitimate when they married. Illegitimacy did not have to be a permanent condition, for the traditional nuclear family might be constructed at any time that unwed lovers chose to marry. Yet just as historical practices established guidelines for sexuality, courtship, and illegitimacy, they equally governed discrimination against those not born in matrimony or never legitimated. To understand how Hispanic law and custom discriminated against illegitimates is to explore how traditional modes of prejudice became embedded as eighteenth-century issues of honor.

THE HISTORIC TEXTURE OF HISPANIC PREJUDICE

When Don Gabriel Muñoz applied for a *gracias al sacar*, he spoke in a code understood by his contemporaries, but one much less intelligible today. Along with every other petitioner, he specifically asked to be legitimated for reasons of "honor." Inherent in this concept of honor were underlying assumptions that had evolved over centuries to distinguish the privileges of those who possessed honor and those who did not. Exploration of the history of Hispanic prejudice reveals how late-fifteenth- and early-sixteenth-century Spaniards evolved legal and popular processes of discrimination that still influenced eighteenth-century American practices.

Just as in any society, early modern Spaniards practiced both negative and also positive forms of discrimination in order to establish a hierarchy of status. Those men distinguished as *hijosdalgo*, or "men of importance," were exempt from some taxes and punishments and positively recognized because of their lineage. Some of them belonged to an even more favored group, the titled nobility, who constituted the apex of Spain's aristocratic society.[31]

In contrast, the statutes that regulated *limpieza de sangre*, or purity of blood, encapsulated a particularly virulent negative prejudice. These developed special force in the fifteenth century and intensified as Spain became a nation. The purity of blood ordinances provided guidelines by which Spaniards could identify each other through a shared obsession with Catholic orthodoxy. The not-so-coincidental result was the forging of a self-conscious national identity intensified by common rejection of the despised "other." Ferdinand's and Isabella's forcible expulsion of Jews and Moors, and the mandatory conversion of those Jews who stayed (*conversos*), was but the most obvious step in this process. Yet their discriminatory measures had been preceded by a century of rising prejudice, and would be followed by centuries more of legislation that sharpened discrimination against the nonorthodox, ethnically different, and eventually the illegitimate. An exploration of four historical trends in Spanish discrimination—whether in favor of *hijosdalgo* or nobles, or against Jews, Moors, heretics, or illegitimates—reveals deeply rooted motifs that underlay eighteenth-century customs and practices.

The first component of Spanish discrimination was the never-questioned assumption that the monarch had the power to alter an individual's rank or heritage. The absence of nobility, or the possession of Jewish, Moorish, heretical, or illegitimate ancestry, was neither theoretically nor even necessarily permanent.[32] What one Spanish historian described so succinctly for purity of blood holds true for nobility and illegitimacy: "The king counts more than blood" ("*Mas pesa el rey que la sangre*").[33] Underlying the royal ability to transform status was a mentality that accepted that there might be a distinction between private reality and publicly constructed reputation.

The statutes of *limpieza de sangre* form a particularly interesting example of potential disparity between private and public spheres. The traditional benchmark for increased discrimination against those without *limpieza* was the 1449 ordinance of the city council of Toledo, which was directed especially against *conversos*, the converted descendants of Jews.[34] In the next two centuries, universities, the military, and religious orders would begin to pass even more discriminatory ordinances. Obsession with purity of lineage and ferocious prejudice against those who could not prove "clean blood" became a distinctive theme of corporate entities throughout Spain.[35]

Yet monarchs might go against this tide of prejudice. Even descent from Jewish ancestry, the most prejudicial condition in early modern Spain, might be officially altered at the will of the king. In 1604 Philip III effectively laundered the blood of the descendants of a famous Jewish *converso*, Pablo de Santa María. Although the decree conceded that the case was "unique," it then conferred *limpieza de sangre* on Don Pedro de Ossorio de

Velasco, as well as all the descendants of this converted rabbi. The royal grant provided that his heirs would be eligible for "all the honors, offices, benefices and patronage" that would go to "gentlemen, nobles, [and] Old Christians free of taint."[36] Other monarchs bestowed less sweeping concessions to individual *conversos*.[37]

The monarch also used his royal power to grant legitimations, changing private status for an enhanced public condition.[38] By the eighteenth century, legitimations had become part of a long list of status changes dispensed by the king and Cámara through the process of *gracias al sacar*. Petitioners might purchase citizenship, a title of nobility, and—in the Americas—even whiteness.[39] This later option developed because at some unknown point American colonists added "mulatto" to the historical *limpieza de sangre* discrimination against "commoner, Jew, Moor . . . [and] *converso*."[40] Transformations from nonnoble to noble, from illegitimate to legitimate, from *pardo* to white, were possible because Spaniards and Spanish Americans accepted a dual reality, one in which private conditions of birth, blood, or race, might have different public faces if the king or his ministers chose to intervene.

A second theme that linked discrimination in both peninsula and colony was the concept of a statute of limitations. Inherited negative characteristics were often limited to members of two past generations—that is, the candidate and the candidate's parents and grandparents. This limitation was traditional, deriving from a time when written documentation was scarce and living witnesses necessarily supplied the preponderance of testimony. A 1492 pragmatic of the Catholic Kings obligated petitioners to establish the identity of their father and grandfather for proof they were *hijosdalgo*, a requirement repeated in 1528 and 1538.[41] A similar two-generation rule applied in 1530 when the Cathedral of Córdoba wrote some of the first rules for the proof of *limpieza de sangre*; the candidate had to name his father and grandparents so that investigators might corroborate the testimony.[42]

As time passed, some private corporations such as *colegios*, congregations, and military orders went beyond the two-generation mandate and carried the *limpieza* obsession to greater extremes, calling for genealogies that stretched back to the seventh generation or beyond.[43] Nonetheless, the two-generation rule still governed certification of *limpieza* for holders of ecclesiastical positions such as parish priests or bishops.[44] By the eighteenth century, most Spanish-American universities, *colegios*, or military regiments accepted the two-generation limitation.[45]

Eighteenth-century *gracias al sacar* petitions reflected these discriminatory limitations. Several cases exist in which legitimate colonists sought to purchase *cédulas* for parents or grandparents whose defective birth threatened their own status. Yet in no instance did petitioners ever request that more distant ancestors be legitimated. Presumably there was no necessity, given the usual statute of limitations.

This temporal restriction also applied to racial prejudice in the Americas. If the percentage of mixed blood over time descended to less than one-eighth, the individual was technically white and met the requirements for *limpieza de sangre*. In two *gracias al sacar* cases petitioners provided the requisite description of the mixtures of previous generations to prove that they were under the critical one-eighth, and thus already met the requirements for purity of blood.[46] Spaniards and Spanish Americans shared an understanding that prejudice might be limited by generational or even quantitative considerations.

A third and even more fundamental theme that linked Spain and the colonies was the historical congruence of penalties applied against those who lacked *limpieza* and against those who were illegitimate. While statutes concerning purity of blood and legitimacy developed separately, by the eighteenth century they incorporated remarkably similar penalties. Both those without *limpieza* and illegitimates suffered what one seventeenth-century writer aptly characterized as a "civil death," since their birth or heritage barred them from access to political or economic power.[47] Some understanding of how such penalties developed, what they entailed, and how they merged provides another vital link between discrimination in Spain and the Americas.

The dearth of studies on illegitimacy in Spain in the fifteenth through seventeenth centuries obviates any easy conclusions concerning the development of discriminatory legislation and practice. An early if vague statement appears in the *Siete Partidas* (1256–1265) that included those "not born of legal matrimony according to the command of the Church" as among those classified as "*infamado*."[48] Such unfortunates lacked "*fama*" or "reputation," which the *Partidas* defined as "the good state of [a] man who lives rightly, and according to law and proper customs."[49] Those without *fama* were unable to achieve "any dignity or honor [*honra*] among those who might be chosen as men of good reputation." Although the *Partida* specifically forbade those without *fama* to serve as counselors to the king, the law conceded that they might still serve as judges of *audiencias* and in "all the other offices."[50] The wording of the *Partida* suggests a very early linkage between defect and civil effect: Since illegitimates lacked "*fama*" they could not achieve "*honra*" and thus should not be permitted to serve in designated prestigious public capacities.[51]

Another benchmark in discriminatory legislation against illegitimates occurred in 1414, when Pope Benedict XIII approved the foundation and the constitution of the Spanish *colegio* of San Bartolomé. Notable in this constitution is the explicit linkage between illegitimacy and *limpieza de sangre*. The constitution not only required entering members to supply proof that they were "of full fame and reputation" but also that they possessed "pure blood" ("*integrae fama & opinionis ex puro sanguine procedentes*").[52] By 1430 the conceptual linkage between illegitimacy and *limpieza* had become even clearer: The constitution of the college of Naples demanded that medical doctors have "no excommunicated or infamous ancestors. . . . If dead they must be publicly declared good and serious men without spurious or otherwise illegitimate birth."[53]

As the fifteenth century progressed, ordinances against *limpieza de sangre* proliferated and became ever more detailed in their discrimination. While illegitimates who could name their parents and their grandparents might be able to prove their *limpieza*, the traditional obfuscations that accompanied illegitimacy meant that many could not, and they suffered under these new penalties. For example, one of the first candidates to face discrimination under the Toledo city council statute of 1449 may or may not have actually been a *converso*.[54] Inasmuch as he was "a secret bastard of unknown father and mother," he was unable to name his ancestors or prove his *limpieza*, whatever his origin. He was, as historian Albert Sicroff commented, "without father, without mother, and without genealogy."[55] Thus, almost from the start, given the inability of many illegitimates to document their ancestry, legitimacy and *limpieza* became linked.

The Toledo *limpieza* statute proved but the first in a series of prejudicial directives that were leveled directly against *conversos* and indirectly against many illegitimates. Public offices were an obvious target of the discriminators, and indeed the Toledo city council based its original authority on the nebulous tradition that the city had royal permission to deprive *conversos* of such posts. The 1449 Toledo ordinance demanded that those unable to prove *limpieza* be "deprived of whatever notaries and other offices that they have and have held in this city and jurisdiction . . . and that from now on they neither swear nor hold such public offices, neither publicly nor secretly, especially the aforementioned notaries."[56]

Although the ordinance did not explain why Toledanos specifically targeted notaries for discrimination, the functions of that office suggest a rationale. While notaries did not exercise any particularly significant political power, they customarily handled privileged information, inasmuch as they certified sensitive documents such as testaments or business contracts. They had access to information that could destroy a family's reputation or provide insight into its investments. *Conversos* could not be trusted and were thus banned from such posts.

During the seventeenth century, imperial legislation both forbade *conversos* from operating as notaries and expanded the prohibition to illegitimates. As late as 1609, the royal provision for notaries had required only that they be of a certain age and demonstrate their expertise before obtaining their title. By 1679, however, such candidates not only had to provide proof concerning their "life and customs" but also had to prove both their *limpieza* and their legitimacy.[57] By the eighteenth century, *gracias al sacar* legislation reflected this development; it included a separate provision for legitimating those who wished to serve as notaries. Thus a local proscription against those without *limpieza*, which also incidentally discriminated against those illegitimates who could not prove their ancestry, eventually expanded to become civil regulations that explicitly prejudiced illegitimates.

A similar progression may well have occurred with the enforcement of the Royal Pragmatic of 1501, which first discriminated against those who could not document their *limpieza*, but that later prejudiced the public careers of all illegitimates. Promulgated by Ferdinand and Isabella, this law originally provided a specific list of more than forty offices barred to those who could not prove *limpieza de sangre*.[58] Unlike the *Siete Partidas*, which while excluding illegitimates from service on royal councils had permitted them to serve elsewhere, the prohibitions for those without *limpieza* extended to every civil post. Not only royal councilors but also judges in *audiencias* and chancelleries, secretaries, *alcaldes, alguaciles, mayordomos,* and other imperial officers had to demonstrate *limpieza*. Even local officers such as *corregidores, regidores,* and *alcaldes* had to meet such requirements, which now affected every public office throughout the realm.

Unlike the case of the notaries, the *Pragmática* was not followed by subsequent legislation that explicitly expanded discrimination to illegitimates.[59] Although the Laws of the Indies required that local *alcaldes* be "honored persons," there was no elaboration exactly what that meant.[60] Yet the connection between honor, legitimacy, and public office was unambiguous and appears in some of the earliest legitimation decrees issued in the Americas. When the son of Huascar Inca legitimated numerous *hijos naturales* in 1544, the decree noted that his offspring would now be "more honored" and therefore would be able to serve in "royal offices" and "councils."[61] A royal *cédula* in 1549 implied that "laws and pragmatics" kept the racially mixed and illegitimate from holding public office, although it did not cite any specific legislation. A 1591 decree gave the viceroy of Peru limited permission to legitimate selected mestizos who, given both their "illegitimacy" and their "mixture," could not hold office.[62] In the seventeenth century a decree assured a newly legitimated Quiteño that he "would . . . be admitted to all the royal offices, councils and public [offices] . . . as fully as [if he were] of legitimate marriage."[63]

By the eighteenth century the link between *limpieza*, legitimacy, and honor was fully institutionalized, for discriminatory traditions in Spanish history had merged. Added to the original *Partida* definition of illegitimates as without "*fama*" and thus prohibited from certain offices of "*honra*" were the more detailed *limpieza* ordinances that expanded and detailed such discrimination.[64] *Gracias al sacar* petitioners explained that their birth deprived them of honor, and thus the ability to hold honorific posts. Lack of honor had produced a civil death that barred those so marked from most prestigious and authoritative positions in society.[65] Honor was less a "personal quality . . . than a social condition."[66]

Eventually, both *limpieza* and legitimacy became preconditions not only for holding office but also for practicing certain professions. The 1501 *Pragmática* had included occupations barred to those who could not prove their *limpieza*, a restriction that necessarily included many illegitimates as well. In addition to public notaries, lawyers, surgeons, pharmacists, and assayers had to provide proof of their purity of blood, and, as time passed, of their legitimacy and honor. Such discrimination was contemporaneous with the sixteenth- and seventeenth-century practices of military orders, religious congregations, colleges, and universities, which also excluded those without *limpieza*.[67] Some of these groups expanded this prohibition to include even those illegitimates who might have been able to document their ancestry. When colonial American institutions such as colleges and universities wrote their own ordinances, they based them on Spanish models and included these prohibitions as well.[68] Even though the Laws of the Indies did not specifically discriminate against illegitimates, the ordinances required that seminarians be "honored gentleman" and that lawyers be able to prove their "quality" and "birth."[69]

Illegitimates who sought ecclesiastical careers faced dual prejudice, from both church and state. Religious orders wrote their own constitutions demanding *limpieza* and proof of legitimacy for entrance. Canons of the Council of Trent discriminated against illegitimates who wished to become priests; even if they were ordained, their advancement was limited.[70] The state also regulated entry to the priesthood, discriminating against illegitimates because, as one royal official noted in 1789, "Ministers of the altar ought to be persons of all honor and estimation," and "those with this defect do not have such estimation."[71] Although such regulations might be overcome with ecclesiastical waivers called *habilitaciones*, these grants removed prejudice for ecclesiastical purposes only.[72] Illegitimates who hoped to graduate from universities before undertaking an ecclesiastical career, or who wanted to avoid social discrimination, preferred a civil legitimation that erased ecclesiastical as well as all other barriers to acceptance.[73]

To some extent there was a direct connection—a link of cause and effect—between these patterns of discrimination and eighteenth-century applications for *gracias al sacar*. Although not all petitioners stated exactly why they were asking for legitimation, the detailed testimony that accompanied each request often noted the particular situations that had prompted the petitions. For example, fifteen illegitimates asked to be restored to honor primarily so that they might hold public office. Eleven requested the special legitimations necessary to receive appointments as notaries. Five mentioned that they were applying so that they might matriculate or graduate from American universities. Four asked for dispensations to practice medicine, two to become lawyers, two to serve in the army, one to practice as a smelter, and twelve to enter or advance in the priesthood.[74]

Even a cursory examination of legitimation cases, however, shows that the link between historic agendas of discrimination and the daily prejudices faced by illegitimates was seldom consistent. Written laws and traditions set overarching guidelines: They established customary agendas for discrimination that might or might not be carried out, depending upon a multitude of other variables.

In some situations illegitimates had already informally passed, for they had overcome discrimination, achieved office, or practiced occupations officially barred to them long before they sought formal redress. This Hispanic propensity to create social space for individual mobility through informal passing marks a fourth link between patterns of discrimination in Spain and the colonies. An examination of several examples of Spanish discrimination against *conversos* indicates that the underlying assumptions that permitted passing in colonial America derived from deeply rooted tradition.

Antonio Domínguez Ortíz's masterful study of Spanish *conversos* provides illuminating instances that illustrate passing: Although his analysis does not use that word, he carefully notes that not every descendant of Jewish ancestry suffered equivalent discrimination. Wealth or personal achievement might make it possible for a *converso* to create, and have others accept, an alternative public personality distinct from the private reality.

Such was the case of Francisco Díaz Pimento, the illegitimate son of a Jewish mariner and merchant, who rose to become an admiral of the Indies fleet, thereby amassing a personal fortune. In 1642 he applied to become a member of the Order of Santiago, which, as one of the more restrictive and antisemitic of the military institutions, required that candidates prove their *limpieza de sangre* through the fourth generation.[75] Yet, even though at least one witness submitted a report noting that the admiral's father was a Jew with involvement in the slave trade, Francisco was accepted into the order. No doubt this was because the candidate found "more than one hundred witnesses" who testified to an invented Viscayan mother and who were willing to attribute his lack of ancestral documentation to his having been born as his parents "passed through" Cuba.[76] The construction and the acceptance in the public sphere of a false persona permitted the *converso* admiral to enter the Order of Santiago, its discriminatory ordinances and his private "defect" notwithstanding.

An even more self-conscious expression of the bifocal vision that facilitated such mobility appears in a seventeenth-century debate over what should happen when witnesses testified that a candidate had *converso* origins.[77] One commentator, Francisco de Amaya, took an extreme position, arguing that colleges should not admit any candidate if witnesses produced any negative information—even if that charge eventually proved to be false. Respondent Escobar de Corro refuted that stance, specifically differentiating between the public and the hidden ("*publice et occulte*") components of an individual's reputation. He declared, "It is evident that purity and nobility are not something essential, corporeal, real or palpable, but something that is held by human opinion, the opinion of the general public." As historian Domíngues Ortíz later pointed out, "The meaning of this phrase could not be more clear: nobility and *limpieza* are not things in themselves, they do not have an objective existence, they are products of the human mind."

In a footnote, Domínguez Ortíz took his analysis a step further. He mused that the "extraordinary consequence" of Escobar de Corro's reasoning was that "a witness not only can, but ought to swear that a candidate is noble and clean, even if the contrary is evident, if the stain is not public." This suggests that the ultimate effect of the distinction between public reputation and hidden reality was the creation of a social space through which individuals such as the admiral could pass. Rather than the "facts" of the case—in his instance, a Jewish father and a questionable mother—popular opinion was the ultimate arbitrator of whether the admiral's constructed public personality might be accepted in lieu of the actual facts of his birth. Yet if the admiral's informal attempt to pass had failed, he still had an alternative, because just as the state officially discriminated, it might also provide formal redress. The continuities and alterations in the history of legitimations provide another example of how practices from the Hispanic past influenced late colonial Spanish America.

'GRACIAS AL SACAR': A HISTORICAL PERSPECTIVE

The precedents for civil legitimation stretch back to the Roman empire, with peninsular roots that precede the formation of the Spanish state.[78] Legitimacy was a fundamental marker of social and material status, for only legitimate births, the post hoc marriages of the unwed, or civil legitimations securely transferred family honor and property from one generation to the next. Because they were so important, legitimation decrees were marked with the royal seal (*sello*) and preserved among the important documents issued by Iberian monarchs. Such *sello* registers are mentioned as early as the *Siete Partidas* (1256–1265), and the Cortes of Toro (1371) and of Toledo (1462) insisted that such documentation be preserved.[79] More than twenty-three hundred surviving legitimations issued between 1475 and 1543, as well as an unindexed and unknown number from the seventeenth century, are preserved in the Spanish archive and castle of Simancas.[80] Three hundred more from the eighteenth century can be found in the National Archive in Madrid. The 244 legitimations from the Americas—the heart of this investigation—remain in the Archive of the Indies in Seville.

Although the Spanish state issued legitimization decrees for more than three hundred years, their civil effect altered importantly from the late fifteenth and early sixteenth centuries on the peninsula to the eighteenth century in the colonies. Ricardo Córdoba de la Llave's preliminary analysis of the first twenty years of fifteenth-century legitimations establishes that they provided comprehensive redress for serious transgressions. Almost 70 percent of the legitimated were bastards whose fathers had been priests (sacrilegious) or whose parents had been married to someone else (adulterous), while fewer than 20 percent were *hijos naturales*.[81] These early peninsular legitimations were powerful social and legal instruments that restored both civil status and the right to full inheritance. Later chapters will explore how their eighteenth-century American counterparts were typically granted to *hijos naturales*, rarely improving inheritance birthright.

While prominent nobles no doubt made personal pleas to monarchs to legitimate favored sons and daughters, a process developed early on for consideration of applications. Most requests arrived at the Councils of Castile and later the Council of the Indies, where royal officials made recommendations to the monarch. The early Hapsburg kings (Charles V and Philip II) seem to have read and commented on some of these dispensations; later monarchs usually gave a pro forma approval to legitimations sanctioned by royal officials.[82] To understand who made these decisions and how the paper flowed is to explore another essential component of the legitimation process.

Since its establishment in 1524, the Council of the Indies had functioned as the paramount colonial authority over the colonies. Staffed by a president, councilors, and attorneys, the council rose in power in the sixteenth century and fell during the next, along with the fortunes of the Spanish state.[83] In 1600 a new body known as the Cámara, expressly charged with patronage, was formed (1600–1609) and re-formed (1644–1700) within the Council of the Indies. The Cámara's responsibilities included the naming of important civil and church appointments as well as the dispensing of special favors, including legitimations. Although the Cámara would be abolished and reinstated several times during its history, when it existed and there was patronage to be dispensed, the *Camaristas* were usually the decision makers.

While only six seventeenth-century legitimations can be found from the early colonies, no doubt many remain scattered in archives throughout Spain and the Americas. The crown usually reserved the issuance of legitimation petitions to itself, although special conditions led to exceptions in the Americas. A 1591 royal decree temporarily permitted the viceroys of New Spain and Peru to legitimate mestizos, presumably the offspring of the conquistadors and first settlers, and Indian women. The goal was the "social assimilation" of these mixed offspring, whose legitimation would enable them to inherit the properties and *encomiendas* of their Spanish fathers.[84] The monarch granted this permission to the Peruvian viceroy for only three years, although the right to legitimate remained in effect in Mexican jurisdictions until 1625.[85] Little is known of the effect of this decree, nor how many legitimations resulted.

Such provisions were eventually rescinded, although it was not until 1631 that the Council of the Indies reminded the viceroy of Peru that it alone had the right to issue legitimations.[86] Additionally, a single reference exists to a later, 1654 royal decree that permitted the president of the *audiencia* of Quito to grant legitimations as a money-making device for a five-year period. Yet by 1663 an Ecuadorian illegitimate again had to apply to Spain for relief, as local permission to grant such measures had expired.[87] This 1663 petition joined with two others from the viceroy of Peru and three from Mexico as the six legitimations that can be discovered from the seventeenth century.[88]

The Bourbon accession to the throne in 1700 produced a systematic reorganization of civil administration (1701–1717) that profoundly reduced the authority of the Council of the Indies. Consistent with the Bourbon goal of making government more efficient, that ruling body lost its authority in matters of finance and military affairs while retaining its judicial and patronage responsibilities. Administratively the Council of the Indies no longer reported directly to the king, but indirectly through the Ministry of the Indies (1717–1787), then the Ministry of the Indies for Gracias y Justicia (1787–1790), and finally the Ministry of Justice (1790–1808). Within the Indies council, the Cámara also experienced significant changes in fortune, being abolished in 1701, re-established in 1714, and abolished again in 1717. Only in 1721 did an uninterrupted history of dispersal of patronage begin, which included legitimations.[89] Even though the Council of the Indies was shunted between Bourbon ministries, Jacques Barbier concludes that it not only retained its remaining responsibilities but also served as an important consultative body throughout the eighteenth century.[90]

Although much within the Council of the Indies changed throughout the eighteenth century, certain structures and procedures remained essentially the same.[91] A president or governor headed the council, which was staffed by nobles (*de capa y espada*) some of whom (*ministros togados*) had training as lawyers. A smaller group of councilors also staffed the elite Cámara de Gracias y Justicia. These *Camaristas* had often served on the Council of the Indies before they joined the more prestigious Cámara, and they received extra stipends in view of their additional responsibility to dispense patronage and favor. Crown attorneys known as *fiscales* assisted both the Council of the Indies and the Cámara.

Throughout the eighteenth century petitions for legitimation followed a similar path from the Americas. Letters, petitions, and memorials from royal officials and private citizens were channeled to the Cámara through the crown attorneys who represented the two major geographical divisions of the Indies. The *fiscal* for the viceroyalty of New Spain routed documents that arrived from the Caribbean, Central America, and Mexico, while the crown attorney for Peru directed the correspondence from most of South America.[92] Internal comments on legitimation petitions show that these two attorneys first read the cover letters, the depositions of witnesses, and the supporting documents, and then summarized the data. Their commentary might or might not include a recommendation. The Cámara then met and discussed the application. Sometimes it came to a decision without comment, sometimes it asked for further information, and sometimes members debated the outcome. A summary of its comments was typically included in the documentary record. Only if a decision were affirmative might the Cámara consider what price should be charged. The decision then was forwarded for what was usually a pro forma approval by the minister of the Indies and signature by the monarch. The final stage in the process was the issuance of the official legitimation decree (*cédula*).

While the administrative paper flow remained essentially the same, two aspects of the process changed significantly by the middle of the eighteenth century. The first was the transformation in the expertise of Cámara personnel, the second a dramatic increase in applications for legitimation. Although detailed analysis of those trends must await later chapters, it is worth noting here that the phenomena coincided during the decades of the most concentrated American Bourbon reform activity.

The early-eighteenth-century Bourbon reforms had brought the Council of the Indies to a low point, reducing its size to nine members and significantly diminishing its jurisdiction. As the decades passed, the Council of the Indies grew again in numbers, effectiveness, and influence. A new series of reforms (1773–1776) made the status and the salaries of councilors equal to those of the premier Council of Castile, and increased the number of officers to fourteen. It was not so much the increase of numbers but the experience of the new appointees that brought striking change. Both the Council of the Indies and the Cámara were increasingly staffed by officials who had had decades of service in the Americas. Mark Burkholder has noted that from 1717 to 1739 only 30 percent of newly appointed councilors had American expertise, but that this figure increased to 52 percent between 1740 and 1773, and to 80 percent between 1773 and 1808.[93] Familiarity with the Indies had always been important for Cámara officials, who had to evaluate applications for colonial appointments. While roughly half of eighteenth-century *Camaristas* had American experience, after 1773 70 percent of new appointees had served in the colonies.[94] It was those officials, who had, as Burkholder underlines, both "personal knowledge" as well as a "variety of experience" in the Americas, who would shape enforcement of the Bourbon social reforms.[95]

It was to this knowledgeable Cámara that a torrent of legitimation applications began to flow from the Americas. During the first half of the eighteenth century the Cámara received few petitions: seven in the 1720s, two in the 1730s, ten in the 1740s, and five in the 1750s. It was only after midcentury that a widening stream—fourteen in the 1760s and eleven in the 1770s—was followed by a flood: fifty-nine in the 1780s, and seventy-one in the 1790s. The early years of the new century saw a decline to twenty-seven in the first decade and twenty-eight in the second. Just as the decades of increased applications corresponded to the peak years of the Bourbon Reforms (1759–1808), so the geographical distribution of petitioners seems to have reflected regions whose societies and economies had been particularly affected by change. The Caribbean, primarily Cuba, provided a noteworthy 36.5 percent (N. 89) of applications, because an expanding slave trade and a booming sugar economy created propitious dynamics for upward social and racial mobility as well as for elite discriminatory response. Yet Cubans were not the only seekers of redress, for 39 percent (N. 95) of illegitimate petitioners came from South America, with 24.5 percent (N. 60) originating from Panama northward (see Table 1).

In the early decades of the eighteenth century Cámara officials generally legitimated most applicants. Later, however, the increasing number of petitions, the greater American experience of the *Camaristas*, and the policy agendas inherent in the Bourbon reforms led to gradual and then to increasing selectivity that started in the 1760s, accelerated during the 1770s and 1780s, and altered yet again in the mid-1790s. Although that is an important part of this story, it will be best told later. Just as the newly appointed Cámara officials could bring decades of colonial experience to bear as they read legitimation petitions, so we, too, must first understand the underlying patterns of life in the Americas. There is much to learn from the collected biographies of the 187 mothers and fathers and their 244 illegitimates, as well as from the testimonies of their innumerable relatives, friends, and neighbors, who listened to their problems and responded—in one way or another—to their plight.

PART TWO

Life Course

THREE

Mothers: Pregnant Virgins, Abandoned Women, and the Private and Public Price of Sexuality

In 1754 Doña Margarita Martínez Orejón of Tasco, Mexico, discovered that she was pregnant.[1] She was eighteen, unmarried, and belonged to one of the town's most distinguished families. Her brothers were priests, her ancestors had been conquistadors.[2] The choices that she, her lover—silver mine owner Don Antonio Villanueva Telles Xirón—their families, and their friends would make concerning her pregnancy would alter their lives as well as those of the next generation. While it seems unlikely that eighteen-year-old Doña Margarita ever dreamed that her sexual affair or her pregnancy would be chronicled decades later in notarized documents, much less preserved for centuries in the Archive of the Indies, her story joins the collected biographies of 186 other such women to provide contemporaneous evidence of the spoken as well as unspoken assumptions that shaped elite attitudes toward female sexuality in colonial Spanish America.

A first conclusion that emerges from these histories is that the underlying rhythms that shaped gender relations in the eighteenth century differed substantially from those that governed late-nineteenth-century or twentieth-century interactions. Although stereotypes such as machismo and *marian-*

ismo have figured largely in scholarly literature as models for exploring male-female relations in Latin America, they prove an inappropriate starting point for this analysis. That is not to deny that certain aspects of machismo and *marianismo* strike accurate chords in the colonial past. The sexual promiscuity associated with machismo was typical of colonial men, who paid substantially lesser prices for their sexual activity than did their female counterparts; the reverence for the Virgin Mary and the female chastity associated with *marianismo* were equally familiar to colonial women.[3] Religious devotion was a prized female attribute and virginity a material asset. Nor is there any question that the ultimate effect of sexual codes, whether in the colony or later, was patriarchal control of reproduction through insistence on female virginity or marital faithfulness.

Yet the constraints that controlled female sexuality are necessarily social, and therefore necessarily historical. They were constructed and reconstructed within the discrete contexts of epoch, race, and class. This is why modern versions of the *marianismo* complex lack analytical subtlety. In its most exaggerated form, *marianismo* presumes that virginity is an absolute. Women are supposedly either "in" sexual control or "out" of such control, and society does not recognize any in between. Unmarried women who lost their virginity, or wives who strayed, lost any claim to respectability; they were "out of control" and therefore approximated the moral, if not the actual, state of the prostitute.

The collected histories of the mothers of illegitimates reveal that eighteenth-century men and women had complicated views concerning rules of courtship, norms for the initiation of sexual activity, and the necessary response and social price when pregnancy ensued. Underlying their actions were conscious and sometimes unconscious assumptions that patterned social responses. Further consideration of the plight of the pregnant Doña Margarita provides an introduction to these interconnected themes.

UNDERLYING CONSTANTS

Eighteen years after Doña Margarita gave birth, she, her lover, her family, and her friends came forward to testify about those traumatic days of her pregnancy.[4] Tasco silver miner Don Antonio Villanueva acknowledged that it was "certain and true" that he had "known" Doña Margarita, "from which

MOTHERS 61

union she became pregnant." He vividly recalled how he had plotted to hide her pregnancy and protect her from public scandal:

> and in order to guard this fact, which was totally hidden and so without discredit for him or for her, it was not made public knowledge, but their indiscretion remained totally hidden, for the contacts they had in her house were not suspicious nor scandalous, given the high standing of both of them and the luster and reputation of her family.

The couple decided "that they would hide the pregnancy," and Don Antonio remembered that their plans had worked perfectly; "and after she gave birth without rumor or scandal" he had taken the newborn to "Zacoalpa to the house of Dr. Don Joseph de Torres, a priest who knew of this, and who received him as an orphan and in whose power he was baptized." After it had become clear that the birth had remained "hidden and silenced," Don Antonio retrieved the baby. He brought him as an "orphan" to Don Miguel de Rivera, an "intimate confidant" and a "companion in his dealing and businesses" who shared a house with him. For the next two decades these men carefully and lovingly supervised the upbringing and education of the young Joseph Antonio.[5]

While Don Antonio raised their son, the unmarried Doña Margarita remained in her family home. As the years passed, she achieved a reputation for her "extraordinary Christianity, retirement, and public reputation of virtue." This was one reason, Don Antonio reminisced years later, that it had been proper to conceal her pregnancy. He conceded that the "fragility" that had led her to consent to sexual intercourse had been "the effect only of a natural weakness and not of incontinence or custom," and "until this day very few persons, and [only] those of the most exalted and best circumstances have knowledge of what happened."

It was only when her eighteen-year-old son was about to leave for the university that Doña Margarita publicly acknowledged that she had, by "mere fragility," conceived, although she hastened to add that the existence of her son had been cloaked in "such secrecy that she has not lost the credit that she and her family have in Tasco." Her testimony revealed the high price exacted for her youthful love affair, for she confessed that:

> she never had anything to do with any other man, neither before nor after she conceived the said Joseph Antonio, nor even after this incident has she

ever had relations with Don Antonio, but she has lived with honor and sense, and with no loss of her good reputation.

Doña Margarita came forth as an unwed mother because the future welfare of her son began to outweigh any detriment to her own reputation. She did "not want to take away the good that could come to him if he knew who his parents were." Personal priorities and social strategies could change depending on life course; the concealment considered essential for an unmarried mother of eighteen might not be as critical for a spinster of thirty-six.[6]

Embedded within several decades of decisions by Don Antonio, Doña Margarita, and their friends and family are assumptions concerning gender, the moral and social consequences of sexuality, the division of their worlds into private and public spheres, the importance of honor, and the prerogatives of hierarchy. Not surprisingly, the gendered and double standard for sexual activity emerges as a first theme, for colonial codes disproportionately punished women who did not control their sexuality. There even seemed to be an approving note in Don Antonio's comment that Doña Margarita had essentially "paid" for her youthful indiscretion through decades of religious devotion, seclusion, and sexual abstinence. Yet even though women suffered disproportionately, the loss of virginity was not considered evidence of a fatal moral flaw. At the core of Catholic religion and culture was the understanding that both men and women would sin, and that such transgressions could always be confessed and forgiven. Although more sexual control was expected of women, there was also the recognition that they might be "fragile."

Doña Margarita and Don Antonio were not alone in their use of "fragility" to explain their lapse into passion. A Cuban mother of twelve illegitimate children also testified to the "human fragility which so combats the strongest spirits so as to conquer them."[7] An illegitimate wrote of the "fragility" of his parents.[8] A Mexican petitioner explained her parents' sexual affair as the result of "the frailty and passion [of which] they could not rid themselves."[9] Obviously, resort to the frailty or fragility excuse was commonplace in colonial Spanish America.[10]

But such toleration had limits. Society conceded that women might be subject to temptation, but it still judged the context within which they yielded. Don Antonio was not the only commentator who specifically differentiated between women who succumbed to temptation because of "natural weakness" and those who did so fairly regularly and promiscuously through "incontinence or custom."[11] Comments by lovers, family, friends, townspeople, and even royal officials are striking in their tolerance rather than in their censure of women who succumbed to passion. One of the most telling silences in *gracias al sacar* testimonies is the absence of condemnation of women who surrendered their virginity, or even of those who engaged in longer term but monogamous sexual liaisons. Elite women could live their lives "in between" the dyad of the saint and the whore. Unlike the Anglo world to the north, Hispanic America had no equivalent of the morally flawed, permanently shamed Hester Prynne.

While the sin that accompanied sexual acts might be confessed and absolved, society could exact a formidable price from women who lost their virginity, became openly pregnant, and produced illegitimate babies. Embedded within Don Antonio's description of Doña Margarita's pregnancy is a telling paradox illustrating how the private-public duality might mitigate social punishment. On the one hand, Don Antonio emphasizes how the couple concealed the pregnancy, for it was "without rumor or scandal," and the birth was "silenced." Yet on the other hand, he also admits that Doña Margarita's sexual activity and resulting pregnancy were not a total secret, for those of "the most exalted and best circumstances [had] knowledge of what happened." Why would Don Antonio testify that the affair was "totally hidden" and still concede that the most important people in the town knew about it?

Underlying Don Antonio's comments was his division of the world into private and public components. Since Don Antonio and Doña Margarita belonged to prominent families, they counted a significant number of the Tasco elite among the intimate acquaintances who composed their private circle. The responsibility of these notables would be to maintain silence and not to admit in public what they knew in private. It was not a contradiction for Don Antonio to say that Doña Margarita's pregnancy remained a secret, yet also to concede that many local notables knew what had happened.[12]

Elites commonly embedded this dual mentality into their testimony, for witnesses might relate detailed knowledge concerning a woman's sexual relationship and pregnancy yet decline to identify her in public. In Chile, witnesses were "very specific" concerning an unwed mother's "ancestry and connections," which were of the "best quality," but they "suppressed" her name because of her "honesty and decorum."[13] In Cuba, a witness clearly knew the identity of one unwed mother but conceded only that she was "a white person, the daughter of noble parents . . . who have always recognized her as their daughter."[14] In colonial Colombia, an illegitimate was produced by "a lady who due to her distinguished quality is not named."[15] One Quito spinster would admit her motherhood to a judge only "privately," as she wanted to maintain her public "unmarried and honorable state."[16]

On some occasions years might pass before the identity of mothers would be revealed. One Venezuelan woman had originally been protected by witnesses in a 1777 deposition because "she was a woman of reputation and for that reason it was impossible to discover it [her identity] in any manner."[17] Ten years later, when further testimony was taken, she was dead, and so commentators were disposed to be more explicit. One recalled that he had originally protected her name but that he was now willing to admit "that the woman that he spoke about in the other declaration and that he expressed to be the mother of the declarant, was called Doña Antonia Luisa de Mata, that before he did not express her name for she was a person of distinction and married." Such bifurcation between the private and public created protective interstices whereby women who had engaged in prohibited sexual activity need not immediately, or even necessarily ever, pay a public price. Doña Margarita was not the only women who lost her virginity, produced an illegitimate baby, and yet experienced "no loss of her good reputation."[18]

Such conscious distinctions between the private and the public were integral to elite negotiations concerning honor. Elite women possessed public personalities and positions in the civil sphere precisely because they possessed honor that they had to maintain and to pass on to the next generation. They might lose their personal honor and damage their family reputation if evidence of their sexuality or pregnancy became "public and notorious." Yet if such information were suppressed, and acknowledged only in the private sphere, they might maintain their public standing. One Venezuelan witness specifically linked the private-public duality and honor when he explained that his mother's name did not appear on his baptismal certificate because she was "a white woman of distinction for whose honor her name has always been suppressed."[19] Chilean historians Caviéres and Salinas provide another telling example of such elite rationalization of the distinction between private conduct and public reputation. One lover maintained that, even though he had had a sexual relationship with a woman of "quality," he had not damaged her "honor," precisely because the "coupling had been without anyone knowing of it."[20]

Honor was not an all-or-nothing affair, but rather an elastic commodity, somewhat analogous to a bank account. Elite women received honor through deposit at birth. Their own proper actions, such as control of their sexuality, marriage, and the production of legitimate children, maintained their reputation and passed an honor account on to the next legitimate generation. However they might suffer potential losses of their own honor balance if they made unfavorable social investments, such as the loss of virginity or out-of-wedlock pregnancy. Honor might also be maintained or restored with good investments, either by commitment to an immediate or to an eventual marriage, or by keeping sexual activity or pregnancy private.

Strategies to maintain or restore honor were furthered by the self-serving assumptions of a hierarchical society that gave the benefit of the doubt to peers unless confronted with striking evidence to the contrary. Even elites who were not within a private circle presumed that their social equals were acting properly and were innocent of any violations of the honor code. This was so even though circumstantial evidence might arouse suspicion. Don Antonio, it must be remembered, testified that the couple had found a private place for their sexual encounters in Doña Margarita's house. Presumably the fact that a man and woman spent time alone together might have raised some question. However he added that their meetings were "not suspicious nor scandalous," precisely because of their "high standing" as well as the "luster and reputation of [Doña Margarita's] family."[21]

This presumption of innocence benefited upper-class women especially, for peers commonly presumed engagements or marriages that did not exist. One witness vouched that an unwed mother "would never have accepted his communication unless he promised to be her husband."[22] Although one Colombian admitted that he did not know from "certain science" he "had heard truthful persons say" that if the woman in question had had a sexual relationship, it "would not be less than under the promise of matrimony."[23] In Mexico and Chile witnesses assumed that couples living together were married—even though they were not.[24] Elite willingness to provide peers with the benefit of the doubt provided additional maneuverability to women whose sexual activities gave them something they preferred to conceal.

Although their strategies might differ, elite women who faced the birth of an illegitimate child shared the same ultimate goal—to minimize or to avoid public loss of honor. The simplest and probably the most frequent solution was for the pregnant woman and her lover to marry immediately, to have a "premature" but legitimate first child, and thus to avoid scandal totally. Additional arrangements might protect or restore honor only if they maintained the public facade that no sexual activity had occurred, or if they linked public knowledge of sexual intimacy to the process of matrimony.[25] The greatest risk to female honor occurred when sexual relationships were public and marriage did not follow. Yet even in that worst case, the popular acceptance of human "fragility," the mental construct of dual worlds, and the presumption of innocence combined to create social space in which women might preclude or delay judgments concerning their honor.

PRIVATE PREGNANCY

In societies where premarital chastity is the ideal, expedients naturally arise to mitigate consequences when the norm is violated, and especially when pregnancy ensues. The most radical solution is to hide the evidence. Historians have chronicled such concealments, occurring with particular frequency in Mediterranean culture zones including Spanish America.[26] The history of Doña Margarita has already introduced a classic example of the variant that I have described elsewhere as private pregnancy.[27]

While marriage was the most acceptable solution when an elite woman surrendered her virginity and became pregnant during the betrothal, the experience of Doña Margarita demonstrates that couples had other options if they did not wed. Doña Margarita rather cryptically commented that "they had this intention [to wed], but certain circumstances, not of any difference of quality, but others, stopped it at that time."[28] Since the marriage was not to occur, the couple decided to hide their affair and their baby. Doña Margarita's social sin was not the loss of virginity to her fiancé, nor even her illegitimate baby, but that she would not be married afterward. Although women might not remain virgins before a wedding ceremony, they paid a high price if they did not eventually bind their lovers in wedlock.

Private pregnancy was a social conspiracy that permitted women to be pregnant and give birth while maintaining public reputations as virgins and women of honor. The social response to pregnant spinsters was complex, as peers reacted not only to empirical reality—that is, whether Doña X was

TABLE 3
Classification of Pregnancies in Legitimation Petitions

Type of Pregnancy	N	%
Private	67	35.8
Public		
With *palabra de casamiento*	11	—
Concubinage	13	—
Other	20	—
Subtotal	44	23.5
Unknown status of pregnancy	76	40.7
Totals	187	100.0

SOURCE: DB 4-187.

pregnant, or whether Doña Y had had an illegitimate child—but also whether that reality was publicly acknowledged. Even the Catholic Church participated in such cover-ups, given that women's names were not identified on their babies' baptismal certificates. Yet to maintain a public reputation as a virgin, such a mother could not openly acknowledge or raise her children. The traditional arrangement in such cases was for the father or relatives to take the babies. Of the 187 mothers of illegitimates who appear in petitions, 67, or 35.8 percent, had identifiable private pregnancies (see Table 3).

The private pregnancy of Doña María del Carmen López Nieto demonstrates the lengths to which an unwed mother might go to hide her pregnancy, and the degree to which family members would support her.[29] Doña María and her family belonged to the highest levels of Spanish colonial bureaucracy, for her father, Don José López Lisperguer, was a judge on the Bolivian high court, or *audiencia*. Nor was Doña María's fiancé and lover, Don Ramón de Rivera, unequal to her in rank; he, too, sat on the high bench. Doña María and Don Ramón could not initially marry because Spanish law forbade the marriage of bureaucrats such as judges to women in their jurisdictions. This antinepotism and anticorruption measure meant that Doña María and Don Ramón had to receive dispensation from Madrid before they could consecrate their union. It was for this reason that Don José, Doña María's father, had absolutely prohibited an early marriage.[30] He felt particularly vulnerable, he later admitted, because a relative of his in Chile who had married without the necessary royal permission had found his later career at a standstill. "Fearful of losing my own post," Don José later remembered, "I resisted the marriage, even though I could not stop the union of wills."[31]

Doña María and Don Ramón were not disposed to wait, but by the time Don Ramón had finally engineered a transfer and a promotion to Lima it was too late: Doña María was pregnant and Don Ramón out of reach. Ashamed, and possibly afraid of confessing to her father, who appears to have been an authoritarian figure, Doña María sought help from her sisters and brothers. They assisted her in faking an accident so as to receive parental permission to recuperate while on a visit to her brother, Dr. Don José Ignacio, a priest with a parish in Puna. There she gave birth to a baby girl, Gregoria, and died of complications after the birth.

The secrecy surrounding Doña María's pregnancy did not end with her death, for her siblings rallied to protect her reputation beyond the grave. One of her sisters, Doña Nicolasa, a member of the nouveau riche Bolivian silver aristocracy and a countess (Condesa de la Casa Real de Moneda), traveled to Puna to collect her illegitimate baby niece. She took the child back to La Plata and raised her in secret. While Doña María's mother and father mourned the death of their daughter from complications of the "accident," her brothers and sisters maintained a conspiracy of silence. It was only when her father was about to die that the countess confessed to him that Gregoria, who was now approaching nine years old, was his illegitimate grandchild; Don Joseph changed his will to provide for her. Years later, her aunts and uncles pressed for her official legitimation, which was granted when Gregoria was twenty-two, in 1795.

Such elaborate cover-ups were not uncommon, and similar family concealments occurred elsewhere in the empire. In Mexico, Doña Magdalena de la Vega engaged in sexual relations with Regidor Don Vicente de Borboya.[32] This couple, like their Bolivian counterparts, needed official permission to marry because Don Vicente was a major officeholder. Years later, Doña Justa, the natural daughter of this couple, described how her parents' desire to save face had led to a private pregnancy:

> Seeing that Doña Magdalena was pregnant and recognizing that marriage could not then take place . . . in order to ward off, and guard against the danger to her honor and good reputation, . . . and the blushes and the emotions to which she would be exposed, they adopted the expedient of moving her to the city of Puebla, under the excuse that she was sick, to the house of her sister, Doña Teresa, where she remained hidden until she gave birth.

Like Doña María, Doña Magdalena died soon after childbirth. A friend of the Mexican couple later remembered that "this result was so hidden that [Doña Magdalena] died with the reputation of a virgin." In both cases collusion with brothers and sisters and removal from the scene had temporarily saved these women's reputations. But what would have happened if these women had survived the ordeal of childbirth?

The evidence strongly suggests that both women would have married their lover-fiancés. In a letter written to the Bolivian countess two decades after the event, Don Ramón affirmed that:

> I recognize [Gregoria] as my natural daughter born of your sister Doña María del Carmen who is in heaven and with whom I would have married, as you know, if the royal permission had arrived to do it, but as God chose to carry her away, I was not able to put in practice my desires after I obtained the necessary license and my transfer to Lima.[33]

Father Joaquín del Moral, a confidant of Don Vicente de Borboya, confirmed the Mexican couple's circumstances:

> Because of the close friendship and confidence [I had] with the subject [Don Vicente] he told me various times that when he was trying to contract marriage with Doña Magdalena de la Vega, he had a daughter named Doña Justa Rufina by her . . . and that he was not able to verify [the marriage] due to the death of Doña Magdalena.[34]

What would have been the next step of these unwed mothers if they had survived childbirth and married their prospective husbands? The marriage ceremony would have automatically and fully legitimated their children. Couples might continue to hide their indiscretion by introducing these recently legitimated children into their homes as "orphans." They might write "private wills," which were not in the public domain and which, while fully explaining past circumstances, would protect the legal rights of their first-born.[35] Or, since honor was no longer threatened, given that the mothers were married and the children legitimated, couples might permit the circumstances surrounding their first child's birth to become public knowledge.

Even if a woman lost her virginity and became an unwed mother, honor might be restored if she eventually married. One unwed Peruvian mother produced two illegitimate sons with her fiancé and then ran off and married someone else after her first lover abandoned her. To protect her "honor," her name had not originally been put on her children's baptismal certificates. Yet after her marriage one commentator confirmed that Doña Marsela now had that "same honor" and "even more because of [her married] state."[36] Marriage at most points in a woman's life might go a long way to restore her honor.

There must have been many unwed mothers who, in conjunction with their lover-fiancés and close kin, successfully engineered private pregnancies, survived childbirth, married, and automatically legitimated their children. These families never needed to apply for *gracias al sacar*. Thus *cédula* petitions can never reveal the frequency with which the premarital activities of colonial elites led to private pregnancies followed by marriages. However, they can disclose how such pregnancies were organized, and the customary roles and responsibilities of the unwed mothers, fathers, and families who engineered them.

From the perspective of a pregnant spinster, the optimum result of a private pregnancy would be to guard her public honor until she became a wife. This was not the sole use of this strategy, for colonists also resorted to private pregnancy at the other extreme, when marriage was not a possible conclusion. At times men simply refused to wed their pregnant lovers; others could not, as they were already married or were priests; and sometimes married women bore children not their husbands'. In these instances, the involved parties had to take extraordinary precautions to save the honor of the mother, as well as to care for her newborn.

Secrecy was not maintained without personal sacrifice. The history of Doña X illustrates such costs, as she endured not only rejection by her lover but also the loss of her baby. Witnesses agreed that Doña X belonged to one of the most honored families in Buenos Aires society.[37] It is unclear whether she had a firm promise of marriage from Don Manuel Domec, a merchant with an extensive commerce in the Argentine interior, but her actions suggest that she hoped that a marriage would take place. Their relationship resulted in a pregnancy, and in early 1753 Doña X gave birth to a baby boy. Apparently she had the child at home, which suggests that family members conspired to protect her and their own good name.

Immediately after the birth, Don Manuel collected his natural son and deposited him at the house of Doña María Josepha de Abalos, whom he paid to care for him. Don Manuel openly and publicly acknowledged the child as his—the double standard applied here, as paternity did not harm the repu-

tation of the elite man. He also protected the name of the mother; the birth
certificate issued in February 1753 listed Pedro simply as "the natural son of
Don Manuel Domec, a Spaniard, and of a lady who is also Spanish."

Consistent with the goal of maintaining the privacy of Doña X's pregnancy, Don Manuel did not reveal her identity to baby Pedro's nurse, Doña
María Josepha. However, Doña X could not tolerate such a separation from
her son. She arranged to be introduced to Doña María Josepha, cultivated
her friendship, and began to frequent her house. The marked attention she
paid to the baby, the many presents she brought him, and the kisses she lavished upon him soon aroused Doña María Josepha's suspicion. Finally, Doña
X confessed that she was the mother. In testimony that still remains pitiful
centuries later, Doña Juliana, the daughter of the nurse, recalled how Doña
X had begged that "when she would not be able to come and see him, in order not to arouse suspicion, that they send a servant with the baby to her
house under some pretext."

Doña X's obsession with secrecy—to hide from society her identity as an
unwed mother—dictated that she deny her relationship with her child. Yet
she continued to visit Pedro and apparently still hoped that her private pregnancy would end in marriage to Don Manuel. It was only after he announced his engagement to another woman that Doña X faced bitter reality. The nurse's daughter remembered that Doña X "continued to visit as
long as Don Manuel Domec remained unmarried, but when she found out
that he was engaged, she became furious and never returned to see her son
again."

With Don Manuel now openly engaged, Doña X had to abandon her
child if she wished to maintain her public honor. Her wrenching decision illustrates the hard choice faced by an unwed mother whose identity had been
protected. If she could keep her pregnancy secret and not become linked
with the unattached baby that mysteriously appeared in local society, she
might maintain her reputation. However, if marriage to her lover did not
occur, an unwed mother had to abandon her child. The story of Doña X,
unlike that of most of her peers, ends on a somewhat happier note. Although witnesses still refused to identify her, they did comment that after
she relinquished her child she eventually married, had other children, and
held an honored place in Buenos Aires society.

Although an unwed mother might have a public reputation as a virgin
while she carried or even after she bore a child, subsequent recognition of

her offspring would stain her honor. Such was the fate of Doña Gabriela Marquez, whose early profile—a youthful romance, promise of marriage, and a secret birth—repeats the private pregnancy pattern.[38] Even though her lover, Don Antonio de Aguilar, was under twenty himself, he came from a prominent family of Chilean landowners. He recognized his illegitimate daughter, María, at her birth, insisted that he be named the natural father on her baptismal certificate—which did not name the mother—and arranged for his sister, Doña Mercedes, to raise the baby secretly. For two years Doña Gabriela waited for Don Antonio to make good his promise to marry her and legitimate their child. Like Doña X, Doña Gabriela was betrayed, because Don Antonio announced his engagement to another woman.[39] Unlike Doña X, Doña Gabriela chose her child over her honor. She arrived at Doña Mercedes's house, reclaimed her two-year-old baby, and openly spent the remainder of her life as an unmarried mother.

Private pregnancies guarded the honor not only of spinsters who did not marry their lovers but also that of already-married women who lacked such an alternative. Married women engaged in extramarital affairs at great personal risk to themselves and to their lovers. Such cases are rare, and in all instances the husbands of these women had been long absent. After Doña Y from Havana was abandoned by her husband, for example, she eventually had two daughters by Don Juan Antonio Morejón.[40] He protected her name during and after their affair, effectively "adopted" their two daughters, and eventually achieved their legitimation. In Cumaná, Venezuela, Don Francisco Betancourt arranged such a private pregnancy for the married Doña Antonia Luisa de Mata. Witnesses expressed much sympathy for her sufferings, because her husband, Don Esteban Lizcano, had abandoned her long before running off to the Llanos. They remembered "that he even refused to support her, and it was these events that no doubt led her to fall into her present situation."[41] In these two cases private pregnancy saved the honor of these elite women, as their married state foreclosed any other options.[42]

To what extent might the number of private pregnancies have changed during the eighteenth century, and what might this reveal concerning elite attitudes toward courtship and sexual intimacy? Analysis of the 139 cases in which applicants supplied the date of birth include fifty-four private pregnancies. Such pregnancies accounted for approximately one-quarter to one-half of the total per decade, with no obvious trend over the century (see Appendix 2, Table 1). Nor does there appear to be any obvious change in the percentages of engaged couples who organized private pregnancies, as these fluctuated similarly throughout the century (Appendix 2, Table 2).[43] Additionally, there were no alterations in the reasons why couples chose private pregnancies: Half of the pairs who made such arrangements were unmarried, another quarter were already married or the man was a priest, while the status of the rest is unknown (Appendix 2, Table 3).

Such absence of change can be as telling as any alteration in pattern. It suggests—although it does not conclusively prove—that the public penalties for extramarital sexual relationships did not much alter over the century: Elites were just as likely to arrange private pregnancies at the beginning as at the end. Nor does the efficacy of the promise of matrimony seem to have varied throughout the century, for the proportion of pregnant fiancées who hid behind private pregnancies neither dramatically increased nor decreased. Nor were there notable changes in the use of private pregnancy to hide adulterous, sacrilegious, or incestuous sexual liaisons. Unlike mid-eighteenth-century Europe and America, where courtship customs were in flux, the underlying reasons why Spanish American elites resorted to private pregnancy remained unchanged throughout the eighteenth century.

PUBLIC PREGNANCY AND EXTENDED ENGAGEMENTS

Although private pregnancies could preserve honor, they entailed extraordinary precautions on the part of the woman, her lover, and their families. At least forty-four, or 23.5 percent, of legitimation petitions reflect an alternative strategy—that of "public pregnancy," in which elite women carried, bore, and raised their illegitimate children under the full scrutiny of their social peers. "Extended engagements" as well as certain forms of consensual unions figure as public pregnancies (see Table 3).

One-fourth (N. 11, 25.0 percent) of public pregnancies can be defined as "extended engagements" in which unmarried women exchanged promises of matrimony and then lived openly for years and even decades in public, monogamous relationships with their lovers. Although some of these women expressed shame, and all risked their reputations and honor, their situation was not irreparable. Public knowledge that there had been a marriage promise provided a mitigating circumstance; marriage could at any time transform an unwed mother into an honorable wife, and her children into legitimate heirs.[44]

Doña María Josepha Pérez de Balmaceda of Havana had such an expectation of marriage, although she seems to have carried her belief in her lover's promise to neurotic extremes.[45] During her courtship, Doña María had taken the rare step of demanding—and receiving—a written promise of marriage from her fiancé before agreeing to have sexual intercourse with him. The couple then lived together for years and produced three illegitimate children. Finally, witnesses agreed, the marriage was imminent: "After the birth of Pedro Antonio . . . [Don Pedro Díez de Florencia] tried very earnestly to fulfill the word that he had given to Doña María Josepha, and [the couple] prepared clothes and finery, and fixed up the house." But just before the ceremony, Don Pedro must have had second thoughts. He discontinued the preparations, took off to Spain to look for a better job, and then sailed to Mexico to assume a new position. Even so, for years he sent pleading letters, envoys, and money to Doña María begging that she join him and be wed. Doña María may well have had enough of his delays and broken promises. She claimed "fear of the sea" and refused to follow him.

Nonetheless she never let her relatives or local peers forget that she was an engaged woman. She kept her lover's written promise to marry knotted in a ball tied to the rosary she wore around her neck, and she repeatedly opened his note and read it aloud to relatives and town officials. As one witness somewhat wearily recounted:

> Many times [Doña María] read that paper in the presence of this witness and of all of her house and family, and many other persons . . . and even many years after the absence and death of [her fiancé] Doña María carried [the paper] hanging from the rosary she wore around her neck which proved her good faith and her well-founded hope that she would have married.

Doña María was not the only scorned fiancée who took solace from a broken promise of matrimony, for it distinguished her from women who engaged in sexual intercourse outside of the marriage process.

Although men might use promises of matrimony to convince women to agree to sexual intercourse, such commitments also gave women leverage. A long-suffering fiancée might sue in church courts to force a prospective husband to the altar, although this proved a less effective option as the century drew to a close.[46] Even if the relationship did not end in marriage, a betrayed woman might prevent or delay her fiancé from marrying another. Promises of matrimony remained serious vows, creating formidable obstacles that might surface years later to haunt the bestower.

Don Francisco Muñoz discovered the endurance of such a pledge when he proposed matrimony to Doña Josepha de Estrada of Medellín, Colombia, in 1760.[47] Decades before he had similarly promised to wed widow Doña Catalina Casafús, and the couple's sexual intimacies had resulted in a son, born in 1746. When Doña Catalina learned that her long-absent fiancé had proposed to another, she went to the parish priest and demanded that Don Francisco not be permitted to wed, "given the impediment of the word" he had given her some fourteen years before. Local cleric Dr. Don Juan Salvador de Villa remembered that Don Francisco admitted the promise, although it had been years since the couple had quarreled and separated. The priest finally convinced Doña Catalina to agree to his "persuasions" and abandon "now [any hopes] of marriage."

Some intriguing evidence suggests that Doña Catalina—an entrepreneurial widow with interests in property, slaves, and mines—used the lever of the fourteen-year-old promise to bargain with her former fiancé.[48] It seems a suspicious coincidence that Medellín notary records reveal that the same year in which Doña Catalina finally released Don Francisco from his vow, he finally made formal provisions for an inheritance for his natural son, Gabriel. This legacy may have provided the start for Gabriel's mercantile career, as well as eventually paving the way for that confrontation decades later over a greeting on a Medellín street.[49]

Since the *gracias al sacar* chronicle only those instances in which marriage never occurred, it is impossible to calculate the frequency with which elite couples became engaged, produced *hijos naturales*, and then eventually married. It is indicative, however, that colonists throughout the Indies familiarly spoke of this practice, and it was commonplace enough to produce its own customs. Such couples were not only distinguished by their mutual exchange of the *palabra de casamiento* but were also much more likely to record the names of both mother and father on the baptismal certificates of their natural children. Such a public acknowledgment both indirectly informed society of the couple's marriage promise and, presumably, put pressure on the parties to fulfill it.

The baptismal certificate of the illegitimate daughter of Doña Thoribia María Guerra Míer and her fiancé, Lieutenant Don Lorenzo de Parga, provides an example.[50] Don Lorenzo had arrived in Valledupar (Colombia) sometime before 1779, where he met Doña Thoribia, the daughter of Don Juan Guerra, who belonged to one of the "first families" of the city. Don Lorenzo remembered that he had "proposed matrimony with . . . Doña Thoribia . . . and under this belief and word had a daughter named Doña María Josepha." The couple was waiting for the required permission from the military authorities to wed when war broke out and Don Lorenzo was transferred to Cartagena.

Doña Thoribia may well have postponed the baptism of her illegitimate daughter, born in 1779, in the hope that she might first be married, allowing her child to be baptized as a "legitimated" offspring. After three years she and her family could wait no longer, but they made certain that the circumstances of Doña María's birth were public knowledge. Perhaps the family's exalted position led the cleric to take the rare option of omitting any reference to the baby's status on her baptismal certificate; he simply noted that she was "the baby, María Josepha," rather than an illegitimate child.[51] Such delicacy did not extend to her parents, who were clearly identified as "Don Lorenzo de Parga, Lieutenant of Granderos of the Fixed Regiment of the Plaza of Cartagena" and "Doña Thoribia de la Guerra, legitimate daughter of Don Juan de la Guerra of the Kingdoms of Spain and of Doña Ana Mestre."[52]

To clinch the case, Doña Thoribia's family routed out the town notables, including her mother's kin, to attest on the baptismal certificate to the extenuating circumstances surrounding the birth: "Also present in this act the Captain Don Diego Facundo Mestre and the Señor Alcalde Ordinario Don José Francisco Mestre to witness that this aforementioned baby was conceived under the promise of matrimony." If Doña Thoribia hoped that this certificate might spur the lieutenant to return for a wedding, she proved mistaken. He later cited the demands of war as a rationale for his continued postponements, and Doña Thoribia died in 1787 still unwed. Yet this family's insistence that the promise of matrimony appear on the official baptismal certificate is striking. It demonstrates, as does a similar case from colonial Colombia in 1766, that sexual relationships that figured as stages in a marriage process were viewed differently than other arrangements.[53]

It is suggestive that one of the clearest statements concerning the customs surrounding extended "engagements" comes from a Cámara official who customarily reviewed colonial applications for the *gracias al sacar*. His official commentary appears in the legitimation petition of Doña Antonia del Rey Blanco of Havana, who was born under murky circumstances.[54] Her unwed mother, Doña Beatris Blanco de la Poza, had spent her young adult years in a Havana convent but was forced to leave because of ill health. Even while living at home she did not participate in local society but remained a recluse in the interior rooms of the family house.

Perhaps this inexperience explains why she was particularly vulnerable to the advances of Don Lázaro del Rey Bravo, a business associate of her brother. Although Don Lázaro had been married in Spain, he had had word that his wife had died during his absence. He proposed matrimony to Doña Beatris and the couple began a sexual relationship. It was only after the birth of her child that Doña Beatris and her family learned—to their horror—that Don Lázaro's first wife had been alive when the baby was conceived, although she had since passed away. Her family refused to permit Doña Beatris to marry Don Lázaro, even though he remained willing to do so. It was only decades later, when the legitimation petition of Doña Beatris's daughter was considered by the Cámara of the Indies, that the legal question of young Doña Antonia's status was raised. Was she an *hija natural*—the much more socially acceptable product of a sexual union between unmarried parents—or was she an *adulterina*, the despised result of an adulterous alliance?

The royal official who reviewed the case followed custom and did not rule solely on the facts: When had Doña Beatris and Don Lázaro begun their sexual relationship, and when had Don Lázaro's wife actually died? Instead, the official also took into account the couple's intent, especially the extent to which their actions reflected their perception, even if it were an erroneous one, of reality. The official accepted the couple's belief in Don Lázaro's eligibility and ruled that Doña Antonia was an *hija natural*, for she "was conceived under this belief and the good faith of Doña Beatris, her mother." He noted that her father had "thought he was a bachelor and able to carry out the promise of matrimony he seems to have given."[55]

The official was clearly swayed by Doña Antonia's baptismal certificate, in which her parents had identified themselves as her mother and father. This public recognition of their daughter was compelling proof that the couple planned to marry: "for it is not customary to declare it this way except when the parents are commonly conceived to be unmarried, and with the disposition or the desire to legitimate their offspring by a subsequent marriage." Engaged couples marrying after they had conceived natural children was so common that a body of generally understood practice had developed.

Examination of the 139 cases in which the year of the sexual relationship between lovers can be ascertained suggests little change during the century in the propensity of couples to exchange a promise of matrimony. Although there were fluctuations from decade to decade, approximately one-fourth of couples had substantiated pledges of matrimony (N. 33, 23.7 percent), between a quarter and a half did not (N. 42, 30.3 percent), and the relationship between the rest is unknown (N. 64, 46.1 percent) (Appendix 2, Table 4). Such statistics bear an unlikely relationship to the "real world" of colonial America, where, it seems likely, substantial percentages of couples not only promised to wed but also carried out marriages and so never needed to apply for *gracias al sacar*. Yet it is telling that there are no changing trends in those courtship patterns among *gracias al sacar* parents.

What was life like for these unwed mothers who lived for years or even decades in the expectation of matrimony? Their case histories show that if they or their fiancés did not flaunt their situation publicly, their social position might remain ambiguous. As in the case of private pregnancies, elite women customarily benefited from an initial presumption that they were innocent. Even when relatives and neighbors knew that a questionable liaison was occurring, they did not always choose to acknowledge it openly. As time passed, and particularly as extended engagements seemed less and less likely to end in matrimony, the situation of such unwed mothers became more difficult.

Public awareness that an unwed woman was having an affair with her fiancé, or that she had borne a child, or even that the couple were living together, was not always immediate. Colonial architecture could cooperate to hide incriminating evidence, as the homes of the prosperous tended to be large, with many rooms for family, servants, and servants' children. Courting couples might find private spaces for amorous activities, and later an extra baby might not make much of a spatial impact.[56]

Since it was an accepted custom for Spanish American women and their families to shelter orphans and homeless children, the presence of minors with vague antecedents was common. The few cases detailed here—the private pregnancy in which the Bolivian Countess de la Casa Real de Moneda took in her illegitimate niece, Gregoria; the Argentine example of Doña María Josepha, who received money to care for the infant Pedro; or the instance of the Chilean sister of Don Antonio, who sheltered his illegitimate baby—illustrate the frequency of infant fostering. Since not all women who took in children were guilty of sexual transgressions, the practice provided a context in which unwed mothers might care for their sons and daughters without scandalous notice.[57]

The tale of Chilean Doña María Rosa de la Torre provides some rare details as to the kinds of social interactions that might take place as friends and neighbors discovered that a spinster was now an unwed mother.[58] Even though Doña María and her fiancé, Don Felipe Briceño, belonged to the Santiago elite, their economic resources were not substantial. Doña María did not have the backing of powerful kin; her father had died in Peru, and she lived alone with her mother. Don Felipe came from a notable Santiago family; his father had held the prestigious position of *alcalde*, but Don Felipe himself was not prosperous.

Lacking the presence of a father, Doña María's home must have provided a convenient locale for Don Felipe's courtship, promise of matrimony, and the intimacy that led to the birth of an infant named José Félix in 1755. A friend and neighbor who was also the baby's godfather remembered that Don Felipe had ordered that both his and Doña María's names appear on the baptismal certificate, because "he wanted to legitimate him."

Although the promised marriage did not occur, there was no immediate public recognition that Doña María had given birth to an illegitimate child, for she received the traditional benefit of the doubt. Even Don Felipe's brother, the priest Fray Agustín, was not initially suspicious. Years later he remembered how he had discovered the truth:

> With the entry and communication that I had in the house of Doña María Rosa de la Torre, I saw there a little boy whom she loved very much, but I was unclear who his parents were for some time until my brother Don Felipe told me that he was his son, and also the child of Doña María, although they were hiding this, no doubt to protect her honor. But once I was knowledgeable of this, she no longer hesitated in my presence to kiss her son.

Another witness remembered that he had heard a rumor that the infant Doña María was raising was hers, but that "because of her honor there was secrecy about this, even though the boy was raised at her side and in her own house." As time passed, Doña Rosa and Don Felipe no longer hid their affair, and, still promising marriage, Don Felipe moved into her house. Some neighbors even thought they were married. As one witness later commented:

Because of the friendship and continuous entry that I had in the house of
Doña María Rosa, in the beginning I was persuaded that she was married
to . . . Don Felipe, although later I knew the opposite because he told me
that he wanted to marry her.

The precariousness of Doña Rosa's situation became manifest when Don
Felipe, seeking his fortune, left her and their son and took off to the Andean
mining districts, a customary escape haven for Chilean men.[59] There he experienced his "total ruin."[60] Even though the signs were not propitious,
Doña María did not abandon hope that he would return and fulfill his
promise to marry her. One of their neighbors remembered that "it was impossible to pry him away for many years from that mining area, in spite of
the continual letters that Doña María Rosa wrote him begging that he return." Another friend spoke of the "tears and pleas" that Doña María directed to her erring lover. Don Felipe never returned to Santiago, and he
eventually married someone else. Even though this marriage was childless,
when he died he willed his estate to his mother, leaving nothing to Doña
María or his son.[61]

Doña María's case illustrates the long-term ambiguities that might sur-
round the lives of unwed mothers as society gradually discovered and acknowledged their situations. Even Don Felipe's brother did not immediately
know that Doña María's child was his illegitimate nephew, nor did neighbors seem eager to clarify the marital status of the couple. The initial social
assumption was toward innocence. Even after the passage of years, when the
pretense could no longer be maintained, Doña María's neighbors seemed
more inclined to sympathize than to criticize.

Women such as Doña María Rosa might spend years in limbo waiting for
their fiancés to marry them, only to discover in middle or old age that their
hopes would never be fulfilled. The legal securities of matrimony, such as inheritance or reliable maintenance for children, could be denied them. Many
such "engaged" women found that their positions moved beyond ambiguity
as the men they had lived with for decades abandoned them to marry, or to
engage in affairs with, other women.

Such abandonment naturally produced bitterness between the unwed
mother and her lover, and it often soured the relationship between the father
and his illegitimate offspring. This clearly happened in the case of widow
Doña Antonia Hernández of Havana, who had lived for years with Don
Nicolás Joseph Rapún as he rose from office to office and eventually attained

the important post of intendant of the Royal Treasury in Havana.[62] Doña Antonia had had three children by her first husband, and, almost annually from 1747 to 1752, she presented Don Nicolás with a child, four of whom survived. Although Don Nicolás did not share her home, all the town knew of their affair and of his daily visits. Don Nicolás promised to marry her, although their illegitimate offspring later explained that he "put her off with flattering hopes that he was going to do it when he reached the heights that he was destined by fortune." Once he became an intendant "he continued delaying from day to day" and it was "impossible to compel him to fulfill that obligation." Even though Doña Antonia sued to force him to marry her, Don Nicolás never gave in. He broke off their long-term relationship and had an illegitimate son with another woman.

Although Doña Rosa and Doña Antonia were eventually abandoned by their fiancés, they never appear to have been ostracized by friends or neighbors. There were some natural reasons why social peers might initially be disposed to show tolerance toward women trapped in such "extended engagements." Colonial Spanish-American cities were full of older, unmarried women who might have shared the plight of Doña Rosa and Doña Antonia, or at least might have been disposed to sympathize with them. Demographers, especially for Mexico, have produced striking statistics that show the extent to which unmarried women formed significant social groupings within colonial cities. In Mexico City (1811), unmarried women accounted for 32 percent of the heads of households; in Antequera (1777), 39 percent; in Atlixco (1792), 25 percent.[63] Although some of these women might have been widows, and many were of the lower classes, they formed a substantial cohort of unmarried women in which *cédula* mothers might mingle.

Unwed elite mothers might also find sympathy from their married peers, for their status remained ambiguous. Although Don Felipe may have failed in the mining districts, there must have been others who succeeded, returned in triumph to marry their fiancées, and thus legitimated their offspring. Even if society were disposed to criticize the relationship of Doña Antonia and Don Nicolás, he was a man of power in Havana, and Doña Antonia would have shared his position if the couple had ever wed.

Although the strict dictates of honor might suggest that engaged women who bore illegitimate children be rejected by their peers, in practical, day-to-day living such was not the case. Instead, neighbors moved with ease and familiarity in and out of such houses. The illegitimate children of these unions played and were educated along with legitimate offspring of equal rank.[64] The pervasive tolerance of a Spanish Catholic society in which human frailty was conceded, and in which sins could always be forgiven, seems to have eased the exigencies of social discourse. Yet there were limits to this tolerance, for unwed mothers generally remained spinsters all their lives, and they and their children suffered the civil and social barriers imposed against those who lacked honor.

PUBLIC PREGNANCY AND CONSENSUAL UNIONS

As time passed, women such as Doña Rosa and Doña Antonia must have realized that they would pass the rest of their lives as aging "fianceés" and as mothers of illegitimate offspring. If they had any consolation, it must have been that they were honorable women who had engaged in sexual relationships as a prelude to matrimony. Although their honor may have been tarnished by public pregnancy, the real fault resided with their lovers, who had failed to honor the marriage promise. Such rationalizations could not provide comfort to a last group, those who had publicly entered into affairs without a promise of matrimony, or who had become the acknowledged mistresses of clerics or of married men (N. 13, 29.5 percent)[65] (see Table 3). Their sexual indiscretions were public knowledge, neither mitigated by extenuating circumstances such as a *palabra de casamiento* nor hidden by private pregnancy.

Colonial historians have uncovered evidence that a substantial cohort of single couples lived together without the promise of matrimony. Thomas Calvo has noted that concubinage was common both among the lowest as well as the highest levels of seventeenth-century Guadalajara society; María Emma Mannarelli observed a similar "high grade of acceptability among the inhabitants" of seventeenth-century Lima.[66] Chilean historians have commented that "concubinage was practiced massively" among most social groups.[67] Elisabeth Anne Kuznesof concluded that for eighteenth-century Mexico the "cohabitational union of two people lacking other commitments might well be considered as marriage in all aspects except the legal."[68] Relationships between unmarried men and women without any commitment to matrimony were presumably more tenuous than those in which the parties vowed to wed. In most other respects, however, such affairs are indistinguishable from extended engagements, although the reputation of the woman may have suffered more because she was not able publicly to justify her sexual affair as one that would lead to matrimony.

The identifying marks of such a relationship emerge in the history of Doña Josepha María Valespino of Havana, who lived with Canary Island ship's captain Don Amaro Rodríguez Pargo and who eventually bore an *hijo natural* named Manuel.[69] Doña Josepha was a woman of means, owning two houses, some slaves, and valuable jewelry. The captain lived with her during those years when he traded in Havana. He paid her bills, carried the infant Manuel with him on visits to neighbors and to his ship, and was generally acknowledged as Manuel's father. Yet he never promised to marry Doña Josepha, and when neighbors described their affair they characterized it as "illicit." Eventually the captain sailed back to his home port in the Canaries. Although he occasionally sent Doña Josepha some wool and other items to sell to support Manuel, he never returned to Cuba. The final break between the couple occurred when the captain wrote and asked Doña Josepha to send Manuel to live with him in the Canaries. When she refused he broke off all contact, and at his death he failed to acknowledge his son. Doña Josepha exhausted her resources in raising Manuel. When he petitioned for legitimation at twenty-six, he described her as "blind . . . and in the most extreme poverty."

The most salient feature of this affair is the absence of the promise of matrimony. However, other more subtle characteristics—the temporal limitation of the relationship, the lack of paternal commitment to mother and son, as well as outsiders' descriptions of the affair as "illicit"—may also serve to locate it within the realm of consensual union rather than that of extended engagement. The word "illicit" may well have been a signifier for relationships without the promise of matrimony, given that Richard Boyer and Guiomar Dueñas-Vargas found it used in similar contexts in Mexico and colonial Colombia.[70]

If an open relationship without any pretense of marriage was seen as "illicit," even greater opprobrium must have attached when women publicly defied the code of honor, the state, and religion to engage in sexual affairs with clerics, with married men, or with a man other than their husband. Documents do not provide much information as to how society treated those who trespassed those boundaries. No doubt petitioners wanted to make the strongest case possible for legitimation and would naturally omit any discussion of the public reputation of their mother or father. Instead, more than others, such requests emphasized the discretion of the lovers, detailed the exalted personal connections of the participants, or confirmed a willingness to pay exorbitant sums to achieve the desired legitimation. Only the most powerful and wealthy made such applications, as the Cámara of the Indies was less likely to approve them, especially as the century drew to a close.

It is probably no accident that two of the most extraordinary of such cases originated from Bolivia, for the silver magnates of La Plata and Potosí combined the wealth and connections essential for such pretensions. The petitions of Don Melchor and Don Agustín Varea y Lazcano of La Plata emphasized their notable parental backgrounds.[71] Their mother, Doña Gertrudis (de Varea y Lazcano), belonged "to one of the principal, distinguished, and richest families" of Potosí. Her lover, Don Domingo Herboso y Figueroa, was a priest and dean of the cathedral of La Plata. He belonged to an extremely powerful political clan, his father having been president of the surrounding *audiencia* of Charcas and thus ranking among the top dozen executive officers in the Spanish empire. Don Domingo's uncle was an archbishop, his brother was a high treasury official in Lima (*Contador Mayor del Tribunal Real de Cuentas*), and another brother was governor of the nearby province of Cochambamba.

Family rank and wealth could not obscure the fact that Doña Gertrudis was an unwed mother and that the father of her two sons was a priest. Witnesses who testified in this case emphasized the care that the couple had taken to avoid public scandal. Although Don Domingo openly visited Doña Gertrudis, the lovers maintained separate residences. The couple did not recognize their sons on their baptismal certificates but listed them as "*expósitos*," or "abandoned." One local remembered that Don Domingo "in particular used a certain caution and reticence because of the dignity and nature of his position."

After Don Domingo's death, his now-adult sons found acceptance in La Plata society. Witnesses testified that they were looked upon "with reputation and honor in all their dealings . . . in the houses of . . . distinguished persons." The position of their still-surviving mother remained more ambiguous. Although the deposition contains much information on family pedigree and wealth, the sole comment on her immediate situation is the rather defensive note that her sons "maintained . . . [her], looking on her with respect and veneration."

During the same years that Doña Gertrudis and Don Domingo carried on their affair in La Plata, a few blocks away the spinster Doña Juana Risco y Agorreta was living openly with a married man.[72] Although Dr. Don Francisco de Moya y Palacios, a *regidor* and *alcalde* in the rich silver town of Potosí, was married to the daughter of a royal official, his residence was with Doña Juana in La Plata. The adulterous relationship produced five children, all of whom reached high positions in local society. Money from silver seemed to smooth all paths, and when one of Doña Juana's daughters, herself a silver magnate, petitioned for legitimation, she received it. The few comments on the fate of Doña Juana resemble those concerning her neighbor, Doña Gertrudis. Witnesses noted that a son still lived with her—even though he had the means to establish a separate residence—because of "the love and veneration that he feels for her."[73] It is difficult to know what the rest of society might have thought.

Even though these Bolivian women trespassed religious and social boundaries when they engaged in sexual relations with a priest and a married man, they themselves were unmarried. Far rarer in the seventeenth century, as well as the eighteenth, were instances in which married women engaged in sexual relationships with men other than their husbands. The two existing examples of female extramarital sexuality share important characteristics. The women either considered their spouses to be dead or to have left them permanently, so the cuckolded husbands were not physically present in the community when their wives carried on their affairs. Both women had suffered physical and emotional abuse at the hands of their spouses.[74]

Women seem to have been especially at risk for extramarital affairs when their husbands had permanently left them, or had spent months or years away from home. Such a pattern fits the already discussed private pregnancy of Doña Antonia Luisa de Mata, who had been badly treated and then eventually abandoned by her husband, Don Esteban Liscano. Even years later witnesses recalled the "bad life (*mala vida*) that the said Liscano [gave her] given his troublesome disposition for he even denied her food."[75] Lack of any spousal loyalty to such an abusive partner was certainly understandable. In contrast, her lover, Regidor Don Joseph Francisco Betancourt, arranged a private pregnancy to protect her reputation and took responsibility for their baby son.

For married women, public knowledge of extramarital affairs could be fatal, not only to reputation but to life as well. The horror experienced by Doña Teresa Medina must have been a common nightmare of many colonial women married to long-absent husbands who might or might not still be living.[76] This Córdoba matron was married to merchant Don Manuel de Urquire, who had left for a "large absence" in Chile. After she received word of his death, she wore mourning and she "was known by all as a widow." Doña Teresa had been a widow for about two years when she began a sexual relationship that left her pregnant. She had been nursing a baby boy for fifteen months when word arrived that her presumably long-dead husband was now about to enter the city. Years later, this son remembered how his mother, rightfully fearful for his life, had entrusted him to Pedro de Olmedo a "*pardo*, but a very honorable man." There are some fairly strong indications that this Pedro may have been his father.[77]

Meanwhile, Doña Teresa was left alone to face the "calamity" of her absent husband's return, including his almost immediate awareness of her extramarital affair.[78] At first, he apparently refused to live with her, but he was "persuaded" to do so because of the "notorious state of her reputation." Doña Teresa now had to bear the brunt of his physical abuse. Even a male observer who was critical of her affair was struck by her "suffering" and conceded that she "had much to bear in a painful enough life." Doña Teresa's female neighbors were even more sympathetic. One testified that she was visiting a nearby house when "the said Theresa entered, and seeing her so spent, [she] asked the cause of it." Doña Teresa responded that her husband had "notice" of the baby and that "the bad treatment that he had given her because of this had put her in that state." The witness remembered that "ultimately" such "ill treatment and pain" proved fatal, for it "caused a fever from which she died." In contrast to their male counterparts, married women risked not only their honor but also their lives if they sought sexual partners other than their husbands.[79]

AFTERMATHS

It is important to remember that the large majority of women whose stories appear here were women who did not fully benefit from protective strategies. Once an unmarried women engaged in a sexual relationship, the surest method of protecting or restoring her honor was through matrimony. The

TABLE 4
Later History of 'Cédula' Mothers

Later Fate	Private Pregnancy		Other		Total	
	N	%	N	%	N	%
Spinster, widow	13	19.4	38	31.7	51	27.3
Married lover	2	3.0	12	10.0	14	7.5
Married other	3	4.4	4	3.3	7	3.8
Died in childbirth	4	6.0	5	4.2	9	4.8
Religious	2	3.0	0	0.0	2	1.0
Unknown	43	62.7	61	50.8	104	55.6
Totals	67	100.0	120	100.0	187	100.0

SOURCE: DB 4-187.

most "successful" private pregnancies, extended engagements, and consensual unions were those that ended in marriage, automatically legitimating the offspring, and thus never figuring in petitions for *gracias al sacar*.

What was the fate of the *cédula* mothers? While the later stories of more than half (N. 104; 55.6 percent) remain unknown, depositions provide glimpses into the rest (see Table 4). Since these women failed in strategies to marry their lovers, it should come as no surprise that the large majority (N. 51; 27.3 percent) remained spinsters and widows.

The next most common fate of *cédula* mothers has not been considered here, for some fourteen, or 7.5 percent, eventually married their lovers. For various reasons these marriages could not automatically legitimate children conceived prior to the ceremony. Affairs between first cousins fell under this classification, as such couples needed official church permission to wed. Also included were cases in which one of the lovers was married but the lovers married nonetheless, after the death of the existing spouse. There were a few instances—among them was Doña X of Buenos Aires—in which a woman had an illegitimate child and then married another man (N. 7; 3.8 percent). The infrequency of this option is suggestive, for it shows that elite women who lost their virginity dramatically closed out their options of marriage to anyone other than their lover.

Equally noteworthy is the absence of interest that mothers showed for the religious life, as only two (1.0 percent) eventually entered convents. Perhaps the existence of other women whose status was equally ambivalent provided sufficient peer support so that *cédula* mothers did not feel they had to reject secular society. The large number of women whose fate remains unknown leaves many questions unanswered, particularly if *cédula* mothers were likely to engage in other sexual liaisons later in their lives.[80] Since their offspring would not be likely to volunteer such potentially damaging information to the Cámara of the Indies, their subsequent history remains unrecorded.

The life course of a woman was not much different whether her honor had been protected by a private or by a public pregnancy. Women with private pregnancies still tended to remain unmarried, nor were they any more likely to marry a man other than their lover. It is also notable that the mothers who had had private pregnancies were much less likely to marry their lovers than were the women who had had public pregnancies. This makes some sense, for couples who took the extreme measure of organizing a private pregnancy must have been either much more likely to marry when they could—and thereby avoid later applications—or much more likely to hide the pregnancy because they knew that they would not marry, either because of personal antipathy or inability. Unmarried women rather than widows produced the majority of *hijos naturales*.[81] And then there was the last group of *cédula* mothers (N. 9; 4.8 percent), who suffered the worst fate of all, as they died soon after the birth of their illegitimate babies. Their maneuverings to protect their honor paled in comparison with their ultimate tragedy.

FOUR

Fathers: Life Course and Sexuality

Habanero Don Diego de Alarcón y Ocaña was a captain in the Armada de Barlovento in the 1690s when his ship first docked in Vera Cruz.[1] There he began to court Doña Juana Díaz de Estrada, the daughter of a former governor of the province. The couple exchanged a promise of matrimony, and as their engagement proceeded their sexual intimacies increased as well. Doña Juana put more and more pressure on her lover to fulfill his pledge of matrimony. The captain's secretary, Don Agustín Henríquez, remembered those days with great clarity: "I was there on occasions when the lady rightfully pleaded with him to fulfill his word, reminding him of the damage to her reputation and the discredit of her family." Even though the captain "swore not to defer it," he did not fulfill his promise. Instead, Doña Juana's pleas became even "more forceful when she found out that she was pregnant." Still the couple remained unwed.

Mother and father treated the birth of daughter María Cathalina in strikingly different ways. His secretary remembered that the captain "took her in his arms. . . . He recognized her as his natural daughter, and he publicly celebrated her as such in view of all the city." In contrast, the new mother "withdrew into great privacy" and proved reluctant to face public scrutiny. Doña Juana's reticence impressed a frequent visitor to her house, who remembered that "her modesty was such that before the dawn [she had dressed herself so that] not even her fingers could be seen." Now publicly marked as an unwed mother, Doña Juana literally went into mourning for an honor that could be restored only by marriage.

The circumstances of this Vera Cruz couple reflect familiar gender stereotypes: the image of the sexually aggressive, celebrating, boasting man contrasts vividly with that of the culpable, betrayed, and shamed woman. While such impressions reflect fundamental realities, they also obscure substantive variations on the theme. Although shamed, Doña Juana was not necessarily a pariah, much less permanently outlawed. Her situation was the natural consequence of a classic pattern of colonial courtship wherein elite women exchanged promises of matrimony, began sexual relationships, and did not hide the resulting pregnancies. In the usual course of events marriage sanctified such liaisons, validated female honor, and automatically legitimated any children. While Doña Juana had justly expected her lover to marry sooner, rather than later, her situation at the birth of her daughter was not that rare, nor was her status irretrievable. Although Hispanic women always paid a higher price than men for premarital sexuality, society still offered discounts to those who eventually produced a man willing to take vows at the altar.

But what of Captain Don Diego? To what extent did his actions reflect the prevailing standards of elite masculine conduct? The disapproving comments of secretary Don Agustín, who clearly sympathized with Doña Juana, suggest that the captain had fallen rather short. The secretary's censure was no doubt intensified by later events, for the promised marriage never took place. Instead, Doña Juana suffered an "accident," and, although Don Diego sped to her side, she never regained consciousness and died before the couple could be wed. The captain was stricken with remorse. He later confessed that he believed that his subsequent "reverses" were "a punishment of God" because he had "delayed the fulfillment of his obligation."

This unhappy story from Vera Cruz raises many questions concerning the private lives of elite men in colonial Spanish America. To what extent was the honor of men such as Don Diego affected by public knowledge of their sexual activity and fatherhood? Were certain kinds of men more likely to find themselves in such situations than others? What were the traditional obligations of men who loved outside of matrimony and who fathered illegitimate children? How did such responsibilities alter over the course of their lives? Did they fulfill them? Such inquiry into the personal, emotional, sexual, and familial lives of colonial Spanish-American men necessarily enters unknown territory. Yet some pioneers have blazed a trail, for the questions raised by feminist scholars concerning the forgotten and neglected histories of women serve to structure research into the concomitantly lost histories of men.

MALE HONOR

Elite men and women shared certain concepts of honor. Both strove to preserve their public reputations as persons of honor, worthy of the perquisites of hierarchy. Both recognized that they had inherited honor from their ancestors and that they could pass it on to the next generation through legitimate marriages and births. However, biological differences established divergent patterns for sexuality and for procreation, as well as distinctive cultural norms for the masculine and feminine expressions of honor. Since men could never physically demonstrate proof of virginity at the time of first sexual intercourse, male sexual abstinence could never be an issue of honor. Men could not become pregnant, and so they never risked physical alterations that signaled that they had been sexually active, which might pose a risk to their honor. A critical corollary was that men could never be absolutely certain to the last positive shred of doubt that they had fathered a particular child.

This biological double standard underlies patriarchal cultural codes that aimed to restrict female sexuality and to authenticate fatherhood as far as possible. The striking images of the funereally clad Doña Juana and the celebratory Captain Don Diego underline the fundamental differences between the sexes. Although the couple's sexual activity outside of wedlock meant that neither could presently pass on honor to their baby daughter, Doña Juana's motherhood had additionally compromised her own honor, while Don Diego's honor was not damaged by his fatherhood. Even the captain's sympathetic secretary never even hinted that Don Diego had forfeited his honor because of his neglect. Instead, the secretary acknowledged that the damage was to Doña Juana's "reputation" and that the "discredit" was to her family. A similar expression of the double standard was expressed by

Chilean Don Pedro Fermin de Necochea. Even though he had fathered an illegitimate son, he still considered himself to be a man of "honest dealings" who "in the private and in the public" had maintained "harmony and good conduct."[2] These denials that extramarital sexuality, or fatherhood, or broken promises of marriage impacted the honor of men is provocative. It signals one of those documentary vacuums where the absence of evidence may be as telling as any contemporaneous testimony.

Public knowledge of male sexual activity neither threatened honor nor diminished the privileges attached to it. Men who seduced elite virgins or who fathered illegitimate children were not excluded from public office because of such activities.[3] Nor were they barred from serving as public notaries, lawyers, or military officers—positions that required that their holders possess honor. No ordinance forbade unwed fathers from graduating from the university, nor denied their entrance to the priesthood. Nor did men who had produced illegitimate offspring reduce their potential for later matrimony, for they often married another elite woman after they had fathered out-of-wedlock infants with a first (see Appendix 2, Table 5).

But what if a man had promised matrimony before engaging in a sexual relationship with a female peer? Was his honor damaged if he subsequently failed to fulfill his word? Previous research has assumed that men who broke promises of matrimony forfeited honor, and that a man's "word and his honor were interchangeable."[4] The legitimation case histories challenge that conclusion, for they reveal that colonists differentiated between the codes of honor and those of religion. One Mexican cleric made this distinction explicit, praising a young illegitimate who showed exemplary obedience "both to the laws of honor [and] to those . . . of God."[5] Rather, when witnesses testified concerning failed masculine promises, they invariably classified them as obligations of conscience rather than as deficits of honor.

Even women whose families had been damaged by masculine intransigence distinguished between issues of honor and those of conscience. When Peruvian Doña Juana Murillo testified concerning her engaged daughter's love affair, which had resulted in two illegitimate sons, she was forced to admit that her daughter had been "dishonored" in public.[6] Yet she never suggested that her daughter's lover, who had reneged on his promise to wed, had been similarly tainted. Instead, she charged that he had an "obligation in conscience" to marry her daughter.

The demands of "conscience" appear frequently as a traditional rationale that compelled men to proper action. Such considerations motivated Don Pedro Díez de Florencia, the signer of the infamous promissory marriage note that was entwined around the rosary necklace of his Havana lover. When he spoke of his desire to marry her, it was not to protect his own honor but to "fulfill his obligation," and therefore to "discharge his conscience."[7] Similarly, a rejected Colombian fiancée charged that her lover had disregarded the "obligation of conscience" when he abandoned her to marry another.[8] One of her relatives agreed, indicting the erring man as one who had "forgotten the obligations of conscience and justice." Yet another Bogotá man spoke of his "mournfulness" in not having married his deceased fiancée "according to the charge of his conscience."[9]

It was not only lovers in *gracias al sacar* petitions that delineated the conscience rationale. Sam Chandler's research on colonial Mexican *montepíos* reveals that a common explanation given by royal officials for why they must wed was "reasons of conscience."[10] Even farther afield, Margaret Darrow points to a similar use of the conscience rationale when extramarital sexuality resulted in pregnancy in eighteenth-century France.[11]

Unlike honor, which was constructed by outsiders and which reflected public reputation, issues of conscience were internalized matters of ethics and religion. One petitioner specifically contrasted the demands of the "respect of the world," which had initially led his parents to arrange a private pregnancy for his mother and to raise him "secretly," with the "interior sentiments of conscience," which had motivated his father to care for him after he was seven.[12]

It makes at least intuitive sense that the promise of matrimony was seen as an issue of conscience because of its linkage to religion; such pledges had precedents reaching back before the Council of Trent to a practice whereby couples made serious vows and effectively married without formal intervention by the church. Although a marriage ceremony was required after Trent, the popular custom of anticipatory promises continued.

The deep religiosity of colonial Spanish Americans meant that they considered God to be a third party when they exchanged such vows, thus making them matters of conscience. Asunción Lavrin cites one instance from Mexico in which a proposing man actually knelt in front of a crucifix to deliver his promise of matrimony.[13] In Peru, an abandoned fiancée formally cursed her erring lover after he broke his pledge. When he was subsequently shot dead in Spain, she considered her seducer's end to have been a judgment from heaven in her favor.[14] The erring Captain Don Diego also explicitly linked matters of conscience and religion when he commented that God had punished him because of his failure to wed his Vera Cruz fiancée. While masculine honor might not be threatened by sexual affairs outside of matrimony, the birth of illegitimates, or broken promises of matrimony, the pressure of conscience might ultimately serve as a powerful lever to compel action.[15]

The irony was that even though male honor was not personally diminished by sexual activity, or out-of-wedlock fatherhood, men could ultimately be bound by the honor code. Their failure to wed risked the reputation of the closest members of their private circle, for it diminished the honor of a sexual partner who might have become a wife, and it deprived their closest blood kin, their often-cherished children, of a life of honor. Thus men eventually acted—not to defend their own honor, but because their failure to wed damaged the reputations of others.

One traditional masculine strategy to protect women who had engaged in sexual intercourse was the strict adherence to a code of silence. Unlike the stereotypical pictures of machismo described for later centuries, in which masculine boasting of sexual prowess was mandatory, some men preserved the honor of their lover rather than advertise their own sexual exploits.[16]

Private pregnancies required the greatest secrecy. Even though Venezuelan Don Joseph Francisco Betancourt often visited the family to whom he had entrusted the care of his illegitimate baby son, he never mentioned the identity of his lover, for he noted that "she was a white woman of honor, which necessitated silence as to . . . the mother."[17] Don Juan Angel de la Torre, a Mexican, shared such "confidence and friendship" with Don Joseph Minjares that the latter sent his son Pedro to live in Don Juan's house, "so that he might teach him to read and write." Yet Don Juan remembered that "he never knew from him, nor even up to today from any other person, who were the natural parents of the said Don Pedro."[18] In Guatemala a witness would admit only that a certain baby was "the son of that same woman whom he has privately and secretly disclosed to the vicar."[19] Such discretion transcended generations, as fathers impressed on their sons the necessity for continued reticence. Don Rafael García Goyena, the illegitimate son in that case, later confided that he would not name his mother, for he had received "secret information concerning her condition, quality, and unwed state."

Decades after the fact, men maintained strict silence concerning the identities of the women they had protected by means of private pregnancies. The names of fewer than a quarter of such mothers had surfaced prior to the legitimation petitions for their children. Since such requests usually occurred years and often decades after a birth, this silence as to maternal identity is noteworthy. Even more striking was that substantially more than half of the men continued to protect the names of their lovers, and those names remain unknown even today. When the identities of mothers who had had private pregnancies became public, it was more often the result of their own admission than that of their lovers (see Appendix 2, Tables 6 and 7).[20]

Even though concern for the honor of women might keep men silent, it did not necessarily motivate them to wed. Seventy-three petitioners specifically explained why marriage had not occurred immediately or soon after the birth of an illegitimate baby. These cases permit some speculation whether the failure to marry was the result of male or female refusal (see Appendix 2, Table 8). In six instances (8.2 percent) both partners were responsible, because they were related by a prohibited degree of kinship and required ecclesiastical permission to wed. Of the remainder, only in twelve instances (16.5 percent) might the failure to wed be laid at the door of the women—and in eight of those it was because the women had died! The four remaining women became pregnant as a result of extramarital affairs, although two of them had already been abandoned by their husbands. No *cédula* mother who could wed rejected matrimony.

The large majority of marriages failed to occur because men (N. 55, 75.3 percent) could not, or would not, tie the knot. For men who were already married (N. 21) or who were priests (N. 11), a ceremony was never an option. A second group included army officers (N. 3) who could not marry until they received official permission from their superiors; bureaucrats (N. 2) also required licenses from the Council of the Indies.[21]

Most of the "other reasons" given by fathers fall under the category of bad faith rationalizations. Five admitted that they had courted two women at the same time, marrying one and abandoning the other; four rejected their lovers for unknown reasons; three refused to marry because their lover was of mixed race; two escaped because they were away when the baby was born; two delayed because they needed to accumulate more wealth before the ceremony; and one had entered into the priesthood. One unwed father was blameless, inasmuch as he died before his baby was born. Regional studies throughout colonial Spanish America confirm this trend: Although a woman might be pressured to say "yes" to a sexual encounter, it was the man who said "no" when it came to the marriage ceremony.[22]

VARIABLES CONDUCIVE TO ILLEGITIMACY: MOBILITY, COMMUNITY, PRECEDENT

Men had the upper hand. They did not risk their honor when they engaged in sexual intercourse, when they produced illegitimate offspring, or when they broke marriage promises. They decided when a sexual relationship would end in marriage. Yet certain men seem more likely than others to appear as *cédula* fathers: Occupation, mobility, community, and propinquity emerge as distinguishing markers conducive to extramarital sexuality and illegitimacy.

Although the occupations of half of the *cédula* fathers cannot be determined, where professions are indicated, a pattern emerges. Army and navy officers, bureaucrats, and priests proved to be the most common progenitors of illegitimate children. All of these were bound by temporary or permanent restrictions concerning matrimony. Merchants constituted another notable cohort, followed by a diverse group that included lawyers, landowners, *marqueses*, notaries, a miner, an assayer, and even a lamplighter (Appendix 2, Table 9).

Evidence suggests that Bourbon reform attempts to increase efficiency and to end nepotism through regulation of the marriages of members of the military and the bureaucracy may have had the unintended effect of promoting elite illegitimacy.[23] Courting officers were bound by the Military Ordinances of 1728, which required that they have permission from their superiors to marry, as well as by a royal decree of 1741 requiring crown ratification of such licenses. The marriage of bureaucrats had been regulated since a 1578 decree discouraging nepotism by forbidding officials to choose brides in the jurisdictions in which they served. Bourbon reformers stiffened this prohibition in 1764 with legislation that extended the restrictions to the offspring of royal officials and threatened those who disobeyed with loss of office. Such legislation not only delayed the marriages of those officers and bureaucrats who honestly wanted to wed but also permitted others to delay marriage indefinitely or even permanently.

The impact of such Bourbon restrictions was intensified when geography entered the courtship equation, for army and navy officers might be transferred to other posts before they received official authorization. One Venezuelan noted that his father had tried in good faith to marry his mother, but "in that time there were no permissions for any soldier to marry."[24] His father was shipped off to Spain and never returned. Don Lorenzo de Parga of colonial Colombia justified his patently less than strenuous efforts to marry his pregnant fiancée by citing the "war [that] was declared with Great Britain in the year of 1779."[25] After relocating to Cartagena, his regiment was then called upon to repress the Revolt of the Comuneros and so, "because of the disturbances," he marched to Santa Fé, Socorro, Río Hacha, and Darién. His prospective bride died before he had finished his numerous campaigns. Distance also affected merchants: One petitioner explained that his "prolonged absence" from his Spanish wife had eventually prompted him to establish another household in the Americas.[26]

Even men whose professions did not involve travel might employ distance to escape from matrimony. Such was the strategy of Don Antonio Tadeo Tames of Arequipa, who was a student in a *colegio* in La Plata, Bolivia, before he fled over the mountains.[27] Witnesses recalled that he was "soon to [have contracted] holy matrimony" after he "procreated Don Manuel Tames as his son, leaving him in the pregnant womb of his mother." Don Antonio absconded to Cochabamba, where his reputation as an unwed father did not prevent him from eventually living as "a subject of honor . . . employed various times in offices of honor in that villa." Don Juan Bautista Corleto engaged in a similar flight from Santa Marta (Colombia).[28] After he purchased a house and land for his fiancée and their baby daughter, he left the city on the pretext that he had to settle a lawsuit. Nineteen years later he had not returned.

Geographical removal separated lovers not only from their betrayed fiancées but also from the influence of both families. While legitimation depositions do not confirm the stereotype that fathers or brothers of pregnant maidens resorted to violence to avenge the family reputation, male relatives almost certainly must have pressured uneager bridegrooms to wed.[29] Grandparents on both sides might demand that lovers marry and legitimate succeeding generations. No doubt such influence was most effective when directed at unwed fathers whose families had lived in the community for several generations.[30]

Although statistics are sparse, they suggest that *cédula* fathers were more likely than *cédula* mothers to be community outsiders.[31] The families of *cédula* fathers were evenly divided, with half residing in Spain or more distant colonial locations and the remainder living nearby. In contrast, the families of women who produced illegitimates were twice as likely to be Creole and have been settled in their respective localities a minimum of two generations. Men were generally more mobile than women, and the fathers of illegitimates were less likely to be locals—and presumably less responsive to community pressures.

Although the evidence is necessarily anecdotal, family precedent was another variable that promoted illegitimacy. While *gracias al sacar* depositions seldom provide information on the presence of other illegitimates within families, the alphabetized notarial records in Lima and Arequipa make it possible to trace the testaments of the parents and siblings of selected illegitimates.[32] These investigations leave the strong impression that illegitimacy was common in some elite families. It additionally suggests that men who were themselves illegitimate, or who had been raised with illegitimate half brothers or sisters, may have been more tolerant of such practices, and possibly even more likely to father their own children out of wedlock.

Two-generation illegitimacy permeated the family of Judge (*oidor*) Don Gaspar Urquízu, who produced three sons named Don Gaspar, Don Juan, and Don Santiago, and then, with another woman, had a daughter named Doña María del Carmen.[33] Although this judge petitioned to legitimate Don Santiago, he never followed the process to completion. Instead he eventually married the mother of his sons at the end of his life and automatically legitimated them. Perhaps because they spent most of their lives as illegitimates, his sons continued the family tradition of out-of-wedlock births. Don Juan, a captain of dragoons, left an illegitimate daughter in Buenos Aires. Don Santiago had a childless marriage, but his final testament recognized two natural sons: Don Miguel, the commander of a *pardo* infantry regiment, and Luis Urquízu.[34]

Arequipa merchant Don Antonio León Calatayúd was another with close familiarity with illegitimacy, for he had grown up with a half brother who was an *hijo natural.* Don Antonio León's mother had given birth to Don Manuel de Cáceres before she began forty-two years of married life that produced two daughters as well as her legitimate younger son. Don Antonio León's letters reflect his acceptance of and love for this older half brother, who was also a business partner.[35] He not only named Don Manuel as one of the executors of his will but also made him an equal beneficiary with his legitimate siblings.[36] Perhaps because Don Antonio León grew up in a household with an illegitimate brother who was totally accepted into the family, he may have had more tolerance for illegitimacy and too little apprehension—as will soon become apparent—concerning the future of his own two *hijos naturales*.

LIFE COURSE AND SEXUAL ENCOUNTERS

Occupation, geographical mobility, familial pressure, and precedent were distinctive elements to be factored into any equation conducive to the fathering of illegitimates. An even more fundamental determinant was masculine life course, or the changing nature of relationships that developed between men and women as they aged and moved through the discrete stages in their lives. Colonial men fathered illegitimates in distinctive patterns throughout their "procreative careers."[37] They figured as youthful seducers, serious courtiers, confirmed bachelors, married men, older widowers, or priests. Sexual relationships occurred as part of courtship, within long-term consensual unions, or as more casual liaisons.

While *cédula* petitions provide no statistical insight into male sexual arrangements in the "real world" of colonial Spanish America, they do provide guidelines as to how sexual arrangements might have varied over the masculine life course (see Table 5). Unmarried males (N. 104) can be divided into two groups. The first cluster is composed of bachelors (N. 20) who engaged in more restricted, often secret sexual encounters. Included among these were younger courtiers (N. 5) who promised matrimony and seduced multiple fiancées, and those who arranged clandestine sexual relationships (N. 15) that resulted in private pregnancies. A second and significantly larger group of single men (N. 84) publicly lived with their lovers and children in marriagelike arrangements that lasted years, decades, or even a lifetime. Included in this group were bachelors who promised matrimony through extended engagements (N. 29), those who engaged in serial sexual liaisons (N. 13), widowers (N. 8), and lovers who were cousins (N. 6). Another cluster included the ineligible: married men (N. 19) and priests (N. 12), followed by the frequently encountered "unknown" (N. 52).

TABLE 5

*Male "State" and the Nature of Sexual Relationships
Leading to Illegitimacy*

Single Men		
Primarily sexual encounters		
Multiple courtships	5	
Private pregnancy	15	
Subtotal		20
Marriagelike relationships		
Extended engagements	29	
Serial bachelor relationships		
with no promise of matrimony	13	
Couple lived together; not enough		
data to classify	7	
Widowers	8	
Incestuous relationships (cousins)	6	
Bachelor; unknown relationship	21	
Subtotal		84
Total single males		104
Other categories		
Married men	12	
Priests	19	
Subtotal		31
Unknown marital state		52
Total other		83
Total		187

SOURCE: DB 4-187.

One royal official who reviewed this variety of sexual arrangements expressed some sympathy for "the fragility of young, unmarried [persons] who covered their passion with hopes that were generally frustrated."[38] Yet in the cases of young courting men, the passion may well have been theirs while the frustrated hopes often belonged to their lovers. This was especially so when younger bachelors promised matrimony and had sexual relations with more than one fiancée at a time, or when their secret sexual relationships ended with private pregnancies.[39] In both cases, male relationships with their lovers were essentially sexual encounters, since the couples did not establish long-term liaisons or live together.[40]

Witnesses substantiate that younger men might yield more than once to the "passion" described by the royal official and wield the coveted promise of matrimony as a particularly potent weapon of seduction. Such promises and betrayals characterized the multiple courtships of Don Joseph Lucas Concha, a cadet in a *pardo* militia company in Caracas.[41] He had "contracted an engagement" with a Doña Manuela Josepha, and their sexual encounters resulted in a baby daughter. The father of the unwed mother, Don Manuel de Ponce, a lieutenant of artillery in the Venezuelan port of La Guajira, later described his efforts to ensure an eventual ceremony. Since his potential son-in-law was not yet an officer, he had made the cadet sign a "written contract" in which "he had promised to verify [the marriage] and to legitimate by subsequent marriage the offspring that resulted from his engagement." The marriage was to take place after Don Joseph had "ensured his military career" with a promotion.

In the meantime, Don Joseph was courting yet again in Caracas, where he exchanged a "clandestine" promise to marry with Doña María Ana de Vegrete. Doña María Ana had prudently arranged for her parish priest as well as witnesses both to overhear his pledge of matrimony and to pressure the vicar general for its immediate fulfillment. When word of the wedding reached La Guajira, Don Manuel lodged an official complaint with the Council of War, bitterly proclaiming that his own daughter had been "deceived." No doubt he felt particularly betrayed, for if the erring lover had not been forced into an instant marriage, Don Manuel could have brandished the written contract and his daughter might well have received priority. In 1785 his story received a sympathetic hearing from the Cámara and his granddaughter a legitimation.

Men who courted and bedded multiple fiancées faced not only personal but also legal complications. Authorities might delay a desired marriage for months or years while they sorted out genuine from spurious claims. Meanwhile, sexually active fiancées might bear illegitimate children. Such was the dilemma that confronted Don Jerónimo Rodríguez Vanegas of Sancti Espíritu, who admitted that, "after celebrating an engagement" with Doña Ana Beatris de Castro, he "was able to persuade her after repeated pleas to unite with [him,] from which meeting . . . she became pregnant."[42] Since the couple were cousins, Don Jerónimo had to appeal for an ecclesiastical dispensation. When his petition became known, Doña Luisa Chamendía surfaced as yet another fiancée and contested the engagement. The ultimate effect of Don Jerónimo's multiple promises was to compromise the lives of three women in his life. The first was the abandoned Doña Luisa; the second, the pregnant Doña Ana; and the third, an illegitimate baby Isabel who, inasmuch as she was of incestuous birth, could not be automatically legitimated when her parents eventually married.

Alcalde Don Juan Bautista de Armentos of Trinidad, Cuba, was another who had to face the consequences of his dual promises of matrimony, although his desired wife, Doña Luisa Mariana Gonzáles, endured even more.[43] When the couple's engagement was announced, another fiancée appeared and asked the lieutenant governor and the *audiencia* to stop the wedding. While the parties litigated, Doña Luisa gave birth to a daughter and "a short time" later died without being able "to verify the marriage." The lawsuit was still under appeal when Don Juan applied for the legitimation of his daughter in 1810.

Yet another bachelor pattern originated when younger men engaged in short-term, usually clandestine sexual relationships and arranged private pregnancies. Included among these was a naval lieutenant of Havana, Don Francisco Garro, who was twenty-five when he concealed the pregnancy of his lover.[44] She appeared on their baby daughter's baptismal certificate as an "unknown mother." He then deposited the infant with his widowed mother before sailing off to his own premature death at age twenty-nine. The secrecy attendant on private pregnancies also gave men license to hide the identity and motherhood of one lover while they courted another. Chilean Don Antonio de Aguilar and Argentinian Don Manuel Domec were but two who orchestrated private pregnancies with one fiancée while planning marriage with another.[45]

The unifying themes that linked multiple courtships and private pregnancies were the comparative youth and inexperience of the fathers and the privacy attached to such liaisons. Yet the comment of the royal official that illegitimacy commonly resulted from the "fragility" and the "passion" of those who were "young" and "unmarried" is not borne out by the majority of *gracias al sacar* applications. Rather, a striking number of unwed fathers lived publicly in marriagelike relationships during those decades in their lives when most of their peers were married. The resulting sexual relationships proceeded less from the elevated hormone levels of the young than from masculine desires to form serious ties with lovers and to establish households, temporary or permanent.

MARRIAGELIKE RELATIONSHIPS

Extended engagements in which men promised matrimony, engaged in sex-ual relationships with their fiancées, cared for their natural children, but never married proved a common pattern during the middle or later years of the life course. Although such unions resembled matrimony, they lacked the religious vows that pledged marital faithfulness and permanency, nor did they ensure the transmission of paternal inheritance to offspring. Slightly more than half of extended engagements ended when *cédula* fathers aban-doned their fiancées, either to remain bachelors or to marry someone else (N. 16); the rest terminated with the death of one of the betrothed (N. 13).

Surviving personal letters and documents from Seville, Arequipa, and Lima provide exceptional details concerning the extended engagement of Don Antonio León Calatayúd, who eventually deserted his fiancée and two small sons.[46] The life course of this Peruvian merchant is worth exploring at some length, for it provides a rare record of that usually undocumented process by which a lover broke his promises and established emotional and, in this instance, geographical distance between himself and his fiancée and children. His story reveals that a benchmark in extended engagements was whether men transferred their primary emotional loyalties from immediate kin, such as parents, brothers, and sisters, and began to identify with their lover and children.

Don Antonio León Calatayúd was an Arequipa merchant of standing, for he had accumulated goods worth more than seventy-five thousand pesos.[47] He apparently shared his wealth with his family, because, even though his mother stated that she had "married poor," she now lived in a house sup-plied by her solicitous son.[48] No doubt Don Antonio appeared as a particu-larly eligible bachelor to Doña Marcelina Hidalgo, who lived with her mother in comparatively modest circumstances.[49]

Early in the 1760s the pattern of courtship, sexual relationship, illegiti-macy, and eventual abandonment began.[50] Don Antonio León exchanged the *palabra de casamiento* with Doña Marcelina, and she surrendered her vir-ginity, eventually giving birth to sons Mariano in 1761 and Agustín in 1762.[51] At first Don Antonio León fulfilled what witnesses agreed were the typical responsibilities of a lover and father-to-be. He arranged and sent for the midwife, was present at the birth of both sons, and hired nurses for the in-fants. Yet he did not officially recognize his first son on the baptismal certificate, for he asked the midwife to have Mariano baptized as of "unknown parentage." When Agustín was born, the next year, Don Antonio admitted paternity, although he still protected the name of the mother.

Even though Doña Marcelina's identity did not appear on her sons' baptismal certificates, she was not guarded by the typical arrangements of a private pregnancy, and she kept her sons with her after their birth. Although Don Antonio provided her with a house and supported her, he also maintained a separate residence over his store. In most other aspects Don Antonio gave public but informal proof of his paternity. One of the merchant's nephews later testified how Don Antonio played with his children, and "many days he kept them in his store, treating them as his sons."[52] The merchant's family also acknowledged the relationship, for his "parents recognized them as their grandchildren and took them to their house."

It was only because Don Antonio failed to fulfill his promise of matrimony that this affair ever became known outside of the neighborhoods of Arequipa, for Don Antonio used his mobility as a merchant to put distance between himself and his lover and their children. He apparently told his fiancée that he had to visit Lima on a trading trip but that he would return in a "short time." However he was already prevaricating, for his Arequipa testament, which he customarily updated before any journey, suggested an alternative destination. He confessed that he was "soon to leave for the court of Madrid, kingdom of Spain."[53]

It is unclear if Doña Marcelina initially knew that Don Antonio planned to journey to Spain, although it is certain that he promised to return from this trip and marry her. If she had had access to his testament she might have recognized additional omens that their marriage might never occur. His will did not treat her as a future wife, nor did it formally acknowledge paternity, for Don Antonio referred to his sons by their mother's surname of Hidalgo rather than his own of Calatayúd. The testament provided Doña Marcelina with only two thousand pesos. Even though Don Antonio left each son four thousand pesos in a religious trust (*capellaniá*), such sums were substantially less than the traditional one-fifth reserved for *hijos naturales*. These provisions were particularly stingy given that Don Antonio had no legitimate children and could legally leave his entire estate to his sons. Instead he maintained his loyalty to his birth family, willing his possessions to his father, his illegitimate half brother, and other siblings.

As Don Antonio traveled to the viceregal capital, he did not immediately break all ties to Arequipa. A remarkable series of personal letters to Doña Marcelina reveal a gradual loosening of the ties between the couple and between Don Antonio and his sons.[54] His first letter is particularly revealing, given that the merchant both expressed his love and concern and also made obvious efforts to provide Doña Marcelina with details that would interest her.[55] Yet a reading of this letter several hundred years later still raises the questions of whether Doña Marcelina would have shared Don Antonio's obvious enthusiasm for his new experiences and whether she perceived in subsequent missives his progressive emotional distancing.

From the first, Don Antonio's letters portrayed a man who was moving beyond the familiar circle of his known world and embracing a larger and more exciting milieu. Even his entrance into Lima established him as a person to know. He wrote Doña Marcelina that he

> entered around three in the afternoon and with the bustle of so many mules loaded with ingots and leather bags . . . that I assure you that they came from the balconies and galleries of the houses to see who it was with such wealth, such that I felt it necessary to close the little windows of the litter.[56]

After establishing himself in a house "a block and a half from the plaza," Don Antonio lost no time in making new friends and sampling the delights of the capital. He found himself "loved and estimated by many gentlemen who knew [him] only by reputation, but now by acquaintance," gentlemen who granted him many "singular favors." These included "taking me out for excursions," and he added that "the most diverting are the comedies, for it is certain that there are no better in Spain." Especially impressive were "the players who suddenly fly through the air," as well as those "good fellows who sing excellently accompanied by more than twenty instruments."

News of Don Antonio's expeditions must have sent especially mixed signals to his waiting fiancée, for the merchant made a trip to Lima's port of Callao. There his companions "invited me to embark, but I did not want to because I might get seasick and they would laugh at me." However Don Antonio finally boarded one ship "and so enjoyed it that [he] did not want to get off . . . without feeling any seasickness." Don Antonio disembarked for a short period and then: "I got on the ship again as if I had always been on the sea without suffering any movement in my head, and thus I knew that neither would you become sick, and in four or six days you could be here."

Although it is uncertain if Don Antonio understood that there might be some difference between the movements of a ship at harbor and one at sea, this experience possibly overcame any lingering apprehensions he might have had about a future ocean voyage. Yet in these early days he still loved and missed Doña Marcelina, for he still—if only half-heartedly—suggested that she join him. He reminded his "little heart" that "there is not a day that I do not think of you," and he sent "all [his] love and appreciation . . . I care for you and want to see you."

Subsequent letters from December until his March 1765 departure for Spain reveal a lover and father establishing further distance from his previous life. In December, even though his letter chatted concerning family business, recent deaths in Arequipa, and of his "love and invariable affection," he also wrote that he was glad to hear that "you and your children remain well." It may be no accident that, when Doña Marcelina's mother eventually submitted these letters as proof of paternity, Don Antonio's proponents noted that nowhere did he ever clearly admit that he was the father of two sons. Never did he speak of "his" sons or of "their" children. The question remains open whether this was a traditional way to refer to children, whether he was deliberately avoiding providing any evidence of paternity, or whether he already thought of his sons as belonging to Doña Marcelina and no longer as much a part of his life.

Don Antonio's letter in February struck a pious tone, partly in response to what seems to have been a frenzy of religious observance on the part of Doña Marcelina. She had apparently written and begged him to make a "general confession" of a lifetime of sin. Admitting that his sins were "great," he wrote her of his compliance with her wishes, and his visits every Friday morning at dawn to a convent a half-league from the city. He also took "much comfort" from the "novenas and many prayers" of his lover. However he wondered if "after so many novenas, prayers, rosaries, and runnings to all the saints of heaven" she might be "falling short in the house" and "not attending to [her] necessary obligations and responsibilities." Even though she was "acting as if [she were] a saint," he begged her to use her "good sense" in the matter.

A later reader can only wonder if Doña Marcelina had begun to comprehend her precarious position, to suspect that her lover might not fulfill his promise of matrimony, and to fear that he might abandon her. Perhaps she hoped that the priestly admonitions that accompanied the general confession of a lifetime of sin might encourage Don Antonio to heed the obligations of conscience. Her own religious exuberance may also have served to beg heaven for his safe return, as well as to buttress her own reputation if he did not. Religious scrupulosity was traditionally expected from elite women whose honor and public reputation were on shaky ground.

By the end of March 1765, Don Antonio did not have much time to write, as he was "ready to leave for Spain." He still assured Doña Marcelina that "the longest [he would] be away is a year." He charged her to "take great care and provide those children with a good education," promising that "with the favor of God we will see each other soon." He signed off as "your loving León" and sailed for Spain, never to return.[57] He continued his mercantile activities, remained unmarried, joined the order of Santiago, and died thirteen years later in December 1778.[58] After "a long absence . . . and no hope of his return," Doña Marcelina took her fate into her own hands. She ran off and married someone who "did not know beforehand that she had had two sons by Don Antonio."

Behind each extended and eventually broken engagement must have been similar tales of temptation, broken promises, and abandonment. Men might choose marriagelike arrangements for phases of their life course without any permanent commitment or price to their honor. The "demands of conscience" could prove a particularly weak reed when the responsibilities of maintaining a wife and children were balanced against personal freedom and the lure of the outside world.

BACHELORS AND CONSENSUAL UNIONS

Marriagelike options were not confined only to men who promised to wed; elite men might live in pseudo-conjugal relationships for years or decades without such pledges. Consensual unions resembled extended engagements in that lovers were unmarried yet could marry and legitimate their affair and their offspring at any time. They also reflected aspects of the medieval *barraganía*, in that the relationship often had temporal limits, although couples no longer signed a notarized contract defining the terms of the agreement. Instead, unmarried men who entered into consensual unions could freely abandon their lovers without fear of complications arising from either church or state.

Although dedicated bachelors might establish consensual unions with elite women without a marital commitment, the theme that emerges most strongly is not their desire for casual sexuality but rather their attempts to establish familylike relationships. Even when bachelors never wed, or married late in their lives, their life course might include one or several relationships in which they lived for years with lovers and children.[59] The career of Peruvian bureaucrat Don Anselmo Camborda provides a colorful portrait of one lover and father who produced four illegitimate children with three different women.[60] His history illustrates how multiple liaisons might complicate not only private lives but public reputations as well.

Documents from Lima and Arequipa confirm that during his lifetime Don Anselmo rather ineffectually faced a barrage of small and large problems: His sister cheated him of his family inheritance and sold his goods as her own, his slaves refused to give him their earnings and instead bought their freedom, the renters of his house reneged and refused to pay. In the midst of these difficulties he also confronted the usual jealousy and backbiting that accompanied service in any royal post—including serious charges leveled against his term as auditor (*contador*) of the royal accounts in Arequipa. His lovers and children only added to his problems.

Don Anselmo's sexual liaisons fell into three stages, which correlate with the beginning of his career as an auditor in Lima, his later years in Arequipa, and his eventual return to the Peruvian capital. His first documented affair was his long-term relationship with Doña Josepha Grados, which began around 1764 or 1765. Since he was a royal official and she was the daughter of a lawyer who practiced at the Limeño court, Doña Josepha was her lover's social peer, although there is no indication that the couple ever exchanged any promise of matrimony. They lived openly together in Doña Josepha's house, where they raised their two sons, Don Vicente and Don Cayetano, born in 1770 and 1776, respectively. In July of 1778 Don Anselmo traveled alone to Arequipa to take up his post as auditor. At this point it is uncertain what happened to Doña Josepha, but she did appear at the Lima church of San Marcelo in 1780 to recognize her sons and to place her name on their baptismal certificates.

Don Anselmo spent most of the years from 1778 to 1793 in Arequipa, where he eventually set up a new household and acquired a new lover, Doña Antonia Corso Negrón. Documents are vague as to whether Don Anselmo ever promised her matrimony, but she was both his social equal and a woman of property. Doña Antonia was fully committed to the interests of

her lover; in a closed will, written in March 1793, she transferred her loyalties away from her own family and relatives, leaving her estate solely to Don
Anselmo and his natural sons.[61] What she did not know was that in a few
months she would become pregnant herself, and a few months after that she
would be alone in Arequipa without her lover.

By 1793 Don Anselmo faced charges of mismanagement and embezzle-
ment. Critics said that he had taken four thousand pesos from the Arequipa
royal coffers to curry favor with the interim governor by acting as his guar-
antor.[62] His private affairs also figured obliquely in the public charges, for
detractors questioned where he had obtained the resources to support two
households. Some wondered where he had obtained the 480 pesos he had
sent to Lima to repair his family home after the May 1780 earthquake. Others questioned how he had raised fourteen hundred pesos to purchase a
house in Arequipa for Doña Antonia. Perhaps fearing imprisonment, Don
Antonio prepared to flee to Lima to answer his accusers.

Doña Antonia actively supported her lover. One of Don Anselmo's ene-
mies, Don Ignacio Rodríguez, later described the following drama: "At the
twelfth hour of the night" he had decided to satisfy his "curiosity." He had
"disguised himself" in a "cape and sombrero" and skulked around Doña Antonia's house, where he saw Don Anselmo with four or five Negroes and
slaves make "three or four trips" with "hidden bundles" between her home
and that of the notary public, who happened to be "a subject very partial to
the said Don Anselmo Camborda." The implication was that Don Anselmo
was using his connections either to hide property with a friend so that it
would not be confiscated after his flight, to prepare articles of contraband for
possible smuggling, or both. Either that night or soon afterward, Don Anselmo fled to Lima to mount his defense.

The loyal Doña Antonia was left to face what turned out to be her last
crisis without her lover, for she succumbed to the all too common complications of childbirth. Her last hours were chronicled in more than usual detail by the seven women—including her midwife, servants, and friends—
who attended her. Midwife Doña Bernarda Calle remembered that she had
slept for two nights in Doña Antonia's house to be ready for "the hour in
which she would feel the birth."[63] First pains began around three o'clock in
the morning of May 21. A baby boy was born, but Doña Antonia could not
propel the afterbirth and she became "tired with a great noise in her belly
and cold sweat." By nine in the morning she was dead, although her baby

son Ignacio Bernardino still lived. The eyewitness testimony to a live birth effectively disinherited the absent Don Anselmo. It also encouraged Doña Antonia's relatives to seize both the infant and the control of her estate. With her death and Don Anselmo's removal from Arequipa, the second stage of his sexual relationships came to an end, although the fate of this son and the disposition of his lover's property would preoccupy him throughout his life.

The last phase of Don Anselmo's sexual relationships can be traced from his 1794 return to Lima through his 1816 and his 1822 testaments.[64] During these years the *contador* tried to deal with the difficulties occasioned by his love affairs, his illegitimate children, and his professional life. In 1795, when his two eldest sons were nineteen and twenty-five, he applied for their legitimation. His letter to Spain identified himself as an auditor of the royal house in Lima and provided his sons' baptismal certificates, which now named both parents and proved that they were *hijos naturales*. He noted that his older son planned to be a priest, while the younger was still attending the College of Nobles in Lima. He explained that he could not marry their mother because "Doña Josepha Grados had embraced the religious state."[65] It is notable that Don Anselmo did not attempt to purchase a *gracias al sacar* for yet another illegitimate child, a Doña Blas, whose mother was unknown but whom Don Anselmo later acknowledged in both of his testaments. It may be that Doña Blas was not yet born in 1795, or that Don Anselmo did not choose to spend money to legitimate a girl.

Also not included in the 1795 *gracias al sacar* petition was Don Anselmo's newborn son in Arequipa. Throughout the remainder of his life, Don Anselmo fought unsuccessfully to obtain custody of Ignacio, as well as of Doña Antonia's Arequipa estates. Although he had originally been named as guardian, Don Anselmo had never assumed jurisdiction; he remained in Lima while his son lived with his mother's relatives in Arequipa. It seems unlikely that father and son ever met, for in 1822 Don Anselmo's will contained an incredible charge. He proclaimed that Doña Antonia's relatives had committed major fraud: that his son had died and that the Arequipa relatives had "substituted" a youth who was "not the son of Doña Antonia but a nobody whom they have given [the name] so as to enjoy the inheritance."[66]

As if these complications were not enough, between 1816 and 1820 Don Anselmo's private life took—if it were possible—an even more dramatic turn. By now this apparently confirmed bachelor must have been in his sixties, but he finally embraced the married state. The identity of his wife is even more surprising, for she proved to be Doña Josepha Grados, the mother of his two oldest and now legitimated sons. Left unclear is whether Doña Josepha had belonged to a lay branch of a religious order and had taken simple vows that could be revoked by a priest, or whether Don Anselmo had lied about her presumed vocation on the legitimation petition.

What seems certain is that Don Anselmo must not have contemplated any union with Doña Josepha in 1795. Given constant money problems, it is unlikely that he would have spent eight thousand reales that year to legitimate his sons when he might have done so without cost with a marriage ceremony. Nor is it likely that Don Anselmo was married prior to his 1816 testament, which did not mention a wife.[67] Yet by 1820 the lifelong bachelor had become a husband. That year Doña Josepha wrote a will that proclaimed her to be "married and a wife . . . to Don Anselmo Antonio Camborda" and that recognized her two sons. It is questionable if by now a sexual relationship was part of their marriage, for in her testament Doña Josepha revealed that she was "sick in bed from an accident."[68] Two years later, Don Anselmo's last will acknowledged that he now had a "legitimate wife" who was "incapacitated."[69]

Don Anselmo spent his final years defending his "honor." His single documentary reference to the word had nothing to do with his lovers, nor with his illegitimate offspring, however, but involved his professional reputation as an auditor. His 1816 will asserted that he had "never lost [count of] not even a cent . . . nor even an ounce of mercury."[70] He defensively blamed any problems with the accounts on his successors' use of the "new method of double entry, which I and the other older ministers do not know." Yet Don Anselmo's last testament (1822) also seemed to concede the merit of the fraud charges leveled against him: The auditor suggested that, if he were to receive any money from his Arequipa lover's estate, four thousand pesos be deposited in that local treasury, given "the just reasons that I owe them."[71] Since the original charge of Don Antonio's detractors was that he had embezzled exactly that sum from the treasury, such a final concession seems suggestive, if circumstantial.

Don Anselmo's life course illustrates how a long-term bachelor might establish a series of marriagelike liaisons. Serial consensual unions provided unmarried men with the emotional, familial, and material advantages of matrimony without the permanent commitment. No doubt royal officials or military officers found such arrangements particularly amenable, given the regulations concerning their marriages and their geographical mobility as well as their need to create supportive private circles wherever they served. Unfortunately, legitimation documents cannot reveal how often such trial marriages were transformed into the real thing.[72] Yet Don Anselmo's endless problems demonstrate that even when bachelors avoided commitment, they did not escape the host of personal complications that accompanied such irregular liaisons.

WIDOWERS

Compared with men who became engaged to several women at once, or those who broke extended engagements, or those who were confirmed bachelors, widowers seem to have managed their sexual affairs more sedately, although they were another noticeable group who produced illegitimate offspring. *Cédula* widowers exhibited two related patterns of sexual activity. The first was a tendency to engage in a relationship near the end of their lives and to produce an illegitimate child after years spent as husbands and widowers. The second pattern is seen in the widowers who "sandwiched" affairs, initiating between-marriage sexual relationships after one wife had died and before they remarried. Testimony leaves the strong impression that widowers were less likely to use a false promise of matrimony to initiate sexual relationships. Perhaps since these men were older, they were more responsible; perhaps they had significant material incentives to offer prospective lovers. It is suggestive that none of the *cédula* widowers were ever sued for breach of promise. Nor did geographical mobility play much role in their liaisons, which usually occurred within the widowers' communities, often within their homes.

The life history of widower Don Bernardo de Miranda Villaizán of Guadalajara, Mexico, provides a typical example of the "last fling," postmarriage pattern of sexuality. The father of two sons who were priests, Don Bernardo was a "subject of first distinction" who had served in the prestigious posts of *alcalde* and *regidor*.[73] After his wife died, his typically observant neighbors began to record the "frequent entrance" of Doña María Gertrudis Castro into his house. No one seemed surprised when she produced a daughter whom the *regidor* recognized as his own, and whom his sons also loved and treated as a sister, even after their father died.

Cases from Havana provide a similar pattern. Don Miguel de Cárdenas Véles de Guevara was a widower with seven legitimate offspring when he began a sexual relationship with Doña Lucía Ordoñez in 1768 and fathered a baby daughter.[74] Before his death four years later, Don Miguel not only provided for the support of the infant but also left Doña Lucía sufficient money for a dowry. Lieutenant Don Agustín Herrera had been a widower for fifteen years when, in 1774, he "had carnal intercourse for a short time" with a Havana women who bore him a daughter.[75] Although, typically, he had not promised matrimony in exchange for sexual favors, he supported his daughter with particular responsibility and eventually paid for her legitimation.

A variant of the widower-as-unwed-father theme occurred when men pursued relationships between marriages. Since widowers were not likely to promise matrimony to such lovers, they often sought women who would not expect permanent commitment, since they were at the edge of racial or social acceptability. Such a profile characterizes the affair of Guanajuato assayer Don Ignacio Martínez de Lejarzar, who spent almost twenty years as a widower between the death of his first wife in 1746 and his second marriage in 1766.[76] In between he lived with Doña María Antonia García y Abalos, and the couple produced an illegitimate son and daughter. The assayer never promised to marry Doña María, who may have already been compromised, since at some point she gave birth to yet another illegitimate son with another lover.[77] By the time Don Ignacio died, sometime in 1773 or 1774, he had married yet again. The assayer thus fathered three sets of children by three different women. First were a legitimate grown-up son, who was also an assayer, and a daughter who had taken the veil in Querétaro. Second were his illegitimate son and daughter produced during his years of widowhood. Finally were two legitimate sons under the age of three, the product of his second marriage.

A sexual relationship between marriages, one that did not promise matrimony, and one in which the father scrupulously cared for illegitimate children, also characterized the middle years of widower Don Manuel José de Escobar of Cartagena, Colombia.[78] After the death of his first wife and before he received a dispensation to marry her cousin, this retired *regidor* lived for at least five years in the early 1780s with María Trinidad Miranda. Race and racism complicated the affair. María—who, significantly, did not use the honorific of Doña—was one-fifth racially mixed, or a *quinterona*. The relationship between this couple balanced on an extremely delicate racial cusp. If the *regidor* had married María, the union could have been condemned as racially unequal, or as a difference of "quality."[79] However, their two illegitimate children passed the critical racial divide, for the union of their white father and their one-fifth *pardo* mother meant that they were regarded as only one-tenth racially mixed. This number fell beneath the one-eighth proportion that traditionally designated whites in colonial Spanish America.[80] Even though their mother had been baptized under the racial classification of "*pardos and morenos*" her children were officially white, and indeed one was baptized as "apparently white."

When Don Manuel José wrote to the Cámara, he took special pains to document the background of his affair with María. Perhaps fearing that her racial mixture might prejudice his case, he presented her conduct in an especially favorable light. He produced witnesses who testified that her father "wore a dress coat and carried a sword [and] show[ed] by this [his] grade of quality."[81] Others described María as "of white color with straight hair" and noted that she still lived "with the same seclusion and honesty as when raised by her parents."

Don Manuel José was even more complimentary. He admitted that it was his own "impulse of human fragility" that had led him to begin the sexual relationship. Even though he was about to "separate himself from this communication" and to marry another, he praised María's "modesty, the state of virginity in which he found her, the assistance and care that she has taken with his interests and the house he gave her." The *regidor* spoke even more wistfully of the "love and affection that he had for their children" and his "just desire" that they enjoy the "honors and privileges" due their birth.

While class and race may have discouraged Don Manuel José from marriage to a woman he respected and perhaps still loved, María gained as well as lost in this relationship. Although she did not marry, this affair may have been her last chance for motherhood, given that she was thirty-three and thirty-seven years old when she gave birth. Her relationship also promoted the racial and social mobility of her family, for her children were born white and, ultimately, legitimated.[82] In this respect, her choice resembled a well-chronicled Cuban pattern: Verena Stolcke has noted that *pardo* women might prefer liaisons with white men and subsequent lightening of the next generation rather than marriage to darker-skinned peers. The popular saying expressed it succinctly: "Rather the mistress of a white man than the wife of a Negro."[83]

Analysis of the relatively few cases of widowers suggests that they tended to be responsible lovers and fathers. Whether such inclination translated in the real world of colonial Spanish America into a greater tendency for widowers to marry their lovers and thus automatically to legitimate their offspring is impossible to tell. Yet older men seemed more ready than their younger counterparts to recognize the price that women paid when they consented to sexual intercourse and to provide the necessary support for lovers and children.

An intriguing question remains unanswered concerning not only widowers but also all other eligible men: Why didn't they marry? Unfortunately, *gracias al sacar* depositions provide only hints as to why men chose to renege on marriage promises, live in consensual unions, or remain bachelors. Yet a life course analysis of these *cédula* fathers provides some context for the trends noted by demographers and historians of colonial Spanish America. Juan Javier Pescador C. concluded, for example, that men in Mexico City (1700–1850) were more likely to marry peers either when they were young or at an advanced age.[84] This propensity for early and late marriage may also be reflected in witness testimony that suggests that passionate younger men and older widowers were—for entirely different reasons—more willing to wed than their middle-aged counterparts. Young men were motivated by peer pressure to be sexually active and to begin a family, while older widowers had both the means and the maturity to welcome a bride. In contrast, a geographically mobile and middle-aged cohort of professional men may have been more disposed to settle for a series of sexual liaisons.

Regional variations of female supply and demand may also have affected the ultimate outcome of sexual liaisons.[85] In regions such as Florida, California, Sonora, and Vera Cruz, where suitable women were comparatively scarce, elite men might have to "go all the way" and agree to marriage to secure an eligible companion. In locales such as Guadalajara or Bogotá, where the male-female ratio was more in their favor, such men might be able to make less permanent commitments and still secure an eligible consort.

INELIGIBLE STATES: PRIESTS AND ADULTERERS

Priests and husbands constituted another distinct cluster of men who fathered illegitimates (priests N. 12; husbands N. 19). The prevalence of clerical sexual liaisons must have served as a backhand protection to parishioners who also lived in forms of consensual unions, since priests had little moral authority to chastise others when they themselves lived in sin.[86] With the occasional exception of a rampaging bishop who swept into localities, separated or married lovers, and cast mistresses out of rectories, there must have been more of a live-and-let-live attitude than is generally acknowledged.[87] In his recent study on the Mexican clergy, William Taylor suggested that there was a "general acceptance of discreet heterosexuality" as long as priests kept their sexual liaisons private.[88]

Such popular tolerance did not extend to governmental circles when sacrilegious affairs had to be confessed to the Cámara of the Indies. One of the more telling criticisms in Antonio de Ulloa's midcentury *Noticias Secretas* had been its "strident condemnation of the colonial clergy," particularly of its "failure to observe the rule of celibacy."[89] Bourbon reformers manifested little tolerance for clerical sexual misbehavior; when the sons and daughters of priests appealed to the Cámara for redress, they faced an uphill battle.

Silence concerning the sexual affairs of priests is particularly striking and equally understandable. Even if priestly liaisons may not have been rare, they nonetheless crossed social and religious boundaries. It was not in the best interests of clerics to provide royal officials with telling details of their meetings with their lovers, nor of their subsequent child-care arrangements. Nor was it a good tactic for priestly fathers to initiate legitimation requests themselves, for officials might be less disposed to grant such offenders any favors. Rather, in seven of the nine cases their sons and daughters applied, for they could present themselves as the innocent victims of their fathers' imperfections.[90]

When witnesses did reveal details of clerical sexual relationships, it was to stress the secrecy of the arrangements. No doubt the goal was to impress royal officials that the principals had at least tried to reduce local scandal. One priest confessed that he took his baby daughter into his household only after he had "discovered" her as an abandoned infant on his doorstep.[91] When Celaya Abbot Don Luis de Rueda fathered a son, he sent him and his mother to Mexico City, away from local gossips.[92] The will of another Mexican priest left his two young children property but referred to them as his "minor heirs" rather than identifying them as his sons.[93] The dean of the La Plata cathedral acknowledged his fatherhood only to his intimate friends.[94] The dearth of information forecloses much exploration of clerical sexual arrangements. The propensity of colonial men to enter the priesthood either as vocation or as occupation, and their proclivity to take and break vows of chastity, will have to rely on sources other than the *gracias al sacar*.[95]

Married men who fathered *adulterinos*, offspring of the other forbidden union, fell into three discernible groups: Approximately half (N. 9) of the men simply confessed to an extramarital relationship but provided little further information. In a second category, five of the remaining fathers married their lovers after their wives had died.[96] Since such marriages could not legitimate the couple's children, such formalizations must have reflected a significant emotional commitment between the pair. The remaining fathers (N. 5) were out-of-town adulterers with wives in one locale and lovers and families in a second. One father had a spouse in the Canaries and a family in Caracas; another a wife in Spain and a household in Guatemala; another a bride in Potosí and a family in La Plata; and another a lover in Spain and a wife in Havana.[97] One military officer seemed willing to marry everywhere, as he had wives in Ceuta, Mexico, and Puerto Príncipe.

The *cédula* cases suggest that adulterous affairs proceeded as much from serious emotional commitment or geographical absence as from desire for casual extracurricular sexual relationships.[98] However, it is essential to remember that legitimation petitions most usually chronicled sexual relationships between social peers. The extent to which elite married men initiated sexual affairs with women of other races or classes is impossible to determine from these sources.

THE CRISIS OF CONSCIENCE AND HONOR

As *cédula* fathers entered middle or old age, a striking number faced a crisis of conscience and honor. Men who took great pride in their own elite ancestry had to confront the unpleasant reality that they could not pass on honor to their beloved sons or daughters. Paternal distress of this kind was a natural result when deep bonds developed between fathers and their illegitimate offspring. Some men had raised their children on their own; others had lived for years in extended engagements, or as bachelors or widowers caring for their sons and daughters in a family atmosphere. Even men who did not personally raise their illegitimate children had legal responsibilities toward them. Understanding the minimum expected of fathers by law provides some perspective on the obligations that linked fathers with their legitimate, as well as with their illegitimate, progeny, and that led to this final crisis of honor.

The *Siete Partidas* (1256–1265), the fundamental law of medieval Spain, placed great emphasis on the act of *crianza*, or the upbringing and education of legitimate children. It defined *crianza* primarily as a male responsibility, "one of the greatest deeds that a man can do [for] another."[99] Although the law recognized certain biological necessities, such as the infant's need to nurse, it gave mothers a special obligation for babies only until the age of three, after which fathers should shoulder the primary responsibility. The law insisted that both "piety and natural duty should move fathers to care for their children, giving and doing for them what is necessary." Paternal obligations included the provision of food, drink, clothing, and shoes, as well as a dwelling place. The law also urged fathers to love their progeny, for "even the beasts, who do not have reasonable understanding, naturally love and care for their children, much more ought men do it."[100] Such prescripts show the other face of the patriarchal control of *patria potestad*. Men may have had supreme authority over children, but they had supreme responsibility as well.

In cases of illegitimacy, the *Siete Partidas* distinguished between paternal obligations to natural children and to bastards. Bachelors who had engaged in sexual relationships with marriageable women who had acted "in the place of a wife" were bound to the emotional as well as some of the material dictates of *crianza*.[101] Fathers were obligated to love and support *hijos naturales* until they could take care of themselves. There were no monetary limits to such maintenance if a father lacked legitimate heirs. However, if he procreated legitimate offspring, the totality of expenses for *hijos naturales* could not exceed one-fifth of his estate.[102]

The *Siete Partidas* relieved fathers of any obligation to support bastards born of "adultery, or of incest, or other fornication." Even if men chose to provide for such offspring, the law insisted that they did so as a "favor, such that they might do to other strangers." This double standard was considered justifiable because women who bore bastards were sexually out of control. The *Partida* explained that "the mother is always certain of the child born to her, that it is hers, but the father is not, of those born to such women." Since men could not be assured of paternity when they had sexual intercourse with such women, they were correspondingly relieved of responsibilities.

Of course not all fathers fulfilled their legal obligations, nor identified with the interests of their illegitimate offspring.[103] Subsequent events after the flight of Arequipa merchant Don Antonio León Calatayúd are instructive in this regard; his neglect of his two sons not only produced a lawsuit but also led to private condemnation by his relatives and friends.[104]

When the letter-writing Don Antonio León sailed from Peru to make a new life in Spain, he had left his parents and relatives as well as his fiancée and his two natural sons, Don Mariano and Don Agustín. It was only to these last two that the merchant owed any legal obligation for maintenance. Yet more than a decade after his departure he had still not paid, and grandmother Doña Juana Murillo finally sued for child support. By then her daughter had run off to marry another and had left the grandmother to support the two boys "with her possessions and at the cost of [her] sweat and work." She petitioned when the boys reached the ages of twelve and thirteen, for her expenses had substantially increased given their need for "education."

The grandmother's lawsuit pitted her against Dr. Don Juan Antonio Tristán, who was a priest, a lawyer, and the rector of the local *colegio*. He was also Don Antonio's cousin and the absent merchant's legal representative (*apoderado*) in Arequipa. His actions are particularly striking, given that he acted differently toward the merchant's boys in public and in private. In public he fought the lawsuit and defended Don Antonio's property; in private he recognized that his cousin had acted improperly, and he tried to aid his two abandoned relatives.

The priest-lawyer's official stance was to fight Doña Juana's lawsuit on the grounds of proof and responsibility. He argued that the letters Don Antonio had written from Lima, and which the grandmother had submitted as evidence of the relationship between her daughter and the merchant, "said nothing of the relationship of Mariano and Agustín respective to Don Antonio, nor even a word of the support that is the proper quality of paternal recognition and obligation." He also asserted that Don Antonio's "good conduct" meant that he would have necessarily fulfilled such obligations if they had existed. "How," he asked the judge, "could Don Antonio forget such an important obligation without telling me anything of it? . . . How could Don Antonio ignore an obligation to support his sons[?]" The absence of any instruction concerning the two boys was particularly telling, given that Don Antonio had directed him to support his "father and sister and others, even when these have the capacity to take care of themselves."

Grandmother Doña Juana contended that Don Antonio had failed to fulfill his legal responsibilities:

> Their father is obligated by all the laws to contribute to the support and expenses of their upbringing according to his fortune, his rank, and that of the mother who had them. My daughter is of decent circumstances, Don Antonio is a Gentleman Knight, and his goods are notoriously numerous.

Although the grandmother admitted that the "letters do not express with material words, clearly and individually that Don Antonio is the natural father of Mariano and Agustín, my grandchildren," she assured the judge of her reliance on his "discreet and penetrating intelligence" to see to the truth of the matter. Her confidence was rewarded to the extent that the official awarded her three hundred pesos, although only one hundred pesos materialized, and the grandmother had to sue again in 1777.

Even while Don Antonio Tristán fought the grandmother publicly, he privately recognized the justice of her claims. In the second lawsuit, one witness testified that the priest-lawyer had confessed to him that "he could not deny that Don Mariano and Don Agustín were sons of . . . Don Antonio León." In fact, since their father provided so little for them, Don Antonio Tristán later admitted that he had paid "from his own pocket" to enroll them in the Arequipa college seminary where he was the rector. When he left Arequipa to take up another position in Cuzco, he asked his successor as rector to watch over the boys. In an affectionate play on words—given that "León" means "lion" in Spanish—he hoped that his friend might "be able to help the little lions (*leonsitos*) as they deserve." He then confessed that "their father is a great miser and goat who causes me a thousand burdens by the small amounts that he spends on them . . . but my powers do not extend to more." The man of "good conduct" that Don Antonio Tristán had defended in public became the "miser" in private because of his failure to attend to his paternal responsibilities. Even though their father failed them, these abandoned schoolboys benefited from the keenly felt obligations to kin.

In contrast to the irresponsible and parsimonious Don Antonio, a substantial percentage (N. 107; 49.5 percent) of *cédula* fathers took the responsibility of *crianza* seriously and provided for their illegitimate children.[105] Many went beyond the basic responsibilities of maintenance and petitioned that their offspring be legitimated. Men who lacked the competing responsibilities of a wife and legitimate offspring proved to be three times more likely to support such applications.[106] Some must have shared the plight of Captain Don Joseph de los Ríos, who confessed that he "did not have any other legitimate son nor daughter, nor natural [offspring.]"[107] Another father acknowledged that he was "without any legitimate succession, nor hope of having any, given his advanced age."[108]

Although the evidence is necessarily anecdotal, fathers might also petition selectively and not legitimate every son or daughter. Even though *Oidor* Don Gaspar Urquízu wrote eloquently of the problems of one illegitimate son, he failed to mention that he had two others as well as a daughter in similar circumstances.[109] Lieutenant Colonel Don Lorenzo de Parga was another father who seemed eager to legitimate one daughter but not another.[110] When he purchased a *gracias al sacar* for sixteen-year-old heiress Doña María Josepha in 1795, he explained that he had not fulfilled his promise to marry her mother, for she had died while he was on (his everlasting) campaign. Yet immediately after he had left his pregnant fiancée, Don Lorenzo had marched to Cartagena, where he had another affair and another natural daughter named Doña María Andrea. In his 1799 testament the officer referred disparagingly to the mother of this second child as "a someone named Candelaria whose name he doesn't recall."[111]

Don Lorenzo showed little consideration for this second daughter, marrying her off to a sergeant of artillery and eventually disinheriting her. His 1799 testament declared that he "had never thought to give this girl anything more than that [which she received] as a dowry for her marriage." It "excluded and deprived her as permitted by law" from any right to his possessions. Doña María Andrea did not take this abandonment lightly. Identifying herself as white, as an *expósita*, and as the daughter of a Doña María Candelaria Ricardo Sevallos, she sued her father for his rejection.[112] Don Lorenzo's actions suggest that paternal concern for illegitimates might vary as a result of the race, wealth, or family connections of the mother.

Behind the dark stories of fathers who abandoned or rejected illegitimate offspring were others about men who not only took their paternal obligations seriously but also identified emotionally with the interests of their sons and daughters. As time passed and infants became young adults, these fathers faced the ultimate repercussions of their failure to wed and pass on honor to their blood kin. A father might cherish a beloved daughter yet understand that her lack of honor would limit her choice of an eligible spouse. He might recognize that a favored illegitimate son might never be able to hold public office, nor be accounted a man of honor in the community. Fathers had to confront the reality that their children had become innocent victims of their sexual promiscuity, or their failure to fulfill their promises. Even though a man's personal honor might not have suffered when he engaged in sexual intercourse with a social peer, broke a pledge of matrimony, or abandoned a lover or an illegitimate child, he still might become caught in the trap of honor when his actions prejudiced the next generation.[113]

Many unwed fathers expressed their guilt when they saw how their failure to marry had hurt their children. Even when his illegitimate daughter was still young, naval lieutenant Don Agustín Herrera spoke of his "remorse," and saw her as an "indispensable obligation and charge to [his] conscience."[114] *Oidor* Don Gaspar de Urquízu was burdened by the "weight" that illegitimacy exacted against the "admirable person" of his adult son Santiago, given that he "loved him."[115] Don Juan Antonio Morejón was tortured by his knowledge of society's "lack of charity" and thoughts of how his actions had hurt his two much-beloved but illegitimate daughters. He "could not dissipate from his imagination" the effects on his daughters, who could not enjoy the "ingenuousness and the natural [behavior] which [wa]s . . . the right of those procreated in legitimate marriage."[116]

Such crises of conscience and honor seem to have dominated the last years of *cédula* fathers, some of whom repented almost literally on their deathbeds. Several made fruitless plans to fulfill the demands of conscience by last-minute marriages to their long-suffering fiancées and automatic legitimation of their adult offspring. One Cuban priest remembered that sixty-year-old *Regidor* Don Joseph Antonio Echevarría, "shortly before he died . . . and while still sick . . . visited the church inquiring concerning marriage, . . . for he was firm in wanting to contract this marriage."[117] Guatemalan Don Joseph García was "in his last extremity" when he confessed to his natural son, Don Rafael, that "he had some thoughts that he might legitimate [him] . . . by subsequent matrimony."[118] While some unwed fathers prevaricated ineffectually, others collected testimony and purchased legitimations.

Even a successful petition might fail to assuage the guilt of some fathers. Cuban Don Nicolás de Castro Palomino's affair with Doña Josepha de Arias had produced an illegitimate daughter named Manuela, baptized as of "unknown parentage" in 1748.[119] The couple later returned to recognize her as their *hija natural,* and Don Nicolás purchased her legitimation in 1776. But when Don Nicolás asked his priest for a revised copy of his now twenty-eight-year-old daughter's baptismal certificate, the cleric provided him with an authentic copy that showed that his daughter's baptismal status had changed, from being listed as of "unknown parentage," to recognition by her unwed parents, to legitimation by the king.

Don Nicolás refused to accept this document, "because it makes very clear the defect of her origin." He re-petitioned the Cámara in 1784 and asked it to erase all evidence of the irregularities surrounding his daughter's birth. He begged officials

> to take out . . . the pages that contain the baptismal and marriage certificates of the aforementioned Manuela Josepha, my daughter, and in their place to substitute others . . . without such references but [which] [state] only that she is my legitimated daughter.

Don Nicolás did not want only to confirm the public status of his daughter; he wanted to wipe the slate entirely clean.

As might be expected, bureaucrats were horrified at any hint that an official record might be altered. They spoke of Don Nicolás's "strange request," which was "not of the best decency" given the "very clear defect in the origin of his daughter." One official concluded: "The petition is repugnant in every respect . . . for it directs that a falsehood be placed in public records that hides the truth . . . and makes them unworthy of trust." The Cámara agreed that it must "entirely deny the petition" but feared that such a determined father might not listen to its remonstrances. The Cámara ordered the bishop of Cuba and the parish priest to guard the documents: "neither to remove the book that contains the baptismal certificate of the daughter of this subject nor to separate out the pages that he requested." The Cámara made it clear that although *gracias al sacar* might legitimate offspring, it could never obliterate the past. As fathers became older, they had to confront the hard truth that the consequences of their youthful actions could never be entirely expunged.

While a father like Don Nicolás might not be able to erase all evidence of his daughter's irregular birth, he could at least legitimate her. Others had to face the even harsher reality that the situation could never be remedied. Havana priest Joseph Miguel Vianes faced an uphill battle when he petitioned twice in 1799, and yet again in 1804, for the legitimation of his son.[120] The priest was so desperate that he gave royal officials a virtual *carte blanche*, offering to pay "whatever [is] necessary without limit" for a favorable solution. However his priestly state, the fact that his son was a *pardo*, and the growing reluctance of colonial officials to legitimate sacrilegious offspring meant that his son remained a bastard.

In yet another instance, a father who anticipated that he would receive an unfavorable decision doctored the evidence in advance. Even though Captain Don Juan Díaz had arranged a private pregnancy and taken sole responsibility for the young Joseph Ramón, he must have known that the Cámara would reject a truthful application, for the mother of his son was a *mulata*.[121] Therefore the captain bribed witnesses to swear that his lover was a "white women." Not content with false testimony, this father went so far as to alter the baptismal records in Santiago, Cuba, so that there were two entries. An original listed Joseph Ramón under the category of the dark-skinned (*pardo*); a false addition placed him under the category of "white."

The Cámara became suspicious and secretly ordered the governor and bishop of Havana to investigate the captain's petition. The word came back that the officer's lover had been a "single *mulata* named Hilaria Cuevas, daughter of Micaela Fromesta who sold milk since she has been freed." Royal officials would not tolerate such falsification of records and began legal proceedings against the captain and his perjured witnesses. And so Captain Don Juan became a victim of his conscience and his honor. If he had married *mulata* Hilaria he would have automatically legitimated his son but crossed racial boundaries and damaged his own reputation. Yet his rejection of matrimony meant that his son could not follow his father's military career. For his son, the captain was willing to risk all, and in this case he lost all, perhaps even his honor.

There is no question that, of the trinity of persons most affected by illegitimacy (mother, father, child), the fathers suffered the least. Analysis of the ultimate state of *cédula* parents demonstrates that men could go on with their lives in ways that women could not (see Table 6). Roughly equal numbers of *cédula* parents remained unwed, which accords well with the general trends noted by demographers that colonial populations contained substantial numbers of lifelong spinsters and bachelors. The remaining *cédula* fathers, however, proved three times more likely to marry than their female counterparts.

Yet even though colonial men might choose between the single and marital state, and might reject and abandon their lovers, they did not totally es-

TABLE 6
Last Known Marital State of Mothers and Fathers

	Women		Men	
	N	%	N	%
Remained single	56	30.0	46	24.6
Nun	3	1.6	—	—
Priest	—	—	16	8.6
Married lover	14	7.5	14	7.5
Married another	9	4.8	30	16.0
Widow, widower	9	4.8	6	3.2
Unknown	96	51.3	75	40.1
Totals	187	100.0	187	100.0

SOURCE: DB 4-187.

cape responsibility from their sexual encounters. Men who promised matrimony faced long-term legal and social pressures to fulfill their word, so that flight and exile were often their only escape. Both law and custom bound men to the responsibilities of *crianza*, and failure in this duty was a failure of manhood. Whether in private pregnancies, as long-term fiancés, as bachelors, or as widowers, fathers not only provided for but also loved, cared for, and took responsibility for their children. As men grew older and their children became adults, fathers faced the bitter moment when they understood that their actions had deprived a new generation of honor. Although colonial fathers did not pay the price demanded of mothers, nor of illegitimate offspring, their conscience and guilt could exact a heavy toll.

FIVE

Babies and Illegitimacy: The Politics of Recognition from the Font to the Grave

Born in 1744, Habanera Doña Rita Josepha Gonzáles had passed a conventional life before she became a victim of the politics of recognition.[1] She had lived "since infancy" with Don Tomás Gonzáles and Doña Francisca Alvarez, who treated her as "their legitimate daughter." When suitor Don Tomás Avella appeared on the scene, Doña Rita remembered that her parents blessed the match and that "they made on that occasion the most obvious demonstrations that [I] was their daughter." It was only decades later that Doña Rita learned that her father did not recognize her as his own. His will

> did not declare my legitimacy but only that of Don Antonio, his son, forgetting me entirely. I was surprised and full of consternation without knowing who my parents were, and my doubt became greater after I learned that my baptismal certificate said that they were "unknown."

Doña Rita never forgot her anguish, for in "a single instant" she "lost the belief that she was legitimate that she had [had] up until then without any contrary suspicion, and the defect of her birth was made public." Her four sons confirmed their mother's dismay at the recollection, and remembered that it "caused her great pain, and bitterness, and tears."

Although it was traumatic, Doña Rita's abrupt change in status was not that uncommon, being the result of conventionalized patterns of social maneuvering that might extend from the baptismal font to the grave. Fathers and mothers were among the first participants in such politics of recognition, for they deliberately chose what status their illegitimate newborns might enjoy or might suffer in their private and public worlds.

Doña Rita had initially gained status from her parents' maneuvering; the concealment of her illegitimacy had made it possible for her to contract a socially advantageous marriage. Even years later, when she was a widowed mother of eight, she confirmed the efficacy of her parents' strategy, for she testified that her husband would "not have married her" if he had known of her birth. He was from "a distinguished family active in Havana commerce" and her illegitimacy "would have been much noted and badly seen by the entire commercial community." Doña Rita successfully petitioned to remove this "great impediment" that "all the families that are pure and are of some distinction look on . . . with horror and aversion."

The status changes that marked not only Doña Rita's life but also the lives of countless others could occur because Spanish Americans did not have a single definition of illegitimacy, nor did they necessarily recognize it as an unchangeable condition. Although colonists never conceptualized this explicitly, they acted as if an individual's birth status were composed of at least four elements. The first was the newborn's natal status, which depended upon civil and ecclesiastical conventions concerning whether the parents were related and whether they were unwed, married, or a priest or nun at the time of their child's conception or birth. A next determinant was the official baptismal status, which derived both from canon law and from popular traditions as to how babies should be registered on baptismal certificates. Third was the infant's social status, which depended on whether recognition by parents and kin was private or public. Last was civil status, the state's legal acknowledgment of the legitimacy (or lack of legitimacy) of a colonist's child. In the case of legitimate births, a baby's natal, baptismal, social, and civil status were congruent: The parents recognized, baptized, and raised the newborn as their own, and the state acknowledged their legal relationship. Yet Doña Rita was not the only illegitimate who lived for decades with a natal status that was distinct from her baptismal as well as her social status.

Such flexibility meant that birth status could not infallibly mark social place: It was not necessarily an ascriptive condition, but rather a layered and changeable construct.

NATAL STATUS

Eighteenth-century Spanish Americans employed a precise vocabulary when they differentiated between the layers that composed the birth status. The first determinant, natal status, varied according to the parental "state," or the couple's potential to marry. The least onerous illegitimate category was the *hijo natural,* or the child conceived or born to unwed parents; their subsequent marriage could completely erase the stigma of out-of-wedlock birth.[2] Other illegitimates were classified as "bastards," or as *spurii,* as they were born "against natural reason" given that either blood ties or previous vows created impediments to parental marriage.[3] Included among these were *incestuosos, adulterinos,* and *sacrílegos. Incestuosos* were the offspring of parents who could not marry without prior ecclesiastical permission because they were related within prohibited degrees of kinship. In *cédula* cases such relationships were usually between first or second cousins.[4] More opprobrium attached to *adulterinos,* the product of adulterous affairs between a married parent and a lover. *Sacrílegos,* the offspring of religious who had taken vows of chastity, were marked with the greatest stigma.[5]

Even though these unambiguous definitions clearly located newborns within a continuum of illegitimacy, such initial determinations of natal status were subject to change. By far the most usual transformation occurred when unwed parents married and automatically legitimated their *hijos naturales.* Since marriage effectively resolved the situation, these most common of cases never figured among the *gracias al sacar.* Yet at least one undecided petition reveals how such a process might unfold, as parents belatedly resorted to the post hoc marriage option.

Don Gaspar de Urquízu Ibáñez, *oidor* of the *audiencia* of Lima, has already made an appearance, for this royal official had experienced a classic crisis of conscience and honor.[6] Don Gaspar had not only promised to marry his lover, Doña Jacoba Sanchez de Alba, but he had also applied for the necessary royal permission in 1742.[7] The ceremony never took place, however, for some twenty-six years later he petitioned that the Cámara legitimate his natural son, Don Santiago, who was an official in the Casa de Moneda. Don Gaspar expressed his "grief" concerning his son's lack of honor, for he now saw how it "tarnished and discouraged him."[8] Although the *oidor* conceded that his son's mother was still alive, he declared that a post hoc marriage was "precluded," given "her old age and her long-standing condition as a paralytic." At that point imperial officials requested further information from the *oidor*, which never arrived, and so the case remained unresolved.[9]

Lima notarial records show that marriage provided the ultimate solution for the *oidor*, who had fathered more than one illegitimate son by Doña Jacoba. Four years after Don Gaspar's incomplete 1778 petition, the couple had not yet married; in May 1782 Doña Jacoba wrote a will that admitted that "Don Domingo, Don Juan and . . . Don Santiago de Urquízu" were her "natural sons."[10] The marriage must have taken place sometime within the next eight months, for the *oidor*'s last testament, written five days before his death on March 4, 1783, ended what may have been years of separation from Doña Jacoba and what was certainly years of illegitimacy for his sons.[11]

It is notable that Don Gaspar's final will gave no hint that a deathbed or near-deathbed marriage had erased decades of illegitimacy. Instead, his testament simply declared in the most conventional fashion that he had "been married to Doña Ana Jacoba Sánchez de Alba" and that the couple had for "their legitimate children" a Don Juan, a Don Gaspar Domingo, and a Don Santiago Urquízu. His father designated the last, an officer in the Casa de Moneda, as the executor of the will. Two years later, when Don Santiago planned "an absence of some months from this city," he wrote a will that also ignored his previous status as an illegitimate, for it named his parents and declared himself to be their "legitimate son."[12] Only twenty-six years later did Don Santiago clarify in yet another testament that he had been a "son legitimated by subsequent matrimony."[13]

How often colonists of all castes and classes transformed premarital sexual liaisons with natural offspring into legitimate marriages with legitimate children, decades after the fact, will never be known. What is evident is that the birth status of *hijos naturales* was subject to change depending upon parental action, and that the classification of illegitimates might vary from document to document over time.

Even more fundamental than any actual number of *hijos naturales* transformed into legitimates was the social recognition that such transitions might occur. The very concept of illegitimacy necessarily had to remain fluid when colonial Spanish Americans constantly mingled with relatives, neighbors, and acquaintances who had the potential to be transformed instantly into fully legitimate offspring anytime during their lives.

In contrast to *hijos naturales*, bastards could not automatically have the "stain" attached to their birth removed through subsequent parental matrimony. Even so, there seems to have been a popular if erroneous belief that later marriage might erase the stigma of incestuous birth when cousins promised matrimony, became the parents of children technically the result of an incestuous relationship, obtained church dispensation of prohibited kinship ties, and then married. Many people believed that the sacrament automatically legitimated the existing offspring, even though this was not the legal reality.[14] In 1803 royal officials finally clarified the issue, approving subsequent marriage as sufficient to legitimate in these situations.[15]

Civil codes granted no such leniency to the offspring of adulterous or sacrilegious unions; the negative consequences attached to bastardy could be officially mitigated only through *gracias al sacar*. Even if the parents of children conceived in an adulterous relationship eventually married, their offspring remained illegitimate. Priests and nuns presumably lacked even this palliative. Yet natal status proved to be but one layer in an illegitimate's birth status, for the politics of recognition might still intervene to lessen or even obscure the stigma attached to bastardy.

BAPTISMAL STATUS

The second layer of a newborn's birth status was fixed by the baptismal certificate, arguably the premier document in life, for it both admitted the infant to the spiritual community and established familial, racial, and social connections as well.[16] The Council of Trent had charged parish priests to keep "vital event" daily registers that would chronicle marriages and deaths as well as the continual arrival of newborns to be baptized and entered into the spiritual community.[17] Church regulations stipulated that infants should normally be baptized when they were three days old. Historians have discovered that this policy was followed fairly closely, at least in Mexico, where babies were usually baptized by their fifth day.[18]

Baptismal registers detailed two critical variables—race and birth—that located the newborn in local society. Clerics subdivided these annual registers into *partidas,* or sections, that corresponded to the racial categories of the local population, and then specified in each entry whether the birth was legitimate. Clerics always provided a book for "whites" that included the local peninsular and Creole elite, while *pardos,* mestizos, blacks, and Indians might have individual or combined sections as well.[19] In most cases the parents' racial category was clearly known and accepted by all concerned, and the race of their infant was equally uncontroversial.

The Spanish-American vision of race as a continuum rather than a stark dichotomy led to the existence of in-between cases as well. Parents who were racially mixed might use their prosperity to achieve a higher racial designation for their children. Sexual relationships between the white and the almost-white might produce infants whose racial mixture was less than one part in eight, and who then might be officially classified as white. Popular custom, individual personalities, and local politics could be as important as any actual racial mixture in establishing a child's race on a baptismal certificate.[20] Since parents who applied for the *gracias al sacar* were almost uniformly from the elite, most illegitimates in this study appeared in the section reserved for "whites"[21] (see Appendix 2, Table 10).

Colonial social politics permitted not only blurred descriptions of a newborn's racial status but of the natal status as well. In instances of illegitimacy, vague listings tended to be the rule rather than the exception. Only in the case of *hijos naturales* might baptismal certificates literally describe the "real" natal status of illegitimates. An exploration of those instances in which natal and baptismal status were congruent provides a contrast with the more customary practice, in which obfuscation was often the rule.

Even though the baptismal certificate served as an official written record, it accurately recorded an illegitimate's natal status only for some *hijos naturales.* The tacit assumption seems to have been that the dishonor that invariably accompanied illegitimacy might still be mitigated by the newborn's potential for full and automatic legitimation if the parents eventually married. In a colonial world where so many were illegitimate, the natural children of white, unmarried parents benefited when their racial and ancestral origins were unambiguously listed. María Emma Mannarelli's comment regarding seventeenth-century Lima holds true for late colonial Spanish America as well: "To be recognized as the *hijo natural* of a Spaniard was to differentiate oneself from the castas of the city who suffered the strongest discrimination."[22] Yet only fifty-five *gracias al sacar* petitioners appear as *hijos naturales*

- TABLE 7

Comparison Between Baptismal and Natal Status

Baptismal Categories	How Listed Baptismal Certificate	Actual Natal Status Determined by Witness Testimony					
		Hijo Natural	*Adulterino*	*Sacrílego*	*Incestuoso*	Unknown	Total
Hijo natural	55	52	1	0	2	0	55
Padres no conocidos	33	13	10	2	1	7	33
Exposito	31	11	2	4	0	14	31
Legitimo	2	0	0	0	0	2	2
Niño	4	3	0	0	0	1	4
No certificate	91	41	21	6	3	20	91
Total	216	120	34	12	6	44	216

SOURCE: DB 2-216.

on their baptismal certificates, even though more than double that number qualified for that classification (see Table 7).

This difference occurred because the listing of an infant as an *hijo natural* could exact a high and sometimes prohibitive social cost. Before a cleric would identify a baby as *natural,* at least one parent had to appear at the baptismal font, agree to be identified on the certificate, and swear that both parents were unmarried and not related by prohibited degrees of kinship.[23] In effect, the church demanded that at least one of the lovers confess openly to having engaged in a sexual affair.

In private pregnancies the infant might be listed as an *hijo natural* only if the father arrived at the baptismal font and swore to the unmarried status of both parents, although still protecting the identity of the mother. Men suffered no dishonor when they made such appearances. If anything, their presence marked them as responsible adults who accepted their paternal responsibilities. Don Bruno Heceta figured among such fathers, for he not only guarded the identity of his eighteen-year-old lover but also swore at his son's christening in 1788 that the child was an *hijo natural.*[24] In 1753 Don Manuel Domec arrived at a Buenos Aires church to declare that the baby boy about to be baptized was his "natural son," although he guarded the identity of the mother, who was a "lady" and "Spanish."[25]

For couples who lived together in extended engagements or consensual unions, such an official admission of their sexual relationship may not have been onerous, for knowledge of their affair was often public.[26] Parental ac-

TABLE 8
Listing of Illegitimates on Baptismal Certificates

Category	Male		Female		Total	
	N	%	N	%	N	%
Hijo natural	39	70.9	16	29.1	55	25.5
Expósito	18	58.1	13	41.9	31	14.4
Padres no conocidos	21	63.6	12	36.4	33	15.3
Other*	5	83.3	1	18.7	6	2.7
No certificate	60	66.0	31	34.0	91	42.1
Total	143	66.2	73	33.8	216	100.0

SOURCE: DB 2-216.
*Includes *niño(a)* and *legítimo(a)* listings.

knowledgment of natural children may have been but another stage in a longer process that eventually led to matrimony. One Chilean father seemed to admit to such a progression when he ordered the priest at his son's baptism to "put in the parish records the names of the parents," adding that he "had plans to legitimate him."[27] Witnesses confirmed a similar instance in Cuba.[28]

In the *gracias al sacar* cases for which baptismal certificates exist, fairly equal numbers of unwed mothers or fathers appeared alone to identify their infant as an *hijo natural*.[29] The remaining acknowledgments proceeded from couples who lived together in extended engagements or consensual unions and jointly recognized their infants. Parents proved slightly more likely to identify themselves for the sake of their baby sons than for their daughters (see Table 8).[30]

If both parents refused to identify themselves, their infant could not be listed as an *hijo natural* but received instead the less desirable baptismal designation of *expósito*, (abandoned, foundling) or *padres no conocidos* (unknown parentage). Witnesses in legitimation petitions provide particularly valuable information concerning the popular usage of these designations, which have sometimes been misunderstood by historians both regarding their definitions and their social consequences.[31]

The baptismal listings of *expósito* and *padres no conocidos* were functionally interchangeable to the degree that they were equally opaque as to parental origin. Infants officially became *expósitos* when they were deposited at institutions such as orphanages or *casas de expósitos*. Yet it is important to underline that babies did not have to be abandoned at public institutions to receive this baptismal designation. Instead, they might be privately "exposed" on a mother's, father's, or relative's doorstep for but the instant required before their presumed "detection" and "adoption," followed by eventual baptism.[32] Legitimation petitions confirm that even though thirty-one babies were baptized as *expósitos* and thirty-three as *padres no conocidos*, only four of these had ever been left at an institution. Rather, the large majority had been immediately taken in by parents or relatives or had been adopted (see Table 7). Nor were these baptismal designations used in a consistent manner. Of the four infants deposited at the Havana *casa de expósitos*, three were baptized as *expósitos* and one was listed as of "unknown parentage."

Evidence from local studies parallels the trends disclosed in *gracias al sacar* documents. José Luis Aranda Romera and Agustín Grajales Porras discovered a similar avoidance of orphanages in eighteenth-century Puebla, Mexico, where only 4 percent of those baptized as *expósitos* actually entered an institution.[33] Donald Ramos found that *expósitos* in Ouro Preto, Brazil (1754–1838), were not really abandoned but were often cared for by a parent or a friend.[34] Pablo Rodríguez Jiménez provides telling examples of similar infant adoptions from New Granada.[35] Although María Emma Mannarelli does not trace the direct disposition of *expósitos* christened in San Marcelo in seventeenth-century Lima, she notes that 98.2 percent of such infants were listed as "white."[36] The implication is that elite families were more likely to hide sexual misconduct and protect family honor with the *expósito* or unknown parentage designation, although they did not necessarily abandon their illegitimate infant relatives.[37]

Although the baptismal designations of *expósito* and "unknown parentage" proved functionally interchangeable, clerical or parental preference for one or the other category varied by region. Baptismal certificates from the *audiencias* of Charcas and Santa Fé in South America, as well as those from Mexico, were more likely to list illegitimates as *expósitos*, while those from the Caribbean (Santo Domingo, Cuba) and Guatemala more commonly favored the "unknown parentage" designation.[38] Other regions evidenced no such clear preferences. As the century drew to a close, there was a growing trend toward listing infants as *expósitos*, perhaps because of the mistaken impression that the 1794 legislation favoring *expósitos* did not also extend to those of "unknown parentage."[39]

The baptismal listing of Doña Gertrudis de Herrera provides a classic example of the resulting potential for disparity between an infant's natal and baptismal status, for even though this Havana woman was an *hija natural*, this more favorable listing did not appear on her 1775 certificate.[40] Instead, since her parents refused to be identified, the presiding cleric gave her the vague designation of "unknown parentage." He did so, Doña Gertrudis later recalled, "to protect the honor of both, . . . even though they were unwed and able to marry." Another Cuban illegitimate confirmed this protectiveness when she testified:

> It is a common manner to put in the baptismal certificates of *hijos naturales* that they are of unknown parentage (*padres no conocidos*), as is mine, because of the caution that is always taken to guard the parents and not to make their frailty known immediately and without necessity.[41]

Sometimes unmarried parents denied their newborns because they feared that priests might try to end their sexual relationship. One petitioner explained that Mexican *hijos naturales* were often baptized as foundlings "because in those early times there was bashfulness in confessing their error, or because they feared that with this notice the priest might take measures to separate them from that life."[42] Overall, *cédula* statistics indicate that unmarried parents were somewhat more likely to recognize *hijos naturales* at the beginning than at the end of the century (see Appendix 2, Table 11).[43]

While parental refusal to admit their sexual relationships and to be named on baptismal certificates may have protected the parents, the cost for the *hijos naturales* was extremely high. The baptismal certificate served as the principal record of family lineage. If such a document did not name parents, it cut the newborn off from any written connection with immediate or extended family members, or with any link with that historical chain of shared honor and blood that was the collective family birthright. A first and decisive moment in family politics occurred literally at the baptismal font as unwed parents either acknowledged or refused to surrender their identities, thus either promoting or denigrating the baptismal status of their newborns. Illegitimacy precipitated generational conflict between parents and children, for the honor and anonymity of the parents became balanced against recognition of those ties of blood that linked them to their offspring.

The absence of parents' names on a baptismal certificate posed painful as well as practical problems for illegitimates. In the colonial era, the baptismal certificate functioned as the closest equivalent to the social security number or the driver's license of today. Although colonial Spanish Americans might not use their baptismal certificates quite as often, they customarily produced certified copies of this document or referred to the information in it when they applied for admission to or graduation from school; when they sought military or civil office; when they were married or ordained; and even in their last will and testament, just before death. *Hijos naturales* whose parents had denied the family connection were regularly reminded of this omission at the most significant occasions in their lives.

Parental failure to recognize an infant as an *hijo natural* led to a substantive lowering of the newborn's status. The alternative baptismal designations of *expósito* or "unknown parentage" were also used to hide the natal status of those born as a result of incest or of adulterous or sacrilegious liaisons. Since the racially mixed used these opaque listings as well, even the race of some white infants might be challenged. To those born out of wedlock, it was infinitely preferable to be identified as the *hijo natural* of an elite family rather than being classified under an ambiguous designation.

Such accuracy was contrary to the best interests of every other category of illegitimate. Children born to unmarried first cousins, or to parents who were married to others, or to priests, found that the categories of "unknown parentage" or "foundling" embodied a vagueness that disguised less acceptable social realities. Don Melchor Varea y Lazcano was but one who benefited from such a listing, for his father, Don Domingo Herboso y Figueroa, was a priest and dean of the cathedral in La Plata, Bolivia.[44] His baptismal certificate described him as an *expósito* who had been "left at the doorstep of Gertrudis Blanco." Knowledgeable locals might have known that this Gertrudis was his mother, and that the newborn had not been abandoned. Yet in such instances it was preferable to be officially parentless than to be marked as the illegitimate child of a local cleric.

An illegitimate's baptismal status was not necessarily a permanent designation. Just as the natal status of *hijos naturales* might be altered to that of legitimate offspring when parents married, so the baptismal status of other newborns could be changed by later parental action. Historians and demographers who investigate baptismal records have often commented on instances in which mothers or fathers returned to admit parentage.[45] Legitimation depositions provide further details concerning the process by which babies originally baptized as *expósitos* or as of "unknown parentage" might later be transformed into *hijos naturales*.

Nineteen (8.8 percent) of the 216 *gracias al sacar* petitioners had had their baptismal status changed.[46] The most common revision occurred when parents returned and formally acknowledged their natural children. Thus a father's admission transformed the baptismal certificate of Don José Cayetano de la Vega of La Paz, Bolivia; the original August 1761 document had listed him as an *expósito*.[47] Just three days after the baptism, Don Dámaso de la Vega, a priest, came forward and admitted that he had fathered the infant "with Doña Buenaventura Teran when he was free, unwed, and in the secular state," and he declared Don José "his *hijo natural* in order to unburden his conscience." Since Don Dámaso had subsequently entered the priesthood, he could not marry and automatically legitimate his natural son. Yet his admission aided Don José years later, for in 1796 he simply had to produce his annotated baptismal certificate to prove parentage in his successful petition for legitimation.

The baptismal status of Doña Gertrudis Herrera of Havana underwent similar alteration, for even though she was originally christened as of "unknown parentage," her father, a naval captain, returned when she was four to acknowledge her as his *hija natural*.[48] Years later he petitioned for her legitimation. Doña Gertrudis's situation typifies the changing and layered nature of birth status: She started with the natal status of an *hija natural*, although with an official baptismal status of "unknown parentage"; later her natal and baptismal status as a *natural* became congruent upon her father's recognition; yet all of these were eventually overlaid by her civil legitimation.

The writing of the last testament marked another occasion when parents might acknowledge *hijos naturales* whom they had previously failed to recognize. Such a transformation altered the status of sisters Doña María and Doña Caridad of Santiago, Cuba, who had been baptized, respectively, as of "unknown parents" (1771) and as an *"expósito"* (1777).[49] Both sisters had been "abandoned the same day" they were born and left at the home of *Regidor* Don Joseph Antonio Echavarría, who not coincidentally was their real father. Although the *regidor* was a bachelor, he took the babies into his own home and raised them with the help of his sisters. Meanwhile he continued a clandestine affair with their mother, the widow Doña Rosalía Ramos. When he died in 1793 he left a closed will that named them his heirs and finally recognized them as his *"hijas naturales."* Three years later the sisters purchased their legitimations. Don Joseph Valiente of Havana was yet another who took advantage of his father's recognition in his will to change his baptismal designation of "unknown parentage" to that of "natural son."[50]

Illegitimates usually benefited when parents who had denied them official recognition on a baptismal certificate eventually acknowledged their blood ties. Even if they were not honored members of their families, they were sheltered under the family name and could call upon the patronage of their often influential kin. However, in one revealing instance an illegitimate formally rejected parental recognition and insisted that her birth status derive from her baptismal listing as an *expósito*. The extreme case of Doña Francisca Sale illuminates the degree to which colonists might consciously distinguish between their natal and baptismal status, manipulating them to produce optimum social mobility.[51]

The long-term chain of events that would cause Doña Francisca's rejection of her (presumed) mother began around seven o'clock on the evening of January 28, 1735, when someone placed a baby girl in the revolving door of the *casa de expósitos* in Havana.[52] The next day the local priest baptized the baby with the name of Francisca Sale Valdés and farmed her out to a single woman named María de Flores, who raised her until she was twelve.[53] Doña Francisca then contracted an early and advantageous marriage with Don Andrés de Lezama, a royal notary, and two years later she gave birth to her first son, a boy perhaps appropriately named José Perfecto.

There is no question that Doña Francisca had experienced extraordinary if not perfect fortune. Her initial chances for survival had been poor. During the first two decades of operation of the Havana *casa de expósitos*, between 1711 and 1731, four out of every five infants placed there had perished, and even in the mid-1730s, when baby Francisca was left in the revolving door, one out of every two infants met that tragic fate. Yet Doña Francisca had flourished and had married well.

Subsequent events suggest that there might have been more than just luck protecting her during those vulnerable early years, for the will of María, Doña Francisca's foster mother, contained a confession. As Don José Perfecto later noted, it "seemed to be confused, for either because of love or other motives it declared that Doña Francisca Sale . . . was her daughter."[54] This will jeopardized both the status of Doña Francisca and, even more so, that of her son.

As a foundling of the *casa*, Doña Francisca had benefited from the officially prescribed aura of doubt about her natal and racial origins.[55] Yet the consistent omission of the honorific "Doña" before the name of María, her foster mother, strongly suggests lower-class and racially mixed origins. Whatever the "defect," this "mother's" deathbed recognition of Doña Francisca was a particular blow to the honor of her potential grandchildren, including the now-adult Don José Perfecto, an official in the Havana tobacco administration. He initiated a petition in 1789 that begged that the Cámara formally rule that his mother should not be considered the daughter of María. His plea is notable in that he asked that his mother's position not necessarily derive from the "truth" of the matter—that is, whether Doña Francisca was the daughter of María. Rather, he argued that whatever the natal status of his mother, her status should derive from her baptismal certificate listing of *expósito*. He argued that "even supposing that María Flores really was the mother of Doña Francisca Sale, in the very act of having abandoned and exposed her at Saint Joseph's Foundling Home, she lost all the right that she might have had to reclaim her as a daughter in the future."[56]

In effect, Don José Perfecto asked the Cámara to distinguish between his mother's natal and baptismal status, and to rule that the latter established her and her children's position in Havana society. He pleaded that María's "declaration [not] serve as an obstacle . . . [to his] career, and that there should exist no doubt concerning his legitimacy or *limpieza*." Since Don José's legitimacy was above question—after all, his parents had been married two years at the time of his birth—it is probable that María's racial defect was the real threat to his honor.

Whatever María's defect, Don José's petition was a pre-emptive strike. The ambiguous status of his mother combined with his own marginal membership in the Havana elite to make him especially vulnerable. He feared that once María's will became public a competitor might try to deprive him of honor, of promotion, or even of his office. He therefore asked the Cámara to prohibit any future "inquiry whatever concerning the affair." Although royal officials refused to issue such a direct ruling, they did agree that Don José and his mother should derive their status from her baptismal listing as an *expósito*, María's recognition notwithstanding. The resolution of Don José's plea illustrates the popular understanding shared by both Spanish imperial bureaucrats and colonial elites that birth status might be layered, that natal and baptismal categories could be distinct and differentiated.

SOCIAL STATUS: PUBLIC AND
PRIVATE RECOGNITION

A newborn's natal status reflected civil and canonically determined degrees of illegitimacy, while the infant's baptismal status rested upon actual birth circumstance as well as popular custom and the extent of parental recognition. The next layer in an infant's birth status was social status, or the extent to which parents and kin acknowledged their relationship to the newborn within the immediate and extended family and within the larger community. Such recognitions might be either private or public.

Such bifurcated recognitions were another example of the colonial mentality, which consciously distinguished between a private sphere, populated by family, kin, and intimate friends, and the public world of social peers and honor. Elites usually manipulated such divisions when private conduct threatened public reputation. Private pregnancies have already provided examples of how an inner circle might contain knowledge of a woman's sexual activity to protect her public reputation and honor.

A similar manipulation of the private-public dichotomy occurred when families made choices about whether they would recognize illegitimate relations. In public acknowledgments, parents, relatives, and family friends not only welcomed the illegitimate within their private circle but also openly admitted the relationship to the world. In contrast, private recognition occurred when a restricted group of parents, extended family, and intimate acquaintances might secretly and informally recognize an illegitimate as a member of the family but refuse to admit the connection in public. It is no accident that, when illegitimates described their social status, they explicitly used code words such as "private" and "secret" or "public" and "notorious" to designate the extent of recognition by their kin.[57]

Parental recognition could be either official or informal. The first was written, and occurred when parents immediately or eventually placed their names on the infant's baptismal certificate, or acknowledged kinship before a public notary or through a final testament.[58] Yet the absence of such acknowledgment did not mean that parents rejected or even abandoned illegitimate offspring. Rather, infants might receive informal recognition by their kin and still have this relationship acknowledged by the world at large. The comments of María Emma Mannarelli concerning seventeenth-century Lima hold true for eighteenth-century Spanish America as well: "The absence of formal recognition does not lead us to think . . . of a massive lack of concern of parents, as the numbers seem to indicate."[59]

The situation of Doña María Josepha de Acosta Riaza provides a classic example of one Havana woman who enjoyed public yet unofficial status as an illegitimate daughter.[60] Because her father, *Regidor* Don Félix de Acosta Riaza, was married to another, Doña María had entered the world as an *adulterina*. Following custom, her 1753 baptismal certificate listed her as of "unknown parentage." Natal and baptismal status notwithstanding, from infancy Doña María's social status was unambiguous. Everyone knew that she was the *regidor's* illegitimate daughter, and her birth was, as one family friend later recalled, a "notorious public fact in this city." Doña María herself emphasized that she was fully—that is, both privately and publicly—accepted into her father's family:

> My father throughout his life not only recognized me always in private as his daughter, but also in public. He carried me to his own home after my infancy and maintained me there until he had established me in a state that was equal with that of the children of his marriage.

Dr. Don Francisco, one of Doña María's half brothers, also emphasized the duality of her recognition, testifying that the family treated her as a sister "in domestic and public acts." Doña María's informal recognition by her family enhanced her social status to the extent that she was able to marry Don Antonio de la Paz, a royal treasurer in Havana.

Even after her father's death, Doña María remained a welcome member of the family. Her half brother, Don Joaquín, confirmed that Doña María "has by himself, his sister and brothers, and all our blood relations been treated, admitted, and reputed as a true sister and relation not only during the life of our father but also after his death [and] continuing until the present." It is suggestive that Don Joaquín emphasized that the family accepted Doña María within its private circle even after the death of their father. Presumably, it might have been only upon the *regidor's* insistence that his children received and acknowledged their half sister. Through these comments, however, Don Joaquín chose deliberately to emphasize that the family continued to recognize Doña María as a sister. Doña María's case was not unique, inasmuch as illegitimates and relatives typically cited evidence of continuing recognition as proof of family acceptance and solidarity.

Yet even though Doña María grew up with her half brothers and sisters, took the family name, and all of Havana knew her story, she apparently had no written, legal connection with her family until her legitimation petition. Even on his deathbed her father failed to acknowledge that she was his daughter, for his will named his legitimate children as heirs and never mentioned Doña María. It is possible that the *regidor* indirectly provided for her welfare, however, for his will contained an enigmatic clause giving one-fifth of his estate—the amount he could legally designate freely—to a family friend. He asked that friend "to do with it what I have communicated in order to unburden my conscience." Yet at the time of her father's death, Doña María's birth status was a layered composite of her natal status as an *adulterina*, her official baptismal designation as of "unknown parentage," and her unofficial public acceptance as the illegitimate daughter of the *regidor*.

Doña María's life illustrates how such informal public recognition might be transformed into written and official family acknowledgment. Her case was comparatively simple, as she had lived in her father's home and her half brothers and sisters had testified to their common ancestry in documents she submitted for her legitimation. Their willingness to support her legitimation combined with the high standing of her husband to win her a reluctant agreement from Spanish bureaucrats. Doña María's situation reveals a colonial world in which written, official proscriptions could be overwhelmed by popular, informal custom. Neither baptismal certificates nor wills could serve as sole guides to an illegitimate's role within the family or status within the community. Equally important were local and spontaneous modes of recognition that governed interpersonal discourse.[61]

Colonists had to be sensitive to such social cues, for the misreading of an illegitimate's family status might lead to embarrassment, or worse, deadly insult. On the level only of her baptismal status, rather than that of her informal social status, Doña María might have been in jeopardy of being snubbed. But her public status called for more respectful attention. She was an accepted member of an elite Havana family whose position was guaranteed by her kin. To treat her with less than the required respect would have been to insult the family that had openly chosen to admit her as one of their own. The multiple layers attached to birth status meant that colonists had to know at what level to respond to illegitimates whose natal, baptismal, private, and public social status could be ambiguous, changing, or even contradictory.

Legitimation petitions provide tantalizing hints about the ways in which eighteenth-century Spanish Americans signaled each other concerning appropriate modes of behavior. Some of the most revealing comments come from outsiders. They watched and listened, knowing that the illegitimate's private circle would provide traditional cues to the degree to which the family acknowledged the illegitimate within the private and public spheres.

At times there was not much need for enlightenment. After all, when an unmarried father and mother carried on an open and long-term affair, outsiders would have a very good idea of the natal status of any resulting children. Yet even in such instances elite peers awaited the appropriate cues. Such a process unfolded in Mexico, where Don Joseph de los Ríos lived openly with Doña Gertrudis Rubio in the mining area of Zimapán.[62] The couple's sexual relationship was public knowledge; one witness recalled that he was "certain" . . . that Captain Don Joseph de los Ríos "was living within the same house and supporting in his company . . . Doña Gertrudis Rubio, the mother of the . . . child, who was unwed, as was the . . . Captain." Yet even though everyone seemed to know that Don Joseph and Doña Gertrudis were having an affair, the couple did not provide any official signal to outsiders that they recognized their illegitimate son. Although the natal status of the infant Joseph Francisco was that of *hijo natural*, his parents protected their own identities and demoted him to the category of "unknown parentage" on his 1744 baptismal certificate.

How then did the miners of Zimapán know that Don Joseph and Doña Gertrudis informally yet publicly accepted him as their son? One cue was that they openly took their baby into their house, rather than arranging for the child to be cared for by someone else. Another significant sign was that Don Joseph and Doña Gertrudis conspicuously spoke to Joseph Francisco as their son, and they permitted him to address them as "mother" and "father." Although the couple eventually ended their affair, and Doña Gertrudis married someone else, Don Joseph offered another indication of paternity when he continued to support his son financially. One witness remembered that Don Joseph had placed his son "in the city of Mexico for his education, teaching, and good upbringing at his own cost."

Public acknowledgment might also be signaled when parents permitted illegitimates to use the family name. Witnesses in one Mexican case took this as a cue; not only had the parents "raised, educated, and called him son" but in addition he had "called them parents, using their surnames without any embarrassment whatsoever."[63] Yet the adoption of the family name was not an infallible sign of kinship, for families who took unrelated babies or children into their homes for charitable reasons might also give them their surnames.[64] In one Mexican town an illegitimate boy ended up with three last names, for he had been raised by a succession of men and so became a Torres, a Rivera, and a Villanueva, although only the last designated his real father.[65]

In small towns like Zimapán, where everyone probably knew everyone else and everyone's business, the social position of an illegitimate may have been fairly unambiguous. In larger cities, however, especially ones in which there were many newcomers, families might have to make constant efforts to alert the newly arrived to the status of illegitimates who were publicly, if informally, accepted within their kinship group. Most members of the Havana elite probably knew that the Intendente Don Nicolás Rapún was carrying on an affair with Doña Antonia Hernández. Although the couple did not live together, they continually visited each other's houses and produced four illegitimate offspring.[66] As noted in an earlier chapter, the *intendente* eventually ended the couple's extended engagement and abandoned Doña Antonia for another, although he maintained contact with their offspring. Because Havana was a port city that received constant infusions of strangers, the *intendente* had to take special care to let newcomers know that he publicly acknowledged his illegitimate sons and daughters. It is through the testimony of the newly arrived in Havana that clues emerge as to how Don Nicolás ensured public social status for his illegitimate offspring.

Don Joseph Aguilar was one newcomer who quickly picked up the signs: "I became aware that Doña Josepha, Don Fernando, and Don Timotéo Rapún called the intendant *'taita'* [which here means father], and that he made much of them, and I know that he has educated and maintained them." On another occasion the intendant purposely showed off his daughters to newly arrived fellow officials. In this way he not only acknowledged that they were blood kin but perhaps also gave a discreet warning that his daughters were under his protection. Years later, when he testified in favor of their legitimation, Don Juan Antonio Barrutía showed that he had never forgotten this introduction, for he recalled:

> One night as I entered his house a few days after arriving from Europe, [the intendant] said to me, "Would you like to see my daughters?" and, [after I had responded] "yes," he introduced Doña María del Pilar and Doña Josepha Antonio, who were there . . . and they took the mantillas from their faces, and I met them.

However he treated their mother, and whatever their natal and baptismal status, the *intendente* gave clear and public cues to the social position of his illegitimate offspring.

Yet another instance of such conscious public behavior emerges from Quito, where Don Joseph Pérez, the treasurer of the Santa Cruzada, remembered the occasion on which Doña Leonor Ana Suáres let him know that her son, Don Francisco Javier, had had an illegitimate child by Doña Rosa Miño.[67] Don Joseph recalled that "[I never forgot the day] I encountered Doña Leonor Ana Suáres in the Plazuela de San Francisco, and after we exchanged the usual conversation she said these exact words to me: 'I really love Don Joseph Miño, who is my grandson.'" It was then, Don Joseph concluded, that he first knew of the connection. Because her illegitimate grandson had taken his mother's surname, Doña Leonor had to make a special effort to acknowledge both her affection and kinship.

The remarks of eighteenth-century legal commentator B. Tristany suggest that his contemporaries were acutely sensitive to informal modes of recognition signaling kinship. This legal analyst provided a guide to additional cues: the listing of the illegitimate in the family Bible, the payment of wet nurse wages, letters that acknowledged the relationship, paternal presence when the illegitimate was sick, and the father's invitation of neighbors to a birthday party or other similar celebration.[68]

Such informal acknowledgments could create a momentum of their own, for even without official parental recognition, observant relatives, friends, and neighbors might years later confirm the relationship. While only fifty-five of the *gracias al sacar* applicants could produce baptismal certificates in which one or both parents directly and officially recognized them as *hijos naturales*, more than double that number (N. 120) could call upon witnesses to testify that they were natural offspring (see Table 7). Thirty-four children of adulterous and twelve of sacrilegious relationships also relied upon family and friends to confirm their parentage. Years of verbal acknowledgments and informal social interactions might translate into unofficial forms of recognition that facilitated civil legitimation.

A contrasting form of recognition was private acknowledgment. In these instances, parents neither recognized illegitimates at baptism nor provided any informal signs to peers that they publicly recognized the infant as their own. Such children were usually not sheltered within the family home, treated as equal members, or given the family name. Parents could also be circumspect in arranging for the care of such children.[69] Details concerning only three such cases appear in *gracias al sacar* petitions, but they provide striking examples of the extent to which elites might go to make fine distinctions between recognition in their private and their public worlds.

The outlines of the private recognition pattern emerge in a petition from Cuba, in which the marquis de Justiz de Santana, Don Manuel Manzano, both fought public knowledge of his illegitimate son and also actively opposed his legitimation.[70] The marquis was already a married man when he visited Santiago de Cuba in 1755 and had a sexual relationship with "one of the most illustrious" unmarried women of the town. When she became pregnant the couple arranged a private pregnancy, and their son was born in February 1756. Consistent with the private pregnancy pattern, the marquis protected the identity of the mother and assumed sole responsibility for his son. He arranged for baptism, hired a wet nurse, and eventually handed his son to Don Manuel Gonzáles Préstelo, who effectively adopted the child and named him after himself. The marquis continued to support his child financially, even after the fourteen-year-old joined a Santiago cavalry company. It was only when his son turned thirty that the marquis discontinued his financial contribution.

Although supported in secret, Don Manuel was never publicly recognized by his father. He was raised by another far from the paternal household in Havana, he did not take his father's name, and he seems to have been excluded from his father's private circle of extended family. At one point Don Manuel rather bitterly commented that his father "would not let him visit Havana because of the grave consequences that would ensue." The final blow came when his father ceased his remittances. Don Manuel "asked him in a friendly way . . . if he might contribute with some kind of support, which he denied absolutely."

Don Manuel then applied for legitimation, but his documentation proved incomplete. It was only because Cámara bureaucrats took the initiative and requested more information that details concerning a cover-up emerged, for the evidence showed that Havana officials had cooperated with the marquis to keep the recognition of his son a private matter.

Havana officials had drawn up their ranks and taken what measures they could to protect the marquis as one of their own. The *audiencia* noted that the marquis had many obligations: "legitimate sons, a granddaughter, and a multitude of poor relations sheltering under his shadow." Royal ministers had little sympathy for Don Manuel, for they felt that a father should no longer provide "maintenance to an illegitimate adult who through his age and sex should be able to acquire by himself what he needs for his sustenance." Yet the *audiencia* had gone far beyond sympathy for the marquis, for they had also agreed to "burn or archive [the documents] denying [Don Manuel] any approval."

When they later defended their actions to the Cámara in Spain, Havana officials rested their case on the perquisites of hierarchy and of honor. They noted the "recommendable circumstances of the . . . marquis, the honor of his marriage, the distinction and delicacy of the constitution of the marchioness his wife." Left unresolved was whether she even knew of her husband's adulterous offspring. The *audiencia* concluded that Don Manuel planned "to shame" the marquis, and so it had decided that "it would not be just to publicize a thing which would wound his honor and estimation." And so the male establishment, first local officials, and eventually imperial bureaucrats cooperated with the marquis. They refused to grant any of Don Manuel's requests for either maintenance or legitimation.

Unwritten and perhaps unspoken, but certainly underlying this father-son conflict, was Don Manuel's desire that his father fulfill more than just the technical commitments of paternity. The marquis had no obligation to take his illegitimate son home and introduce him to the outside world as kin, or to love or support him as a son. Yet Don Manuel may well have been aware that other illegitimates, for example Doña María Riaza, who lived in Havana during these same years, had been accepted, loved, and recognized both privately and publicly by her father and her kin. His legitimation application vented what must have been years of accumulated frustration concerning "the blameless stigma that he has above himself . . . even though he is of distinguished parents." Nonetheless, Don Manuel's pleas that the Cámara "dissolve the obstacle of illegitimacy . . . with the infinite prejudices that it occasions" remained unfulfilled.

The "infinite prejudices" that Don Manuel endured must have been even further multiplied for Doña Justa Rufina Bueno de Borboya, because the lack of public recognition accorded to this Puebla, Mexico, woman by her father meant that she lost standing not only in the social but also in the racial sphere.[71] Seen from the perspective of the inhabitants of Puebla, it becomes clear how such a situation eventually developed. All that most Poblanos must have known was that one day in 1736 the widow Doña Teresa de Vega and her *morisca* maid, Ana de Villegas, carried a newborn girl to Saint Joseph's church and had her baptized as a foundling. It was also obvious that immediately afterward Doña Teresa's household experienced a series of tragic deaths, for first Doña Magdalena de la Vega, a sister and houseguest of Doña Teresa, died, and then the widow herself passed away.

With Doña Teresa's household broken up, the *morisca* Ana took the surviving baby and raised her on her own. Some Poblanos may have noticed that *Regidor* Don Vicente de Borboya visited Ana's residence from time to time—perhaps some even speculated that he and Ana were the parents of this baby girl. In any case, given little evidence to the contrary, the infant Justa grew up with the public reputation that she was the illegitimate daughter of the *morisca* Ana. It was almost half a century later that Poblanos learned Doña Justa's secret history. Her application for legitimation proved that Doña Justa was not the illegitimate *morisca* daughter of Ana but rather the *hija natural* of two members of the regional elite, Doña Magdalena de la Vega and Don Vicente de Borboya. Doña Magdalena was the classic case of a successful private pregnancy, for even though she did not long survive childbirth she had "died with the reputation of a virgin."

This reputation was apparently maintained for almost half a century. The testimony of the *morisca* Ana, and of Doña Josepha de Priego y Vega, the niece of Doña Magdalena and Doña Teresa, revealed how the family had preserved her honor even if at the expense of her baby daughter. Ana provided an inside picture of the collaboration between female relatives and servants during the family crisis:

> [She] was as always serving Doña Teresa de Vega . . . when they brought to her house a relative of Doña Teresa from a hacienda with the pretext to cure her of a certain illness, and having ordered the witness to serve her, I could not help, *I could not help* but discover that she was pregnant, and when the time came she gave birth to . . . Doña Justa Rufina. . . . [italics in original]

Doña Josepha, who was also present at the birth, remembered how she "took [the newborn] in her arms and in company with . . . her mother and Doña Teresa, her aunt, she helped to dress her; and later the same Doña Teresa carried her to be baptized at Saint Joseph's parish of this city, and to do this Ana Teresa de Villegas, servant of Doña Teresa, carried her in her arms." Doña Josepha's testimony proved particularly important, for it helped to establish the physical improbability that Ana was Doña Justa's mother. Doña Josepha affirmed that "clearly Ana Teresa is not the natural mother of the said Doña Justa Rufina (although some think so), for she would not have been able to give birth and [then immediately] to carry her to be baptized."

While a conspiracy of women protected Doña Magdalena during pregnancy and childbirth, it was Don Vicente who took the customary responsibility for his baby daughter, although he offered her only a private recognition. When first Doña Magdalena and then Doña Teresa died, he asked the *morisca* Ana to care for the infant. For the remaining twenty years of his life he fulfilled his promise to support Doña Justa, and he even provided for her after his death.

Perhaps it was because Don Vicente later married that he never awarded Doña Justa those public marks of attention that would signal to outsiders that she was his natural daughter. Instead, consistent with the private recognition pattern, he did not take Doña Justa into his own home; he neither openly called her daughter nor publicly provided her with financial support or education. Even though he must have known that town gossip reported that his daughter was the illegitimate offspring of the *morisca* Ana, he apparently never tried to correct this mistaken public impression.

Don Vicente did, however, let those within his private world of friends and relatives know of his connection with Doña Justa, and at times he even invited them to visit this daughter, whom he described as "very lovely." It is through their testimony that a picture emerges as to how a closed circle might know of the relationship between the *regidor* and his daughter but still cooperate with him so that his private acknowledgment did not extend to Puebla's public world.

Don José Joaquín Carranco de Villegas was one who made such visits, no doubt because he was related to Doña Teresa and Doña Magdalena, and also because he had a "very special friendship" with Don Vicente. Don José later testified that on his first visit he was not entirely certain of Don Vicente's connection with the young Doña Justa. Within the privacy of Ana's home, however, the *regidor* supplied the customary sign, for Don José remembered how "Don Vicente took some twelve pesos and, giving them to Ana, said, 'This is for your expenses.'" Since Don José was curious to discover what was going on, he recalled that he had later taken Ana aside and asked her, "What was the money for?" She had responded, "For the support of Doña Justa Rufina." And so, Don José concluded, "since I had seen that Doña

Magdalena was pregnant, this confirmed the truth of what had happened." Another visitor was Fray Joaquín del Moral, a priest in the local Augustinian monastery, and someone who had such "intimate friendship and confidence" with Don Vicente that the *regidor* had told him of his illegitimate daughter. Fray Joaquín remembered how Don Vicente took him "various times" to the house of Ana, where "on each occasion he gave her money up to ten or twelve pesos and he told this witness that this was for the support of the child, his daughter, who was then about six or seven years old."

Almost half a century later, Doña Justa's legitimation petition summarized testimony of numerous such visits by friends and relatives to prove that she was recognized within their private world. Don Vicente had, the petition noted: "confessed to some confidentially and in secret . . . while others saw him give Ana de Villegas the twelve peso maintenance for the support of his daughter, while he made it evident to others with no less effective means." Her case emphasized the degree to which colonial Spanish Americans saw themselves as actors in two worlds. Their vision proved sufficiently bifocal that a family could permit an illegitimate member to have the public social status of a *morisca*, even though they recognized her "confidentially and in secret" in their private circle as white.[72] Doña Josepha acknowledged this private-public duality directly in her testimony when she spoke of her cousin Doña Justa's reputation as a *morisca*: "And even though many people still think and believe this was so, even today, this witness and all the relatives of Doña Teresa know that this was not so." In her legitimation petition Doña Justa herself acknowledged that her parents had tried "to bury the event [of her birth] in the region of silence," and how "to hide one error, they engendered another." Her relatives proved eloquent witnesses to that hidden past when Doña Justa applied to Spain not only for legitimation but also, in effect, for transformation of her racial status.

Doña Justa's story exemplifies the ways that birth and racial status might be shaped in colonial Spanish America. Although her natal status was that of *hija natural*, her baptismal status was of "unknown parents." In day-to-day life she enjoyed informal social status within a restricted circle as a white natural daughter related to the Vega and Borboya families; her public reputation in Puebla was as the illegitimate daughter of the *morisca* servant Ana. Finally in 1785, Doña Justa received a civil legitimation. Each element of her status proved to be a logical consequence of the politics of recognition, even if the composite proved to be both complex and contradictory.

PASSING AND THE POLITICS OF RECOGNITION

Private recognitions were not the only instances of illegitimates having a different status in their private and public spheres. It was probably even more common for families to collude in helping illegitimate relatives to construct false public persona. This deceptive variant of the politics of recognition shared characteristics with both public and private acknowledgments. As in public recognitions, the private circle of family and friends provided cues to the outside world that they accepted the illegitimate as blood kin. The difference was that these were misleading cues designed to establish a more advantageous public reputation than the natal or baptismal reality. Such cases resembled private recognitions as well, for such a private-public disparity meant that an illegitimate had a dual persona: one within a closed social circle of parents, family, kin, or friends who knew the truth, the other an enhanced if false public version. Unlike private recognitions, the public persona was superior to the private reality.

A common marker of such deceptive politics of recognition was the "discovery" episode. This occurred when petitioners remembered their shock when they discovered that they were illegitimate, and that their family had concealed their irregular birth. Yet it is questionable whether such stylized revelations reflected real disclosure, or if they were constructed as part of strategic ploys to manipulate the Cámara to rule favorably. The discovery episode seems suspiciously neat, for it gave illegitimates the best of both worlds. On the one hand, they could argue that since they already enjoyed public reputations as legitimates, a *cédula* would not disrupt the social status quo, but simply restore their rank. Yet to make this argument, illegitimates had to disclose the cover-up that had given them false public reputations in the first place. This revelation could be damaging, since the Cámara might be inclined to reject cases in which collusion had created false public status. The discovery episode solved this dilemma, permitting the illegitimates to assert their innocence of the deception and to blame family and friends. Presumably, royal officials would be more sympathetic to parents and relatives who had only evidenced family solidarity when they strove to enhance the status of their illegitimate kin.

The case of Doña Rita Gonzáles of Havana, whose story opened this chapter, contains a classic discovery episode.[73] Doña Rita recalled that, when her father disinherited her, "in a single instant [she] lost the belief that she was legitimate that she had had up until then without any contrary suspicion, and the defect of her birth was made public." It may be true that Doña Rita's parents hid the irregularities surrounding her birth, and that her illegitimacy came as a nasty shock. Yet tantalizing hints in this and other cases suggest that illegitimates might often have been able to deduce their status significantly prior to the formalized discovery episodes they describe.

Although Doña Rita said that she never knew until her mid-thirties that her "parents" were not her parents, and that she was almost certainly illegitimate, her marriage lines suggest otherwise.[74] The presiding cleric listed her husband-to-be in the conventional manner when he noted that he was the "legitimate son of Francisco de Abella y de María Bajados y Ruya."[75] Doña Rita, on the other hand, did not receive the customary parallel notation. Instead, the priest simply commented that she was "from this city." Such vagueness was a customary circumlocution that appears in the marriage certificates of other illegitimates as well.[76] As in the case of private pregnancy, the Catholic Church cooperated in shrouding contradictions between private reality and public reputation. Yet any knowledgeable colonist, including Doña Rita and her bridegroom, would have been alerted by such an obvious omission of parentage on the marriage document. If Doña Rita could read, she certainly must have known of her clouded origin at the time of her marriage, and therefore long before the birth of her eight children, the death of her husband, and her subsequent discovery episode with her father's will.

Mexican lawyer Don Juan Joseph Rueda de Aguirre was another who provided royal officials with a model discovery episode.[77] He recalled that his mother, Doña Teresa Aguirre de Yrazal, had taken him away from his birthplace in Celaya and raised him in the more anonymous locale of Mexico City. Don Juan insisted that he had always considered himself to be legitimate, although he had never questioned his mother as to the absence of a father. Instead, he somewhat ingenuously noted that, since he had been educated "at the expense of Doña Teresa . . . his mother, and . . . since he never knew his father, he believed that she was a widow." After Don Juan graduated from the university and was accepted at the bar, he and Doña Teresa returned to Celaya. It was only then—at least according to Don Juan's recounting of the tale—that he found out that his mother was unmarried and that his father was the abbot of the local monastery. Such a discovery was not only a direct blow to his personal honor but also threatened his occupation: University codes forbade sons of priests from graduating, and imperial legislation frowned upon illegitimates practicing at the bar. Don Juan's reaction was characteristically dramatic: "I was so surprised by that news that I would have taken my own life." However, he was eventually "sustained with soothing and continuous council from the All-powerful."[78]

Although Don Juan's reaction rings true, it is doubtful that he had never previously suspected the secrets surrounding his past. It seems unlikely that a son would be so incurious concerning his father, or that he and his mother would have never met visitors from Celaya who realized his origin. Whether he knew or not, his history provides an example of how kin might use geography to create a false public reputation. While Don Juan was considered legitimate in Mexico City, in Celaya he was known as the illegitimate son of the local abbot.

The artificial creation of a false public reputation produced a similar duality and crisis in the life of Don Pedro Minjares de Salazar, a Durango merchant who was thirty before he discovered that the couple who had raised him and whom he had always considered to be his parents, were not.[79] Don Pedro had grown up on a hacienda outside Durango, "always in the belief that . . . Joseph y Minjares and Josepha de Amessaga were my legitimate and natural parents, for I never knew anything to the contrary." The couple, who were hacienda overseers, treated Don Pedro as their son and he reciprocated, "minding them, looking at them with the respect and veneration that was their right and due given the love and affection that they gave me."

When Don Pedro was twelve his "parents" apprenticed him to one of Durango's most important merchants, and as the years passed he proved so adept a learner that he became first a trusted partner and finally a major city trader in his own right. It was only when Don Pedro was thirty and planning to marry that he requested his baptismal certificate in order to prove his "legitimacy and racial purity." He found instead that the certificate listed his parents as "unknown."

Don Pedro never discovered the true identity of his parents. His "mother," Doña Josepha, had acted as his godmother at baptism, and since canon law forbade a child's mother to serve in that capacity, it is doubtful that she was his natural parent.[80] Possibly Don Pedro was the illegitimate son of the "father" who raised him, or even of the Durango merchant who started him on his career and who treated him as a son. Although Don Pedro eventually married his fiancée, he could never conclusively identify his parents, and therefore could not receive a *gracias al sacar*.

Yet Don Pedro's wealth and his reputation had achieved such a level that even when his private secrets became public knowledge, members of the Durango elite continued to support his passing as a man of honor. One of the many testimonies in his favor was one that captures the essence of what it must have been like to be fully accepted as a social peer:

> I have never known nor have I even seen anyone, no matter how exalted or decorated, who has failed to give him [Don Pedro Minjares] the best treatment; but instead all have cooperated to honor him, to attend him publicly and privately, frequenting his house, having particular confidences and correspondence with him, inviting him to their functions, being next to him and finally, according to him the same respect as to any person as equally distinguished.[81]

In Don Pedro's case, the local elite deliberately chose to accept him as a peer, public knowledge of his obscure origin notwithstanding. Witnesses agree that he became not only one of the richest and the most prominent but also one of the most beloved citizens of Durango.

Family attempts to enhance the status of illegitimate kin usually employed informal strategies. Parents might collude to keep pregnancies and baptismal certificates secret, and to give the impression in public that an illegitimate was a legitimate person of honor. Apparently families rarely tried, or were seldom effective in employing, the more direct tactic of placing false information on baptismal certificates. Those *cédula* cases in which natal and baptismal status can be compared reveal only three instances in which parents successfully lied to create deceptive baptismal listings.[82] Local clerics strictly controlled such entries, as they must have known who was pregnant and who was not, who was related to whom, and who was married and who was not.

An exception to this rule reveals the special circumstances that permitted one Caracas couple to place false information on their baby daughter's baptismal certificate. Even though Don Bartholomé Gonzáles and Doña Ana Rita Pérez told the baptizing priest that infant Doña Margarita was a natural daughter, she was actually an *adulterina*; her father had left a wife in the Canary Islands when he moved his business to Caracas.[83] Don Bartholomé set up a new household in Venezuela with Doña Ana, although he did not attempt to marry her, for such a ceremony would have been bigamous and prosecutable.[84] Most of Caracas, including the neighborhood priest, likely presumed Don Barthólome was a bachelor living in a consensual union or an extended engagement. As the years passed Don Barthólome and Doña Ana added a son and a second daughter to the family. Years after Don Barthólome's abandoned first wife died, he eventually married the Caracas mother of his children. This produced a most complex situation.

Don Barthólome's two youngest offspring had been born while he was a widower but before he had married their mother. Their natal status, presumably their baptismal status (their certificates are not provided), and certainly their private and public social status was that of *hijos naturales*. Since their father was a widower and their mother unmarried when they were born, these two children were automatically legitimated by their parents' subsequent marriage. They now enjoyed the natal, baptismal, private, and public social status of legitimated offspring.

The situation of first-born Doña Margarita was not so fortunate. Her natal status was that of *adulterina*; her baptismal certificate carried the false listing of *hija natural*, which had established an erroneous private and public reputation. While her parents' marriage had automatically legitimated her siblings, it could not alter her status. At the same time, her public reputation changed, along with that of her siblings, from its original false classification of *hija natural* to the more false one of legitimated daughter. Thus Doña Margarita had the natal status of an *adulterina*, the false baptismal status of an *hija natural* legitimated by subsequent matrimony, the private social status as a child of adultery, and the public social status of a daughter legitimated by subsequent matrimony. Nor did Doña Margarita's parents contradict her false public reputation when their fourteen-year-old daughter was courted by Don Joseph Bosque, who presumed on "good faith" that she was their legitimated daughter.

The unraveling began with the death of Don Barthólome, the subsequent marriage of Doña Margarita to Don Joseph, and his assumption of some of the family business affairs. Since his wife was part heir to her father's estate, Don Joseph scrutinized the will that kept Don Barthólome's property intact and divided the income equally among his children, the two youngest of whom were still minors. It was in the family papers attached to the will that Don Joseph experienced what was perhaps a real "discovery episode," for he was horrified to find that the baptismal certificate of his wife predated the death certificate of Don Barthólome's first spouse.

At one stroke Don Joseph found that the wife he had assumed to be le-

gitimate and the inheritor of a third of her father's estate was instead the result of an adulterous relationship and potentially disinheritable. This affected both Don Joseph's purse and his self-esteem. He must have feared
eventual betrayal, because at any time in the future her two now-legitimated
siblings might sue and deprive Doña Margarita of her inheritance. Instead
of going along with the family cover-up and hiding the situation, Don
Joseph applied for his wife's legitimation, and it is only for that reason that
the family secret became public.

Don Joseph's feelings of self-pity and betrayal emerge clearly in his letters
to the Cámara of the Indies. Styling himself as a "vassal submerged in the
worst misery without any fault of his own," he begged the royal ministers to
legitimate his wife and thereby release him from the

> ugly stain that has been placed on my clean family and that has to cause per-
> petual disquiet and feelings from his relations and rivals who would not let
> pass any occasion to throw in his face the defect of his wife, which would be
> passed to all his children.[85]

Although Don Joseph's petition may sound somewhat whining to modern ears, he did feel his honor had been blemished and that he had been cruelly tricked by his wife's family. As a prospective son-in-law and member of
the private circle, he had had the right to be told the truth before the wedding. Although the Cámara was sympathetic to his plight, it refused to guarantee his wife's inheritance. Officials reluctantly legitimated her to the limited extent that her *adulterina* status would not prejudice the honor of her
husband nor descend to the couple's children.[86]

What is missing here is any word from fifteen-year-old Doña Margarita
herself, who, once the family conspiracy had unraveled, faced a scornful and
outraged husband. During the first years of her life she had already under-
gone numerous transformations of status, but now with her husband's discoveries and the ensuing public depositions, she finally received a limited legitimation by the Cámara of the Indies. Doña Margarita's case, with its
roller-coaster rises and descents in birth status, reflects the flexibility that
colonial society attached to birth status as well as the abundant possibilities
for manipulation. Many families may have used the private-public duality to
hide similar difficulties. They may well have been successful, if family solidarity held, and if—unlike the unhappy Doña Margarita—they avoided the
difficulties raised by a proud and outraged husband.

The politics of recognition illuminate those complex ways in which the Hispanic world constructed illegitimacy and treated illegitimates. Colonial Spanish Americans lived in a society in which kinship and intimate friendship divided the social world into private and public spheres that permitted illegitimates multiple kinds of status. Families could manipulate such social spaces to provide restricted, full, or even false acknowledgment of their illegitimate kin. For illegitimates, birth status was not solely ascriptive; rather, it was layered, changeable, and constructed. For those born out of wedlock, the politics of recognition proved a potent force that operated not only at the moment of their birth, or at the baptismal font, but throughout the rest of their lives as well.

SIX

Children: Growing Up Illegitimate

In Panama City one afternoon in 1759, an eleven-year-old boy named Joaquín passed the hours in hiding while his father, his uncle, and their companions searched for him in vain.[1] His uncle, Dr. Don Francisco Javier de Luna Victoria, had recently been appointed the bishop of Trujillo, Peru, and he was leaving that day for his new post. One of the bishop's men later remembered how "his excellency had to delay his leaving for an entire afternoon because [Joaquín], who did not want to leave home, hid himself." Eventually Joaquín was found, he said good-bye to his father and to Panama, and he departed with his uncle for Peru.

Joaquín's home for the next several years was the Episcopal palace, where he lived as a member of the bishop's extended family. When he grew up he married the daughter of a prominent Trujillo official, had seven children, owned haciendas, and served in high office in the city.[2] His life course exemplifies how patronage by an eminent relative and geographical distance might mitigate the consequences of illegitimacy. To erase any doubts concerning his social standing, Don Joaquín purchased legitimation when he was forty-eight.[3]

It is not the accomplishments of the adult Don Joaquín that are the focus here, but rather that haunting image of his childhood afternoon in hiding. The anxiety and fear shown by this eleven-year-old, who did not want to leave his father and home, underscores the insecurity faced by children who suffered dislocations because of their illegitimacy. Understanding their plight necessitates exploration of some unfamiliar pathways, for historians know little about the childhood years of colonial Latin Americans.[4] The marginality of illegitimacy opens windows into this lost world, for when witnesses remembered the infancy and childhood of illegitimates, they verbalized generally unspoken assumptions concerning the traditional roles of parents, family, and friends.

Testimony confirms that the childhood years unfolded almost exclusively within the private sphere. Mothers and fathers, sisters and brothers, half sisters and half brothers, aunts and uncles, cousins, relatives by marriage, and intimate friends of the family effectively defined the child's emotional and physical milieu. For legitimate children, acceptance within this closed circle was virtually automatic; for illegitimates, the situation was less certain. Those who received formal and public recognition no doubt enjoyed more secure childhoods than those recognized informally, or only privately, or not at all.

The naturally circumscribed place of children spared illegitimates much public discrimination. Lack of recognition might deprive them of the family surname; they might not receive equal treatment with a legitimate half sister or brother; they might not inherit if a parent died. Yet children could not be expected to anticipate future difficulties: An illegitimate girl of six might not worry if her lack of honor would affect her marital choices, nor might a boy of eight wonder whether he would ever hold political office.

Far more crucial from children's viewpoint must have been the reliability of relationships within the private sphere. Who took care of them? Where did they live? Did they grow up with both parents or with only one? Did they have brothers or sisters? Were they accepted by their aunts, uncles, and cousins? Who loved them? Our concern follows theirs in an exploration of those ways in which illegitimacy did, or did not, distort the private relationships that were at the core of most Latin Americans' childhood.

While out-of-wedlock children had no monopoly on crisis in the private sphere, the personal crises that underlay illegitimacy created especially propitious breeding grounds for distinctive problems. The very presence of such children testified to a history of family trauma, be it broken vows, failed relationships, or premature deaths. Such circumstances created classic patterns of family stress. Some children lived with unwed parents, others divided their time between dual residences, and still others lived with relatives. If both parents wanted them, they could become the object of fights over custody. If parents abandoned them, they could become the center of lawsuits over financial support. Many lacked a stable family home as they were shifted within the private circle of nurses, guardians, or relatives, or shipped away to school. Some suffered geographical dislocations, and all must have faced moments when they felt that they never quite belonged.

The childhood years unfolded within three distinct yet interconnected stages. *Infancia* spanned the ages from birth until two or three, which coincided with the baby's need to nurse and its greatest dependency and potential mortality. The intermediary years were marked by typical cognitive and physical developments culminating around the ages of ten through fourteen. It was then that adults made obvious preparations for their charges to leave the protective private circle of family and friends and enter the adult and public world. When Don Joaquín's father decided to send his son at the crucial age of eleven from the only home he had known to make a new life in Peru, he was acting within a well-established tradition. Yet the pain experienced by young Joaquín during his afternoon of hiding was indicative of the price exacted from such innocents because of their illegitimacy.

'LA INFANCIA'

Both Spanish law and Spanish American elites explicitly recognized the developmental stages of the earliest childhood years. The *Fuero Real* (1255) marked the age of three as the first critical transition point, for law obligated mothers to nurture infants before that age, after which fathers assumed responsibility.[5] *Cédula* witnesses confirm that *infancia* constituted the first three years, during which infants developed and grew and began a fuller acculturation into family and society. The end of *infancia* marked a natural transition point as children were commonly moved from one caregiver to another, or from outside to inside the family home.

Little is known of the customary arrangements that colonial Latin American elites made for the care either of their legitimate or their illegitimate babies. While depositions reveal that many out-of-wedlock infants enjoyed un-remarkable first years, they are silent as to the characteristics of such nor-mality. Illegitimates Joseph, Gregorio, María Mercedes, and María Dominga were among those who passed unexceptional infancies.[6] Born in Trujillo, Peru, in the 1730s and 1740s, they were "notoriously known" as the offspring of Don Manuel Espinosa de los Monteros and Doña María Vicente Flores, "at whose side they have always been raised." The infancy of Juan Joseph Bernuy of Lima must have been equally commonplace, given that his par-ents lived together in an extended engagement and raised him as their child. He remained illegitimate solely because of the sudden death of his unwed mother.[7] The early years of Don Francisco Antonio and Don Antonio Jo-seph Escalada of Buenos Aires were also typical, as they were raised by their parents who, for "various accidental reasons," never married.[8] The lives of some illegitimate infants were so ordinary that outsiders assumed that they were legitimate. Don Marcos Vicente Gutiérrez was a twin born in 1772 in Teotihuacán, Mexico.[9] Since his parents lived together, many townspeople were probably in accord with the witness who had "always held him to be a legitimate son of a legitimate marriage . . . and thus he is considered in his birthplace." Where parents had long-term commitments to each other, the lack of a marriage certificate did not rule out years of normal childhood for their illegitimate offspring.

One of the first parental decisions that affected the infancy years was whether the mother or a wet nurse would suckle the newborn. Although his-torians of Europe have explored the extent to which fashion as well as neces-sity led parents to pay others to nurse their babies, there is little comparable data concerning such practices in the Americas.[10] It is not clear whether popular custom encouraged Latin American elite mothers to nurse their ba-bies, or whether families chose to delegate this necessity to wet nurses who might care for the infant either within or without the family home.

European trends suggest possible clues to colonial practices. One demog-rapher observed that northern Europeans seemed more likely to send babies to be nurtured outside the home, while southern Europeans and, by exten-sion, Spanish Americans showed a preference for bringing wet nurses into family residences.[11] Other historians have noted how class affected decisions concerning the employment of wet nurses; prosperous families had the best selection and were more likely to introduce such women into their house-holds, where they could be more closely supervised.[12]

The most accessible information about colonial Latin American wet nurses comes from institutions such as *casas de expósitos,* or infant orphanages. Mothers would customarily arrive at dawn or dusk to deposit their newborns in the *torno,* or revolving door, in the hope that their child would be adopted.[13] Since these babies were usually just hours or days old, they were very vulnerable and in need of immediate nourishment. The priests who ran the institution in Havana solved this problem in a manner most likely emulated elsewhere. They had a regularly available pool of lactating mothers who could be hired upon short notice to nurse abandoned infants in their homes. Presumably such lower-class women were equally available throughout the rest of Spanish America, not only to orphanages but to private families as well.

At first glance the abysmal mortality rate of infants in orphanages suggests that wet nurses must have been almost criminally neglectful of their infant charges. Abandonment at the Havana *casa de expósitos* and assignment to a wet nurse proved a virtual infant death sentence. Of the 373 babies deposited from 1711 to 1731, 80.2 percent (N. 300) died soon after their arrival; mortality rates halved by 1735, when 44.4 percent (N. 12) of the 27 entering babies succumbed.[14] After that time notations on infant death were no longer kept, so it is impossible to determine if the *casa* continued to improve its survival rate. Since illegitimacy, either by itself or in conjunction with poverty, was one of the main reasons that women abandoned their babies, the death rate for illegitimate babies in Havana must have been significantly higher than that of their legitimate peers.

The blame for such a high death rate cannot be laid solely to Havana wet nurses. The less-than-salubrious conditions of that capital must have led to a generally high level of infant mortality. Yet compared with situations elsewhere, Havana wet nurses proved to be relatively successful nurturers of abandoned infants. The Mexico *casa de expósitos* registered a 67 percent rate of infant mortality from 1767 to 1774.[15] One historian calculated a 75 to 80 percent mortality rate at the seventeenth- and eighteenth-century orphanage in Seville, and concluded that "practically every *expósito* is a dead child."[16] As in Havana, the death rates for some European foundlings dropped as the eighteenth century progressed, although conditions varied widely from country to country and city to city. Foundling mortality in mid-eighteenth-century Paris was around 68 percent, while 90 percent of abandoned infants in late-eighteenth-century Rouen died before they reached a year.[17] By the

TABLE 9
Who Took the Baby Immediately After Birth?

	N	%
Both parents	30	13.9
Mother	26	12.0
Father	20	9.2
Relatives	12	5.6
Wet nurse	12	5.6
Adoptive parents	4	1.8
Unknown	112	51.9
Total	216	100.0

SOURCE: DB 2-216.

late nineteenth century the mortality rate in Paris foundling homes hovered around 32 percent, while death still claimed 72 percent of such infants in St. Petersburg, 80 percent in Naples, and 86 percent in Moscow.[18] Abandoned babies in Spanish America as well as throughout the Western world must have experienced at least double or triple the mortality rate of their legitimate counterparts.[19]

Compared with these abysmal statistics are the vastly more flattering descriptions of the care that wet nurses lavished on *cédula* infants. Here nurses appear as much more than paid providers of milk; they are affectionate and loving caregivers who treasured their charges. Inasmuch as these characterizations appear in legitimation applications, they obviously describe wet nurses who were successful, for their charges grew up. Yet the warmth of the testimony is striking.[20]

Legitimation petitions do not provide much useful statistical insight as to how many families made arrangements for wet nurses; in half the cases, witnesses never commented on the infancy of illegitimates. When they did so, it was usually to note who took responsibility for the baby immediately after birth (see Table 9). Statements suggest that the natural mother had the potential to nurse her newborn in a quarter of such cases, for babies were either raised by both their parents or by their mother. Even in these instances, however, it is unclear if parents resorted to wet nurses. Nurses might have lived in, or parents might have sent the infant to stay at the home of such providers, deeming such arrangements so perfectly ordinary that they were unworthy of comment.

In another quarter of legitimation cases wet nurses were a necessity rather than an option, for infants had been separated from their mothers at birth. In instances of private pregnancy or the mother's death in childbirth, the father often took sole responsibility for the baby. In one Havana case officials noted that father Don Diego del Pino had not only provided for the "raising and education" of his two illegitimate children but he had also paid for their "suckling."[21] At other times relatives or adoptive parents sheltered the newborn, and sometimes witnesses specifically noted that the first home of the infant was with a wet nurse. Although it is impossible to know the extent to which elite families customarily employed wet nurses, it is clear that the social dislocations characteristic of illegitimacy must have sent a greater proportion of such infants to foster mothers.

The infancy of Don José Antonio Esquerra y Mustelier provides a glimpse both of the types of arrangements made between parents of illegitimates and their wet nurses as well as of the natural affection that developed between these women and their charges.[22] Don José was the out-of-wedlock son of Doña María Mustelier and Lieutenant Colonel Don Antonio Esquerra. The couple had exchanged a promise of matrimony, begun a sexual relationship, and became parents in 1765. Immediately after the birth, Doña María "exposed" her child at the house of Gregoria Herrera, who took primary responsibility for Don José. However, the parents had also arranged for a wet nurse, the mulatto Margarita Romera. In 1813, when she was seventy years old, Margarita remembered those early days and how she had "raised him whose costs Doña María Mustelier paid the first month, and afterward when the lieutenant colonel arrived, who had been absent, he came to visit the baby, whom he caressed very much, recognizing him as his son." The officer gave her eighteen pesos "as well as a milk cow." Margarita added that she never received any further "friendly presents" because "she asked for nothing more, as she had developed much love for the child." It is unclear whether Margarita cared for the infant in her own home or in Gregoria Herrera's, but in this instance she apparently terminated her care when the baby was weaned. Wet nurses often ended their stay at the family home or returned the infant there or to the father, relatives, or others when the baby no longer needed their milk.

The intimate responsibility of wet nursing meant that these women as well as their families became part of the private circle of elite families. Sometimes they not only cared for one of its members but also shared and kept its secrets. Such cases occurred most often when either a private pregnancy or a private recognition limited the public acknowledgment that an elite family might accord an out-of-wedlock child. Such cooperation emerges in Peru, in an affair between Doña Catalina Morales de Amarburu and royal official Don Joseph Cantoya, both of whom had survived their spouse. Their relationship led to a secret pregnancy.[23] Doña Juana Laso de la Vega, one of Doña Catalina's intimates, remembered how her friend "had secretly confided that she found herself to be pregnant." Doña Juana acted as godmother at the birth, and "as such she received into her hand the creature who was given the name of Josepha." Also present at the birth was the wet nurse, for the baby was given "to be raised with great secrecy by Micaela Gamboa."

Since baby Josepha's parents granted her only private recognition, the number who knew of her parentage was strictly limited. Yet necessarily included within this inner circle of knowledgeables was the wet nurse, Micaela, and her family. Years later, Micaela's son Alberto Salazar, a carpenter, recalled how his mother had "raised [Doña Josepha] at her breasts from the moment that she left the belly of Doña Catalina Morales de Amarburu, keeping her until the age of fourteen." Doña Catalina visited her illegitimate daughter and "beneath the same secret that she told only to his mother" confessed that Doña Josepha "was her daughter."

This conspiracy was so well maintained that not even the legitimate daughter of Don Joseph Cantoya knew that she had a half sister. Only decades later, when the husband of Doña Josepha pressed for her legitimation, did family friend Doña Juana testify to the knowledge "in possession of all the [maternal] family . . . guarding the secret until the testimony of this witness today." By then the mestiza wet nurse Micaela was dead, and it was her son who came forward to attest to the truth of those long-past events in which his family had also kept the secret and preserved the honor of the Amarburus.

While some wet nurses primarily provided milk until infants could be weaned, others followed the pattern of Micaela Gamboa, who made the transition to dry nurse and cared for her charge until she was fourteen. This progression from wet to dry nurse seems to have been common as well as natural, since the initial affection that developed between nurse and baby made such women obvious caregivers during later years.[24] The bond became particularly important to illegitimates who had no parental home ready to receive them. Such was the situation of Don Joseph Antonio de Betancourt of Cumaná, Venezuela, who was adopted by the family of his wet nurse: His mother was married, and his father had proved unable or unwilling to raise him.[25]

It was María Petronila Ortíz de Torrejón, the daughter of wet nurse María Manuela, who provided a child's remembrance of those days, when she had been "very little," and when "they carried him so that her mother might nurse him." Included in her reminiscences were the "daily appearances" of the baby's father, Don Joseph Francisco Betancourt, who "made faces and hugged . . . Don Joseph Antonio." Although Don Joseph paid the family for approximately ten years to care for his son, he eventually left for the Valley of the Río Caribe, where he married and let contact lapse. Luis Beltrán Rendón, the husband of wet nurse María, became the boy's foster father until he left their home at sixteen. Luis later testified that he had known Don Joseph Antonio since he was less than a month old, "for from that age until 1769 he has lived in the house of this witness." Such relationships may have been common, as not only the nurse but often her family as well cared for illegitimate infants of the elite.[26]

In one instance the love that bound such a nurse and her charge was so strong that foster mother Doña María Josepha Abalos actively campaigned to maintain the infant in her home.[27] Buenos Aires merchant Don Manuel Domec had, as part of the private pregnancy he arranged for his lover Doña X, sent their newborn son Pedro to be cared for by Josepha. When the merchant eventually married, he tried to move his illegitimate son to his new establishment. The nurse's niece remembered how

> after his marriage with Doña Rufina Ortega he wanted to carry him [baby Pedro] to his house so that his wife might care for him, but as my aunt so loved the baby, she successfully interceded with Doña Rufina that she would not let her husband Don Manuel take [the baby] away.

In this case a coalition between a foster mother and a new wife determined that young Pedro would spend not only his infancy but his childhood as well with the woman who had cared for him since birth. Although Pedro was not moved at that time, the end of infancy marked a natural point when many other illegitimates left their wet nurses and were transferred to the home of one or both parents, relatives, or strangers.

CHILDHOOD: CHILDREN LIVING WITH PARENTS

Doña María Josepha Acosta Riaza of Havana was not the only illegitimate to comment that it was "after infancy" when her father carried her to his family home to be raised with her legitimate half brothers.[28] Although elite parents by design or necessity might find it natural to delegate the care of young babies to others, the end of infancy forced parents to choose to leave the child with nurses or take the toddler into the family home. The most important variable affecting the childhood of illegitimates was who assumed responsibility for their upbringing.

As in infancy, so in childhood the lives of some illegitimates differed little from those of other youths. This was especially so when their parents lived together for decades in extended engagements or concubinage. Yet the lack of official commitment inherent in such arrangements must have made them potentially more fragile, particularly to pressures from church and state that encouraged lovers to end unsanctioned sexual arrangements.[29] The prime sufferers in such dissolutions were illegitimate dependents.

One readily discernible pattern was for children to begin their family lives cared for by both mother and father but to endure eventual parental estrangement. Men usually precipitated this domestic crisis by moving away, often to begin a relationship with another women. Such was the situation encountered by young Manuel de la Trinidad Rodríguez when his father, a ship's captain, ended his affair with Doña Josepha María Valdespino and sailed off to the Canary Islands never to return.[30] During the years his parents had lived together, Manuel had received much attention and affection from his father. Observers remembered the "love" shown by father to son, and the "gratefulness" of the captain to those who paid attention to his child. When Manuel's father visited friends he carried the young boy with him. He took him on board his ship, where the boy sat at his desk and was eventually put to sleep in his bunk, "all with extreme paternal love and tenderness." What was the effect on young Manuel when his father no longer returned to Havana, and when even the occasional remittances of goods and money for his support eventually ended?

The offspring of *Intendente* Rapún Hernández remained bitter into adulthood because their father had broken off his affair with their mother and had begun a relationship with another woman. The young children of Don

Antonio León Calatayúd may also have had mixed feelings as they remembered the times their father had taken them to visit his store in Arequipa, before he sailed off to Spain. It would not be surprising if illegitimate children suffered feelings of anxiety and guilt as they watched their parents' relationships collapse. Both their childhood environment and their future expectations would depend on whether they were taken by their father or their mother.

CHILDREN LIVING WITH FATHERS

Although women might more commonly raise children alone, men also cared for illegitimate children. This often occurred when they terminated extended engagements or consensual unions, and it was even more common in instances of private pregnancy or of maternal death. After noting the existence of such male-headed households in colonial Mexico, one demographer suggested that "a sense of family and love of children" should also be entered into the historical equation and balanced against the "proverbial thoughtlessness" that was the stereotypical negative picture of father/child relationships.[31]

Children taken by their fathers grew up in environments distinct from those typically provided by mothers. The double standard inherent in colonial patriarchy tolerated greater sexual freedom for elite men, who did not find their marriage prospects reduced by the existence of illegitimate offspring. As a result, such children often had to adjust to the introduction of stepmothers, as well as the eventual arrival of half sisters and half brothers.

Children raised by an elite father also benefited from his superior status and wealth. His patronage could provide a comfortable or even luxurious standard of living as they grew up, as well as bringing them enhanced opportunities in adulthood if he used his influence in their behalf. Paternal affection could also be manifested in testamentary bequests, given that *cédula* fathers proved almost four times more likely to leave property to offspring than *cédula* mothers.[32]

The childhood of Don Gonzalo de Leazgui of Guanajuato, Mexico, illustrates this pattern.[33] He passed both his infancy and his childhood with a stepmother, and eventually with his legitimate half sisters María and Aurelia and half brother Manuel. His father, *Contador* Joseph Gonzalo de Leazgui, was in the midst of an affair with a Doña Isabella de Villa while he was courting a Doña Sebastiana Vásquez, whom he eventually married. Soon after the marriage the deserted Doña Isabella found out that she was pregnant. Shortly after she gave birth, Don Gonzalo and his new wife took the infant Gonzalo into their home, where he grew up as one of the family.

Documents from Guanajuato provide surprising evidence that the *contador* was not the only one who brought an illegitimate child to this marriage, for, contrary to the prevailing pattern, his new wife had also been an unwed mother.[34] In the traditional will written by women before undergoing the mortal threat of childbirth, Doña Sebastiana confessed that she was the mother of an illegitimate daughter named Juana Francisca. At the time of this 1699 testament Juana was seven, while María, Doña Sebastiana's and the *contador*'s first legitimate child, was five. Since Doña Sebastiana wrote a public as opposed to a private will, and since she gave her husband custody of her illegitimate daughter, the child must have been publicly acknowledged and may well have lived with the family along with Gonzalo and later with the couple's three legitimate children.

As he grew up, Gonzalo benefited from his proximity to his father, who paid for his education at the *colegio* of San Ildefonso in Mexico City and his training as a lawyer. By the time he was an adult, the private reality of his illegitimacy had become so blurred that he essentially "passed" as legitimate in Mexico City, where few knew of the irregularities surrounding his Guanajuato birth. His father's petition specifically asked the Cámara to exercise a special discretion in this regard because "there are very few who know of the defect of his [Don Gonzalo's] illegitimacy."[35] The request for legitimation was yet another projection of paternal influence in behalf of a son whom the *contador* "recognizes, loves, and esteems" and for whom he desired "all good, honor, and estimation."

While Don Gonzalo's stepmother may have had particular reasons for accepting her husband's out-of-wedlock child into their household, other newly married women also assumed this additional role. Some of them may have been like Doña Josepha Ruis of Cali, who became engaged to *Regidor* Don Juan de Varón Fernández even though she knew he was living with Doña María Betancur and that the couple had two *hijos naturales* with a third on the way.[36] One can only speculate what young Juan and Margarita must have thought of subsequent events as their pregnant mother left them behind as she fled from their father's hacienda in rage and gave premature birth on the road to Cali. She eventually moved to Pasto, where she raised their newborn brother on her own.

Juan and Margarita had to cope with their father's rejection of their mother, the sudden loss of their mother and a baby brother, the arrival of their stepmother, and eventually the couple's legitimate children. It was one of these, Doña María Ignacia Varona, who supplies the only light to this tale, for she remembered that her mother had treated Juan and Margarita "as if they were her own children."

It is interesting to speculate concerning the relationships that developed between Juan and Margarita and the *regidor*'s legitimate children, and generally between legitimate and illegitimate siblings who shared the paternal home. While legitimation documents rarely detail such daily interactions, they do provide scattered reminiscences suggesting that childhood connections could lead to close and loving ties lasting into adulthood. The compelling bonds of shared blood and years of daily life together were more important than any social conventions that discriminated against illegitimates. The observation of one historian of colonial Brazil that illegitimates might lead "fully integrated family lives indistinguishable from those who were born legitimate" seems an equally appropriate characterization for many of their Spanish-American counterparts.[37]

Ties between legitimates and illegitimates could be formed even when relations did not grow up in the same household. At least the adult connections between *hijo natural* Pedro Domec and his two younger legitimate sisters, Doña Rufina and Doña Michaela, show every evidence of such family affection.[38] The Domecs have appeared before, for Pedro's birth was not only a classic private pregnancy but, in addition, his wet nurse had successfully lobbied to keep him in her Buenos Aires home rather than transfer him to his father's residence after his marriage. Pedro lived with his nurse until the age of ten, but, after Don Manuel's wife died, he was brought to live with his half sisters for four years before he joined his father on his mercantile expeditions to Paraguay. As an adult, Don Pedro established his own commercial establishment in Asunción, where he married and began a family.

Even though Don Pedro had lived but a few years with his two legitimate half sisters and now was far away from them, the ties of love and blood remained strong. Whenever business took him to Buenos Aires, he paid them visits. One family friend remembered that "Don Pedro Nolasco and his sisters treat[ed] each other with the greatest care, attention, and familiarity." The intimacy between them was such that his sisters "washed his underwear" and he "took care of what was necessary for their clothing," including on one occasion ordering their shoes. Meanwhile his sisters made baby clothes for his two small children in Asunción. Even outsiders noted that attentions between the legitimate and illegitimate Domecs were familiar in the most profound sense of that word.

Legitimation petitions document loving relationships between a father's illegitimate and legitimate children. A typical example comes from Havana, where an adulterous affair by the first marquis of San Felipe and Santiago led to a private pregnancy for the mother and an illegitimate daughter named Gertrudis.[39] The marquis introduced the baby into his home, where she grew up with his legitimate son and heir, who treated her "as a sister" and with "particular love." While such cases were the rule rather than the exception, the *cédula* sources are selective in this regard. It would not be in the best interests of illegitimate petitioners to present Cámara officials with a chronicle of family fights, or of their mistreatment by their half brothers or half sisters, but rather to stress their acceptance by their legitimate kin.

There were some fathers who—even though they recognized and took responsibility for illegitimate children—seemed reluctant to introduce them to new wives, or to raise them with their legitimate offspring. The early years of Don Domingo Antonio de Zapiola of Buenos Aires fit this pattern, for while he may have received an excellent education, he spent little time with his father or his father's family.[40] His parents, Doña Manuela Sosa and Don Manuel Joaquín de Zapiola, had had a long-term affair that led to the birth of Domingo in 1767. The couple may have had plans to marry, for they listed both their names on the baby's birth certificate. However, they must not have lived together, for Don Manuel took charge of the newborn, and he paid a Doña Cathalina Artillaga to raise his son for the next six years. During this period the couple ended their relationship, and in 1771 Don Manuel married another woman with whom he had four legitimate children.

Young Domingo seems to have spent little time at the paternal home. Even though his father married when his son was four, he left the child with his nurse rather than introducing him into the family residence. When Domingo was six his father carried him off to Spain, where he spent the next eight years attending school. Since his father was a Buenos Aires merchant, he may have visited him on business trips during these years, although there is no evidence of such contacts. His father arranged for Domingo to return to Buenos Aires when he was fourteen only because he had become sick, and so Don Manuel "kept him in his own house until he recovered." This was apparently the only time Domingo ever spent at his father's home. Once he had recuperated, his father sent him to a priest who tutored him before he left for the *colegio* and university at Córdoba. It is difficult not to conclude that Domingo's illegitimacy deprived him of a home with his father. Yet he did receive what must have been a superior education for any youth of the time, and he eventually inherited the one-fifth of his father's estate permitted by law.

The demands of a father's profession also meant that children who lived with him tended to be more geographically mobile than if they had resided with mothers. Such was the fate of young Joseph Francisco de la Luz of Havana, Algeçiras, and Seville.[41] His father had been a captain in the Royal Armada whose affair with a prominent Havana maiden had ended in a private pregnancy. By then Captain Bruno Heceta had sailed away, but he made arrangements for the care of his baby son, who eventually arrived at his posting in Spain. When his father became the commander of Spanish naval forces at Algeçiras, young Joseph Francisco accompanied him and lived in his "house and company" until he was ten. His father then sent him to school in Seville "to conclude and perfect his education." Don Cayetano Ramírez Camborda was another who moved from Lima to Arequipa and back to Lima as he followed his father's bureaucratic posts.[42] Don Rafael García Goyena grew up with a nurse in Quito until he was seven, at which time his merchant father, who now lived in Guatemala, sent for him.[43]

CHILDREN LIVING WITH MOTHERS

While illegitimates raised by mothers may have benefited from her special maternal attention and affection, in almost every other way they were disadvantaged compared with children raised by fathers. *Cédula* mothers suffered lasting consequences as a result of their sexual activity and were less likely to marry or to enjoy a traditional family life with legitimate children. Equally restricted were the woman's financial prospects, for although elite mothers of illegitimates were seldom left destitute by their families, neither were they apt to enjoy the same level of wealth as men.[44] Women were also less mobile and more likely to live and raise their illegitimate children in localities where the shadow cast on their and their children's honor was known.

The effects of this double standard molded the lives of illegitimate children raised by mothers. They more commonly lived as only children or with other illegitimate brothers or sisters, and were less likely to grow up with legitimate siblings.[45] Their standard of living was often lower than that of their father's household, nor were they as able to call on his material assets.

A contract between Doña María Josepha Vásquez and her fiancé Don Félix Palacios illustrates the basic, and probably even the most generous, support provided to illegitimate children who grew up with their mothers.[46] Even though Doña María had exchanged a promise of matrimony with Don Félix, and this Havana couple had had a baby, named Antonia, he refused to marry her. Although Doña María never forced him to the altar, she did successfully sue through church courts for some restoration of status as well as financial support. The resulting settlement mandated that Don Félix provide her with "a house in that city free of all burdens." He had to give up all hope of custody of his daughter, "so that [at] no time can he take her from her mother," and he had to pay eight pesos per month for her maintenance. An additional clause stipulated that his daughter's honor be secured, for the settlement gave Don Félix three months to apply for her legitimation. Yet even though young Antonia grew up in her mother's new home and lacked for few basics, the distancing from her father meant that she was less likely to benefit from his social prestige or to receive a mention in his will.[47]

The life course of Don Francisco Javier de Betancur reveals how a child raised by a mother became obsessed by his lack of connection with his father's superior name.[48] Part of Don Francisco's story appeared earlier, for he was the baby born prematurely on the road to Cali as his mother fled the hacienda of *Regidor* Juan Varón Fernández, leaving her older illegitimate children, Juan and Margarita, behind. These two followed the classic pattern of children raised by fathers, growing up with the *regidor*'s new wife and the couple's legitimate children. When they became adults, Don Juan entered the priesthood and Doña Margarita married and lived in Buga. Neither felt sufficiently burdened by illegitimacy to apply for *gracias al sacar*.

Their story emerges only because their brother, Don Francisco Betancur, sought legitimation when he was seventy-three years old. After his untimely birth on the road, his mother had taken him to Cali. However, his father's threats to take the child prompted Doña María Betancur to take him over the mountains to Pasto, where she raised the boy on her own. Even though Doña María deliberately omitted any reference to his father on Francisco's birth certificate, the *regidor* publicly recognized him as his child, visited him in Pasto, and brought him presents including a fancy-gaited riding horse. When he grew up, Don Francisco married into "one of the principal families of that place," yet he never lost the feeling that he had been deprived of his rightful patrimony. One of his legitimate half sisters seemed to agree with him, for she commented that he "had not enjoyed the benefits and favors that [his illegitimate siblings] Dr. Don Juan de Varón and Don Margarita had gained."

The question still remains why a man of seventy-three years would seek legitimation. For Don Francisco Betancur such a decree confirmed his official link with his ancestors and the family chain of honor. He rather defensively wrote that all in Pasto knew of his ancestry, and that he "ought to use the name of his father." Yet unlike his illegitimate brother and sister, who always used their father's name of Varón, Don Francisco petitioned under his mother's family name of Betancur. His legitimation both validated his paternal ancestry and ensured that his descendants would not be burdened with "a stain that would serve as an obstacle to impede [their] imitating the glories of their elders."

Illegitimates raised by mothers suffered because they lacked access not only to paternal status but also to material resources. Such situations naturally resulted when fathers were estranged from lovers, rarely saw their children, and established new families and new lives of their own. As the years passed, the traditional bonds of responsibility and affection that linked fathers with their illegitimate children stretched thinner, so that fathers became less likely to provide for offspring after their death. Such rejection could be especially cruel when fathers with no legitimate children, and thus with total freedom to dispose of their assets, chose to leave their estates to other relatives, ignoring the futures of their illegitimate sons and daughters.

While the impact of illegitimacy on inheritance will be explored later, the relative freedom given Latin American men to dispose of their assets is worth noting. There was one upper limit: Fathers with legitimate offspring could never leave more than one-fifth of their estate to their illegitimate children. Fathers with no legitimate children could will their possessions as they chose. In either case, paternal disposition of assets to illegitimates was an option, not a requirement. Children raised by mothers apart from fathers proved particularly vulnerable to loss of paternal inheritance.

Such was the fate of Don Manuel de la Trinidad Rodríguez, whose father, Don Amaro Rodríguez Pargo, had shown him much affection as a child.[49] When this Canary Island wine trader ended his business in Cuba he sailed away, leaving young Manuel to grow up as the only child of his mother, Doña Josepha Valdespino. At first the two were relatively well off. Doña Josepha had "two houses, various slaves, and many valuable jewels," and the captain sent presents and goods to be sold for his son's support. Eventually Don Amaro asked Doña Josepha to send their son to the Canaries. She initially refused "because he was too little," and later she decided that "while she lived she would not send him from her company and care." After that, the captain "refused . . . to send her anything."

This tussle over the child and the estrangement between the couple meant that when the captain died he left his possessions to a cousin rather than to the now-adult Don Manuel. By then Doña Josepha was blind and living in "the worst extreme of poverty." Don Manuel and his family also lacked "a thousand necessities" and lived "without any comfort." Even though his legitimation petition was rejected on technical grounds, it would not have served his purpose in any case, for he had hoped—against all precepts of law—that it might have given him some claim to his father's estate.

A case from Santiago de Chile demonstrates how affective ties between fathers and illegitimates might weaken to the point of disinheritance when children grew up with only their mothers. Unwed mother Doña Gabriela Márquez, who has appeared earlier, waited two years for Don Antonio de Aguilar to fulfill his promise to marry her.[50] When he became engaged to another, Doña Gabriela took their baby girl from his sister, who had been secretly caring for her, and raised the baby on her own. Perhaps because María Rosa spent her first two years with her father's relatives, the ties between them remained strong, even into adulthood. Her acceptance within this private circle was complete, for witnesses commented that "even today all her aunts and uncles and cousins on her father's side receive her in their houses and treat her as an immediate relative."

In the beginning, the young María Rosa saw much of her father, who had recognized her on her baptismal certificate. Doña Rosa de la Fuente, who lived in a house next door to Doña Gabriela, remembered that Don Antonio "loved her as his daughter, given the frequency and communication that

he had . . . with both [mother and daughter]." Don Antonio told one intimate friend that "Doña María Rosa looked very much like himself, and that
he had no trace of doubt [that] she was his daughter." The proud father also
pointed out the family resemblance to a brother-in-law whom he brought to
visit his daughter. This relative remembered "that the same Don Antonio . . .
remarked to me how much the features and body structure [of young María
Rosa] resembled that of my deceased wife . . . the sister of Don Antonio."

As time passed, contacts between daughter and father must have become
less frequent, and at some point Don Antonio married and transferred his
loyalty to his wife's family. Eventually, he stopped supporting the child financially. A cleric testified that Doña Gabriela had to care for the young
Rosa "at her own cost and from her own property" until her death. Nor did
Don Antonio remember his daughter in his will, even though his testament
expressed some apprehension about his worldly transgressions.[51] At the last
minute he canceled his order for a large grave cross and bought instead a less
expensive one, so that extra masses might be purchased in his behalf. Yet he
had no concern for his natural daughter, for he simply noted that he had had
no children from his marriage. He left all of his property to his wife. She
eventually founded an entail for her nephew.

Years later the husband of Doña María Rosa would comment bitterly
concerning his wife's exclusion from the paternal estate. He detailed the
"abundance of cattle," the "worked silver," and the "rich furniture," that
were part of the "increased wealth that Don Antonio . . . enjoyed during his
life, that he left after his death to his wife . . . without agreeing to leave his
poor daughter anything for her decency and maintenance."[52] Perhaps if
Doña María Rosa had been raised by her father, she might have been remembered at his death. What is certain is that Spanish law empowered fathers to disinherit illegitimate children at their whim.

Don Manuel and Doña María Rosa were not the only petitioners who
may have lost access to financial resources because they were raised by their
mothers. One Cuban saga is notable for demonstrating how conflicting family loyalties might pressure fathers to disinherit their absent illegitimate children. This extraordinary battle developed because relatives in Puerto
Príncipe considered themselves more worthy of inheritance from Don
Joseph Guerra than his illegitimate son, Fernando, who had grown up with
his mother in Havana.[53] The conflict was remarkable because relatives raised
the issue and fought over their possible inheritance while Don Joseph was

still living and apparently in the best of health. The relatives initiated this pre-emptive attack because Don Joseph did not have any legitimate children. They felt threatened when his natural son began collecting his credentials in 1772 in preparation for a legitimation petition.

The roots of this struggle stretched back more than thirty years to when Doña María Brito and her Havana family had visited Puerto Príncipe. She had become engaged to Don Joseph and then found herself pregnant. The couple's relationship must have deteriorated fairly rapidly, for although baby Fernando appeared in June 1743, Don Joseph was married to another woman by December of that year. Doña María took her baby back to her family in Havana, where she eventually married a close relative.

As the years passed Don Joseph fulfilled his obligations as a long-distance father, for he publicly recognized his illegitimate son, sent provisions to his mother's home in Havana, wrote letters, and housed his son when he visited him in Puerto Príncipe. By the time Don Fernando was thirty, it was apparent that his father was not going to have any legitimate children, and so Don Fernando petitioned not only to restore his honor but also to "ensure the interests of fortune." It was at this point that his father's relatives stepped forward to insist that Don Joseph promise that they, rather than his illegitimate son, would inherit his estate.

Don Joseph felt so pressured by his relatives that he wrote a letter to the Cámara asking for total freedom to dispose of his assets. He admitted that he found himself "without legitimate children from [his] marriage" but noted that he did have "many brothers and very honorable relatives who are very poor." He asked the Cámara to legitimate his son, but "without the qualification that he has to be my necessary heir," therefore freeing his assets for distribution to relatives as well as to charity.

When Don Joseph sent a copy of this request to his son, he added a personal letter that tried to comfort Don Fernando for his apparent rejection in favor of more distant blood kin. He told Don Fernando that it "was necessary to give his relatives the pleasure of getting in the first blow," and so he had given in, although he still hoped "to conserve the harmony" that he had always had with his son. He explained that "he had made the representation that you see" because of the "great objections" they had raised, and in order not to "trample their sentiments." He reassured his son that "when I make my last will I will keep your merits in mind, and you will then see how much I esteem you."

Whether Don Joseph left his goods to his importuning relatives or to his newly legitimated son remains unknown. There may have been excellent reasons why Don Joseph's relatives deserved such consideration: Perhaps they had lent him money, or they had lived with him and worked with little compensation. Or perhaps he felt particular affection for them. Yet the question remains whether Don Joseph's relatives would have pressed their claim if Don Fernando had spent years as a child and later an adult in his father's household. Precisely because fathers had options regarding whether they would remember illegitimates in their wills, proximity and emotional attachments played as important a role as blood ties in any final dispensation.

GROWING UP INSIDE AND OUTSIDE THE PRIVATE CIRCLE: RELATIVES AND ORPHANS

Although most illegitimate petitioners passed their childhood with one or both parents, a few were taken in by relatives or outsiders (see Table 9). Such adoptions were often informal, and commonly occurred when parents could not care for offspring either because they had orchestrated private pregnancies or private recognitions, or because they had died. The *cédula* histories usually reflect the most fortunate of possible outcomes, for these illegitimates tended to find loving homes with their adopted families.

Don Diego de la Riva of La Paz, Bolivia, passed his childhood with a substitute mother from his family's private circle.[54] He was adopted into his aunt's household when his unmarried mother entrusted him to her married sister to raise as her own. The young Diego proved especially welcome, as this couple had only one child, named Sebastián. Another son had died young, and Diego may have helped to fill that void. The couple treated him as their own, and he assumed their family name.

The childhood ties that developed between Diego and his legitimate cousin Sebastián were very close. Don Sebastián, a priest, changed his will to leave his possessions to his cousin, who was then a married lawyer with a growing family. In a letter to the Cámara, Don Sebastián spoke of the "great love and goodwill" he had always had for Don Diego, whom he called his "brother." The priest recalled the "union and brotherhood" that the two had "maintained from their boyhood without separating the one from the other until the present."

An illegitimate was also warmly enfolded within a Mexican private circle. Don Joseph Martin de la Rocha, mentioned earlier, had written to his spinster sister Doña Elvira in Vera Cruz and asked her to care for his baby daughter Josepha when her mother died after a private pregnancy.[55] Merchant Don Angel Morillo was a family friend and a member of the Rocha inner circle who later described the environment in which the young Josepha grew up. He used the sensitive social indicator of clothing as one proof of her total acceptance: He came "to understand how much they have loved her, treating her as a daughter of the house and dressing her equally to that of its lady." Another family friend who had "always had much intimacy in the house of the Rochas" was also impressed by the public nature of the family acceptance of Doña Josepha, and by their open affection: "One cannot doubt the love of her relatives, who do not hesitate to call her cousin and niece."

Although some aunts and uncles might stand ready to adopt illegitimate nieces and nephews in their home, other *cédula* illegitimates did not end up living with relatives. Such adoptions usually occurred when the extended family was not available to take charge, such as in cases of poverty or disaster. An adoption occurred in Córdoba, Argentina, in which the resort to private pregnancy, the absence of supportive kin, and paternal protestations of poverty combined to orphan young Manuel and Joseph Gaspar Casas.[56] Their mother was a widow who so fiercely maintained her private pregnancy that even years later she refused, within the protective secrecy of the confessional, to admit her relationship to her two sons. Nor was their father, a foreigner, willing to assume the traditional role as provider. Don Mathias Antonio Figueredo, a Portuguese, later justified his neglect because of the "meagerness" of his "fortune." Thus, he "was put in the pitiful plight of leaving [his sons] at the doors of Don Ramón Casas, and he . . . in effect through charity . . . has educated them until the present, providing them with the learning appropriate to their youth."

Even more dramatic circumstances led to the eventual adoption of the Mexican baby Francisca Navarro who, because of death and distance, lacked nurturing kin.[57] Seventy-six-year-old Don Antonio Masias was one of the close friends of her merchant father, Don Vicente Navarro, and could still vividly recall the tragic months surrounding her birth, almost a half-century before. Don Antonio sailed with Don Vicente from Spain "in the year of thirty-seven or thirty-eight," and the merchants had taken a house together in Jalapa for the commercial fair. Because of Don Antonio's friendship and "confidences" with Don Vicente, he learned that his companion had exchanged a secret promise of matrimony with Doña María Segura. Don Vicente planned a fast trip to Spain to put his business in order, but, even more important, to retrieve his "papers of nobility" so that he might "verify" the marriage. Just before he sailed he asked his friend Don Antonio to "give the girl anything she lacks, because he had left her pregnant."

Meanwhile the pregnant Doña María faced mounting difficulties. Her parents were dead, and she lived with relatives whom she thought would be unsympathetic. At least one friend remembered the couple's "fear" that her relatives would discover her pregnancy. As her condition became obvious, this apprehension must have become a reality, although her relatives apparently helped Doña María maintain a private pregnancy. She was in "the last stages" of this pregnancy when Don Antonio received a letter from Don Vicente's Spanish relatives announcing that her lover had "scarcely arrived in Cádiz when he died of a violent fever." Apparently Don Antonio had not considered the effect of such traumatic news on Doña María. Her "grief" precipitated her labor, she gave birth to a baby daughter, and died shortly thereafter. Doña María's relatives still attempted to maintain the secrecy of her pregnancy; Don Antonio remembered that "above all there was concern in hiding [the birth]."

With both her father and her mother dead, with her father's Spanish relatives apparently unaware of her existence, and with unsympathetic maternal connections in Jalapa who clearly wanted to keep the birth secret, the newborn baby girl became an obvious candidate for adoption. Therefore "at the instant" of her birth, the relatives "exposed" her at the house of Don Francisco Ortíz, "a subject of circumstance in that town." He immediately had her baptized and served as her godfather, perhaps naming her "Francisca" after himself.

Don Antonio witnessed the baby's christening, even though he was not invited to the ceremony. At this point, Doña María's relatives understandably had little inclination to include him within their private circle. He was not only an intimate friend of the man who had gotten Doña María pregnant, but in addition his impolitic announcement of Don Vicente's death may well have contributed to her death. Even so, Don Antonio remained faithful to his friend's last wishes, for he transferred Don Vicente's parting charge to watch over Doña María to concern for the now-orphaned baby daughter. Don Antonio crept into the baptistry and "clandestinely attended [the christening] in order to observe the end of that misfortune." Almost a decade later, "in forty-six and forty-seven," when he returned to Jalapa after years in Spain, he "tried to find out about the girl Doña Francisca." He discovered that she was being "raised as a daughter in the house of that same Ortíz."

Witnesses never explained why Don Francisco Ortíz was chosen by Doña María's relatives. Whether he was a member of her private circle, married or unmarried, is unknown; but they did affirm that he cared for the young Francisca "with particular love." It is perhaps relevant that upon his death a few years later, no wife appeared to raise his adopted daughter; Doña Francisca seems to have been orphaned yet again, and moved to the house of yet a third "father," Don Juan Atenas. There her personality and talents eased her acceptance into the family, for one admirer described her as possessing a "totally honest modesty, [and] a docile and charitable nature." Her "accomplishments were appreciated in the house of Don Juan de Atenas as if she were his own daughter." The tragic history of her parents did not fall upon this orphaned daughter; she eventually married well and had four sons. Her story underscores how systems of "informal fosterage" might provide backup when kinship systems failed.

PREPARATION FOR ADULTHOOD

A final stage of childhood started around the age of ten, when parents made first preparations for their offspring to leave the security of home and the private circle and to assume adult and public responsibilities. Such a transition had long been customary in Europe, where historians have noted that the beginning of apprenticeship systems, or of employment as servants or other full-time work, often commenced about the tenth year.[58] For the legitimate and illegitimate children of Latin American elites, ten marked the age when many young men were sent away to school or were taken by their fathers to be trained in the family business. Since women played little role in the public sphere, their training was not as obvious—it also occurred, although the education preparatory to marriage still took place within the private circle.

The lives of many of the illegitimate children who have appeared in these pages changed around the age of ten. Young Joaquín was eleven when he unsuccessfully hid from his father and his uncle the bishop so that he would not be sent from Panama to Peru. Josepha was fourteen when her family finally took her from the care of her nurse, acknowledged the family connection, and prepared her for marriage. Pedro Domec was ten when his father took him from his nurse, and fourteen when he accompanied his father on business trips to Paraguay. Joseph Francisco, son of the Algeçiras naval commander, entered boarding school in Seville at ten.

Although these years marked a transition for all elite children, the accompanying changes could be especially pronounced for those who were illegitimate. As they left the protective shelter of the private circle, they began to encounter official prejudices against them. Education outside the home required that boys present baptismal certificates to *colegios* showing not only that they were Catholic and white but also that they were legitimate.[59] This prerequisite proved a particular burden for young Don Pedro Joseph de Necochea of Santiago, for he had to be rebaptized when he was ten and a half years old.[60] His original christening had been so secret—in order to preserve his mother's honor—that no one could find the document when his father tried to enroll him in a *colegio* in Argentina.

As parents faced the fact that their children were growing up and moving into the adult world, some began to apply for their legitimations. Few parents legitimated babies or the very young; the Cámara issued only four decrees for children under the age of eight. Postponement made much practical sense. Men and women living together might still marry and legitimate their children automatically, with no trouble or expense. Young children enclosed within the private circle suffered few immediate effects of their illegitimacy. Some, tragically, would not survive to an age at which their illegitimacy might become a hindrance. Only special circumstances precipitated a petition early in a child's life.

Such a situation moved Don Luis Jiménez de Castañeda from Granada to request the Cámara to legitimate his baby daughter before she reached her first birthday.[61] By then her Havana mother had already died, and so the Spaniard was particularly concerned, given his own "advanced age" and his lack of "legitimate succession." The three other decrees issued to children under the age of eight (ages 4, 5, and 7) also reflect unusual circumstances. In two instances (ages 4 and 5), younger siblings received legitimations as part of family applications that involved older brothers and sisters. The last couple petitioned to legitimate their seven-year-old, who had been conceived in adultery, since only a *cédula* could secure his inheritance rights.

Only after children had survived the earliest years were parents likely to consider legitimation. Unlike petitions for adults, which often specified instances of discrimination, requests for the legitimation of children tended to anticipate such difficulties. Parents feared that their offspring would eventually face obstacles, and so they began petitioning when children were between the ages of eight and fourteen. The fourteen petitions granted to such children fall into three general categories: concerns for inheritance, expressions of general guilt, and the expectation of later discrimination.

Petitions to secure the inheritance of illegitimate children were unusual, because legitimation was seldom necessary to safeguard their property rights under law. However, there were circumstances—for example, when fathers wanted to leave property to *adulterinos* or when parents hoped to bequeath possessions equally to legitimate and illegitimate siblings—in which only *gracias al sacar* might secure succession. Three of the four legitimations for inheritance granted to children between the ages of eight and fourteen fall in these categories, while a last decree was issued to a younger sibling who was legitimated along with older brothers and sisters.

Guilty fathers formed a second category of petitioners. Such requests were typical of the "crisis of conscience" discussed earlier, when men openly repented their actions and sought to minimize the harm that would befall their children, aged eight, nine, eleven, and twelve. More specifically, their concerns prompted petitions to legitimate an eight-year-old so that he might eventually attend university, a ten-year-old to hold public office, and a nine-year-old old girl to find an eligible husband. The worries of their parents also prompted the legitimation of an eight- and a thirteen-year-old, while no reason was given for the legitimation of a boy of eleven. The fact that parents petitioned so early suggests that they knew that they, and their children, had cause for concern. It is no accident that adults in their twenties, thirties, and forties were the most likely to seek official legitimation, for out-of-wedlock birth took its greatest toll at that stage of the life course.[62]

SEVEN

Adults: Passing, Turning-Point Moments, and the Quest for Honor

In 1798, Don Manuel Antonio Gutíerrez of Portobello, Panama, confided to the Cámara of the Indies that "since puberty" he had been "excited by the desire to erase as much as possible the memory of [his] beginning."[1] To achieve this aim he had "observed the most exact conduct in his business, dedicating himself . . . to commerce." There he merited the "greatest credits due to his constant good faith and exact fulfillment of the charges and commissions that have been confided in him." By the time of his petition he felt that his "moral virtues" and "agreeable behavior" had gained him the "appreciation and estimation of superior [persons] of that city and those subjects of the best distinction." Even though Don Manuel Antonio had gone a long way in overcoming his illegitimacy, he still suffered from the "shame" that his birth caused his wife and his children, and so he finally applied for legitimation to "obtain the effects that are attached to those who have had the luck to be born of a legitimate and true marriage."

As illegitimates became adults and moved into the public sphere, they faced the full force of the discrimination resulting from their birth. Their first response was often similar to that described by Don Manuel Antonio, for they used the private-public duality to project the most favorable persona in public and to attempt to pass. Like Don Manuel, many reached strategic moments when they realized that such informal efforts had limits, and that only *gracias al sacar* could overcome continued discrimination.

When illegitimates applied for a *cédula*, they requested to be legitimated for reasons of honor or to better their inheritance (see Appendix 2, Table 12). Their depositions reveal that discrimination in issues of honor was extremely complex. Some written laws and ordinances clearly ostracized illegitimates; others vaguely did so, while popular traditions and local customs contained patterns of bias that varied over time. Discrimination in property issues was much more straightforward and consistent, for a corpus of uniformly enforced written laws governed the flow of material goods from one generation to the next. This chapter explores the quest for honor, and the next will focus on the pursuit of material gain.

Such explorations chronicle much more than just the attempts by illegitimates to achieve a measure of parity with their legitimate kin. The process by which illegitimates circumvented discriminatory norms through passing, and sometimes reached turning-point moments when such efforts failed, exposes the raw dynamics underlying mechanisms of mobility in eighteenth-century Spanish America. Their collected biographies provide a rare context in which to understand the extent to which a colonial society that was hierarchical, patriarchal, and racist might permit individual exceptions to its general rules.

THE ETIOLOGY OF PASSING

A 1781 letter of Don Fernando Guerra of Havana to the Cámara furnishes a self-conscious commentary on the progression that commenced with one individual's informal attempts to pass, led to rebuffs and a turning-point moment, and culminated in an application.[2] Don Fernando confided that he had hoped that his efforts would overcome the negative consequences of his illegitimacy. He had believed that his "orderly behavior combined with the excellence and splendor of his forefathers" would make it possible for him "to blind [others] to the note of illegitimacy" that had been left him "as a shadow among the illustrious prerogatives of his nobility and distinction." Yet Don Fernando's attempt to pass in public as a person of honor ultimately proved unsuccessful. Neither his exemplary conduct nor his noted lineage was sufficient to "dissipate the clouds of his origin." The "legal impediment which he breathed from birth" made it impossible for him "to acquire . . . honors consistent with the quality and distinguished merit of his ancestors."

Most striking in Don Fernando's letter was his open discussion of his informal attempts to pass, and his cognizance that passing was a viable option. It was only when he discovered that he could not sufficiently "blind" others to the facts of his birth that he reached the decisive moment and made an official application for legitimation. Petitions initiated by adults are particularly revealing about the problems of passing, as illegitimates commonly provide evidence of their attempts and the particular incidents or long-term frustrations that eventually prompted their applications.

Passing was never an all-or-nothing affair. It was common for illegitimates to enhance their status in small but meaningful ways, often only to be thwarted when they sought more substantive mobility. Illegitimates sought to be addressed as "Don" or "Doña," for such appellations were given only to those who possessed honor. Not surprisingly, the large majority of *cédula* petitioners had achieved this honorific title long before they received *gracias al sacar*.[3] Illegitimates also passed when they were invited to the homes of local elites and were considered worthy of their trust or shared confidences.[4] While such informal evidence of social mobility may not regularly appear in the historical record, such recognitions must have provided important measures of status and personal gratification, and they possibly marked the first steps toward more significant advancement. Elites may have been more willing to enhance the status of illegitimates with such informal concessions rather than include them on the city council or permit them to marry a son or daughter.

The deposition of Don Joseph Ramón de Olmedo reveals such incremental benchmarks in the process of passing, for this Argentine merchant detailed his struggle to build an honorable public reputation and to be accepted by his business peers.[5] Don Joseph wrote how he had tried to make up for his "defect of legitimacy" with "proper behavior and honorable proceedings." He had been a "faithful, quiet, and pacific subject of your majesty"; he had been "religious," and he had paid his taxes. Don Joseph could produce witnesses to testify that he was accepted by his commercial peers. One merchant noted that he had "always kept his confidences and correspondences with honor and probity"; another vouched for his "excellent credit and integrity," and his acceptance by the "principal commercial houses." Such approval was noteworthy, for other illegitimate merchants testified that their birth hindered their careers inasmuch as commercial peers questioned their trustworthiness given their absence of honor.[6] Don Joseph's application used evidence of his informal acceptance to seek yet further mobility, for he wrote that he hoped eventually to marry and to hold political office, and he did not want his birth to limit his future possibilities.

The three Pro brothers of Lima had also informally passed to achieve substantial mobility on their own, long before they applied for legitimation.[7] Don Martin had served as notary public to the royal *audiencia*—a position usually denied illegitimates. Don Gregorio had become a lawyer, also in spite of restrictions against illegitimates, and he practiced his profession with "no complaint, accusation, or calumny either in public or private." Brother Francisco was a merchant accepted as a person of "honor and luster." One observer noted that "all these brothers . . . had been received very well wherever they presented themselves, [and their] illegitimacy has not served as an obstacle."

If the Pros had achieved so much, why did they bother to apply for legitimation? Unknown numbers of other illegitimates may never have reached decisive moments. Some may have passed so successfully that they never even applied. Still others no doubt experienced such downward mobility that admission to elite circles was improbable, and so legitimation could not improve their social position. *Cédula* petitions resulted when illegitimates encountered limits to their passing and came to believe that state intervention might significantly tip the outcome in their favor.

A complex brew of variables affected passing and led to turning-point moments, although three factors were always paramount. The first was gender, for the extent of personal ambition as well as the type of prejudice varied dramatically with the sex of the petitioner. The second was geography and proximity, for the micro-culture of regional elites affected local propensities to discriminate, the corresponding potential to pass, and the proclivity to seek redress. The third was timing, for as the eighteenth century drew to a close, discrimination intensified, foreclosing informal attempts to pass and prompting increased resort to *gracias al sacar.*

GENDER, TURNING-POINT MOMENTS, AND
THE VARIABILITY OF PASSING

Gender profoundly molded the roles of men and women, and it correspondingly shaped their potential to pass. The patriarchal society that provided significantly wider opportunities to Spanish-American men also permitted more numerous kinds of discrimination against them. An earlier chapter has traced how absence of public honor produced a "civil death" that barred illegitimate men from graduating from the university, practicing law, or becoming a notary, a smelter, a military officer, a churchman, or an officeholder in the local or royal bureaucracy. Illegitimacy also limited personal choice, especially the potential to contract an advantageous marriage with an elite woman or to pass honor to offspring. The burdens of illegitimacy weighed heavily on men, who proved twice as likely as women to apply for *gracias al sacar*.[8]

Inasmuch as Spanish American women were already foreclosed from professional or political careers, their illegitimacy added little to existing discrimination against them. Yet absence of honor could considerably limit their few adult choices. Illegitimate women needed special permission to enter the religious life, although such dispensations did not require a *gracias al sacar*. When an illegitimate woman passed, it was to marry a man of honor and to become the mother of future "honorable" generations. Women sought *cédulas* when illegitimacy restricted their selection of eligible spouses or the transmission of honor to their children.

Not only the traditional roles of men and women but also the personal talents of illegitimates influenced their passing. Men who were hard workers or notably accomplished might enhance their mobility in the public world if their superiors or local elites recognized their merit. Women might use their appearance or their personality to attract particularly eligible men. Yet individual excellence could be a double-edged sword, for men or women who were especially ambitious might "push" the limits of elite tolerance and evoke prejudice.

The degree of support offered illegitimate adults by their private circle also influenced mobility, for not all elite families were equal. Those with notable status or wealth had superior potential to forward the interests of illegitimates. Exploration of *cédula* case histories illustrates not only the distinctive aspects of male and female passing but also how gender interacted with other variables to promote or impede social mobility.

MALE PASSING

For men, one of the most visible proofs of honor was to occupy a leadership position in the imperial bureaucracy or in local government. Some of the more telling histories revolve around men's attempts to pass in order to hold public office. The saga of Don Joaquín Cabrejo provides an excellent introduction, for he was the highest officeholder to apply for legitimation.[9] His prominence as judge advocate, lieutenant governor, and interim governor of Panama left documentary evidence in Bogotá archives that reveals a more candid picture than usual of the variables that affected passing.

When Don Joaquín requested a *cédula* in 1784, he gave no indication that his birth had thwarted his personal ambitions or his bureaucratic career. Instead, he provided minimal information: proof of the marital state of his parents, a copy of his baptismal certificate, and details concerning his public service. He simply asked to enjoy the status of a man of honor that he could pass on to his children. Don Joaquín's application underscores the difficulty of analyzing applications, since it is likely that other illegitimates concealed histories of discrimination beneath equally bland and uninformative requests for the restoration of their honor.

Don Joaquín's birth and infancy resembled those of other seekers of legitimation. *Bogotanos* Don Vicente Timón and Doña Gertrudis Franqui had been unmarried when they courted, began a sexual relationship, organized a private pregnancy, and baptized their son in 1731 as a child of "unknown parents." Don Joaquín may have spent his childhood without much parental supervision, for his mother retained the traditional distance required by private pregnancy and his father failed to take him into his own residence when he eventually married. Don Joaquín never used his father's last name, commenting that he had "arbitrarily t[aken] the surname of Cabrejo." Yet Don Joaquín must have found powerful patronage somewhere within his private circle. Someone paid for his education as a lawyer and subsequent admission to the Bogotá high court. Since illegitimates were generally not encouraged to practice law, he was already successfully passing. In 1759, when he was twenty-eight, his parents appeared before a notary and finally acknowledged him as their *hijo natural.*

It was probably no coincidence that this was the same year in which Don Joaquín received an appointment to serve in the newly created post of judge advocate and lieutenant governor of Panama.[10] Since royal officials represented the king and exercised his authority over elites in their jurisdiction—elites who naturally possessed honor—royal officials also had to be men of honor. His appointment meant that Don Joaquín had passed yet further; as a royal official he was a public man of honor, the private reality of his illegitimacy notwithstanding.

Don Joaquín formally assumed his royal appointment in 1761. As the years went by he assumed greater responsibilities and received consistently favorable ratings from his superiors.[11] His passing proved successful, even though occasions arose when his illegitimacy might have been used against him. Just three years after Don Joaquín arrived in Panama the governor had died, and there was a fierce squabble over who would serve as his interim successor. That honor had previously gone to the governor of Portobello, but since Don Joaquín was the new lieutenant governor he was now first in line to take up the temporary vacancy. Such ambiguous situations could be particularly dangerous for illegitimates who had constructed public persona superior to their private reality. Whenever issues were in conflict or in doubt, detractors might use the "stain" of illegitimacy as a lever to tip the balance against them. Yet no one from Portobello or Panama City sent an indignant letter to the Bogotá *audiencia* that someone without honor held such an important position. Rather, the Panama City council supported Don Joaquín's succession and confirmed him as interim governor. For illegitimates who passed, the absence of challenge to their position was as important an indicator of their success as their actual mobility.

Even though Don Joaquín had overcome his birth to enjoy a status closed to most illegitimates, he continued to press for promotion and higher office. As the years went by he showed greater and greater frustration with his stalled position. In 1766 he asked that his superiors nominate him to be a judge on an *audiencia,* his lifelong ambition.[12] Yet he remained isolated in Panama and eventually complained, "I never get any notice of anything."[13] In 1777 he suggested to his Bogotá superiors that he had been "too long" in his post, and he reminded them of his exceptional services, including a term as interim governor, as well as his promotion of Bourbon reform measures.[14]

The latter included his oversight of expropriated Jesuit properties and his establishment of revenue-producing tobacco and *aguardiente* monopolies. Don Joaquín also complained that his "indispositions" had increased so that he "lived continually ill because of the heat of a climate [that was] totally opposed to his constitution." His doctors had predicted that his "deterioration would be ensured" without a move to a cooler climate.

Don Joaquín's Bogotá superiors forwarded his petition for promotion and transfer to the Council of the Indies. At that point his hopes were crushed. In November 1777 the secretary and governor of the Council of the Indies, José de Gálvez, reiterated to the viceroy in Bogotá the Bourbon policy that increasingly discriminated against Creoles holding high positions in the Americas.[15] He explained that Don Joaquín could not be promoted because he did not include in his vita "the precise quality that he was legitimate nor where he was born." Gálvez concluded that these were "indispensable qualifications for whatever honorific office and even more for a judicial minister."[16] Given Gálvez's notorious personal prejudice against Creoles who were legitimate, both Don Joaquín's birth and his birthplace surely weighed against him.

Years of service in colonial bureaucracy counted for nothing if a candidate could not meet the new prerequisites of birth. Gálvez also dismissed Don Joaquín's petition because there were "various complaints from Panama citizens" concerning his decisions on local suits, although he must have known that judges usually created a coterie of disaffected losers. In the conclusion to his letter Secretary Gálvez asked the viceroy, now that he knew of Don Joaquín's "defects," to keep him informed concerning the "quality, education, and conduct of the said Cabrejo." Left unstated was whether this discreet surveillance was to lead to a possible later promotion or perhaps, more ominously, even to a demotion.

Don Joaquín fruitlessly waited for his appointment. Existing documents do not reveal whether his Bogotá superiors eventually informed him of Gálvez's negative appraisal, or whether he concluded on his own that his illegitimacy was a bar to further advancement. If Don Joaquín knew of Gálvez's remarks, he would have had to have taken them seriously, for his superior had not only refused to promote him but had also challenged his existing status by questioning his informal passing and his public persona as a man of honor.

Whether occasioned by Gálvez's comments, his dismay at not receiving the Quito post, or accumulated years of frustration, Don Joaquín finally reached a critical juncture and applied for a *cédula* in 1784. His application recounted none of these events. Instead, it masked his ambition and his disappointment in a simple request to be considered a man of "honor." At this point Don Joaquín's passing worked in his favor. The official who reviewed his application stressed that his "honors as a minister" and his "conduct and good behavior in . . . service to the king" were reasons why it would be "very proper" to accede to his request.[17] When he was fifty-three, Don Joaquín became a man of honor.

Legitimation did not bring Don Joaquín's long-sought promotion. Eight years later he remained lieutenant governor and judge advocate, still vainly writing the viceroy, still complaining about his health, and still receiving superlative reports from his immediate superiors.[18] Three years later still, near the end of his career, the Panama comandante general reported to the viceroy that Don Joaquín was "one of the most qualified and meritorious ministers that anyone could desire."[19] The official rhapsodized over his "judicious learning, [his] continuous study and practice of forty years as a lawyer, and thirty-two [years] in the laborious employments of general councilor, lieutenant governor, and judge advocate." Even though the comandante praised his "maturity, assiduity, impartiality, and above all . . . [his] faithful and God-fearing Christian life," Don Joaquín never became a high court judge.[20]

In 1784, the same year that Don Joaquín sought legitimation, Don Joseph Antonio Betancourt, a Venezuelan, also forwarded his request to the Cámara.[21] One way to gauge Panamanian Don Joaquín's success is to compare his profile with that of this petitioner from Cumaná. Both men were hardworking, talented, and ambitious, and both served in the colonial bureaucracy. Yet their potential to pass differed substantially.

Without a superior's active encouragement, Don Joseph Antonio might never have applied for a *cédula*. Compared with Don Joaquín Cabrejo, who at least in the early years of his career seems to have had confidence that his achievements might overcome the stain of his illegitimacy, Don Joseph Antonio cherished few such illusions. Instead, he initially was resigned to the fact that his personal talents and ambitions must necessarily be circumscribed by the "defect" of his birth.

Incidents from Don Joseph Antonio's difficult childhood have already been explored; even though his father had arranged a private pregnancy for his mother and had deposited him with a nurse, he eventually abandoned him. Informally adopted by his foster family when he was ten, Don Joseph Antonio lived with them until he was sixteen. By the age of twenty-two he was working as a clerk in the Puerto Rican Real Hacienda (Royal Exchequer). Eventually he returned to Cumaná, where he developed a reputation as an extraordinarily hard worker, for he simultaneously held three jobs: clerk for the governor of Venezuela, accountant for a logging operation, and accountant for the royal tobacco administration.

Don Joseph Antonio deeply impressed his superiors, and their genuine appreciation for his diligence emerges even through the hyperbole that was characteristic of colonial Spanish-American administrative language. His supervisor at the Real Hacienda in Cumaná remembered that Don Joseph Antonio had "served and serves with all honor, application, constancy, and care," and he added that he had worked "many holiday nights and days." Don Joseph Antonio's supervisor at the royal tobacco administration, *Contador* Don Andrés Palacios, lifted his employee's hopes that his hard work and initiative might lead to a promotion. The *contador* was so impressed with Don Joseph Antonio's "honorable way of dealing and his notable ability" that when a vacancy occurred in his office he "spoke to. . . . Betancourt so that he might apply to fill the post."

This offer from a superior constituted a turning point for Don Joseph Antonio, raising his expectations despite the defect of his birth. His reaction to a possible promotion is illuminating, for, although he did not lie, he certainly equivocated. Skirting the barrier of birth entirely, he told Don Andrés that it would "not be possible" for him to apply, as he was too busy with his multiple positions to seek the proffered post. More significant than his words were his actions; it was now that he began to collect the necessary testimony for his 1784 legitimation petition. Admitting that he sought legitimation so as to hold offices of honor, he added that he had already been unable to accept a position in the tobacco administration because of "the mentioned impediment of illegitimacy." Don Joseph Antonio's was an anticipatory action: If another opportunity arose, he would be eligible for promotion.

Most striking about Don Joseph Antonio's application is his unstated but clear presumption that an illegitimate could not aspire to even the lowest rung of offices in the Venezuelan colonial bureaucracy. Don Joseph Antonio assumed that if he accepted such a position he would be challenged on account of his birth. His lack of confidence in his potential to pass as a person of honor stands in sharp contrast to the attitude of Don Joaquín, who served at a much higher level and still hoped for further promotion.

Subsequent events suggest that some of Don Joseph Antonio's insecurity originated from the circumstances surrounding his birth. Although his 1784 petition had protected the identity of his mother, he had produced witnesses who gave the strong impression that both of his parents had been unmarried. When the Cámara demanded further details, he was forced to confess that his mother had been married at the time of his birth, although she had been cruelly treated and then abandoned by her husband.

This omission stepped over the line between acceptable obfuscation, which blurred private realities, and substantive manipulation of the facts in order to mislead officials. The Cámara invariably became obdurate when it discovered such maneuvering. One official expressed what must have been a majority opinion when he grumbled that "the new information, far from bettering his case, makes it worse, for it needs even greater indulgence." Although royal officials had both the power and the precedent to legitimate Don Joseph Antonio, by now they lacked the will, and they turned him down in March 1787. He reapplied, including yet another packet of letters of praise from his superiors, but he was rejected again in January 1788.

Even though Don Joseph Antonio never received a favorable verdict, comparison of his case with that of Don Joaquín reveals both provocative similarities as well as contrasts. Both men shared decisive moments when their illegitimacy thwarted their occupational mobility. Yet their careers prior to their applications reflected significant disparities in their ability to pass. Don Joaquín had served for decades in midlevel royal bureaucracy and had had expectations of being appointed a judge; Don Joseph Antonio felt that he must be legitimated before he could hold the most lowly office in the Venezuelan tobacco administration. Support from the private circle, geography, and chronology additionally affected these colonists' perceived, as well as their actual, potential for political and social mobility.

Even though Don Joaquín had not been raised by his parents, he had received significant support from his private circle. His parents had acknowledged him, and someone had paid for his education as a lawyer and supported his royal appointment. In contrast, Don Joseph Antonio had been abandoned by his father; even though his deceased mother's brothers eventually acknowledged him, that was not necessarily an advantage, given the

adultery that had led to his birth. Nor could his nurse's family further his career, as they were not members of the elite. It was only when Don Joseph
Antonio found a patron in the royal bureaucracy that he began to hope for
any promotion. Family connections and patronage profoundly influenced
the potential for passing of these two men.

Their milieus also molded the expectations of the two applicants. Even
though Don Joaquín disliked the climate, his Panamanian locale improved
his chances for passing, for his move from Bogotá had distanced him from
elites with knowledge of his illegitimacy. His chances were also probably enhanced by his Central American location: Illegitimates passed more easily
there than elsewhere. A man of Don Joaquín's obviously superior talent
might go far in a comparative backwater like Panama City.

Don Joseph Antonio enjoyed none of these advantages. He lived and
worked in the same town of Cumaná where his father had served as a *regidor*, where he had been raised by his foster family, and where locals had personal knowledge of his illegitimacy. Venezuelan elites were among the least
tolerant of passing. Time also worked against him, for the latitude that had
made possible Don Joaquín's Panamanian appointment in 1759 was less evident a generation later, when Don Joseph Antonio sought promotion in
1784. The stories of these two men underscore why passing and turning-
point moments are not easily predictable occurrences. The interplay of variables is so complex that one illegitimate might suffer discrimination at the
very point at which another might pass.

Don Joaquín Cabrejo and Don Joseph Antonio Betancourt were largely
dependent for their passing upon the tolerance of their superiors in the imperial bureaucracy. Yet an even more common opportunity for officeholding
and a corresponding potential for discrimination attached to political service
at the local level. At the end or beginning of each year, cabildos (city councils) throughout Spanish America met to elect new members. This was one
occasion on which local elites conspicuously spoke for themselves in deciding whether they would admit illegitimates to their ranks. While the basic
legal requirement for cabildo office was literacy, there was a presumption
that officeholders possessed *calidad*, and therefore honor.[22] Local elites usually set much higher standards than the legal minimum, for there was a close
correlation between wealth, social status, and cabildo service.[23]

Cabildo service carried with it much more than just a fleeting year of local
power. Men elected to the city council were distinguished in their neighbor-

hoods as persons of responsibility and substance, and such distinction lasted throughout their lives. This was why even though colonists continually griped that city council service was onerous, they still accepted election and marked it as a high point in their public careers. Service on the cabildo distinguished a man as a member of the local inner circle, for a fraternity of peers had elected him as a man of honor to be included among their elite ranks.

Not all city council offices were elected annually, as *regidores* customarily purchased their position and held it during their lifetime. Even these officials, however, had usually served in an elected post before purchasing an office. *Regidores* shared responsibilities with a variety of elected officials including *alcaldes*, a *procurador general*, and a sheriff who assumed the primary burden of town management during their year of office.

Each year that the permanent *regidores* and outgoing annual officers met to elect a new slate, they enhanced the public reputations of a favored few. At times they decided whether they would permit someone who was illegitimate to pass and join their selected group. If their decision was negative, it could provoke turning-point moments for illegitimates who had succeeded elsewhere. Evidence of the extent to which illegitimates could pass in distinct cabildo jurisdictions provides sensitive indications as to the variations in local discrimination throughout the empire.[24]

The situation of Don Manuel Antonio Vásquez y Rivera from Tegucigalpa, Honduras, and that of Don Mariano de las Casas of Havana, Cuba, provide glimpses of the discriminatory differences between Central America and the Caribbean. The contrast is compelling, since both men served, or tried to serve, as *procurador general* of their respective cabildos within the same seven-year time period (from 1786 to 1793). The local elites involved showed vastly different levels of tolerance toward these two ambitious men.

Don Manuel Antonio Vásquez y Rivera encountered comparatively little discrimination in Tegucigalpa.[25] He was the natural son of a royal official and a woman of "first distinction." By the time he petitioned in 1793 he had already successfully passed, for local elites had elected him to be *procurador general* in spite of his illegitimacy. In addition, he had recently purchased the permanent city council office of *regidor*. It was not fear of local, but rather of imperial, prejudice that prompted his petition. He was not sure that royal officials would confirm his new rank if he were illegitimate, so he wrote the Cámara and asked for "your royal dispensation of that defect" before he took up his post.[26]

Spanish councilors not only willingly granted his request but they discounted the usual price as well. They patronizingly commented that Tegucigalpa had "little population" and that public offices were "of little estimation, as they are more burdensome than useful to those that hold them." They noted the difficulty in finding suitable citizens to hold office, for "even in the capital [Guatemala City] those best qualified to serve excuse themselves from public posts." Their remarks imply that absence of competition and of qualified personnel in Central American locales might translate into more tolerance toward passing. This may be why both Don Manuel Antonio of Tegucigalpa and Don Joaquín Cabrejo of Panama City experienced comparatively little discrimination. Such indulgence was virtually nonexistent in Havana, where competition for office was fierce and discrimination particularly ferocious. There the prejudice of local elites transcended the generations to discriminate against Don Mariano de las Casas, a city council candidate who was himself legitimate.[27]

This contretemps began innocuously enough on the first of January 1786, when the Havana city council met to elect officers for the coming year. The cabildo deadlocked twice in its choice for *procurador general* before sparring factions divided their votes evenly between Don Mariano de las Casas and Don Antonio Basilio Menocal. Following legal custom, the two men then cast dice to see who would hold the office, and Don Mariano, a Havana lawyer, emerged the victor. Normally that would have settled the issue, but cabildo factionalism surfaced and the losing side tried to overturn Don Mariano's win by dredging up any possible murk from his family past. This rival faction challenged the validity of Don Mariano's election because he had descended from a "bastard through his maternal line." These officers proclaimed the lottery results were invalid, inasmuch as such casting of lots should occur only "when the subjects are equal." This was not the case, they said, because the "defect" of Don Mariano's illegitimate mother had transcended a generation to blot the honor of her legitimate son.

Faced with a badly divided city council, the governor polled its members as to Don Mariano's suitability for office. Those who supported his candidacy emphasized that he was a "legitimate son," while the other side insisted that "the mother of . . . Don Mariano is not legitimate."[28] Whatever their different positions and the lottery notwithstanding, when the cabildo met later that week, it was his competitor, not Don Mariano, who held the coveted post.

What started as a triumphant election for Don Mariano had now become a public challenge to his honor. Bitterly complaining of his enemy's "daring spirit of malevolence, hatred, and rancor," he tried to repair the damage.[29] In January, March, and April he appealed the decision. He obtained a statement from the governor that he was qualified to hold any position "to which he might be elected."[30] Thus Don Mariano finally reached a decisive moment. In 1789 he began to collect testimony, and in 1792 he appealed to the Spanish Cámara to legitimate his seventy-one-year-old mother, Doña Antonia del Rey Blanco.[31]

By then Don Mariano had trouble finding anyone alive who could testify to events that had occurred more than seventy years before. He eventually found some in their seventies and eighties who recalled what must have been a well-known scandal in the Havana of their infancy and childhood. Doña Antonia's story appeared earlier: It was her mother, Doña Beatris Blanco de la Posa, who after leaving the convent of Santa Catarina for health reasons had been courted, promised matrimony, and seduced in her own home, only to discover that her lover was married. Little is known of her later years, but her illegitimate daughter, Doña Antonia, married Don Juan Andrés de la Casas in 1742, and the couple produced Don Mariano. With her marriage the illegitimate Doña Antonia essentially passed as a women of honor, for she married an accepted member of the Havana elite who had already served on the cabildo in 1739.

One Havana city council faction had directly challenged Doña Antonia's passing when it opposed the election of her son. The refusal to accept her as a woman of honor meant that she would have been unable to pass honor on to Don Mariano, and thus he could not be an "equal" of his competitor. Those on the city council who emphasized Don Mariano's legitimacy had implicitly accepted his mother's informal passing as a public person of honor—and her legitimate son as a peer.

In this case royal officials went out of their way to affirm Doña Antonia's passing and to approve her legitimation. The Cámara noted that she was now "seventy-one years old, that she had been married with a distinguished person and had legitimate succession." It granted her a *cédula* so there would be no "pretext to embarrass" her family concerning "those effects of pure distinction and honor to which they might aspire . . . as has occurred in the case of Don Joseph Mariano, her son." Even though the mother became legitimate, her son never served on the Havana city council.[32]

Several striking themes emerge in this comparison of city council elections. The first is the manifest difference in the attitudes of local elites toward passing. In Tegucigalpa elites elected Don Manuel Antonio as their *procurador general* even though he was illegitimate. In Havana elites denied the same post to a legitimate candidate because of the "stain" attached to his mother. Passing and turning-point moments distinctively mirrored the varying levels of discrimination practiced by local elites throughout the empire.[33]

FEMALE PASSING

Don Mariano's plight serves to introduce the other half of the gender theme, for it was the status of the women of his family—his unwed grandmother and his illegitimate mother—who foreclosed his city council career. Female honor became a public commodity precisely because its absence could prejudice the political and economic mobility of succeeding generations of sons. The transmission of honor became one of those critical nodes where generally private issues such as sexuality and illegitimacy directly influenced the public roles not only of male but also of female family members.

The Havana experience of Don Mariano provides a classic example of how a long-term cloud might hover over an elite family who accepted an illegitimate bride into their midst. Decades might pass with local society treating her as a woman of honor, but if the family became involved in controversy, any skeletons in the family closet could be used against them.[34]

A case from Caracas reveals that royal officials and colonial elites shared the belief that not only elite men but also women had to possess and transmit honor. Don Joseph Bosque, who has appeared earlier, was shocked when he discovered that his Venezuelan wife who he thought had been legitimated by her parents' marriage instead remained an *adulterina*.[35] One royal official commented that this revelation must have been "painful" for Don Joseph, who now had to confront the "shocking accident of the ugly stigma of illegitimacy and adultery, a stain to be passed on to his offspring." Even though Don Joseph had acted properly by "contracting marriage in order to propagate his honor," he had now prejudiced "the progeny he hoped to perpetuate in honors and distinction."

Since Spanish-American elites concerned themselves with the past and present as well as the future implications of honor, it was natural for families to guard against the marriage of illegitimate women into their private circle. The situation commonly arose when illegitimate women reached marriageable age and faced such prejudice. The guardian of Doña Gregoria de Rivera y López of Bolivia applied for a *cédula* for her when she was twenty-two so that she could "contract a marriage worthy and equal to the circumstances and honor of the family."[36] Legitimation made her a more acceptable bride, for it foreclosed any future challenges to her, or her children's, honor.

Evidence of family refusal to accept an illegitimate bride also surfaces in a case from Venezuela. Such resistance must have been formidable, for the love letters that Don Juan Antonio de Echevarría wrote to the widow Doña Juana Figueroa suggest that he was more than smitten by her charms, if not totally committed to a match.[37] Doña Juana included some samples in her petition to the Cámara in the hope that it would remedy her predicament.

Don Juan addressed Doña Juana as the "greatest love of my heart" and pledged his total devotion: "I am dying for you, . . . I never eat nor sleep but I only think of you." The hindrance to any happy ending was his family's resistance to the match, for Don Juan Antonio also confessed that "if I marry as you wish, my brother will not be friendly with me, nor others that I know." Even though Don Juan Antonio repeatedly offered to die for her, he seemed unwilling to marry her if it meant alienating his brother and assorted relatives.

Doña Juana was understandably upset with such tactics. She must have made her position very clear to her fiancé, for Don Juan Antonio lamented that he "felt very upset that you do not treat me with affection." He should have had more sympathy for her situation, however, for his family had challenged Doña Juana's passing. In her petition she defended her public reputation, noting that she "had always behaved with honor and esteem and had been treated as a notable woman of that city." Nor had "that defect served as any obstacle in the first marriage she had contracted with Don Bartholomé Ramírez." Although some members of the Cámara were sympathetic to her plight, her birth as an *adulterina* worked against her, and her petition was eventually denied.

While illegitimacy might limit a woman's marriage potential, it did not inevitably foreclose a union with eligible males. Not all elite men reacted with the horror Don Joseph Bosque did, nor prevaricated as Don Juan Antonio did when considering an illegitimate bride. In a backhand sense the overwhelming patriarchy of colonial Spanish America worked to the advantage of illegitimate women, for the status of a wife could not much damage that of her husband, and the position of a husband might enhance that of a wife.

Illegitimate daughters were viewed as particularly acceptable candidates by upwardly mobile men who might otherwise be unable to marry women with equivalent social connections or dowries. Spaniard Don Eugenio Fernández de Olmedo was one such newcomer, who had arrived in Santiago, Chile, to continue his mercantile career.[38] He found himself "engaged in commerce with some credit" when he decided "to embark upon the state of matrimony with . . . Doña María Rosa." When the merchant investigated and discovered that she was "of good quality and clean of all racial taint," he married her "even though she was not born in matrimony." It was only a decade after their marriage that the merchant then sought her legitimation so that "the legitimate children that we have . . . procreated" would not suffer because of her birth.

Women sought legitimation not only when they wanted to become brides but also after they became mothers. It was fear that her own illegitimacy might deny honor to her children that occasioned the petition of Doña María Josepha Basco of Havana, who "was living sad and full of the blush caused by her illegitimacy, which she will transmit to her three minor sons."[39] Doña María Josepha was the daughter of a naval captain whose stay in Havana had resulted in a private pregnancy for her mother and her own illegitimate birth. Her father recognized her and later even introduced her to the Spanish woman he eventually married. When he and his wife passed through Havana on a trip to Mexico, they had "treated her as a daughter." Her father's brothers also included her within their private circle, for they stayed with her in Havana on route to their colonial postings as governor of the Philippines and as a judge in Guatemala. At the time of her application, Doña María had passed as far as a woman was able; she was totally accepted by her father's distinguished family and had married a *peninsular* from Barcelona, giving birth to legitimate children. Doña María Josepha understood, however, that the prominence of her family would not protect her sons from the prevailing Cuban intolerance for any "taint" of illegitimacy.

Female turning-point moments often occurred, therefore, as children began to make the transition from the private to the public sphere. Legitimation of mothers did not bring them much benefit personally, for with their marriages to men of honor, they had already passed. However, their legitimations might make it possible for their sons to attend colonial universities, usually to study to become a doctor, lawyer, or priest.[40]

Such a combination of circumstances precipitated the 1766 request of Bogotá merchant Don Domingo Soriano y Lombana that the Cámara legitimate his forty-five-year-old wife, Doña Josepha Sánchez.[41] Doña Josepha's parents had exchanged a *palabra de casamiento* and had lived together in an extended engagement until her father rejected her mother and married another woman. He however eventually retrieved and raised his daughter. When she grew up, he provided her with a dowry of 1,500 pesos and arranged for her marriage with an aspiring merchant, Don Domingo, who was no doubt eager to add her assets to his existing capital of 12,000 pesos. Don Domingo's commerce flourished; an inventory at his death in 1773 showed he had almost 30,000 pesos worth of goods in his store. The couple owned six slaves and five houses, including a family home in the Calle of the Plateros valued at 6,000 pesos. The family possessions also included fine china and mirrors, and Doña Josepha owned a mantilla decorated with pearls, a gold chain, and emerald earrings. Her dowry had been invested and had multiplied tenfold into a capital of 15,955 pesos. The couple were blessed with nine living children, six sons and three daughters.[42]

Consideration for the future generation led Don Domingo to plead that his wife's "defect of illegitimacy . . . not serve as an impediment so that [his] sons might enter the *colegio* [San Bartolomé] and obtain honorable posts."[43] The merchant feared that "some subjects of little worth" could bring up the "illegitimacy of their mother as an obstacle and impediment without consideration of the rank, character, and distinction of their parents." In response, the Cámara not only agreed to legitimate Doña Josepha but also specifically noted that her sons "could enter the *colegios* of those kingdoms."[44]

Doña Manuela Antonia Angulo Rizo was another mother who sought civil intervention, not to improve her own status but rather to mitigate discrimination against her son.[45] Circumstantial evidence strongly suggests that she was the daughter of cleric Dr. Don Leonardo Antonio de Angulo, who had deposited her at the door of his own rectory, "discovered" her, baptized her as an *expósita*, and raised her as an act of "charity." Doña Manuela was "raised and educated as a woman of circumstance and of white origin with every decency" and eventually passed to marry Don Joseph Joaquín Rizo. He was quick to inform royal officials of his own honorable ancestry: "Not from the beginning to the end of our lineage have we exercised any vile office nor have we been pettifoggers . . . but always . . . capable of managing our fortune . . . to deserve the approbation of . . . subjects of distinction." Doña Manuela's passing had been successful to the point that the couple's sons had been admitted to "studies in the college seminary, [and] others to the battalion of white militia."

Without legitimation, however, the potential for challenge to the status of Doña Manuela or her children could never be totally eliminated. The crisis arose in 1785, when her nineteen-year-old son, Don Pedro Manuel, graduated from the seminary and applied to the Bishop of Havana for ordination. The prospective cleric remembered that he waited "many days" in Santiago for a response from the bishop, and "even though there had been various mail arrivals to this city from Havana, I still did not have any result about my application, and so I presumed that there must have been some cause of this delay."

His father dismissed the idea that his son might be found unworthy, given his "life, customs, and good reputation," concluding that the only possible "impediment was that Doña Manuela Angulo . . . was an *expósita*." A letter finally arrived from the bishop in February 1785 in which he refused to accept Don Pedro Manuel into the priesthood, because it would be "against the dispositions of law that cannot be contradicted." Embedded within this cryptic comment was horrible news for the family: The bishop had gone beyond challenging Doña Manuela's passing as a woman of honor; he had also refused to accept her baptismal status as an *expósita*. He bypassed her public reputation to accept rumors concerning her private reality as the daughter of a cleric. If this was so, her son would need exceptional dispensation to enter the priesthood.

When Doña Angulo petitioned the Cámara for redress, she did not ask to be legitimated, given her inability or unwillingness to document her parentage. Rather, she and her husband simply requested that the Cámara force the bishop to recognize her public persona as a woman of honor with the baptismal status and special civil rights of an *expósita*.

The family's conscious manipulation of the differences between Doña Angulo's natal, baptismal, social, and legal status, as well as the disparity between her private and public reputations, proved successful. The Cámara firmly supported the cover-up and noted that a "common principle of law" was that "in the case of doubt one should always presume the most favorable." It chastised the bishop whose actions were opposed to the "progress of the nation" and its "greater happiness."

Turning-point moments for men and women occurred at different points in their life course. Women were usually legitimated before marriage to enhance their prospects or later when the details of their birth might threaten the opportunities of the next generation. Men faced such immediate personal discrimination that the fate of their descendants necessarily took second place to their own careers. However, as men became older they increasingly concerned themselves with their posterity. Havana merchant Don Agustín Violete was fifty-six in 1819 when he decided to apply, not to further his own career but so the "stain and defect" of his origin would "not be carried to . . . [his] family."[46]

GEOGRAPHY, PROXIMITY, AND PASSING

Not only gender but also locality proved another determinant of turning-point moments, for regional elites varied in their propensity to discriminate. The Caribbean, notably Cuba, contributed disproportionately to the total number of applicants, followed by the populous Andean and Mexican provinces, followed then by the peripheries. Any interpretation of the degree to which such applications reflected local levels of discrimination can proceed only with a strong caveat. It is a large leap from the personal situations of 244 petitioners to any conclusions concerning wider regional patterns of prejudice against them (see Table 10).

It is at least tempting to speculate that the disproportionate number of Cuban applicants reflected an effect of the Bourbon reforms, for Cuba rose like a "phoenix" because of late-eighteenth-century policies that led to free trade, land grants, massive importation of slaves, and the sugar boom.[47] Such a vibrant economy created significant potential both for upward mobility and for reactive discrimination. Elites in Cuba may have felt particularly challenged by newly created, upwardly mobile cohorts and have been disposed to thwart those who tried to pass. Yet if the balance between upward mobility and discrimination was particularly tense in Cuba, how can it be measured against that of Mexico or Peru? Could passing have been so much easier in the colonial center that candidates never bothered to apply for legitimation? Or were illegitimates so downwardly mobile that *cédulas*

TABLE 10
Distribution of Applications by Region

Region	N	%
Caribbean	84	38.9
Andes	38	17.6
Mexico	35	16.2
Southern cone	22	10.2
Northern South America	19	8.8
Central America	18	8.3
Total	216	100.0

SOURCE: DB 2-216.

could not better their already dismal situation and so they never petitioned? Internal patterns combine with anecdotal histories to provide some finer indications of the parameters of discrimination throughout the empire.

Gender differentials provide a valuable clue to local variations in prejudice, for illegitimate men and women did not apply in equal numbers. On average men applied twice as often as women; yet women were much more likely to petition from some regions than from others. Gender differentials divide the empire into four distinct discriminatory areas: the Caribbean and northern South America, Mexico, the peripheries, and the Andes (see Table 11). In Cuba, Venezuela, and Colombia, as many women as men applied; Mexico approximated the empirewide average of two men to each woman; in the peripheries of Central America, northern Mexico, and the southern cone, four men applied for every woman. Andean Ecuador and Peru registered approximately six times as many applications from men as from women.

Why were Caribbean women so much more likely to apply than their Andean counterparts? Previous analysis has shown that women commonly applied either when they were about to marry or when their own passing failed to secure the honor of the next generation. Given this reasoning, women would be more liable to apply in regions where prejudice was especially fierce, for it hurt not only them but also their children. The Cuban experience supports this formulation, for the island not only produced a disproportionately large number of applicants but, in addition, illegitimate women and men petitioned in equal numbers. This hypothesis suggests that illegitimates suffered the greatest discrimination in the Caribbean and northern

TABLE II

Ratio of Male-Female Illegitimate Applicants by 'Audiencia'

Audiencia	N. Male	N. Female	Ratio Male-Female	Location
Santo Domingo	43	41	1-1	Caribbean
Caracas	4	4	1-1	Northern South America
Santa Fe	5	6	1-1	Northern South America
Mexico	21	9	2.3-1	Mexican
Charcas	6	2	3-1	Andean
Guatemala	11	3	3.7-1	Central America
Panama	4	0	4-0	Central America
Guadalajara	4	1	4-1	Northern Mexico
Chile	4	1	4-1	Southern cone
Buenos Aires	14	3	4.7-1	Southern cone
Quito	5	0	5-0	Andean
Lima	22	3	7.3-1	Andean
Total	143	73	2-1	

SOURCE: DB 2-216.

South America; somewhat less in Mexico and even less in Central America, the southern cone, and northern Mexico; and the least in the Andes.

The profiles of men who passed provide confirmation of these regional patterns of tolerance and intolerance. Ten illegitimate men became office-holders before they applied for *gracias al sacar* (see Appendix 2, Table 13). None of these held political office in the Caribbean or in Mexico, where discrimination was extreme, and the sole exception from northern South America was Don Gabriel Muñoz, who held a minor neighborhood office (*alcalde juez pedáneo*) in Medellín.[48] The remaining nine who passed to hold office before they purchased their legitimacy did so in southern cone, Central American, and Andean locales.

Anecdotal evidence additionally supports these regional patterns.[49] The tolerance extended to the Pro family of Lima, to Don Joaquín Cabrejo from Panama City, and to Don Manuel Antonio Vásquez y Rivera from Tegucigalpa contrasts sharply with the difficulties of Don Joseph Antonio Betancourt in Cumaná or Don Mariano de las Casas from Havana. Yet within these broader regional variations may also lurk individual idiosyncrasy: No doubt someone passed in Cuba at the same time someone else failed in Peru.

Locality played another, more subtle role in prompting turning-point moments, for some applications directly precipitated others. Such cluster applications occurred when petitioners shared similar profiles. Since elites socialized with each other, it is understandable that one family's solution might be imitated by others. *Gracias al sacar* proved to be both an effective and a fashionable solution to the complications posed by illegitimacy.

Cluster applications could occur within families when the solution for one generation provided a model for another. When the Alarcóns of Havana petitioned to legitimate a daughter in 1722, they included documents that showed that a paternal grandfather had received a similar concession in 1631.[50] Another less obvious familial linkage originated in Lima, where the successful petition of Don Gregorio Pro in 1780 provided a precedent for his son-in-law.[51] The connection can be traced through Don Gregorio's 1814 testament, which named his five children, one of whom was Doña María Manuela, married to Don José Antonio Cobían.[52] This same Don José Antonio applied for his own legitimation two years later in 1816. His last testament, dated 1849, confirmed his connections to the Pro family, for he identified his wife and noted that he lived in the house of his deceased father-in-law, Don Gregorio.[53]

Extended family ties link applications from La Plata, Bolivia, and Lima, Peru, and demonstrate how a coterie of imperial bureaucrats moved in the same circles and sought equivalent solutions. The unhappy story of Bolivian Doña María del Carmen López Nieto has appeared earlier; her father forbade her to marry her fiancé *Oidor* Ramón Rivera y Peña until the couple had received the necessary royal permission.[54] Don Ramón transferred from La Plata to Lima, while his fiancée and her sisters organized a private pregnancy that culminated in Doña María's death in childbirth and her daughter's adoption by her maternal relatives.

In Lima, Don Ramón eventually found another bride, Doña María Antonio Herboso y Arburua, whose father was an official in the Royal Tribunal of Accounts.[55] There was illegitimacy in her family as well, for Doña María had two first cousins, Don Melchor and Don Agustín, who lived in La Plata and were the illegitimate sons of the dean of the cathedral. Such family connections linked Don Ramón to several legitimation applications—not only the unsuccessful 1791 petitions of his wife's cousins but also the happier 1795 outcome of his own natural daughter.

Acquaintances forged by professional interactions within communities also produced cluster applications, as one successful applicant provided advice or served as an example to another. It seems beyond coincidence that

Buenos Aires merchant Don Francisco Antonio de Escalada, himself legitimated in 1771, would step forward in 1784 to provide a *gracias al sacar* deposition for fellow merchant Don Manuel Domec, who was collecting testimony to legitimate his own son.[56] Don Francisco Antonio's example may
have influenced yet another of his colleagues to consider legitimation, for he
served on the Buenos Aires city council in 1779 with Don Manuel Joaquín
de Zapiola. Don Manuel's own illegitimate son, Domingo, was just twelve
at that time, but in 1788 his father collected testimony for his eventual legitimation.[57] Two of the three petitions from Cuba in the 1740s originated
from illegitimates who may have been students together, since they succes-
sively applied in 1741 and in 1746 to graduate as medical doctors from the
University of Havana.[58]

Other instances of cluster legitimation are more difficult to document, although circumstance, geography, and chronology make it probable that petitioners knew each other. Applications from Venezuela suggest such circumstantial linkages; after an initial *cédula* granted to a Caracas illegitimate
in 1748, there were no cases from that jurisdiction until 1779 and 1784.
Those involved Caracas couples in remarkably similar circumstances. In
both cases the lovers eventually married, but their union, because of kinship
or adultery, failed to legitimate their children. Both families applied so that
their illegitimate children could inherit equally with their other children.[59]
Since the profile of these cases was unusual, the dilemma of the first family
may well have provided a model for action by the second.[60]

Familial and regional clusters like these provide powerful evidence of the
close if ordinarily undocumented links among local elites. If *gracias al sacar*
proved a solution for one individual, the word might spread and inspire
neighbors with similar problems to seek redress. Colonial Spanish America
was a much smaller world than is usually realized.[61]

TIMING: THE LATE-EIGHTEENTH-CENTURY INCREASE IN DISCRIMINATION

As the eighteenth century drew to a close, *cédula* applications poured into
the Cámara's chambers; three out of every four petitioners applied after
1780.[62] Time became the third variable that affected the quest for legitimation, for as petitioners faced greater obstacles and were less able to pass, they

were more likely to purchase *cédulas*. Why did so many submit applications in the last decades of colonial rule?

Although the answer is extremely complex, it is clear that Spanish America was a different place at the end than at the beginning of the eighteenth century. Regional economies and societies had begun to develop their own internal dynamism as populations increased, old export products revived, new ones flourished, and the Bourbon state promoted further growth through reforms. Peripheral regions such as Cuba, Venezuela, and Argentina experienced booms in sugar, cacao, and in trade generally; the core Mexican and Peruvian economies began to revive. A newly created cohort of the upwardly mobile—recently arrived Spaniards, Creoles, *pardos*, and mestizos—sought access throughout the Americas to offices, professions, and social alliances previously denied them. The reaction of local elites was to raise the barricades and to restrict access to their privileges.[63] The closing decades of the eighteenth century were marked everywhere by a defensive tightening of the social hierarchy.

Gracias al sacar depositions reveal individual portraits within this broadly painted picture, illustrating how elite defensiveness was translated into reduced tolerance toward passing. Discrimination against those who lacked honor became both a shorthand for, as well as a symptom of, attempts to maintain status in the face of challenges from below. Jane Schneider's observation on the uses of honor in Mediterranean societies hits the mark for late colonial Spanish America as well, for she noted that "concern with honor arises when the definition of the group is problematic, when social boundaries are difficult to maintain, and internal loyalties are questionable."[64]

By the end of the eighteenth century the social equation that had always balanced elite efforts to limit access to hierarchy against family attempts to promote the mobility of illegitimate members had decisively swung in favor of the former. The dramatic increase in *cédula* applications and the internal patterns within them—the increase in applications from women, stories of heightened discrimination, evidence of multigenerational prejudice—provide striking verification that the closing decades of the century were marked by heightened discrimination. Illegitimates who might once have passed were simply no longer able to do so.

Prejudice against illegitimate women serves as a particularly sensitive indicator of increased levels of discrimination, since it was generally easier for women to pass than it was for men. If more illegitimate women petitioned as the century ended, intolerance was on the increase. Before 1780, one woman purchased a *cédula* for every three men; after that date one woman applied for every two men (see Appendix 2, Table 14). Their male counterparts must have experienced even greater obstacles.[65] Anecdotal case histories describe previously opened doors now slammed in the faces of illegitimates. The plight of Mexican Don Joseph Manuel Ignacio Martínez de Lejarzal provides a telling example: An occupation open to him one year was closed the next.

Parts of Don Joseph Manuel's story have appeared earlier, for he was the illegitimate child who was "sandwiched" between the marriages of his widower father, an assayer in the silver-rich town of Guanajuato.[66] Although listed as an *expósito*, Don Joseph Manuel was publicly acknowledged by his family. Guanajuato residents remembered that his legitimate siblings treated him "by writing and by word as a brother." Such solidarity extended to his training as an assayer; his legitimate brother confessed that Don Joseph Manuel "had inherited this inclination from their common father." At first he held no official post, although Don Joseph Manuel "practic[ed] with great relish . . . the highest and delicate work of this occupation."[67]

There were historical as well as immediate reasons why Don Joseph Manuel faced discrimination when he sought an official appointment as an assayer. The Spanish Pragmatic of 1501 had included assayers among those practitioners who had to demonstrate *limpieza de sangre*. Assayers refined precious metals both for private individuals and for the state, and they had to be trustworthy men of honor. Given that Don Joseph's parents had not recognized him on his baptismal certificate, he could not meet this requirement. Even more immediately and more ominously, in 1790 the Mexico City assayers' guild passed an ordinance requiring that their members be of legitimate birth.

The Pragmatic and the ordinance notwithstanding, in 1792 Don Joseph Manuel applied to the Mexico City guild. He passed as a man of honor, receiving an appointment to take up a post in Rosario. It may well be that the connections of his family, with its fame as assayers, and his own skill contributed to his initial success. However, he failed to follow through and assume the post in Rosario on account of illness. When his health improved in 1794, he applied for the "first vacancy that might be available, and that might be granted."

Don Joseph Manuel's request for a new post contained no indication that he was concerned that his illegitimacy might hinder his career. After all, he had already passed. However, time had run out, for an illegitimacy apparently acceptable to the guild in 1792 was no longer acceptable in 1794. It rejected his application for a post and even refused to test his proficiency.

Don Joseph Manuel's response to this refusal was intriguing, for it revealed his underlying assumptions concerning his occupational mobility and his passing. He appealed to the guild on the basis that there could always be individual exceptions to general rules. Since he had already received special treatment, he was understandably upset with a body that did "not want to use any indulgence whatsoever in this case, but to carry to its ultimate rigor the letter of the law that asks for legitimacy." He suggested that "even though the ordinance asks for legitimacy it is because it requires the best in everything, and not to exclude absolutely those who are *hijos naturales.*"

Don Joseph Manuel's hope that his "good habits and Christian ancestors" might overcome the guild's reluctance to accept him was in vain. Instead, he became a victim of a rising guild defensiveness as they felt the status of their profession challenged. One Mexico City assayer proclaimed that if members allowed someone with his "defect" to take and pass the examination, that "would be enough to confirm the low opinion that many individuals have that . . . these positions are servile."[68]

Don Joseph Manuel refused to accept the judgment of his fellow assayers; he applied to a higher council (the *Junta Superior de Real Hacienda*), which engaged in the usual fence-sitting characteristic of colonial bureaucracy. On the one hand the junta upheld the exclusivity of the 1790 ordinance against illegitimates; on the other it reminded Don Joseph Manuel that "he lacked only the royal dispensation of [his] majesty." Don Joseph Manuel took this broad hint and applied for a *cédula* in 1795. In October 1796 he presented his new legitimation decree to the guild, took the exam the next month, was "approved in the art of smelting," and received his license to practice. His life course provides a classic instance of an illegitimate who passed as far as he was able, encountered discrimination, reached a critical juncture, and applied for formal legitimation. Equally striking is that he would not have been likely to apply if stricter enforcement of discriminatory ordinances had not challenged his passing.

A series of applications from Mexicans who wanted to be lawyers reinforces the impression that illegitimates encountered increasing restrictions as the century progressed. In 1727 the Mexico City *audiencia* had permitted

Don Joseph Gonzalo de Learegui to practice as a lawyer in spite of his birth.[69] In 1780 Don Joseph Antonio Villanueva y Torres could still attend the royal *colegio* of San Ildefonso to study law, despite a challenge to his credentials.[70] Even though he successfully argued that this institution based its statutes on that of its Madrid counterpart, which admitted *hijos naturales*, the handwriting was on the wall, and he applied for legitimation the next year. By 1814 Don Basilio Joseph Arrillaga found that he could not even begin to study to become a lawyer unless he presented seven baptismal certificates that attested not only to his own legitimacy but also to that of his parents and grandparents.[71]

This general curtailment of occupational mobility was evident throughout the empire. Panamanian Don José Segundo Ibarburu had passed to hold office in the tobacco administration in 1793. He applied for legitimation in 1796 not because he feared local prejudice but because an imperial order of that year decreed that only subjects eligible for "the first employments" should hold royal posts.[72] He worried that his birth might terminate his career.

Illegitimates also found entrance to the priesthood increasingly curtailed. Royal bureaucrats not only intensified their traditional diatribes against clerics who produced offspring but now discriminated particularly against their sons, and generally against any potential religious who was illegitimate. Clerical hopefuls had previously been able to apply for *habilitaciones*, which permitted them to become curates, hold prebends, and achieve upward mobility in the church in spite of their birth. *Habilitaciones* were not as comprehensive as *gracias al sacar*, for they did not provide civil legitimation. Their benefits were confined within ecclesiastical circles. Yet by 1789 royal officials even began to turn down these more restricted exemptions. When Don Melchor de Rivera y Jordán, a lawyer-priest from Charcas, applied for a waiver, royal officials spurned his petition.[73] They charged that fathers of illegitimates "regularly destined" their sons for such religious positions, thereby filling posts that might be held by legitimates with real vocations. The Cámara commanded that local officials "not easily admit to sacred orders those that are not legitimate sons . . . . of legitimate matrimony."

Even more revealing patterns of heightened discrimination emerge from *cédula* petitions that recounted multigenerational family histories. Between 1789 and 1799 a cluster of relatives petitioned to legitimate elderly or even deceased family members whose birth status clouded family genealogies.

These were illegitimates who had successfully passed at the beginning or the middle of the century, so that they had not applied for *cédulas*. Yet at the close of the century their absence of honor prejudiced their legitimate descendants.

An effort to avert social embarrassment motivated a Puerto Príncipe family to admit that one of their ancestors, Don Joseph de Zayas, was the son of a priest.[74] Despite the nature of his birth, Don Joseph had been able to pass in his own time as a person of honor. He both married a woman of "distinguished reputation" and served as captain of the local militia. Nor had Don Joseph's legitimate son, Don Santiago, suffered from his father's illegitimacy, for "he had obtained positions of honor in politics and the military."

It was family concern for the next generation, for Don Santiago's legitimate son, Don Mariano, that led to a petition in 1799. As was common in Cuba militia units, Don Mariano, like his legitimate father and illegitimate grandfather before him, had begun by serving as a cadet.[75] Unlike them, he might face discrimination and be refused promotion because of the stain of his grandfather's birth. Don Santiago and Don Mariano therefore applied so that their ancestor's illegitimacy "would not serve as an impediment to their continuing to enjoy the honors, privileges, and grants" usual to elite families.[76] Left unstated was why Don Mariano encountered this problem, when his father and illegitimate grandfather had not.

The Cámara official who reviewed this petition expressed bewilderment concerning the request. He noted that Don Joseph had held office in the militia even though he was illegitimate, as had his son. The bureaucrat wondered, "Why would [his grandson] need such a dispensation?" Underlying the official's response was the assumption that if the grandfather and father could pass as persons of honor, the grandson should be able to do so as well. The family's answer to this query was inherent in the very fact of the petition itself: The climate in Puerto Príncipe, which had tolerated passing for the son of a priest and for his legitimate son, was no longer as hospitable for his legitimate grandson. If Don Mariano could not document his descent from legitimate ancestors, his career was in jeopardy.

Although family members never stated it directly, the most likely difficulty arose from their inability to document three generations of *limpieza de sangre* and legitimacy. Earlier in the century, such proofs had apparently not been demanded; if they had been, Don Joseph, the son of a priest, would not have qualified. By 1799 rising prejudice against illegitimates had led to greater enforcement of these requirements and so threatened the career of his legitimate grandson.

It is also provocative that Don Joseph did not follow customary procedure and request his own legitimation. Since the Puerto Príncipe archive had burned, the family could not provide his baptismal certificate, and so it is impossible to know how old he was when his son and grandson made their request. The absence of a personal application may mean that Don Joseph was already dead. If so, this case would join three others in which families from Mexico, Peru, and Cuba begged the Cámara in 1789 to legitimate deceased relatives.

Underlying post mortem applications were two interesting assumptions. The first was that elites considered honor to be a commodity that not only passed from one legitimate to another but that could be attached to an individual after death as well. With *gracias al sacar*, the state might effectively reach beyond the grave. The second was that families resorted to this option because they were desperate. They needed to legitimate dead ancestors retroactively because the ancestral "stain" now weighed heavily on their late-eighteenth-century descendants.

Both of these assumptions prompted the plea of Don Ventura Escrivinís, a Mexican, that the Cámara legitimate his "dead wife," Doña Francisca, so that her birth would not prejudice the military career of their sons.[77] Her dramatic early history has appeared earlier. Orphaned when her merchant father died of a fever in Spain and her mother went into premature labor and died after hearing of the death of her fiancé, she was adopted and lovingly raised by a prominent Jalapa family. Doña Francisca had effectively passed as far as she was able when, at the age of twenty-three, she married Don Ventura, who could trace his ancestry back to the seventeenth century and who served as a lieutenant colonel in the militia.

The couple had apparently felt no pressure to legitimate Doña Francisca during her lifetime. It was only decades later that an anxious widower feared for the next generation. Although royal officials provided extensive commentary on this application before they approved it, it is notable that they never considered the fact that Doña Francisca was dead.[78] Instead they noted the "pre-eminence" of Don Ventura and applauded the intentions of his sons to follow a military career.

Familial upward mobility prompted another post mortem petition. Cuban Doña Gabriela Rizo of Santiago wished to clean up the family tree, necessitating the legitimation not only of her dead husband but of his deceased grandfather as well.[79] The family's fortunes were on the increase, perhaps because of Cuba's economic expansion, although Doña Gabriela credited "divine providence," which had "multiplied [the family] possessions." In any case, she and her husband had dedicated a fifth of their fortune to the construction of a church in the barrio of Santa Ephigenía. Although her husband died soon after the work began, Doña Gabriela continued the effort, which totaled the substantial sum of forty thousand pesos, an amount that did not include her yearly donations for maintenance or alms for the poor.

Of course Doña Gabriela had an ulterior motive in her documentation of such laudable public service. She suggested that it provided an excellent reason for the Cámara to restore honor to her dead husband and his dead grandfather. This would preempt any discrimination against her family, so that members would encounter "no obstacles to honorific, political, military, or ecclesiastical offices." The Cámara was so impressed with Doña Gabriela's philanthropy that it issued the legitimations without charge and restored honor to every branch of her family tree.

One issue was left unclear. Had Doña Gabriela's illegitimate husband and her father-in-law so successfully passed in previous decades that they had not needed to apply for a *cédula*? Or had it been only the family's upward mobility that now made its members seek positions of honor? The relative influences of increased discrimination and enhanced socioeconomic mobility are particularly difficult to measure in the dynamic Cuban locale where both variables were no doubt operative.

What is certain is that instances in which families legitimated their dead prove the importance of honor to local elites. Yet it was not only honor that was at stake when petitioners attempted to pass, or when they eventually sought royal intervention. Property was also critical to any maintenance of social hierarchy. The degree to which legitimation might—or might not—influence the passage of wealth from one generation to the next provides the focus for the next chapter.

EIGHT

Adults: The Quest for Family Property

In 1742 Mexican Don Joseph Antonio Mariano Navarro Montes de Oca wrote the Cámara of the Indies and asked to be legitimated, not only "to enjoy the honors and employments of the republic" but also to be "instituted unconditionally and without penalty as the heir of his parents."[1] He understood that he faced an uphill battle, for, as he was the son of a priest, royal officials seldom proved sympathetic. Yet his aspirations were typical; the desire to inherit family wealth consistently motivated applications for *gracias al sacar.*

Just as illegitimacy cut its victims off from the chain of honor that stretched from generation to generation, it also deprived them of family property that passed from one legitimate member to the next. Petitioners such as Don Joseph Mariano often linked these two goals in their applications. Yet discrimination for reasons of inheritance was obviously different from discrimination for reasons of honor. The potential for passing and the etiology of turning-point moments take on distinctive configurations when property was at issue, and legitimation *cédulas* provided uneven relief.

Unlike questions of honor, regarding which historical codes, popular culture, and local practice affected how, or even if, an illegitimate suffered discrimination, prejudice in material issues was unambiguous. An extensive corpus of Spanish law provided formal and enforceable guidelines that regulated the inheritance of property and prejudiced illegitimates.[2] Distinct from honor, such discrimination was uniform. It did not matter if illegitimates were male or female, if they lived in Guanajuato, Tegucigalpa, Havana, or Buenos Aires; if they were a Marqués or a Don; if they wished to inherit in 1700, 1750, or 1810—they were equally subject to the restrictions imposed by Spanish law.[3]

The impact of passing also differed depending on whether the desired mobility was to enhance status or to better one's inheritance. In the case of honor, both the individual and the family benefited from passing. An illegitimate cousin who served on the city council and a half sister who married well not only enhanced their own rank but also reflected favorably on those in the private circle who had supported their passing. In contrast, passing for reasons of property pitted family members against each other. Unlike honor, which could be conceptually stretched to admit favored illegitimates within the social hierarchy, inheritable possessions such as cash, land, mines, animals, or jewels were inelastic. When illegitimates passed to inherit property, they acquired possessions that might have gone to legitimate siblings, cousins, or other kin. Such competition provided obvious grist for intrafamilial conflict. Even when petitioners purchased *cédulas* the ultimate effects differed, for while legitimation always restored honor, Spanish law still restricted inheritance potential.

Given that legal codes clearly prejudiced them, family politics seldom supported them, and *cédulas* rarely helped them, why then did illegitimates either attempt to pass or petition to be legitimated for reasons of property? The collected case histories reveal petitioners engaged in three distinctive strategies: In the first, the issue really was moot; illegitimates sought to obtain honor, given that access to family property was either irrelevant or impossible. The second were instances in which the law was ambiguous or silent, and petitioners applied in expectation that legitimation might better their inheritance. A third category included special pleadings: Petitioners requested preferential clauses that designated them as "exceptions" to law and permitted them to inherit in spite of legal prohibitions. To determine when legitimations could not improve the inheritance potential of petitioners it is first essential to understand when they could.

THE 'GRACIAS AL SACAR' AND INHERITANCE
ACCORDING TO SPANISH LAW

Inheritance did not figure as a goal in many applications because of the personal circumstances of illegitimates. If petitioners did not know the identity of their parents, or if their parents had not recognized them, it was difficult or impossible for them to inherit. For someone like Don Pedro Minjares of Durango, Mexico, who really did not know who his parents were, issues of inheritance were irrelevant; he applied solely for reasons of honor.[4] For others, property issues had been resolved prior to their applications. By the time the sons of Don Francisco de Pro y Colmenares of Lima sought legitimation in 1777, their father had been dead for fifteen years.[5] Legitimations had no effect on an inheritance that had already been distributed.

Although Spanish law discriminated against illegitimates, it also protected them. If illegitimates accepted the legal provisions that detailed what they might and might not inherit, they need never apply for a *cédula*. A myriad of regional medieval laws (*fueros*), which were mostly superseded by the *Siete Partidas* (1256–1265) and especially by the Laws of Toro (1502), combined with other royal legislation concerning inheritance to make up the comprehensive Spanish codes of the *Nueva* (1567) and later the *Novísima Recopilación* (1805).[6] For most purposes the *Nueva Recopilación* embodied the principles of inheritance that guided eighteenth-century practices. Such legal codes demanded that testators follow complex rules concerning proportions as well as kinship when they divided their estates. Since guidelines for the inheritance of legitimate heirs formed the basis against which to gauge the lesser bequests mandated to illegitimates, an understanding of the privileges of the former provides a context in which to measure the prejudices against the latter.

The simplest rules for inheritance applied to the basic nuclear family of parents and legitimate children; it might be summarized as the one-fifth, one-third, "forced heir" rule. One-fifth of an estate could be given freely to anyone, including family, friends, or charitable bequests. The remaining four-fifths, or *legítima*, had to be divided in a prescribed order to "forced heirs" or to a designated list of mandated successors up to a fourth degree of kinship.[7] The first in line were direct descendants, with the priority given to legitimate children. However, this four-fifths did not have to be divided equally, as one-third of this portion, the *mejora*, could be given to a favored child. The remaining four-fifths minus one-third had to be divided equally among all legitimate children.[8]

The calculations became much more complex when parents included illegitimate offspring in their testaments. Prevailing codes regulated such bequests depending upon whether the testator was a father or a mother, whether the inheritor was an *hijo natural* or a bastard, and whether property transferred by testament or through intestate succession.

Fundamental biology underlay the legal differentiation concerning paternal and maternal legacies to illegitimate children. Since males could not be as physically certain about their parentage as females, Spanish law gave them greater leeway whether to recognize or to leave property to illegitimate offspring.[9] When fathers chose to acknowledge such children, legal codes further distinguished between bequests to *hijos naturales* and to bastards.[10] This latter difference was particularly critical, for, as Linda Lewin rightly notes, the indiscriminate use of "illegitimate" as a synonym for "natural child" blurs "a central category in heirship."[11]

The *Nueva Recopilación* permitted fathers to will *hijos naturales* either a maximum of one-fifth or the totality of the inheritance, depending upon the claims of third parties. The presence of legitimate children produced the greater legal restriction, for *hijos naturales* were then limited to that portion of the estate that could be given freely, or to a maximum of one-fifth. The remaining four-fifths belonged to the legitimate children as forced heirs.[12] Spanish law further limited the one-fifth given to *hijos naturales*, for it demanded that executors subtract the costs of *crianza*. Expenditures for food, clothing, and education during infancy and childhood were considered an inheritance that had already been transferred to natural children.[13]

Cédula petitions of *hijos naturales* reflect such inheritance limitations. When Don Manuel Joaquin de Zapiola asked the Cámara to legitimate his natural son, Don Domingo, this Buenos Aires merchant noted that he had four legitimate children, and so Don Domingo could inherit only the fifth upon his death.[14] Since gifts to friends, charitable bequests, and the costs of *crianza* were also subtracted from his fifth, Don Domingo inherited substantially less than his legitimate half brothers and sisters. When his father died he received 8,591 pesos: His legitimate siblings each inherited 15,122 pesos.

Hijos naturales were most likely to inherit when a father had no legitimate children. He could then divide the estate as he chose and bequeath natural children everything, nothing, or anything in between.[15] Such an absence of eligible third parties benefited the *hijos naturales* of Don Francisco Pro; they had received the maximum paternal inheritance fifteen years before they applied for legitimation.[16] Their father had written a will that divided his estate as if his natural children were legitimate. A favored daughter, Rosa, received what was left from one-fifth of the estate after charitable bequests had been subtracted, as well the *mejora*, the one-third subtracted from the remaining four-fifths. The rest was divided equally among all five *hijos naturales*. The Pros' illegitimacy proved less prejudicial, not only because their father lacked legitimate heirs but also because he guaranteed their rights through a written testament.

Paternal inheritances to bastards depended upon their natal status. Unlike *hijos naturales*, who could inherit the entire estate if a father had no legitimate offspring, children resulting from adultery or incest were limited to the one-fifth.[17] The bulk of the inheritance fell to other legitimate relatives, who figured as forced heirs. The 1380 Law of Soria, which formed part of the *Nueva Recopilación*, had been even more harsh concerning legacies to the children of clerics. It specified that such offspring "cannot inherit the possessions of their clerical fathers nor of other relatives on the part of the father."[18]

In certain circumstances, mothers followed the same legal guidelines as fathers concerning the proportions of inheritance that they might will to designated kin. When mothers, like fathers, had legitimate children, these took precedence over illegitimates, who were limited to a maximum of one-fifth. As with fathers, mothers could leave their entire estate to *hijos naturales* in the absence of legitimate offspring. The Law of Soria equally forbade nuns who had had children to pass property to them.[19] Yet the biological certainty of motherhood gave children produced by incest or adultery greater claims to the maternal estate. Unlike fathers, who could never assign such bastards more than one-fifth, mothers without legitimate children or *hijos naturales* could bequeath them everything.[20]

When parents did not write testaments, the inheritance potential of illegitimates became even more uncertain, for they could benefit only if they numbered among the forced heirs. Forced, or necessary, heirs were defined by two linked characteristics: First, they were those relatives that the testator had to favor by law in the designation of heirs to an estate. Second, they stood to inherit in their assigned order if a relative failed to leave a will, and there was an intestate (*ab intestato*) succession. This mandate was so powerful that eighteenth-century jurist Antonio Gómez described such heirs as "those who forcibly [or necessarily] have to receive the goods of the deceased."[21]

An understanding of the phenomenon of forced heirs and of intestate succession is critical to any analysis of the transferral of property from one generation to the next. Although research is lacking, it seems likely that Linda Lewin's observation that colonial Brazilian property transferred more commonly through intestate inheritance than through testaments is also valid for Spanish America.[22] Although elites were more likely than the majority to write wills, intestate succession was common among that group as well. No doubt the large majority of illegitimates in colonial Spanish America inherited parental property according to the guidelines established in intestacy.

Spanish law demanded that parents not exclude legitimate children or grandchildren as forced heirs, so these took first precedence for the four-fifths (*legitima*) of inheritable property. After them came ascendant relatives such as parents, and then collaterals, including sisters, brothers, nephews, and nieces.[23] The biological certainty of kinship permitted *hijos naturales* as well as the offspring of incestuous and adulterous relationships to become the forced heirs of mothers who had no legitimate issue. They could inherit before other blood relatives, even if their mother had not written a will. They were usually not classified as forced heirs beyond their mother and could not succeed as such to the property of grandparents or other relatives.[24]

The extent to which *hijos naturales* were the forced heirs of fathers is one of the black holes of Spanish law. One commentator noted that the issue had been "so debated with such differing opinions by jurists that it has been more confused than clarified."[25] The problem was simple; the answer was complex. Spanish laws provided contradictory guidelines concerning paternal obligations to natural offspring. The earlier *Siete Partidas* had established that if there were no legitimate heirs and the father had died intestate, *hijos naturales* could still succeed (*abintesto*) to one-sixth of the total estate, although they had to divide this inheritance with their mother.[26] The later, and overriding Laws of Toro, however, did not make any explicit reference to the potential inheritance of *hijos naturales* when their father had not left a will, and so the issue was blurred.[27] Furthermore, Spanish legal commentators eroded the rights of *hijos naturales* when they argued that fathers had the option to disinherit them by writing a testament excluding them.[28]

The ultimate result was controversy, for even though *hijos naturales* were not considered to be the forced heirs of fathers, they could under certain conditions inherit a portion of his estate. If their father did not write a testament and did not have legitimate offspring, they could petition, according to the dispositions of the *Partidas*, for the one-sixth portion of his property. However, *hijos naturales* did not meet the definition of forced heirs, for they were not mandated inheritors. The presence of legitimate children nullified their one-sixth automatic inheritance. Their father always had the option—an option he did not have with forced heirs such as legitimate children—to write a will totally excluding them from any inheritance, although he always owed the maintenance attached to *crianza*.

Given such contradictory legal guidelines, what were the possibilities for illegitimates to improve their inheritance with a *gracias al sacar*? Did a civil legitimation automatically convert them into forced heirs who stood first in line to divide their parents' estate with or without a testament?

When parents had legitimate children, the answer was no, given the overriding mandate of Spanish law to safeguard the rights of legitimate generations. The Laws of Toro specifically prohibited giving preference to offspring legitimated by the king over legitimate siblings in matters of inheritance. This restriction generally affected fathers more than mothers, given that men were more likely to have had an affair that produced an *hijo natural* and then (inasmuch as their honor was not damaged by the first liaison) to marry someone else and produce legitimate offspring. When fathers developed close ties to their natural children, the legal restriction that they might leave them but a fifth of their estate could produce much anxiety and guilt.

A case from Peru reveals how one father planned over a period of decades to leave the maximum possible inheritance to his natural son. The situation arose when Dr. Don Antonio de Bedoya, a lawyer in Lima, exchanged a *palabra de casamiento* and engaged in a sexual relationship with Doña Francia de la Fuena, "who was a virgin and with all honor."[29] Although the relationship produced an *hijo natural* named Don Gregorio Antonio, the marriage never took place, and four years after the birth the lawyer married another. Even before this ceremony the father had made provisions for his natural child, to offset the adverse effects of the marriage. He granted his young son a "gift" of two thousand pesos to "make up to him the injury that he might do to him in marrying with another."

In 1792 when his natural son was fourteen, his father applied for his legitimation. Seven years later, when he wrote his testament, Don Antonio recalled that he had particularly asked the Cámara that "my son Gregorio Antonio might inherit from me even if at the time of my death I have other natural or legitimate children." The issue was relevant because Don Antonio now had produced a legitimate son named Don Carlos. Royal officials rejected his request. They legitimated Don Gregorio Antonio for purposes of honor, but cited the Laws of Toro restricting inheritance. Their refusal to make a special exception meant, as Don Antonio later lamented in his testament, that his first son could "be left only the fifth part of my possessions."

Don Antonio's 1799 will went to great lengths to circumvent the limits of the law and reserve additional inheritance for his firstborn. He not only protected the two thousand pesos already in reserve, but he noted as well that he held an additional two thousand pesos that the Señora Marquesa de Corpa had bequeathed his son. The lawyer also made sure that the library "in [his] bedroom" went to his firstborn and was excluded from the calculation of the fifth. This collection, Don Antonio reminded his executors, had "belonged to the Marqués de Corpa, and his widow, the Señora Marquesa, had left it to [his] . . . son Gregorio Antonio."

Although the cost of an *hijo natural*'s education was also subtracted from the fifth, Don Antonio tried to spare his first son this diminution. He commanded that "neither should figure in the calculation of the fifth" the moneys that had "been spent on his degree of doctor in this royal university of San Marcos, for the greatest part of this cost was borne by the Señora Marquesa." Left undetermined was whether the marquesa provided such support out of love and kinship for Don Gregorio Antonio, or whether she functioned as an intermediary for an anxious father who wished to maximize his son's inheritance.

Don Antonio peppered his will with exhortations that his testament not be challenged. The lawyer commanded that, "if there were any doubt" concerning his bequests to Don Gregorio Antonio, particularly as they affected his "other legitimate son, Carlos," he "directly forbade" "even the smallest lawsuit." After pages of provisions and concerns for this first son, for whom he had "the most tender love," Don Antonio's acknowledgment of Don Carlos, as his "only and universal heir," seemed grudging, to say the least.

Would the situation have been different if Don Antonio had legitimated his natural son long before he married and produced legitimate offspring? The answer is again no, for Spanish law protected the interests of even unborn legitimates. The code was clear: If an illegitimate had been "legitimated to inherit the goods of his father or mother or his grandparents" and any of these subsequently had legitimate heirs, "the legitimated party cannot succeed with those . . . of legitimate ancestry in the possessions of the father or mother."[30] Whenever there were existing or future legitimate children, *gracias al sacar* did not convert the newly legitimated petitioner into a forced heir equally eligible to divide the four-fifths of an estate.

Attempts to override such legal effect prompted a petition by Havana merchant Don Nicolás Frías in 1818, for he had a nine-year-old natural daughter named Doña María.[31] Don Nicolás may have been contemplating matrimony, for he asked not only that Doña María be legitimated but also that she "be able to inherit and enjoy [his] possessions, even if in the future [he] contracts marriage and [has] legitimate offspring." Although royal officials legitimated her, they did so "without any prejudice to the legitimate offspring that you might have as disposed by the twelfth Law of Toro." With rare exceptions, Spanish officials consistently rejected attempts by parents or illegitimates to improve their inheritance at the expense of existing or future legitimate siblings. With or without a testament, legitimate children and those legitimated by subsequent matrimony had exclusive claims to the bulk of the parental estate.

But what would have happened if Don Nicolás had decided not to marry? Would Doña María, then legitimated by *gracias al sacar*, have had any superior rights to her father's property? The answer would depend upon circumstances. It could be yes, because she might benefit from civil legitimation if her father died intestate. Then, as his sole legitimate descendant, she would become a forced heir eligible for four-fifths of the estate. Yet the answer could also be no, for Doña María would not benefit to any larger extent than if her father had chosen to write a will in the first place. Her legitimation could not better her access to her father's property if he eventually had a legitimate heir, and he could easily leave her everything in a will if he did not.[32]

If Don Nicolás had legitimated Doña María and then married, had legitimate children, and died intestate, her situation would have been murky, to say the least. Doña María would not have figured as a forced heir, for that would prejudice the claims of offspring born in legitimate matrimony. Nor could she claim the one-sixth inheritance, since there were legitimate heirs. Even though she was now legitimate, if her father did not take care to write a will that gave her the maximum one-fifth of his estate, she might have no claim to his property. Presumably a father who cared sufficiently to bear the cost of the legitimation of his daughter would be equally ready to write a testament to favor her inheritance as far as the law allowed.

If inheritance were the sole reason for the legitimation of Doña María, it would have been much less expensive, time-consuming, and secure for Don Nicolás simply to leave her what she was legally due in a testament, rather than purchase a *gracias al sacar*. This is one reason why the issue of inheritance produced few turning-point moments, for the desired results might be easily accomplished when parents left written testaments.

In the case of bastards, the effects of civil legitimation varied depending on whether property descended from the mother or the father. If the mother had legitimate children, the overriding consideration was for those heirs, and the law limited legitimated bastards to a maximum of one-fifth of the estate. Nor did civil legitimation better the potential of offspring resulting from incestuous or adulterous relationships to succeed from mothers when they were their only offspring. If a mother died intestate, the Laws of Toro already recognized the rights of these bastards as forced heirs who could succeed in the absence of a testament.

The law was silent and therefore more controversial on the question of whether civil legitimation might improve the chances of children resulting from incestuous or adulterous relationships to inherit from fathers. The issue revolved around the extent to which a *cédula* prejudiced the rights of third parties to inherit the estate. If a father lacked legitimate descendants, and if his parents were dead, collateral relatives stood next in line to inherit his property. Did civil legitimation make a legitimated bastard a forced heir who could inherit ahead of such relatives? Without clear legal guidance, the legitimation decree itself became the instrument that determined the extent to which property transmission might be altered. Sometimes such *cédulas* were themselves ambiguous, but at other times they explicitly permitted bastards to inherit the paternal property either with or without a testament.

On the surface, Spanish law did not provide much incentive for petitioners to apply for civil legitimations to enhance their inheritance potential. Wills written according to existing legal codes could ensure property transmission from parents to illegitimates with much less expense and with equal certainty. With the possible exception of fathers' legacies to bastards, the purchase of civil legitimation had minimal effect on the lawful transmission of property from one generation to the next.

'GRACIAS AL SACAR' AND AMBIGUOUS
INHERITANCE

While Spanish law stipulated the terms of inheritance in the large majority of illegitimacy cases, there were uncertain areas of the law or particular family circumstances in which succession was ambiguous. These situations were more likely to produce turning-point moments leading illegitimates to seek *cédulas* in the hope that this might either confirm their inheritance or better their position in a possible lawsuit.

The circumstances under which adulterous offspring might inherit from fathers was one of the more common legal ambiguities resolved by legitimation petitions, although royal officials remained firm in their protection of the rights of legitimate offspring. In 1640 when they granted the request of Limeño Alonso Sánchez Chaparro to legitimate a son born of adultery so that he might "inherit all and whatever goods, [and] moveable property," they qualified that the concession could not "prejudice of your legitimate sons and daughters born or procreated by legitimate matrimony, now or in the future."[33]

The determination of royal officials that the legitimation of children born as a result of adultery would not diminish the inheritance of the legitimate sometimes led them to seek intimate information. In Cuba one couple had engaged in an adulterous affair and—even though they eventually married—petitioned so that their bastard son would be permitted to inherit.[34] Before granting their request, royal officials went so far as to write the bishop of Havana with questions concerning the couple's fertility, and presumably their potential to produce legitimate offspring. Learning that the father was "past fifty," that the mother was "thirty-three," and that both enjoyed "good health," officials approved the legitimation, but only with the stipulation that if either party ever produced "legitimate children" their first son's inheritance as a legitimate would be "void." When Don Morejón Trinidad petitioned in 1793 that his two daughters born in adultery be heirs to his estate, he hastened to assure officials that he was not only single but in addition that he lacked any "forced or necessary heirs" who might complicate matters.[35]

Sometimes the ambiguity that prompted petitions was not in the law but rather in the misguided or unreasonable expectations of illegitimates. Several cases seem to have originated from the wishful thinking of illegitimates who believed themselves deprived of their rightful share of family property. They applied for a *cédula* in the mistaken hope that legitimation might tip the legal balance in their favor.

Such was the expectation of Don Eugenio Fernández de Olmedo of Santiago when he petitioned for the legitimation of his wife, Doña María.[36] Her plight has been explored earlier, for she had been raised by her mother and without her father. He had married and died childless, leaving all of his property to his wife and nothing to his natural daughter. When Don Eugenio received his wife's legitimation decree in 1792, he sued, asking that she be declared the sole heir to her father's estate. Given the length of time since her father's death and the freedom of men to decide whether to leave property to *hijos naturales*, the suit was problematic at best, and it received short shrift from the *audiencia*. Don Eugenio, however, was not the only petitioner who fruitlessly hoped that civil legitimation might enhance access to family property.

A similar motivation led Don Manuel de la Trinidad Rodríguez to apply for legitimation.[37] Don Manuel's story about how his father had abandoned both him and his Cuban mother to return home to the Canaries was recounted earlier. When Don Manuel's mother refused to send Don Amaro Rodríguez Pargo their son, the wine trader cut the boy out of his will and left his property to a cousin. In his petition Don Manuel confessed his desperate hope of traveling to the Canaries and challenging his father's will. He even made an unsuccessful attempt to borrow money from royal officials in Havana to help him do so. Just as the officials rejected that request, so they were unsympathetic to a petition based on such unrealistic fantasies.

Another clouded legality that motivated at least one petitioner was the law's silence as to succession if there were several illegitimates in a family only one of whom had been granted a *gracias al sacar*. Don Manuel Coimbra Guzmán tried to augment his own inheritance by using this loophole when he asked both to be legitimated for honor and also to "be able to succeed his parents . . . with the exclusion of [their] other illegitimate children."[38] As might be expected, royal officials were completely unsupportive. They proclaimed that "the sovereign charity of the king" should never produce a result in which "the concession made to one of his vassals should lead to the detriment and diminution of another." They legitimated him for honor, but not specifically for enhancement of any property rights.

Bureaucrats were also unwilling to help illegitimates convert themselves into forced heirs. Habanero Don Joseph Ignacio Valiente was rejected in his attempt to succeed from collateral relatives who possessed "a quantity of goods."[39] Most attempts to use *gracias al sacar* to prejudice the rights of legitimate siblings or relatives met with rejection from the crown. However there were special cases where royal officials made exceptions, and where civil legitimation might alter the legal rights of succession.

INFORMAL EXCEPTIONS TO INHERITANCE LAW

Colonists explored two potential avenues by which to leave more property to illegitimate relatives than was permitted by law. The first were informal mechanisms, such as private arrangements within the family circle to provide for additional inheritance. In effect the family aided the illegitimate to pass and to inherit as a legitimate. If such efforts failed, they might be followed by a formal petition for an extraordinary *gracias al sacar*. These legitimations contained specific clauses that overrode the usual limitations of Spanish law on the subject of illegitimate inheritance. Both tactics corroborate Linda Lewin's caveat that historians not only understand "the law's basic provisions" but also read "nuances of social behavior" to comprehend how "individuals approached the disposition of their patrimony in imaginative, even ingenious ways."[40]

Informal avoidance of inheritance law must have been fairly rare, for it was liable to several pitfalls. Since family property was not expandable, the private circle and especially the immediate family had to cooperate fully in any extralegal partition. If any member challenged a defective testament in court, the law would intervene to deprive the illegitimate of that portion of the estate not permitted by legal codes. If there were evidence of collusion, those involved might find their own property confiscated. Existing wills reveal the customary strategies followed by parents to attempt to leave additional property to illegitimates, while several *cédula* cases originated from belated efforts to remedy such situations when informal stratagems proved unsuccessful.

Embedded within testamentary clauses was a certain ambiguity concerning bequests to illegitimate family members. Perhaps to avoid embarrassment to themselves or to kin, parents often used cryptic phrases or indirect bequests to leave property to out-of-wedlock kin. In most instances parents probably followed legal guidelines, but the vagueness of the phrases could cover illegal bequests as well. For example even though Guanjuato assayer Don Ignacio Martínez de Lejarzar did not name his natural son directly in his testament, he ordered his executors to look "among my papers" where they would find a "memorandum . . . and it is my will that the said clauses . . . be held and estimated as a codicil that they carry out and execute."[41] In a later will he referred again to this special request, and ordered his legitimate sons, who were the executors, to carry out "their literal context without any interpretation" for they were to "have the same force and vigor as if each one was . . . in this my testament."

Yet another father confided that he had given an illegitimate daughter "in life what she needs to sustain herself" and that he planned at his death to leave her "the most that I am able after previous consultation with wise and God-fearing men."[42] This father then wrote a private will—one not open to public view—in which his daughter received additional bequests "through communication with my oldest son after my death." In Chile, Felipe Briceño left his brother, a priest who knew about his natural son, a note to distribute 150 pesos "with the secret motive that I have told you."[43] Such private wills and phraseology could mark family arrangements not necessarily congruent with inheritance law. María Emma Mannarelli notes that it was "relatively common" in seventeenth-century Peru for fathers to give money to third parties to carry out such confidential and sometimes extralegal bequests.[44]

Even more striking evidence that colonials resorted to private communications to bypass inheritance law comes from late colonial Mexico. There a court issued guidelines that specifically noted the existence of such maneuverings. The 1805 directive commented that "many times testators leave private codicils with secret communications, and they are accustomed to add very forceful commands that [these] in no instance are to be manifested or revealed to any judge."[45] The goal of such secrecy was to "frustrate the laws dictated for the public benefit." The new instruction gave judges the authority to compel the executors to "show confidentially . . . if [the testament] is just and according to the laws."

Parents who tried to leave property to illegitimates through intermediaries walked a fine legal line. Eighteenth-century commentator Antonio Gómez noted that such strategies were legal only if the relevant property was left unencumbered.[46] It was illegal, for example, for a priest to leave property to his brother with the written, or even tacit, understanding that this brother would then transmit the inheritance to the priest's son. If these conditions were discovered, the brother was subject not only to confiscation of the inheritance and of his own properties but also deportation. However, if the priest bequeathed the property to his brother without verbal or written restrictions, his brother could then pass it to the cleric's son, for the son could inherit freely from a third party.

In the real world such fine distinctions may not have impeded the use of this tactic. One modern Spanish expert noted that the prohibitions on the transferral of estates to the illegitimate offspring of clerics could usually be bypassed:

> What efficacy did these prohibitions have? Probably hardly any: The experts and those interested dedicated themselves with great success to looking for ways to elude them, and thus they conceived the intermediary . . . an intimate friend, relative, the daughter-in-law, the son-in-law, the grandchildren.[47]

Another strategy employed by parents for leaving additional property to illegitimates was to pretend that they were legitimate. This utilized the distinction between the private and public spheres, for if illegitimates had "passed" in public, they might be able to enjoy that distinction in legal documents as well. In such instances parents sometimes indulged in wishful thinking, hoping that their final testamentary wishes might be carried out even if they contained provisions contrary to law.

Parental failure to face up to the legal consequences of illegitimacy might cost their offspring dearly. Such a case appeared before the Cámara in 1739 when a Havana husband pleaded, not that royal officials legitimate his wife, Doña María Thomasa Florencia, but that they confirm her father's certification of her legitimacy.[48] The situation arose because Doña María's cousins charged that her father, Don Juan de Florencia, had conceived her with Doña Josepha María while the latter was still married to her first husband, Don Martin. Doña María's father eventually married Doña Josepha, but since neither side supplied the relevant dates it is impossible to know whether Doña María was an *hija natural* legitimated by subsequent matrimony or if she remained an *adulterina*.

The potential challenge to Doña María's inheritance must have surfaced prior to Don Juan's death, for her father took the unusual precaution of providing a notarized statement that she was legitimate. When he died, she became his sole heir. Her cousins protested that his testament was invalid, for it wrongly treated a daughter conceived in adultery as if she were an *hija natural* who had been legitimated. If Doña María was an *adulterina*, the will was nullified and her father had legally died intestate. Since the offspring of an adulterous affair could not inherit intestate from a father, the collateral relatives, not coincidentally her cousins, were now the primary heirs.

Doña María faced a difficult dilemma. Royal officials pointed out that if she really was legitimate, she should be able to prove it and inherit accordingly. On the other hand, if she was not, she could not apply for legitimation after the fact and hope to succeed her father. Had her father acknowledged her as an *adulterina* before his death, legitimated her, and established her as his heir, she might have appealed that his will be carried out.

However, if his strategy had been for his daughter informally to pass as legitimate, his tactics failed. At the moment of his death, when his cousins challenged his will, it became void; he thus technically died intestate, and they became his forced heirs. Even if Doña María were then legitimated she could not succeed intestate, as that would prejudice her legitimate cousins, who were lawful successors. Royal officials left any final decision in this case to local courts, which were presumably cognizant of the crucial details of the matter.

What is notable is the very human conflict between a father's desire to leave his estate quietly, if perhaps illegally, to an illegitimate daughter, and the complicating demands of relatives. Although instances must have been rare, it may have been possible for families to keep such arrangements within the private circle and informally permit greater-than-legal inheritances for illegitimate kin. Perhaps in some instances relatives allowed similar false testaments to stand, which always meant that others received less-than-legal inheritances. When such attempts at passing were questioned, however, the legal system favored the challengers.

'GRACIAS AL SACAR' AS FORMAL EXCEPTION TO INHERITANCE LAW

Parents who wished to leave their illegitimate offspring more than was permitted by law had one final alternative. They might formally appeal for a *cédula* that "really" legitimated their offspring, so that there was absolutely no legal discrimination possible in matters of inheritance. Such extraordinary legitimations placed their recipients above the effects of law, for it gave them special privileges denied not only to petitioners but also to the vast majority of Spanish subjects.

The rationale that permitted such requests was grounded upon a Hispanic concept of law that viewed it less as a universal mandate to be enforced impartially than as an entity to which personal exceptions might be made. Since the monarch was above the law, he might suspend it for individuals under certain circumstances. Bureaucrats who exercised authority in his name could make similar dispensations.

In at least one case a royal official explicitly spelled out this principle. The exemption from law was extreme, since the petitioners were the Muñozes, who were the product not only of sacrilege but also of adultery. Even so, the bureaucrat observed that "these requests . . . do not exceed the power of princes."[49] He went on to explain that while bastards could not really be transformed into "natural or legitimate offspring," the king could "concede them all the civil effects that the law provides for legitimate children, given that the[ir] incapacity . . . springs from positive law, and since the prince is superior to that, he can annul it." The extent to which royal officials chose to override legal prescriptions varied according to time and the particulars of the case.

Unusual personal misfortune promoted one petition in which a Buenos Aires mother appealed that her natural son be able to inherit the estate of a father who had died unexpectedly.[50] Doña María Estefanía Peregrino had engaged in "intimate familiarity" with Don Julián María de Lizarazu, a lieutenant in the Lancers. Don Julián had applied for the necessary royal permit to marry but had suddenly died intestate. Since he had no legitimate children, his parents and then his relatives became forced heirs, with his natural son entitled at best to but a sixth of his estate.

Doña María asked the Cámara to change the normal order of succession so that the couple's son "be able to inherit from his father . . . as if he had been born of legitimate marriage." Officials agreed, accepting her evidence that the lieutenant would have married and the child would have been "legitimated if the unhappy death had not occurred." Their unusual response may have been prompted by recognition that it was the state's military regulations that had delayed the marriage and caused the problem in the first place.

Some of the most dramatic exceptions to law occurred when parents asked royal officials to override one of the strongest taboos in the Spanish legal system: the prohibition that illegitimates inherit equally with legitimate siblings. Such situations commonly arose when a man produced an *hijo natural* and then married and fathered legitimate children. These fathers might then petition to be allowed to divide their estate equally between *hijos naturales* and legitimate offspring who were half brothers and sisters. Royal officials universally rejected such petitions. However, there were some rare occasions upon which children were full-blood relatives yet unable to inherit equally from their parents. It was only then that royal officials might contemplate extraordinary legitimations to nullify the usual effects of Spanish law.

Technical cases of incest formed one of the most understandable circumstance in which royal officials were willing to bypass the law. Since both civil and ecclesiastical definitions of incest covered blood relationships within the fourth degree, first cousins required a bishop's dispensation before they married. If such relatives engaged in sexual intercourse and produced a child before permission arrived for the ceremony, their offspring was not legitimated by any subsequent matrimony. When such parents appealed, it was specifically to bypass the law that forbade *incestuosos* to inherit equally with their legitimate full-blood siblings.

Such a situation led both the parents and the husband of Doña Rafaela Espinosa de los Monteros to beg the Cámara to grant her "a perfect legitimation" so that she might inherit equally with her brother and a sister.[51] The family crisis had begun with the courtship of Doña Rafaela's mother, Juana Inés González, who lived in straitened circumstances near the port of Guajira in Venezuela, and who, significantly, never used the prefix Doña. Juana's father was "exceedingly poor," for he supported his family of six with the proceeds from a few fields of corn, yucca, and flowers, as well as the pittance he received from his maintenance of the alarm cannon overlooking the harbor.

Juana's first cousin, Don Antonio Espinosa, later remembered how "because of the frequent communication [they had] had since [childhood]," since they lived only "a short distance from each other," the couple "fell in good and mutual love." Don Antonio promised to marry Juana, and he began gathering the required testimony to send to the bishop in Caracas. In September 1750 he begged the bishop to approve the petition, since Juana lived in an isolated district and "could not find another white person of equal good quality to marry." Her situation was especially onerous given that her "poverty" meant that she was held in "total disregard" by other persons of substance. He, on the other hand, portrayed himself as "young and able" and willing to support her.

Unfortunately, Don Antonio's request for dispensation was not granted, inasmuch as the bishop expired before taking any action. The couple had to wait from September 1750 until April 1753 before his replacement sent the required permission to marry. By that time the couple had an eighteen-month-old daughter named Doña Rafaela, who was technically a product of incest. The pair later testified that they had believed that their subsequent marriage had legitimated their daughter. Her confirmation certificate noted her legitimacy, nor was her birth an issue when Don Salvador Hernández later courted and married her.

Sometime later, however, Doña Rafaela's parents learned that their marriage had not changed her natal status as an *incestuosa*, and consequently she could not inherit equally with her siblings. Doña Rafaela's husband was particularly disturbed and confessed that this revelation "served in not a few occasions as torment." Royal officials seemed especially understanding of the family's misreading of the law. One bureaucrat noted that "even though there is no lack of those who are persuaded that a legitimately contracted marriage has the power to legitimate any previously conceived progeny even if incestuous," the "more common and secure . . . opinion" limited such post hoc legitimations to *hijos naturales*.

Despite their consideration of Doña Rafaela's position, royal officials debated whether they should grant such an extraordinary legitimation. Their hesitation did not derive from any uncertainty that as representatives of the king they had the requisite power, for one official noted, "There is no doubt that . . . monarchs can confer such indulgences and concessions." Rather, royal bureaucrats questioned if they should tamper with the "rights and natural effect of procreation," which demanded that there be equal inheritance only among legitimate offspring. One official pointed out that the parents had produced two legitimate children who were "free and exempt from all infection" and that it would be an "impropriety" to equate them with a "stained and infamous offspring."

The final decision was a compromise. Doña Rafaela received a legitimation that permitted her to inherit equally with her brother and sister in the *legítima*, or the four-fifths of the estate normally reserved to legitimate children. However, her parents were forbidden to leave her any additional legacies. She could not be given the *mejora*, or the one-third of the four-fifths that might be reserved to a favored child, nor could she or her children in-herit the one-fifth of the estate that might be given without restriction. Doña Rafaela was not permitted to inherit any entailed property or benefit from any property left by intestate relatives. Since neither her mother's nor her father's family appeared to possess great wealth, the ultimate effect of such prohibitions was probably not severe; her legitimation may have roughly equalized the inheritance among all siblings.

By the time Don Ambrosio de Sargunzieta applied for a similar dispensa-tion in 1803, royal officials had had more experience with such requests.[52] Unlike the case of Doña Rafaela, Don Ambrosio could not plead ignorance of the law, since he had certainly manipulated it. He already possessed de-grees in both philosophy as well as canon and civil law when he had engaged in a sexual relationship with his future wife, Doña Joaquina, with whom he shared multiple third and fourth degrees of kinship. The couple's son was born in Madrid in 1784. He was the product of an incestuous relationship, although his natal status was not reflected on his baptismal certificate, which falsely proclaimed him to be legitimate. Don Ambrosio later confessed that he had registered his son that way so as to avoid scandal, given that "public opinion [already] held them to be married." The next year the couple re-ceived the required ecclesiastical dispensation, married, and eventually moved to Mexico, where Don Ambrosio enjoyed a distinguished career and their family increased with the addition of two daughters. There seems little doubt that Don Ambrosio knew the legal complications that might ensue if he did not seek an extraordinary legitimation, and in this instance royal of-ficials readily granted his request.

Royal bureaucrats were much more hesitant to intervene when extraordi-nary legitimations involved adultery. Two cases in 1784, one from Venezuela and one from Guatemala, tested their willingness to use the royal power to equalize inheritances among full-blood siblings, some of whom were the product of adulterous relationships and some of whom were legitimate. Such was the situation faced by Doña Margarita González Bosque of Cara-cas.[53] Her story has appeared earlier; her father, Don Bartolomé, had still been married to a Canary Island wife when he fathered Doña Margarita in Venezuela. Even though her parents eventually married, and Doña Mar-garita eventually passed as a legitimated daughter, she remained an *adulte-rina* in the eyes of the law.

Don Bartolomé took advantage of this gap between her private bastardy and her public reputation of legitimacy to write a false will mandating that his property be equally shared among his three children. This was patently illegal, given that Doña Margarita remained legally restricted to one-fifth of his estate. When her husband belatedly discovered his wife's "defect," he sued to secure her inheritance portion. Yet royal officials refused to prejudice the property rights of Doña Margarita's legitimate siblings. Their only concession was to reserve to Doña Margarita's husband a final appeal "before the governor of Caracas concerning the succession of the property."

Another even more complicated case so divided the Cámara that officials debated whether to appeal to the king himself to resolve the impasse. The differing natal statuses of the four offspring of merchant Don Cayetano Yudice formed the core of the problem.[54] Don Cayetano was a Spanish merchant who left his wife in the mother country and lived the rest of his days in Guatemala. There he had a stable and long-term relationship with the unmarried Doña María Dominga de Astorga, and the couple produced four illegitimate children, who were named Don Esteban, Doña María, Don Joseph Miguel, and Doña Mariana. There was no question that the pair's first two children were the products of adultery, as they had been born while Don Cayetano's distant wife was still alive. Their third child, Joseph Miguel, added an interesting twist; he had been conceived when Don Cayetano was still married but born four days after his Spanish wife's death. Don Cayetano and Doña María had a last daughter while he was a widower. Seven years after his wife's death, the merchant married Doña María.

As the end of his life approached, Don Cayetano realized that Spanish law limited his two eldest children to sharing in one-fifth of his estate. In 1782 he applied to the Cámara and asked not only for their legitimation but also that they might be able to inherit equally with their younger siblings. The stakes were not small, for Don Cayetano's active capital as a merchant approached a half-million pesos.

Don Cayetano's petition illustrates his own understanding of the various degrees of illegitimacy as well as his practical awareness of how these differences affected his children. Don Cayetano assumed that the natal status of his two youngest children was that of *hijo natural,* since he had been a widower at the time of their birth. His subsequent marriage to their mother automatically legitimated them and made them full and equal heirs to his estate, so that they need not be included in his petition. He also seemed to understand that extraordinary legitimations were rarely granted, so he stressed his reasons why the Cámara should make a special exception in his case. Describing the major contribution made by his two eldest to the family business, he argued that it would be unjust to deprive them of an inheritance equal to that received by their brother and sister. He begged the Cámara not to divide his family, and to prevent future "discord and quarreling" among the members. Don Cayetano's existing testament also indulged in wishful thinking, for it divided his goods equally among his offspring. The merchant must have known that such partition could be successfully challenged if the Cámara did not grant his petition.

When Don Cayetano's case reached Spain, the Cámara divided, at first seemingly unwilling even to consider the merchant's plea. Bureaucrats did not hesitate because of any moral reservations concerning his adulterous relationship, however, and indeed the merchant's petition had included some apologetic remarks deploring his "blindness and error." Instead, officials were sharply split on the question of precedent versus equity.

Those bureaucrats who argued for precedent rejected the merchant's case and cited traditional chapter and verse: "Those legitimated by the order of the king cannot inherit from their parents [equally] with those who are born legitimate or who are legitimated by subsequent matrimony." Other councilors considered that justice and family harmony should be weighed against the demands of law. The special circumstances that surrounded this case may well have influenced their position. After all, Don Cayetano and Doña María had lived together for twenty-eight years in a stable relationship, and all of the merchant's potential heirs were full-blood brothers and sisters who had grown up together as in any other family.

After an unusually lengthy soul-searching, the Cámara finally arrived at an imaginative compromise reflective of the best efforts of Spain's imperial bureaucracy. In effect, everyone won. The Cámara maintained its resolve that bastards not inherit equally with legitimated offspring. Yet to maintain family harmony, Don Cayetano's two eldest offspring, conceived in adultery, received the same inheritance as their younger brother and sister, *hijos naturales* fully legitimated by subsequent matrimony. How did the Cámara manage such a legal sleight-of-hand? Since the bureaucrats were unwilling to overrule existing precedent and to make *adulterinos* equal heirs, they took the extraordinary step of questioning the natal status of Don Cayetano's two youngest and legitimated offspring.

The merchant's unconventional living arrangements played into the Cámara's hands. The bureaucrats noted that Joseph Miguel, Don Cayetano's third child, was the product of "punishable adulterous copulation," for he had been conceived when the merchant's Spanish wife was still alive. It is notable that the Cámara deliberately skirted the more pertinent issue as to the boy's natal status, no doubt because Don Cayetano was a widower of three days when Don Joseph Miguel was born. Such specious reasoning was carried yet further in the case of Don Cayetano's last child, who had clearly been both conceived and born at a time when the merchant was a widower. Here, the Cámara wondered aloud as to Don Cayetano's intent. Did he know when he had had the sexual relations with Doña María that had produced his last child that his Spanish wife was dead? If he did not know, the Cámara concluded, this daughter was "probably" also the result of tainted intercourse. Thus the Cámara quickly concluded that all Don Cayetano's offspring had some stain, and the officials magnanimously decided to legitimate all of them and make them equal heirs!

This decision was not only patently absurd but also in opposition to the Cámara's usually careful and cautious consideration of the facts of each case. And indeed, there were official voices that expressed the conventional argument that even if Don Cayetano's third child had been conceived in adultery, he had been born as an *hijo natural*. One bureaucrat noted that with Don Cayetano's marriage the child "without any dispute or any doubt . . . was legitimated." The Cámara also deviated from customary practice through omission. It failed to send inquiries to Guatemala to determine exactly when Don Cayetano had discovered that his Spanish wife was dead. In other legitimation cases in which pertinent information was lacking, the Cámara had showed no hesitation in postponing decisions and requesting that the necessary data be sent from the Americas. Here, it appears, members were not particularly interested in the answer.

Even more extraordinary was the Cámara's action in demoting the natal status of Yudice's two younger children. Admittedly this downgrading of their birth took place for but the theoretical instant required to put them on an equivalent level with their elder brother and sister so that all the Yudice offspring could then be fully restored to honor and inheritance. The Yudice family certainly did not question the Cámara's dubious means to this eagerly sought end. Instead, the Guatemalans were so pleased that they went a step further and immediately re-petitioned the Cámara to declare them nobles as well![55]

The question arises as to why the Cámara ruled differently in these two cases from the same year. While these petitioners shared the same goal—to permit siblings who were *adulterino* and legitimate to inherit equally—there were some important differences. In Venezuela, not only had a father written a false will, illegally dividing his estate, but, in addition, he was already dead at the time of the petition. With his death his will became void, and his legitimate children succeeded intestate to the four-fifths of his estate. State intervention to change this proportion after death would have been especially intrusive. This may explain why royal officials refused to equalize the property distribution, although they left open the option of further tinkering by local officials.

In contrast, even though Don Cayetano Yudice had also written a will that would have been illegal when he died, he was still alive at the time of his petition. He himself could plead the case for an equal division, and, even more important, his property was still his own, so that no one had yet succeeded either legally or illegally. Inasmuch as intrusion at this point did not take away property already partitioned to forced heirs, the Cámara may have been more willing to intervene.

In both the Venezuelan and Guatemalan cases, the Cámara rejected the simple and obvious solution. Each petition originally asked the Cámara to legitimate offspring conceived in adultery, to make them equal with their siblings. Even though the Cámara recognized its power to make such exceptions to law, royal officials consistently rejected such opportunities, proving themselves scrupulous protectors of the inheritance rights of legitimate offspring.

The zeal of royal officials to safeguard the property rights of legitimates may have indirectly abetted successful outcomes in a final category of extraordinary legitimations, those in which petitioners requested permission to inherit from their clerical fathers. Since the fourteenth-century Law of Soria specifically forbade such transferral, such offspring could formally inherit only by means of a special *gracias al sacar*.[56] Although the offspring of priests faced more than the usual difficulty in securing legitimation, they did have one unusual variable in their favor: Few men who became priests ever fathered legitimate children. One royal official even rationalized his support for the legitimation of the child of a priest with the comment that when petitioners lacked "legitimate siblings," legitimation "cause[d] no one any damage."[57]

Technically that was not strictly accurate, for the prohibition against inheritance by the offspring of clerics meant that the relatives rather than the children became forced heirs. The official went on to note, however, that since priests had the liberty to write testaments that left their personal property to whomever they chose, relatives might be disinherited in any case. The legitimation of a cleric's offspring posed no additional privation to more distant kin, who never had had any guarantee of inheriting.

When the offspring of clerics applied, they usually asked for legitimation for honors and inheritance. One Mexican petitioner followed the usual formula when he asked to be "purified from this stain" and to be transformed "as if he had been procreated and born from legitimate matrimony," so that he might inherit "without penalty or any embarrassment."[58] But as the eighteenth century progressed, such potential heirs were less likely to receive good news from the Cámara. Offspring of priests found it difficult even to be legitimated for purposes of honor, for royal bureaucrats classified their birth as "odious," being the product of "damnable and punishable copulation."[59]

Although illegitimates applied for *gracias al sacar* both to restore honor and to acquire property, the former petitions proved more efficacious than the latter. Royal officials steadfastly defended the rights of legitimate offspring and of forced heirs. Every inheritance right guaranteed to illegitimates in Spanish law could be more easily secured by a written testament, and need not be confirmed with a *gracias al sacar*. If the law did not support the transmission of property, parents might make informal, although risky, arrangements for inheritance. They might also try to convince royal officials to bypass the law and to make an exception in their favor—but with rare success.

The very inability of civil legitimations to secure inheritance illustrates— if in a backhanded way—that honor remained fundamental to the mentality of eighteenth-century elites. It constituted the primary reason that illegitimates sent their applications to the Cámara. As more and more did so in the last decades of the eighteenth century, a new dynamic entered the equation. Unlike their predecessors at the beginning and middle of the century, generations of royal bureaucrats who had lived in the Americas and who were committed to reform now staffed the Cámara. The next chapters peer over their shoulders in an attempt to understand how their collective decisions charted new directions for *gracias al sacar*, placed it within the broader scope of Bourbon social reforms, and altered state policies concerning sexuality, illegitimacy, and the family.

PART THREE

The State's Response

NINE

Royal Officials: Prelude (1717–1760) and Early Policy Formation (1761–1775)

In a compelling synthesis that detailed the scope and impact of Bourbon re-forms in the Americas, David Brading still had to admit that "little is known about the administrative revolution which lay behind the new-found vital-ity of the state."[1] While Jacques Barbier has traced the successive Bourbon reorganizations of the eighteenth-century bureaucracy, and Mark Burk-holder has provided profiles of the men who served in the Council and Cá-mara of the Indies, too much remains unknown.[2] Particularly lacking is in-sight into the links between administrative reforms, the reformers, and pol-icy execution. A century of comments and decisions by crown lawyers and Cámara officials who read legitimation petitions provides some understand-ing of that usually hidden process by which Bourbon decrees were—or were not—translated into social policy.

This chapter and the two that follow trace how Cámara officials formed their judgments, which varied over time, concerning which petitioners might be legitimated, both expressing and shaping a Bourbon social agenda. Any attempt to discover coherence within Cámara policy must proceed with sev-eral caveats. It is impossible to pinpoint critical decision makers: A changing coterie of crown attorneys summarized legitimation petitions, suggesting the possible disposition of cases, and almost fifty Cámara officials commented or made judgments throughout the century.[3]

To understand how Cámara officials made decisions it is necessary to try to look into their minds as they evaluated legitimation petitions. *Camarista* changes in policy were not always self-conscious, nor even necessarily consistent. Instead, officials might slightly alter policy or procedure in one case, backtrack in the next, and return to the changed procedure the following time. A crown attorney might propose guidelines in his written comments to the Cámara only to have his suggestion at first rejected but then incorporated sometime later. Only consideration of collective decisions over decades reveals how Cámara officials shaped policy in ways that they themselves may have recognized only years after the fact.

Analysis of Cámara decisions from the "inside out" reveals that officials first gradually, then decisively, took up roles as social gatekeepers. The analogy is apt, for gatekeepers have contradictory responsibilities. Their mandate is to guard what is within, by keeping most people out. Yet gatekeepers also open the door, sometimes letting outsiders in. While the fundamental effect of legitimation policy, indeed of all the Bourbon social reforms, was to practice exclusion and to maintain hierarchy, there were occasions on which the door might swing open and the social and racially mobile might enter. Understanding how Cámara officials evolved roles as gatekeepers through their development of legitimation policy provides insight into that process.

This chapter begins in the 1720s, when few petitions arrived from the Americas and the gate stood open. The Cámara had no rigid standards, and those who "petitioned and *paid*," (between 1717 and 1760) usually received legitimations. But in the 1760s, as Bourbon administrative reforms brought increased efficiency and as officials with American experience served on the Cámara, bureaucrats began to check petitioners' documents at the gate, introducing a period (from 1761 to 1775) of "petition, *prove*, and pay."

The next chapter explores the 1770s and 1780s, when Cámara officials continued to demand detailed evidence and when self-conscious moral overtones began to influence who moved through the gate, in an epoch (from 1776 to 1793) of "petition, prove, *prejudice*, and pay." The third chapter focuses on late-stage Bourbon reforms (1794 to 1820), when there was a disconnect between policy makers and policy administrators. Faced with the radical implications of a 1794 decree on *expósitos,* as well as of the 1795 *gracias al sacar,* Cámara officials relied on their evolved "precedent" to determine whom they permitted through the gate and whom they excluded. The trend throughout the century was for officials gradually to narrow the qualifications of acceptable applicants, even while they approved ever greater numbers who met the designated standards. To understand how this process evolved, it is necessary to return to the early decades of the eighteenth century, when few American illegitimates petitioned the Cámara, at a time when such precedents were still to be made.

PRECEDENTS

Even though legitimations were a hallowed Spanish tradition, the eighteenth-century Cámara of the Indies had to develop its own policies concerning who should receive a *cédula* and what they should pay. This is somewhat surprising, given that Spanish monarchs had approved thousands of legitimations in earlier centuries and that the eighteenth-century Cámara of Castile had issued hundreds on the peninsula. Yet in tens of thousands of pages of legitimation petitions, there are only two mentions of this parallel process. One came from a petitioner who had been born in the Canaries but who lived in the Indies and was unsure whether the Cámara of the Indies or that of Castile should attend to his request.[4] The second reference to the Castilian Cámara confirms that Indies officials knew that their peninsular counterparts possessed standardized policies that they lacked, for in 1790 one official commented that there was a 1773 *arancel,* or a regularized list of prices charged by the Castilian Cámara for legitimations.[5] Reference to this price list reveals the extent to which these two Cámaras operated in isolation, given that one had a written price list for legitimations that the other not only lacked but also consciously ignored.

Such procedural disparity raises a fundamental question concerning the state's ultimate objectives for *gracias al sacar.* To what extent did royal officials consider legitimations to be money-raising propositions, or did other social intentions inform their decisions? Understanding why the Cámara of the Indies disregarded peninsular precedents, and how it evolved its own policies, provides some insight into the development of an American agenda for *gracias al sacar.*

Documents in Simancas and Madrid do not detail the cost of Castilian legitimations from the fifteenth through seventeenth centuries, but it is probable that uniform price lists existed before the eighteenth century. The earliest known *arancel* appears in a 1718 notation by the Castilian Cámara de Gracias y Justicia that the price for the legitimation of children of priests was 176 reales *vellón*.[6] The Pragmatic Sanction of 1722 marked a comprehensive effort by the early Bourbons to fix prices for royal *gracias*. The crown authorized a committee to collect information and then set standard charges. The goal was to provide "equity and proportion" and to "correct the abuse" that worked to the "detriment of the public welfare." The first section of the resulting compilation established a range of prices for the Cámaras of Castile and Aragón. Included were the legitimation of *hijos naturales*, priced at 88 reales *vellón*, of "bastards" (presumably of adulterous or incestuous birth), set at 120 reales *vellón*, and of *hijos espúreos*, or priestly offspring, set at 240 reales *vellón*.[7] This sliding scale suggests that the concept that prices should vary according to the natal status of the petitioner was established early.

This 1722 Pragmatic Sanction did not affect solely the Spanish mainland, for several pages after the Castilian list was one for the Indies. Even though the latter *arancel* listed many of the same royal concessions that might be purchased, including titles of nobility, the privilege of citizenship, and the right to found an entail, there was no similar price list for legitimations. This inexplicable oversight contributed to decades of indecision and inconsistency. Such lack of guidance meant that the Cámara of the Indies eventually had to develop its own guidelines concerning who should be legitimated and what they should pay.

The internal documents of the Cámara of the Indies reveal that bureaucrats consistently separated the issues of merit and cost in matters relating to royal concession. First the attorney and the Cámara evaluated the case on its own merit, according to their standards at the time. Only after they approved a petition did the Cámara direct the lawyer to search the archives for precedents, to help suggest the price to be charged. This gap between the Cámara's judgment and its subsequent determination of charges is a strong indication that money-making was not a first priority. In fact it was extremely rare for officials to weigh the merits of a case against its revenue-producing potential. Since money did not motivate decisions, what criteria did guide the officials? Analysis of the changing rationale given in legitimation decisions reveals how Cámara officials established themselves as social gatekeepers and, in the process, evolved state policies toward sexuality, illegitimacy, and the family.

THE OPEN GATE: THE ERA OF "PETITION AND PAY," 1717–1760

The half-century from the Bourbon institutionalization of the application process in the years following 1710 until the 1760s marked Cámara policy at its most limited, most lax, and most tolerant (see Table 12). Only illegitimates from the viceroyalty of New Spain (Mexico) applied during these decades. The crown issued seven *cédulas* that provide minimal information on the lives of the petitioners or the reasons why the Cámara approved. Analysis of the eighteen cases with fuller data suggests that *Camaristas* made little distinction between natal categories, as they invariably legitimated *hijos naturales* and those of sacrilegious birth, as well as those whose circumstances remained undetermined because of scanty information. Even the two *adulterinos* who were rejected had reason for hope. In both instances Cámara officials hinted that reapplication might lead to positive conclusions, much like those granted four other petitioners in similar circumstances. Essentially, anyone who petitioned and paid received a *gracias al sacar*.

Cámara policy in these early decades of the eighteenth century seems closely linked to Spanish practices in the fifteenth and sixteenth centuries, when the crown readily legitimated all categories of illegitimates, restoring both their honor and potential for inheritance. The Cámara's legitimation of those of sacrilegious birth, the most disdained category of bastard, demonstrates that neither moral nor social considerations affected bureaucratic policy. In later years officials would argue that legitimation of priestly offspring set a bad example to other clerics, as well as to the lay population. Yet in this early period *Camaristas* permitted everyone, including the offspring of priests, to "petition and pay."

When an initial series of four cases, in 1743, 1748, 1750, and 1757, arrived from clerical offspring in Mexico, Cámara officials did not refer to earlier policies for guidelines. Instead bureaucrats wavered, then seemed to arrive at their own independent judgment on the first case, which they then used as

TABLE 12
Legitimations from 1717 to 1760

		Cases with Petition and Decision				
Natal Status	*Cédulas* Only	Yes	No	% Yes	% No	N. Cases
Hijo natural	2	6	0	100.0	0.0	8
Adulterino	4	0	2	0.0	100.0	6
Sacrílego	0	4	0	100.0	0.0	4
Incestuoso	0	0	0	0.0	0.0	0
Unknown	1	6	0	100.0	0.0	7
Total	7	16	2	88.8	11.2	25

SOURCE: DB 2-216.

a precedent for subsequent rulings. The first Mexican petitioner, Don Joseph Antonio Mariano Montes de Oca, sent a short letter that provided minimal information, including the admission that his father was a "priest" and that his mother was "unmarried and noble."[8] Although Don Joseph's parents were alive at the time of his petition—he noted that he hoped to be their heir—they did not testify in his favor. Rather, Don Joseph protected their identities, as did the other witnesses who affirmed the truth of his declarations. The only substantive information contained in his petition was his offer to pay the Cámara two hundred pesos if they would accede to his request. At first the Cámara demurred, deciding in August 1742 that "the petition is not granted." However in July of the next year officials inexplicably changed their minds and approved the legitimation.

This success paved the way for additional applications from Mexico. Don Juan Francisco de la Cruz Sarabia applied in 1748, again with minimal proof, for he equally declined to name either his father (a priest) or his unmarried mother.[9] This time the Cámara simply noted that "it had conceded similar *gracias*" and decided that if the petitioner made "some payment to his majesty" it would "agree to this petition." Two years later, when Don Joseph Antonio Gil de Hoyos, another son of "a priest and an unmarried woman," asked for legitimation, the Cámara "agreed to the legitimation . . . following the terms of cited example."[10] When Don Juan Joseph Rueda de Aguirre, son of a Celaya abbot, applied some seven years later, the Cámara's only comment was to approve the legitimation, noting that a similar decree had been given to another in 1748.[11]

In one sense, the offspring of priests formed one of the most egregious forms of illegitimacy, for if the Cámara was willing to legitimate them, officials would be unlikely to refuse anyone else. Such a conclusion may explain why the Cámara also legitimated petitioners whose documentation was so scanty that their natal state could not be determined. Doing so made little difference, even if such opaqueness obscured sacrilege or adultery, given that officials were willing to legitimate the openly acknowledged offspring of priests and adulterers.

The proclivity to legitimate anyone who applied eliminated the need for verifying the natal state of petitioners. As a result, another characteristic of the first forty years of legitimations is the generally meager evidence demanded from applicants. Among the twenty-five petitions during these four decades, only four provided even baptismal certificates. Thus officials could not determine whether petitioners had been baptized as *hijos naturales* or *expósitos*, much less discover the real circumstances surrounding their birth. Cámara officials were accepting and passive. They accepted the word of petitioners at face value, as well as the information they chose to present. They ignored omissions or possible contradictions in testimony, rather than seeking further information or corroboration. Analysis of the questions that officials failed to ask concerning a 1739 case from Mexico demonstrates what information might have been extracted from applications that instead was disregarded.

Compared with those sacrilege cases in which petitioners named neither the father nor mother, nor sent much documentation or witness testimony, the legitimation request of Mexican Don Mariano Joseph de Soria provided, at least on the surface, much more evidence and proof.[12] Don Mariano's petition included his baptismal certificate, which listed him as a "child of unknown parents," and he provided the names of clerics who would testify to his identity. These corroborated his tale of a successful private pregnancy: His mother's identity had been protected for twenty-eight years after Don Mariano's birth. His father, the marquis of Villahermosa, apparently never recognized his son on his baptismal certificate. Yet he must have informally acknowledged him as his *hijo natural*, for Don Mariano noted that this connection was "public and notorious." Royal officials seemed convinced by his testimony; they found "no inconvenience" in granting his legitimation.

Later Cámara officials would probably have rejected it. First of all, it failed to prove paternity; his case rested essentially on his own word concerning his father's identity. Admittedly there was circumstantial evidence in his favor: The testifying priests noted that his father had cared for him, and he did use the family surname of Soria. However such informal or unofficial recognition did not establish unquestionable proof of paternity, for illegitimate relatives or adoptive children often received similar attentions. Since Don Mariano's father was still alive, the most certain procedure was for him to confirm the relationship. Yet during this period the Cámara accepted the petitioner's word, rather than demanding more exacting standards of proof.[13] Officials would later demand testimony when fathers were still alive to give it.

Don Mariano's petition also failed to substantiate the marital state of his parents. The only evidence that the marquis was a bachelor was Don Mariano's word that his father recognized him as his "natural son," which implied that both parents were unmarried at the time of his conception or birth. In later years, the Cámara was not so trusting of such self-interested testimony. It also may be possible that someone on the Cámara knew that Don Mariano's father was a bachelor, for the marqués was a prominent figure who had served thirty-five years on the Mexico City *audiencia*. Yet Cámara officials made no mention of such firsthand knowledge, as they would in later cases in subsequent years.[14]

The status of Don Mariano's mother was even less certain, as her private pregnancy concealed her identity as well as any sure knowledge concerning her marital state at the time of her son's birth. Throughout the century concern for protecting female honor usually triumphed over the necessity to corroborate a woman's marital status. Yet embedded in the testimony was a clue that a later Cámara might not have overlooked. One witness noted that the mother "was not named in these decrees because she is married."[15] Later officials almost certainly would have pursued this suggestive hint and at least demanded to know whether Don Mariano's mother was married either before or after his birth, and thus whether he was an *hijo natural* or was of adulterous birth. In this first period, when the Cámara seemed unconcerned about the marital state of the parents and the resulting degree of illegitimacy, it either ignored such information or considered it to be irrelevant.

The Cámara's unwillingness to investigate such particulars was paralleled by its inability to arrive at consistent prices. Of the twenty-five cases from New Spain that appeared before the Cámara, the charges for nineteen can be determined. Price bore as little correlation to the outcome of petitions as did natal status. An *hijo natural* might pay more in the same year than the son of a priest (3,000 reales and 2,000 reales, both in 1741); or more than an *adulterino* (5,000 reales in 1723; 3,750 reales in 1729). When prices are averaged, *hijos naturales* generally paid the least (2,292 reales), followed by those of unknown parentage (2,650 reales), *adulterinos* (2,749 reales), and *sacrílegos* (2,800 reales). Overall, officials collected 51,550 reales during this period (see Table 16 in Chapter 11).[16]

It seems likely that the rarity of petitions contributed to such erratic pricing. Only four cases survive from the 1720s, one from the 1730s, eight from the 1740s, and six from the 1750s. Since *Camaristas* averaged ten- to fifteen-year terms, bureaucrats might encounter relatively few petitions during their service on the Cámara. With the press of other business they may not have felt compelled to develop guidelines.

A lack of consistency was also the result of the Cámara's following a case-by-case procedure to assess cost. After a petition was approved, the crown attorney searched the archive for comparable cases. Sometimes he noted which cases or prices might serve as baselines; at other times he just proposed a price. Bargaining might also occur when illegitimates tried to preempt the process with offers to pay a certain amount, or attempted to negotiate for reduced rates. Most, however, paid the price asked.[17] Some colonists used *apoderados*, or legal representatives on the peninsula; others seemed to handle the cases themselves.

From 1720 to 1760 the Cámara opened the gate wide for those few illegitimates who sought royal *gracias*. It proved to be nondiscriminatory regarding natal status, minimalist, passive, and inconsistent. Royal officials seemed ready to restore the honor and the inheritance potential of any petitioner. They accepted scanty documentation and failed to challenge inconsistencies in the information presented to them. The price for legitimation depended upon precedent and negotiation between petitioners and royal officials. Yet this tolerant prelude would change in midcentury as Cámara officials began to forge new policies for *gracias al sacar*.

THE YEARS OF "PETITION, PROVE, AND PAY," 1761–1775

The first decade and a half of Charles III's reign marked a transition from the passivity of the early Cámara. Petitions originated both from the viceroy-

TABLE 13
Legitimations from 1761 to 1775

Natal Status	Cédulas Only	Cases with Petition and Decision				N. Cases
		Yes	No	% Yes	% No	
Hijo natural	0	3	2	60.0	40.0	5
Adulterino	0	0	0	0.0	0.0	0
Sacrílego	0	4	0	100.0	0.0	4
Incestuous	0	1	0	100.0	0.0	1
Unknown	1	2	1	66.6	33.4	4
Total	1	10	3	76.9	23.0	14

SOURCE: DB 2-216.

alties of New Spain and those of Peru, and *Camaristas* issued one *cédula* and resolved thirteen other applications (see Table 13). They approved slightly fewer petitions (76.9 percent, 1761–1775) than in the first period (88.8 percent, 1717–1760). If statistics are the sole guide, bureaucrats continued to award legitimations indiscriminately. But internal documents reveal more negative Cámara comments concerning bastardy than are found at the beginning of the century, although these attitudes were not yet translated into policy or actual rejections.

Statistics are also somewhat misleading concerning Cámara responses to petitions from *hijos naturales* and those of unknown parents, for these received fewer approvals than bastards (60.0 and 66.6 percent, respectively). Yet the notes of royal officials suggest that the rejections of *hijos naturales* stemmed less from their natal status than from their inability to provide proof. This increased demand for documentation was the hallmark of the transitional years from 1761 to 1775, in which officials began to restrict the pool of the eligible for *gracias al sacar*. Exploration of some benchmark cases demonstrates both of these continuities, as well as signaling alterations in Cámara policy.

Of all the legitimations ever granted, those to Don Manuel, Don Sebastián, and Don Francisco Muñoz of Bayamo, Cuba, demanded the greatest latitude, for their father was a priest and their mother a married woman.[18] The dual stain of sacrilege and adultery gave this case a certain notoriety, for later applicants often referred to it, using it as a precedent. They could cite this most egregious case and confidently remind the Cámara that the crown had legitimated petitioners whose birth was far inferior to their own. The case of the three Muñozes additionally serves as a bridge from the first period to the second, for even though the Cubans' application was approved in 1743, their legitimation decrees were not issued until 1766.

The Muñozes' original petition resembled those from the early 1700s; the brothers simply provided baptismal certificates that listed them as of "unknown parentage" and noted that their mother was a married woman and their father a priest. Since they were the sole surviving heirs of their parents, they asked to be legitimated both for honor and for inheritance.

The Cámara's response to the Muñoz brothers' petition also followed the early pattern, for officials seemed predisposed to grant any request. Although the reviewing attorney noted that the Muñozes were the product of "punishable and condemnable intercourse," he added that their legitimation "did not exceed the powers of princes," and the Cámara granted their request. The twenty-three-year delay in issuing their decrees occurred because the British captured the ship carrying the first installment of their payment to Spain. Later exigencies of war combined with personal financial losses by the Muñozes to delay payment until 1765. At this point officials seemed less eager to support their legitimations, but they finally agreed that the issue had been "virtually decided." They did establish a new price, however, which was double the amount charged to *sacrílegos* in previous legitimations.[19]

A similar predisposition not to prejudice children born of sacrilege dominated Cámara thinking on another case from this period, that of Doña Ana de Escurra of Peru.[20] Doña Ana provided little background information, as she did not send her baptismal certificate, nor did she name her father, a cleric, although she did identify her mother. While the official who reviewed this scanty petition condemned the "transgression" of her parents and their "punishable copulation," he did not extend his criticism to the innocent Doña Ana. Instead he spoke of his "compassion" for her "unhappy state," which "she suffered without any guilt on her part," and he recommended her legitimation. Yet even though the Cámara agreed to legitimate her for purposes of honor, it now refused to grant an exception to the law so that she might inherit her father's property.

Elements of these two cases illustrate key continuities as well as alterations of Cámara policy. On the one hand royal approval of both legitimations maintained the centuries-long tradition that the innocent offspring of priests should not suffer from parental misbehavior. On the other, the Cámara made open and derogatory comments concerning such illicit sexual re-

lationships and contemned the children of such unions.. The Cámara's refusal to authorize Doña Ana's inheritance was yet another blow, given that
sacrílegos had customarily been exempted from the Law of Soria and permitted to inherit from their fathers.

The 1761 benchmark that initiated the era of "petition, *prove*, and pay"
refers less to the petitions of the *sacrílegos*, whom the Cámara still legitimated in spite of minimal documentation, than to new standards applied to
other applications. Gradually a new breed of bureaucrats emerged who collected documentation and managed information in a strikingly different
fashion from that of their predecessors. Cámara officials no longer passively
accepted whatever petitioners chose to send them. Instead they actively demanded information and questioned the veracity of testimonies that crossed
their desks. As officials probed beneath the surface, they encountered the
complex persona of their illegitimate petitioners.

Cámara officials found that they had to unravel the differing status made
possible by the private-public duality, and to decide whether an illegitimate's natal or baptismal status would be the basis for their decision. Their
insistence on greater specificity began to alter policy, for officials decided
that illegitimates baptized as *expósitos* and as of unknown parentage would
no longer be eligible for *gracias al sacar*. Yet even while Cámara officials
were narrowing the pool of potential candidates, they still seemed unconcerned as to the ultimate moral, racial, and social impact of their decisions
on communities.

Camaristas no longer just read the documents they received from illegitimates; they began to read between the lines, to pinpoint natal, baptismal,
and social status. Since the desire for a successful outcome naturally encouraged colonists to present the best possible public face, they often blurred or
even deliberately obscured less desirable private realities. Even so, the documents that colonists forwarded to the Cámara often contained a variety of
relevant clues as to incongruities between their private and public spheres.
The more efficient and discerning Cámara officials not only began to inter-
pret these indicators but also to judge by omission and to conclude that
colonists' failure to submit information was obstructionist. Starting in the
1760s bureaucrats began to demand standards of proof and to develop
modes of analysis that they would eventually institutionalize as *gracias al
sacar* procedure.

Don Manuel Trinidad Rodríguez was among the first to confront the altered standards, for this *hijo natural* found officials unwilling to accept his evidence as to the identity of his Canary Island father, as well as to the marital state of his parents.[21] When he applied for legitimation in 1761, he produced his 1722 birth certificate, which listed him as a child of "unknown parentage." However a marginal note dated from 1743 identified both his mother and father, and a number of witnesses corroborated that the couple had lived together and acknowledged Don Manuel as their son. Even so, Cámara officials were unconvinced by this evidence. They expressed "substantive doubts" concerning the parental acknowledgment attached to the baptismal record. They also demanded proof, as opposed to simple statements by witnesses, that both of his parents had been unmarried at the time of his birth. One official lectured that "one can not consider *hijos naturales* as those who allege to be so." Although the Cámara had accepted the word of petitioners before, it now demanded that *hijos naturales* be able to "prove that at the time of their conception or birth their parents would have been able to marry."

The royal officials who now chose to apply a more rigorous standard had some grounds upon which to question Don Manuel's paternity and natal status. Circumstantial evidence suggests that the note on the margin of his baptismal certificate identifying his parents was placed there long after his father had abandoned his mother and sailed away to the Canary Islands, never to return. In that sense it may not have constituted formal paternal acknowledgment. Nor did his father mention Don Manuel in his will, or leave him any of his Canary Island properties when he died. Yet Don Manuel had presented as much proof of paternity and of parental status as had earlier successful petitioners, if not more. The difference was not in his documentation but in the attitude of the Cámara.

Such demand for greater specificity had the most significant impact on applications from those baptized as *expósitos*, or as of "unknown" heritage. Illegitimates who were *hijos naturales* not recognized by their parents, or *adulterinos*, *sacrílegos*, or *incestuosos* were those most likely to have different status in their private and public worlds. Sometimes *expósitos* might have been informally acknowledged or privately raised by their parents, even though they maintained their official baptismal status of "unknown parentage"; others really could not identify their mothers and fathers. Cámara policy now distinguished between these two categories. Officials demanded that those with questionable parentage document their natal status before being granted legitimation. As bureaucrats read between the lines, they implicitly began to distinguish between the contradictory public and private status of petitioners, and explicitly to narrow those instances in which royal leniency would lead to redress.

A first victim of the new policy was Don Sebastián de la Guerra of Guatemala, who originally applied in 1757 to be legitimated to hold the office of public notary.[22] He was turned down two times because the Cámara refused to accept testimony concerning the difference between his private and his public status. While Don Sebastián's natal state remains unclear, his public status derived from his baptismal listing of "unknown parentage." However, as was true in many such cases, his parents were not really unknown, as they had unofficially but informally acknowledged and cared for him. Don Sebastián's documentation reflected these distinct persona; his baptismal record denied any knowledge of his origins, but he could still present witnesses who not only testified that he was "held and reputed to be a Spaniard free of all '*mala raza*'" but who also revealed that they had seen his parents "raise the said Guerra from his young infancy." In previous decades bureaucrats would not have distinguished between this blend of private and public information, and most likely would have granted the legitimation.

Now royal officials refused to approve the petition, specifically because it mixed information on Don Sebastián's private and public states. The crown attorney who reviewed the case noted the contradiction between the baptismal certificate and witness testimony. He presented Don Sebastián with two options. He could resort to his official public status, of being of "unknown parentage." If he did so he could enjoy the traditional benefit of doubt given to such illegitimates, since "those that really and truly are of unknown parents can obtain honorific employments." Alternatively, Don Sebastián could apply for a civil legitimation. However, he would then have to substantiate his natal state and "prove if he is an *hijo natural* [or a] bastard [or of] incestuous, sacrilegious, or adulterous [birth.]"

Don Sebastián's first option, to fall back on his *expósito* status, was chimerical at best, for the honorific employments effectively open to those of unknown parentage were more theoretical than actual. The state seemed unwilling to press for *expósito* mobility into official positions, while local elites everywhere denied them the status of persons of honor. His only effective solution was to apply for civil legitimation.

With this case and others that occurred about the same time, however,

Cámara officials closed the traditional path; bureaucrats were no longer willing to accept statements concerning paternity or natal status that could not be officially documented. The result was that petitioners could no longer blend information from their private and public spheres. Don Sebastián could no longer be "of unknown parentage" and still produce witnesses to testify to the quality and character of his mother and father. The eventual ramification of this bureaucratic reasoning was to deny to *expósitos* and those of unknown parentage the option of official legitimation. Either their parents were really unknown, and they could not prove their parentage and their natal status, or their parents refused to recognize them officially, which had the same ultimate effect because they could still not prove parentage.

This harsh judgment against *expósitos* was somewhat mitigated in the 1760s by the willingness of Cámara officials to experiment with another solution for those who no longer met the evidential standards for *gracias al sacar*. *Camaristas* agreed to issue personal decrees to applicants that confirmed that they were *expósitos* and should enjoy the traditional benefit of the doubt attached to that status. Such a consolation decree was issued to Don Pedro Minjares of Durango, Mexico, who applied not to be legitimated but to be confirmed in his rights as an *expósito*.[23] Even though witness after witness had praised his competence, his charity, his excellence as a merchant, and his acceptance by local society, it was equally clear that he could not document his parentage. A Mexican official suggested that Don Pedro be declared "an *expósito* and of unknown parents and as such he ought to be reputed as legitimate and of legitimate marriage," so that he might obtain the "employments, offices, and dignity that are conferred to noble gentlemen."

Royal officials agreed to this solution and granted Don Pedro a personal decree that said that he could obtain "whatever employments, posts, and honorific offices" that "might be held by any other good and honored man." However, if statutes demanded a candidate prove legitimacy or nobility, he was not eligible, for the only remedy in those instances was "legitimation from your majesty and special *gracias*." As if to underline that the decree issued was not a *gracias al sacar*, officials did not charge him for their services.

Word must have spread in Durango concerning the concession made to Don Pedro, for officials three years later heard from Don Nicolás López Padillo, also from the Guadalajara *audiencia*, who was "disconsolate" because he had been denied a *gracias al sacar*.[24] He had applied for legitimation to become a notary but had been refused because he was an *expósito* and unable to meet the Cámara's new standards. He now asked, in "imitation of the favor given in 1761 to Pedro Minjares, citizen of Durango City," that royal officials grant him the same privileges. The Cámara agreed that he had "revised his petition according to acceptable terms," and they sent the desired certification without charge.

On its face such policy appears contradictory, for what officials seemed to deny *expósitos* in one ruling they mostly returned with another. Yet considered in the context of what would follow, the new policy contained ominous implications. Although the new decree affirmed the traditional prerogatives of *expósitos*, it did nothing to mitigate the equally traditional prejudices against them. The enhanced demands for specificity fell heavily on those of adulterous, sacrilegious, or incestuous birth, who invariably had baptismal certificates that hid both their natal status and their parentage. Although officials still legitimated such applicants, the raised evidentiary standards made it impossible to hide an unfavorable natal status under the less damning rubric of "unknown parentage."

As time passed this new scrupulosity concerning evidence would be combined with growing concerns over the moral implications of legitimation. Cámara officials would go beyond critiques of bastardy or demands for proof of natal status to question whether the adulterous or the sacrilegious should ever be legitimated, since such indulgence might set a bad example. *Expósitos* would eventually fall into a classic Catch-22 situation: If they could not document their bastardy they could not be legitimated; if they proved it they would be denied legitimation on the grounds of immorality. Notable in this period, however, is the continued absence of any sustained expression of moral concern.

Another characteristic of the 1760s and 1770s was the general absence of Cámara interest in the social impact of legitimations on communities. Presumably if *gracias al sacar* were to be effective, local elites had to incorporate the newly legitimated into their midst. During these years the few comments that considered the wider impact of legitimations originated not from *Camaristas* but from the Americas. Colonists, like *Camaristas*, were uninterested in a moral agenda; they were most interested in the social, and especially the racial, implications of legitimations within their tightly knit communities. Local elites sent clear signals to Cámara officials as to whether applicants had already informally passed and deserved legitimation, or whether their petitions should be denied.

Such local intervention may have influenced *Camaristas* to reject the petition of Don Carlos de los Santos, for in 1762 the city council of Buenos Aires wrote to warn them concerning his pretensions and his quest for upward mobility.[25] Don Carlos sought office and social position in the city but feared that the illegitimacy of his mother-in-law, Doña Petronila Peralta, might be an impediment. When he applied for Doña Petronila's legitimation, the city council feared that he would disguise not only the facts surrounding her birth but also her race. Members charged that Don Carlos was trying to "hide and deny the origin of his wife," who, because she was Doña Petronila's daughter, was

> descended from those born as slaves, and it has not been a long time [since her] legitimate grandmother died in this city without ever having taken off her mantilla, which is what servants wear in this place.

Even though a letter from a cabildo was rare, royal officials did not outwardly respond to this local pressure. Although they refused to grant the legitimation, they fell back on all-purpose rationalizations concerning merit and money, deciding that there was "no reason" to legitimate Doña Petronila, since she had failed to show any "merit accomplished by herself, her husband, or her parents," nor had she offered "any monetary payment for the grant." Left unclear was whether a substantial payment for legitimation might have changed the Cámara's mind. Officials pointedly decided to preserve the city council's letter, so that if Don Carlos ever solicited "some honorific office, the report of the cabildo of the city of Buenos Aires could be kept in view."

In another instance local officials clearly conveyed their acquiescence to the legitimation of *pardo* (mulatto) Don Carlos Santos de la Peña of Portobello, Panama.[26] Don Carlos's superiors spoke of his competence and character, and showed that they accepted him as a man of honor in the local community. His superior in the Panamanian bureaucracy, Don Francisco Pérez, noted that Don Carlos was worthy of confidence and intimacy, "for in cases and affairs of the greatest secrecy he is the person whom I value for his observations." He went on to argue that Don Carlos's race and illegitimacy should not be held against him:

> Belying the defect of his color, his influence and actions are as if he had the most elevated birth, such that I have been motivated to treat him as a son, to

love him and to estimate him as such, and he has earned this same acceptance from the Señor Presidente of this city and the ministers of the royal *audiencia*, [and] generally all the town.

Other witnesses took up the refrain when they confirmed that Don Carlos was "esteemed by the gentlemen of this city" and that he was an "honorable man." The Portobello elite made it very clear to the Cámara that Don Carlos had already informally passed both racially and socially, so that his civil legitimation would only confirm, not disturb, the local status quo. Although his case was delayed—he applied in 1748—he eventually received the coveted legitimation in 1761.

During the 1760s and 1770s there were only fourteen petitioners from New Spain or from Peru. Only two prices are extant from the first group, and three from the second. These reveal that the Cámara of the Indies continued to charge in a most unsystematic manner. The daughter of a priest from Peru paid less than an *hijo natural* from Buenos Aires (2,250 reales, as opposed to 4,450 reales). The Muñozes from Cuba, of both sacrilegious and adulterous birth, paid the most (6,666 reales each). Officials collected 36,250 reales from legitimations during this period (see Table 16 in Chapter 11).

Such inconsistency stands in sharp contrast to the Council of Castile, which updated prices during these years. A 1773 price list (*arancel*) standardized the legitimation of an *hijo natural* at 150 ducats (1,650 reales), an *adulterino* at 900 ducats (9,900 reales), and a *sacrílego* at 1,100 ducats (12,100 reales).[27] If price is any indication, the Castilian Cámara was more willing than its Indies counterpart to discriminate against bastards.[28] Although the Castilian and Indies Cámara charged different prices, they seemed to share a new willingness to discriminate against bastardy, a trend that would intensify in the last quarter of the century.

The question naturally arises as to what extent Bourbon administrative reforms contributed to this more diligent and scrupulous Cámara. Tracing any direct cause and effect between reorganization and changes in policy, particularly on moral issues, is difficult. However it is notable that this period (1754) was characterized by change: Ferdinand VI divided the Bourbon ministries, including the Indies, into "distinct units," each with its own head, a division that Jacques Barbier judged to be "inherently more efficient."[29]

While *Camaristas* in the 1750s and 1760s never consciously articulated the ways in which these decades marked a turning point in their analysis of petitions and increased demands for proof, they did seem to be actively seeking guidance. A particularly difficult case in 1762 produced some unusual research: The Cámara decided to search its own archive for *gracias al sacar* precedents.[30] The crown attorneys for Peru and New Spain produced lists of legitimations preserved from earlier centuries. The secretariat of Peru preserved five sixteenth- and one eighteenth-century *cédula*, while the secretariat of New Spain found five from the period from the 1740s through the 1760s.[31] This search for guidance was consistent with the heightened preoccupation of Cámara officials toward accumulating data and shaping policy. This trend would only intensify as the Cámara entered the height of the American reform era, in the 1770s and 1780s.

TEN

Bourbon Reformers: The Activist Cámara, 1776–1793

By 1793 a Cámara official could recite the profile of the perfect candidate for legitimation. Such was Doña María Antonio de Haro of Havana, whose case, the *fiscal* concluded, combined

> all the circumstances that justice requires for legitimation: that is, an offspring born and recognized by unmarried parents with the desire to legitimate her by subsequent marriage, and no prejudice to a third party since they have no other children.[1]

To understand how officials arrived at this end is to trace the evolution in Cámara policy from 1776 to 1793, the most defining period of the American *gracias al sacar*. During these years the number of petitions for legitimation increased dramatically, reaching a peak of fifty-nine in the 1780s and seventy-one in the 1790s. As Cámara officials debated these applications, they continued to define their role as gatekeepers, narrowing the definition of who would be permitted through the door and fully accepted as persons of honor, and who would find the door shut and mobility curtailed.

The 1770s and 1780s also marked a general intensification of Bourbon reform in the Americas. Greater administrative efficiency translated into increased state intrusion into colonial life, which in its most extreme form produced violent reactions such as the Revolt of Tupac Amaru in Peru or the Comuneros in Colombia (1781). Included among the political and economic Bourbon initiatives was an important social reform, the Royal Pragmatic on Marriages (1778), which gave both parents and royal officials the authority to prevent marriages that crossed natal and racial boundaries.

A tempting conclusion immediately emerges. Might the increased applications from illegitimates be a direct response to the Royal Pragmatic? Certainly elite fathers might consider the illegitimacy of a potential daughter- or son-in-law a sufficient reason to petition to end a liaison, and they might expect local officials to support them. Yet despite the timing, the comments of *gracias al sacar* petitioners provide no direct evidence that even one application was directly occasioned by the Royal Pragmatic. In thousands of pages of testimony, some of which was extremely chatty, there is only one mention of this measure, and in an entirely different context.[2]

It seems unimaginable that this royal legislation on marriage partners did not increase elite sensitivity to natal defects and prompt more illegitimates to apply. Yet even when petitioners requested legitimations directly occasioned by their wish to marry, they never mentioned the Pragmatic but always posed their difficulties within traditional references to honor—that the lack of honor hurt their marriage prospects or impeded the social mobility of their children.[3] It may be that the Pragmatic Sanction was just one additional overlay to an already exaggerated and self-conscious defense of honor and hierarchy that characterized the mentality of late colonial elites.

Whatever its effect, the Cámara had to respond to this flood of applications that now poured from the Americas. Its reaction was to maintain and sometimes even to tighten standards of proof. State activism took new forms as officials with decades of American experience used their expertise to solicit more detailed information from petitioners. They not only consciously delayed decisions but also initiated independent investigations, ordering colonial administrators and ecclesiastics to furnish them with background information. Their ultimate goal remained the determination of the natal status of the illegitimate. Those unable or unwilling to divulge the circumstances surrounding their birth received less sympathetic consideration from officials. Yet even while bureaucrats increased their demand for specificity, they were still inconsistent in their treatment of *expósitos*. Only in the subsequent period would the crown issue a royal decree (1794) on the *expósito* issue, which itself would pose even greater challenges to royal officials as they debated how to enforce it.

The most notable change—and the reason why this period might be only somewhat facetiously termed that of "petition, prove, *prejudice*, and pay"— was that Cámara officials began to weigh legitimations on a moral scale. Those whose parents had sinned "too much" in the eyes of the *Camaristas* were less likely to receive a favorable verdict. This discrimination took several forms. Cámara officials commented negatively about the more "odious" forms of bastardy and began to show concern that the legitimation of *adulterinos* and *sacrílegos* might undermine moral standards. By the end of the period, officials wondered if the legitimation of *hijos naturales* might encourage sexual license, and not serve the best interests of the state.

"PETITION, PROVE, PREJUDICE, AND PAY," 1776–93

From 1776 to 1793 the number of applications for legitimations increased dramatically (see Table 14). There were twenty-three cases with final *cédulas* and seventy-three that can be traced from the initiation of the petition to a Cámara decision. While officials approved three of every four requests, that figure masks substantial differences: The success rate varied according to the natal status of the petitioner. Royal officials legitimated the two *incestuosos* who applied. *Hijos naturales*, who made up the greatest number of applicants, were the next most likely to be legitimated, with a success rate of 87 percent. After those were *adulterinos*, with a 75 percent approval rate. Only 33.3 percent of *expósitos* and those "of unknown parentage" received *cédulas*, while none of the *sacrílegos* passed the test.

The "hands on" experience of a growing number of Cámara officials with service in the Americas emerged in the only legitimation case in which politics almost certainly determined the outcome. By the time the fifty-five-year-old Paraguayan Don Joseph Cañete de Antequera requested a decree in 1779, he had already passed to hold numerous offices in Asunción, including those of *alcalde* and *regidor*.[4] The name of Antequera was notorious to Cámara officials, for Don Joseph's father had been a fellow bureaucrat who had been tried and convicted of treason and eventually executed.

TABLE 14
Legitimations from 1776 to 1793

Natal Status	*Cédulas* Only	Yes	No	Unk.	% Yes	% No	% Unk.	N. Cases
		\multicolumn{6}{c}{Cases with Petition and Decision}					
Hijo natural	9	40	4	2	87.0	8.7	4.3	55
Adulterino	0	9	3	0	75.0	25.0	0.0	12
Sacrílego	0	0	2	0	0.0	100.0	0.0	2
Incestuous	0	2	0	0	100.0	0.0	0.0	2
Unknown	8	4	8	0	33.3	66.7	0.0	20
Total	17	55	17	2	74.3	23.0	2.7	91

SOURCE: DB 2-216

James Saeger has skillfully traced the crossfire that the elder Antequera was caught up in when he was sent by the *audiencia* of Charcas to Asunción in 1721 to try to resolve the endemic disputes between the pro- and anti-Jesuitical factions. Governor Antequera became genuinely popular with the locals as he attempted, but eventually failed, to arbitrate the vicious disputes between Jesuits and Franciscans, Jesuits and locals, and the *audiencia* of Charcas and the viceroyalty of Peru. When it became evident that the pro-Jesuitical faction had the upper hand, Antequera's supporters deserted him. His efforts to compromise produced a charge of treason against him and led to his eventual flight in 1724. A questionable trial in Lima resulted in a guilty verdict. Here, too, the local population rallied to his defense. A riot in his favor so accelerated his execution march that soldiers panicked and killed him with bayonets and muskets before he could receive his official punishment, and so he was only belatedly beheaded.[5]

Behind the public controversy lay Governor Antequera's private life in Paraguay, which had included repeated visits to the house of Doña Micaela Sánchez, who had been married but whose union had been annulled. She lived conveniently near a cart factory owned by the governor, and he had combined visits to his business with those to her home. Captain Don Sebastián de Cáceres proved a particularly vivid witness to these visits, for he stood sentry while the governor was inside. The couple's son was born "almost drowned" in November 1724, just six months before events forced the governor to flee the province.[6] Even in the midst of preparations to depart, he sent for his infant son, "in order to see him."

Don Joseph's petition almost fifty years later included proofs of paternity that he had been collecting for more than twenty years. He made no reference to the scandal surrounding his father's name, but Cámara officials made pointed comments; clearly they were very familiar with the case. When one official asked if Don Joseph had sufficiently proven paternity, another noted that "everyone knew" that his father had neither married nor produced legitimate children. Another suggested that the "disgraceful death" of his father as well as the "persecutions" that preceded it might have explained why the governor had not officially recognized his son.

Given the prevailing anti-Jesuit sentiment of Bourbon reformers, culminating in the Jesuit expulsion from the Americas in 1767, the initial indication was that Cámara officials sympathized with the plight of father and son. The lawyer who initially reviewed the petition recommended legitimation. The reputation of the elder Antequera had risen as the fortunes of the Jesuits had fallen. Powerful Pedro Rodríguez Campomanes, the president of the Council of Castile, had written sympathetically of Governor Antequera's plight, portraying him as a victim of the Jesuits, who had subjected him to a "remorseless campaign of defamation."[7]

Yet when the Cámara met, it rejected the application and continued to do so in spite of a series of letters from Paraguay that testified to Don Joseph's service to the king. Cámara officials may well have been of two minds. On the one hand many had served in the Americas, and they certainly understood how a former peer might have been crushed by Jesuit manipulations and whipsawed by the ruthless politics of his age. On the other, such seasoned administrators were equally cognizant of their mandate to uphold royal authority, and so they eventually refused to extend any indulgence to the son of a convicted traitor.

THE QUEST FOR "THE FACTS"

During these years, the Cámara focused most of its attention on the moral issues surrounding illegitimacy and the potential role of the state in shaping orderly behavior. Cámara officials not only began to demand details concerning the lives of petitioners but also to process the data through moral filters and to formulate policies accordingly.

One of the first indications that royal officials were now differentiating between *hijos naturales* and those of adulterous, sacrilegious, and incestuous birth occurred in a 1776 case from Bolivia. The petitioner, Dr. Don Diego de la Rivera, had informally passed as a man of honor, for he had graduated from the royal university in La Paz, was a lawyer accepted for practice at the viceregal court, and had held royal office.[8] In fact his achievements were so impressive that one Cámara official wondered why he needed legitimation, given "that he has the degree of doctor and the title of lawyer of the *audiencia* of La Plata and Lima [and] enjoys as such the prerogatives and essences of [a] noble."

Don Diego took a shortcut in his petition, sending neither his baptismal certificate nor information on the marital state of his parents, essentially conceding that he was a bastard. Although the Cámara official who reviewed his petition might have demanded further information on Don Diego's natal status, his commentary took another direction. He accepted the admission of bastardy and then proceeded to weigh his merit against the defect of his birth. The official conceded that it was "of much greater difficulty [for] *sacrílegos, adulterinos,* or bastards to achieve legitimation . . . than when *hijos naturales* solicit it." He suggested that bastards needed "some particular merit or service" before they should be legitimated; *hijos naturales* had only to provide "relevant proof" to show that their parents "could have been able to marry without impediment or dispensation."

Such commentary confirms a conscious change in Cámara thinking that eventually transformed policy. Officials had always recognized the legal distinctions between *hijos naturales* and bastards, and had always conceded that natural offspring were a less "onerous" form of illegitimacy. But now an official explicitly suggested that the Cámara's approval of petitions should depend upon the category of the illegitimacy. He implied that if *hijos naturales* could prove that their parents had been eligible to marry at the time of their conception or birth, and could pay the fee, they should receive certain legitimation. Those of adulterous, sacrilegious, or incestuous birth, however, had a much heavier burden. Previous Cámaras had suggested that they could no longer hide their natal status under an ambiguous category such as "unknown parentage" and expect to be legitimated. Now they were forced to admit to a despised birth as well as provide evidence that they were deserving before their petition might be granted.

In Don Diego's case, the reviewing lawyer decided that his service to the state had been so extraordinary that he merited legitimation. Yet the Cámara overturned this recommendation and refused to grant a *gracias al sacar.*

While the lack of documentation may have contributed to the decision, discrimination against illegitimates was obviously on the rise.[9]

As the percentage of *Camaristas* with service in the Americas increased, they evaluated the submitted documents with greater sophistication, intensified their demands for evidence, and clearly articulated criteria. In one 1785 case a reviewing lawyer provided an unofficial checklist of the new standards. He noted that petitioner Doña Justa Rufina Borboya had not proved that she was an *hija natural,* for she had not provided a baptismal certificate, nor an "authenticated declaration" of parental recognition, nor evidence that her parents could have married "without dispensation."[10] Although bureaucrats sought similar clarification from all petitioners, they were particularly interested in identifying *hijos naturales,* whom they then readily legitimated.

Even though bureaucrats had now developed guidelines, they remained willing to make exceptions. They eventually did legitimate Doña Justa, for although she had not answered all of their questions, she had presented detailed testimony. *Camaristas* recognized that she had informally passed as a woman of honor, given that she was "married with a subject of importance, and with various children." Gender may also have played a role in Doña Justa's favorable verdict. Although they did not admit it here, bureaucrats would later openly express a preference for legitimating women.

Even though the Cámara legitimated Don Manuel Coimbra y Guzmán in the same year as it did Doña Justa, officials had originally shown him no similar leniency. It had rejected his first application and demanded additional proof, including direct testimony from his parents.[11] The attorney who had reviewed Don Manuel's original application in 1782 noted that his "father and . . . mother . . . are still living, according to what can be deduced from the documentation." He then speculated that it was "strange" that the petitioner had not asked them to provide testimony in his favor, especially "since they live in the same city of Havana [and] it would be very easy to obtain it." Such close and inferential reading of documentation was becoming common, as officials openly expressed skepticism concerning the quality and authenticity of the documentation submitted to them.

Four years later the Cámara rejected the testimony of both the mother's and father's families concerning events that had occurred within their private circle in Lima. The case was an extraordinary one in that both parents had recognized their illegitimate daughter, Doña Josepha, only in private.[12] Years later the family of the now deceased unwed mother, Doña Catalina

Morales de Amarburu, remembered how her identity had been protected. Although Doña Catalina had recognized her illegitimate daughter secretly, family members affirmed that "this was known by no one except [them]selves." Consistent with the fact of her private pregnancy, Doña Catalina did not raise her daughter herself, but first entrusted the baby to a mestiza nurse and then to her sister, who later testified to these events.

The lover and father in this case, Don Joseph Cantoya, had never told his family that he had fathered an illegitimate daughter. Only years later, after Don Joseph had died, did the illegitimate Doña Josepha approach a legitimate half sister, Doña Andrea, and request four thousand pesos, which she said that their mutual father had promised her. Doña Andrea remembered how she had "privately made inquiries and investigations to know the truth." Persuaded that Don Joseph was indeed Doña Josepha's father, she had passed over the money "because it was just, given the obligations she had to her." Yet this conviction on her part, even when combined with corroborating testimony from Doña Josepha's kin, was not sufficient to persuade officials of paternity, and they refused legitimation.

Cámara bureaucrats not only showed mounting skepticism concerning testimony that they would likely have accepted a decade earlier but they also continued to read between the lines and root out information not necessarily favorable to petitioners. When the four offspring of Havana *intendente* Don Nicolás Rapún first applied for legitimation in 1776, they included with their documentation a copy of their father's will, which recognized them and left them property.[13] After his affair with their mother, however, their father had had another illegitimate son by another woman, and his will left that son even more property. Apparently the four applicants felt that any mention of this half brother, whom they resented, would only complicate their own legitimations. When they sent their documents to Spain they did not include the middle portion of the testament, which dealt with their half brother.

The *fiscal* who reviewed their documentation pointedly noted the missing information. He explained his "suspicion in view that the whole testament is not presented, and only the beginning and end of the instruction with insertion of some of its clauses." He suggested that members refuse the application until the Cámara could review the full testament. When they did so, officials remained dissatisfied, since the will revealed the presence of the half brother. Royal officials openly wondered if the *intendente*'s last son had been especially favored because he was a superior category of illegitimate "and had the quality of *natural . . .* which the others lack." They therefore demanded all baptismal certificates, and even initiated their own investigations.

Their first question centered on Doña Antonia and whether she had been unmarried when she gave birth to the *intendente*'s four illegitimate children. One official openly mused that Doña Antonia "had been widowed for some time before she had a child by the *intendente* Rapún, and so it is not impossible that she might have been married to someone else." The *Camaristas* revealed their American experience in their decision to use personal connections to investigate the *intendente*'s status, "since there is no lack in this court of subjects who have been, and lived in Havana and who have had intimate contact with Don Nicolás Joseph Rapún."[14] It was not until 1782 that the Cámara confirmed the unmarried status of both parents and granted the legitimations.

Such close reading of documentation and speculation as to the plausibility of received information became common in the 1770s and 1780s. When *Camaristas* were not satisfied, especially concerning the identity of the parents and their marital state, they now delayed decisions, sending questions back to petitioners with demands that they prove crucial points. Thus petitioners from Lima (Urquizu, 1778), Havana (Pérez Volcán, 1771; Garro Zayas, 1779), Guadalajara (Soto y Cevallos, 1776), and Buenos Aires (Domec, 1783) found their petitions rejected or postponed until they could satisfy the demands of the Cámara.[15]

Many cases ended like that of the Pro family of Lima, who were initially turned down in 1777 because they had neither provided baptismal certificates nor shown that their parents "could have contracted marriage."[16] When in 1780 they remedied these deficiencies, the Cámara readily granted their legitimations. Through such initial rejections and eventual acceptances, the Cámara engaged in a dynamic interaction in which royal bureaucrats instructed petitioners and their legal representatives concerning their changing and enhanced standards of proof.

Several cases hint that not all Cámara officials uniformly supported such strictness. In 1781 although one lawyer negatively reviewed the petition of Don Joseph Ventura Estanislao de la Mar of Lima, others on the Cámara were more willing to accept lesser standards.[17] Compared with that of many petitions, Don Joseph's documentation was fairly complete; he had provided his baptismal certificate, which listed him as an *hijo natural* and named his parents. The reviewing official, however, recommended that the Cámara deny the petition until Don Joseph had also proved that his parents were not closely related and that there was no other "legitimate impediment to contract marriage." A second official who reviewed the documents was much less meticulous, for he noted the practical problems of communication between Lima and Spain in time of war. He suggested that the Cámara forward the legitimation to the *audiencia* of Lima and have it investigate these final points, and, if there were no difficulties, to issue the *gracias al sacar*. The Cámara rejected this alternative and demanded the further proof, which never arrived.

Three years later Cámara papers reflected an even more revealing interplay as bureaucrats debated whether to postpone action on the case of Don Joaquín Cabrejo of Panama.[18] Although Don Joaquín's baptismal certificate had listed him as of "unknown parentage," his mother and father had returned to recognize him officially. The problem was that neither had certified that both were unmarried when they had their affair, which would have made Don Joaquín an *hijo natural*. The Cámara's initial decision was to ask Don Joaquín "to forward evidence concerning the state of liberty of his parents at the time of his birth."

Don Joaquín's *apoderado*, or Spanish legal representative, tried to speed matters up, perhaps because his client was anxiously waiting his cherished promotion to become a judge. He asked the Cámara if it might waive its objection, given the time and effort that the production of the additional documentation would consume. The *fiscal* who reviewed this request recommended that the Cámara agree to do so if Don Joaquín was willing to pay five hundred pesos (seventy-five hundred reales) for the legitimation. He reminded his fellow officials that the operating expenses of the Cámara were "notoriously exhausted," and extra money might be especially welcome. Yet the Cámara refused to go along. It insisted that Don Joaquín produce the proper information, and when he did so charged him two hundred pesos (three thousand reales) for legitimation. The Cámara's decision to insist on proof rather than accept additional payment signaled a determination to maintain rigorous standards even in the face of financial temptation.

Royal officials showed their increased activism both by requesting further information and by initiating investigations of their own. At times they ordered civil and church authorities in the colonies to collect information for them, and sometimes even to investigate possible fraud. The greater famil-

iarity of Cámara officials with the Americas no doubt facilitated their inquiries, since they knew which officials might have access to the information
they sought. Cámara activism also reflected a heightened awareness that legitimations had real impact on families and communities. Unlike previous
periods, when colonists had to take the initiative if they wanted their inclinations or feelings to be known, officials now actively solicited their opinions. Usually the primary concern of bureaucrats was to ensure that a *gracias
al sacar* would not cause controversy or disturb the status quo, yet it was
probably no accident that the first evidence of imperial concern for local
feelings occurred in 1781, contemporaneous with colonial uprisings. The
Peruvian Revolt of Tupac Amaru and the Colombian Revolt of the Comuneros may have reminded Cámara officials of the need to be more consider-
ate of American sensibilities.

A 1781 case from Cuba highlights these many facets of Cámara activism.
Officials questioned the information presented in the petition of Don Fernando Guerra of Havana, investigated his claims, and considered the impact
of his legitimation on third parties.[19] They did so even though Don Fernando had supplied detailed witness testimony concerning his parents' affair, as well as a baptismal certificate that listed him as an *hijo natural* and
named his mother. Yet the reviewing lawyer still proclaimed his "vehement
suspicion," given that Don Fernando's father had not testified in support of
the petition, "because this is the common, the most secure, and the
[method] which produces the best effects." Since Don Fernando had expressed the hope that he might inherit from his father, the official was particularly suspicious about the absence of paternal testimony: "In the thirty
years that have intervened since the birth of Don Fernando until the present, there has been much time to prepare the material."

The Cámara sent a note to the governor of Havana asking him to investigate the circumstances. In response Don Fernando's father sent a personal
letter to the Cámara in which he acknowledged his son and supported his legitimation, although he admitted that other relatives were pressing to be the
primary legatees. Although officials granted the decree, they emphasized
that Don Fernando's father could leave his possessions as he chose.

Even when property was not a consideration, the Cámara increasingly
considered the impact of legitimation on the petitioner's private circle. When
Doña María Josepha de Acosta Riaza of Havana petitioned in 1784, the Cámara refused to act until it heard from her closest relatives.[20] Since she was

the product of a private pregnancy, her father had taken responsibility and introduced her into his own home, where she grew up with his legitimate children. Officials solicited their comments, not to substantiate her birth but rather to discover if they minded if she were to be legitimated.

One Havana notary went from house to house asking Doña María Josepha's relatives if they favored her petition. Her brother-in-law provided a typical response when he said that "all the family" would experience "great pleasure [if] her application was accepted." Her half brother was even more supportive, telling officials that he "treated her as a sister within the household and in public, giving her that place and estimation that her fair talents and circumstances [merit]." He concluded that he would be "pleased" if the king "would give her the grace to which she aspires." Assured of such family support, the Cámara readily granted her petition.

At times Cámara officials sent their colonial counterparts scurrying after even more elusive information, demanding not only facts but also judgments as to whether illegitimates seemed worthy of *gracias al sacar*. In 1780 they asked the Mexican *audiencia* to describe the character of twenty-three-year-old Don Joseph Antonio Villanueva y Torres, a student at the University of San Ildefonso in Mexico City.[21] They approved his petition only when they were assured of his "judicious conduct," his "constant application to the literature," and his "manifest progress." Four years later the Cámara continued to snoop: It asked the bishop of Havana to engage in "delicate inquiries" concerning the ramifications of a case of adultery.[22]

Although Cámara activism no doubt increased the accuracy of the information submitted to it, cases still occurred in which its procedures failed to uncover fraud. In at least two instances the testimony that petitioners sent to Spain contradicts documents in archives in the Americas. It is difficult to know the circumstances behind such examples, but in both instances men named as fathers in legitimation petitions officially denied parentage in their wills. Since these repudiations remained in local repositories and never reached Spain, the two petitioners received their legitimations.

On the surface, the case of forty-five-year-old Don Juan Joseph Bernuy of Lima seemed typical and convincing.[23] In 1789 he provided testimony from family friends, a nurse, and a priest that his parents, Doña María Josepha Vargas and Don Toribio Bernuy, had recognized him and raised him in their home. The couple lived together in a very extended engagement, for young Juan Joseph had already reached the age of ten when his still unwed mother died suddenly of a pain in her side. Witnesses recalled that Don Toribio dressed the boy in mourning after her death, but that the father had eventually entered the priesthood and now served in a parish in La Paz. Since those who testified in 1789 did not refer to Dr. Don Toribio as *difunto*, or dead, they must have presumed that he was still alive at that date. Even so, Cámara officials did not follow what had become their more usual practice and demand that the cleric submit testimony and admit paternity; they simply approved the legitimation.

What these bureaucrats would never know is that a 1783 will in the Lima notarial records casts some doubt on Don Juan Joseph's story, and specifically on Dr. Don Toribio's paternity.[24] In this testament a Dr. Don Toribio Bernuy, canon of the church of La Merced in La Paz, directly denied that he had ever fathered an illegitimate child. In an unusually specific clause for a testament, the cleric insisted "on his priestly oath" that "[he had] never had any natural son whatever." He then, with never a mention of Don Juan Joseph, proceeded to leave money, silver, and jewels to his sister, cousins, and the poor.

An equally suggestive repudiation of paternity occurred in a 1770 will left by Don José de Grijalva of Ecuador, although in later years members of his family contradicted his testimony.[25] Don José was a notorious womanizer who was eventually convicted of murdering his third wife following an orgy of drinking and gambling at their hacienda outside of Quito. Sentenced to exile in Valdivia, Don José wrote his last will the month before he left Quito; he never reached his destination because his mule foundered in a stream en route and he drowned. Don José declared: "I do not have a natural son, that even though [they] are raising a boy named Ramón, he is not mine." Although this rejection seems unequivocal, Don José clouded the issue when he left the boy two hundred pesos, "because he raised him."[26] Given his reputation, Don José's refusal to admit paternity was probably a blessing.

This was not, however, the attitude taken by Don Ramón Grijalva, who, aged nine at his father's death, had grown up to become a royal official in Popayán and to apply for legitimation in 1796.[27] No hint of the scandal attached to his father's name, nor of any testamentary repudiation of paternity, appeared in any of the documents he forwarded to Spain. Don Ramón provided a baptismal certificate that listed him as of "unknown parentage" but included a later attachment naming his parents. Witnesses testified that his mother had become engaged to Don José after his second wife died, and she then became pregnant with Ramón. When marriage failed to ensue and Don José married another, he presented her with two thousand pesos "as a form of recompense," and also "contributed to the maintenance of . . . his son Don Joseph Ramón." Even members of Don José's family testified to the connection; one witness remembered that Don José had left "a short note" to his eldest son to "look on Don José Ramón as a brother," given that he was "born from [my] loins."

Although officials apparently did not know of the scandals that had racked this Quito family a quarter-century before, they did seem suspicious of the testimony. One bureaucrat reflected how "it was very easy to encounter witnesses, especially in these matters, who commonly believe they can shade the truth, because it does not cause any prejudice to anyone, and it favors the [person] who seeks [it]." Although it may have had reservations, the Cámara approved the legitimation.

Left unclear in both of these cases is how such contradictory information should be interpreted. Should such clear denials of paternity be taken as "official" or "public" statements, which still might have hidden another "informal" or "private" reality? Or were these official public rejections real denials of paternity? Either assessment is possible, given the dual world inhabited by colonial Spanish Americans.

DISCRIMINATORY TRENDS AND MORAL OVERTONES

The period from 1776 to 1793 was marked by the Cámara's more rigorous pursuit of "the facts," and its search increasingly took on moral overtones. While royal officials had always distinguished between *hijos naturales* and bastards, they now openly expressed prejudice against the offspring of adulterers and priests, only reluctantly legitimating them. More and more officials demanded that the latter show particular cause why they merited a *gracias al sacar*. The bureaucratic response to petitions from *hijos naturales*, however, was much less discriminatory. Yet internal comments demonstrate that the Cámara increasingly wondered whether the benefits that resulted when *hijos naturales* were legitimated might be negated if the state conveyed the impression that the sexually active and their illegitimate offspring need not pay.

The one exception to the Cámara's changed attitude toward bastards was

its continued legitimation of those conceived as a result of incest. The incest
in these cases, however, was always an ecclesiastical technicality, not that between parents and their children or between siblings. Rather, it encompassed
relationships that fell under the Catholic Church's broad definition of kinship. Usually it involved first or even second cousins, who required ecclesiastical dispensation to marry. The situation of Don Jerónimo Rodríguez
Vanegas of Espíritu Santo, Cuba, was typical, for he was related "in second
and third degree" to Doña Ana Beatris de Castro.[28] His will described how
after they had "celebrated their engagement" he had finally "persuaded her
after repeated arguments to unite with him, from which union resulted the
aforementioned Doña Isabel." When the couple finally received church permission to marry, their daughter was already five years old. Their marriage
could not automatically legitimate her, since she was not classified as an *hija
natural*, given the prohibited degrees of kinship. In this case, as in similar
ones, the Cámara generally treated the petitioners more like *hijos naturales*
than bastards and readily granted the legitimation.

Such leniency contrasted sharply with a series of decisions in which the
Cámara either refused to legitimate, or only reluctantly legitimated, *adulterinos* and *sacrílegos*. In 1787, when the Cámara's insistent requests for more
detailed information finally revealed what Venezuelan Don Joseph Antonio
Betancourt had hoped to conceal—that he was "of adulterous [birth] on the
part of his mother" and therefore of "punishable circumstances according to
the laws"—officials denied his legitimation.[29] When fellow Venezuelan
Doña Juana Figueroa applied the next year, she discovered that even a frank
admission concerning her origin did not help her case, for a bureaucrat concluded that "since she is of adulterous [birth] . . . she needs much more indulgence and favor."[30] In this instance the crown attorney seemed sympathetic and suggested that her "good reputation" might tip the balance in her
favor, but the Cámara refused to legitimate her. Even when they ruled favorably, officials did so reluctantly, and often with denunciations that adultery was a "crime" that was "detestable and punishable."[31]

In a further departure from its earlier attitude, the Cámara now extended
the sins of the parents onto their children. Comparison with an earlier case
suggests the degree to which officials had changed their position. Although
the reviewing lawyer in 1771 had condemned Doña Ana de Escurra's clerical
father for his "punishable copulation," he had also been sympathetic to her
"unhappy state" and cognizant that "she suffered without any guilt on her

part."[32] By 1785 officials condemned the sinners but were no longer as willing to forgive the innocents. Bureaucrats now argued that the state could exert moral and social control by punishing the offspring of adulterers and clerics. In one Havana case the *fiscal* noted that the law discriminated against *adulterinos* so as to "contain" illicit sexual activity. He suggested that the ultimate goal was to make couples "keep the faith that is required in matrimony," and for that reason only a "grave and justifiable motive" should move the Cámara to legitimate *adulterinos*.[33]

Subsequent cases found officials searching for a balance between particular circumstances that might favor *adulterinos* and *sacrílegos* and their more general concern that such legitimations might encourage promiscuity. Precedent was an argument that always impressed bureaucrats, and so petitioners often cited decisions from an earlier time, when the Cámara had been more lenient. The legal representative of Doña Juana Zayas-Saldívar used this tactic with some success in 1791.[34] Even though his client was the product of a double adultery, he reminded officials that they had legitimated others with even more inferior status, and he specifically referred to the Muñozes of Bayamo.

The Cámara's policy had changed greatly in the nearly three decades since the decision on the Muñoz brothers, however. The reviewing lawyer willingly conceded that their birth circumstances were worse than that of Doña Juana. But he went on to express grave reservations, arguing that the state should discourage such legitimations, to "keep men to their duty so that they might cease from committing such excesses so prejudicial to religion and to society." He suggested that if the state refused to legitimate bastards, it might discourage couples from producing them, "not only because of fear of incurring the penalties prescribed against themselves, but also for consideration of not making so unhappy the innocent offspring that proceed from their punishable incontinence."

Although the Cámara now hesitated to legitimate *adulterinos* and *sacrílegos*, bureaucrats still made exceptions to their rules. The reviewer in Doña Juana's case noted several factors in her favor. First of all she had already effectively passed as a woman of honor, and her legitimation would only "honor and qualify a women, who even though of defective origin, already enjoys a reputation as the widow of an officer of the infantry, and so [is already] necessarily distinguished." The lawyer reasoned that legitimation would enable her to maintain her status and make it "easier" for her "to undertake a second matrimony equal to her quality." This, he continued, "would be most useful to the state."

In the most striking departure of all, this official then turned his particular analysis of Doña Juana's situation into an even more sweeping argument. He suggested that the Cámara might generally favor the legitimations of women over those of men. Although Cámara officials may have given some benefit of the doubt to women before this case, this was the first time that a bureaucrat explicitly suggested, and then went on to explain why, the Cámara should actively discriminate in their favor. The core of the argument was that there were fewer "inconveniences and consequences" attached to the legitimation of women than of men. That simple phase encapsulated some of the essential ways that gender differentiated the Hispanic patriarchy. The legitimation of women posed fewer "inconveniences" precisely because it restored the traditional order in which men, rather than women, determined status.

In a series of explanations the *fiscal* articulated some of the generally unspoken assumptions that governed gender relationships. Perhaps he still had Doña Juana's case in mind when he noted that women traditionally take their status, or, using the eighteenth-century word, their "quality," "from the family of the man that they marry." He then added a provocative caveat:

> It *always* follows that his quality and not that of the woman, is that which *generally* decides if his descendants do or do not enjoy the privileges of nobles, and their civil and political [effects]. [italics mine]

This statement is critical because it embodies some unwritten assumptions concerning gender and the transmission of status. On the one hand the *fiscal* asserted that male rather than female "quality" was "always" dominant, a statement certainly compatible with the traditions of patriarchy. Yet the official did not totally validate male supremacy, for he admitted that the father's status could only "generally" determine the "privileges" of the next generation. Men could only "generally" and not "always" ensure status because inheritance of honor, which was the first constituent of elite status, was transmitted both from the father and the mother. The *fiscal* implicitly conceded the duality of this transfer when he noted that illegitimates of "both sexes" passed their defects on to their offspring. This explains why male status could not "always" but only "generally" be determinant, for if a woman lacked honor she also prejudiced the status of her descendants. Earlier chapters have provided examples in which a woman's lack of honor dramatically restricted the office-holding or occupational status of succeeding generations.

Understanding the link between patriarchy and honor explains how the legitimation of a woman worked to restore the status quo. Female illegitimacy disturbed the traditional pattern of patriarchy, in that an elite man married to an illegitimate woman could not be certain that his descendants could hold political office or honorific occupations, given the "stain" inherited from their mother. Once a woman was restored to honor, however, the couple's offspring then followed the norm, deriving their primary status from their father, with no diminution resulting from their mother's illegitimacy. Legitimation of women resolved the conflict between the elite code that governed the transmission of honor and the traditional perquisites of patriarchy.

The case for men was very different, which is why the lawyer concluded that their legitimation "is never comparable." In a patriarchal society in which the status of men was determinant, men "propagate[d] and extend[ed] to all their descendants" the family name and rank. The legitimation of a man brought change. By empowering him and his heirs, legitimation could radically disturb the present and the future status quo. Considered from this perspective, the legitimation of a woman served only to strengthen patriarchy; the legitimation of a man worked to challenge it.

This reasoning seems to have influenced later Cámara decisions. When royal officials balanced the negative and positive effects of the legitimation of *adulterinos*, they commented on the gender variable. In 1793 when Don Juan Antonio Morejón sought legitimation for the two daughters he had fathered with a married woman, royal officials worried about the "bad example" that such a legitimation might provide.[35] The *fiscal* wrote the Cámara of his reluctance to approve this petition, unless the father could show "grave and urgent motives" or pay "a considerable sum." The latter had to be great enough to "show [that] such dispensation of the law would not be easy to secure, and [that it would] serve as a brake so as to prevent such detested disorders, so opposed to the good of the state."

Although the Cámara spoke harshly, it still acted only after consideration of extenuating circumstances. The crown attorney referred to the Saldívar precedent two years before and concluded that the "reason of their sex" favored the *adulterino* Morejón sisters, given the "fewer inconveniences and effects of the dispensation," which was eventually granted. Yet even though

Cámara officials self-consciously announced that they favored female applicants, statistics suggest that women were not disproportionately successful after 1795.[36]

Cámara policy and practice proved more consistent when officials considered petitions from *sacrílegos*. During these years only two cases reached the Cámara, perhaps because applicants rightly suspected that the well-known anticlericalism of Bourbon reformers would lead them to reject the product of priestly incontinence. In sharp contrast to earlier periods, when bureaucrats had legitimated the offspring of priests with little negative comment, both cases demonstrate the lengths to which the state would now go to prejudice the offspring of clerics.

Evidence concerning the 1785 petition of Dr. Don Manuel Borda, a priest, has to be pieced together from various sources, a fact that is significant in its own right, for it suggests that the decision was not made through regular bureaucratic channels.[37] Only a short note from the cleric asking that the Cámara legitimate the two sons he had had by an unmarried woman appears in a *legajo* of issued *cédulas*. The only clue to the Cámara's decision was that its judgment was cited as precedent in the other petition concerning *sacrílegos* from these years, that of Don Melchor and Don Agustín Varea y Lazcano, sons of the dean of the cathedral of La Plata, Bolivia. When Cámara officials reviewed this petition, they commented that they had first denied Dr. Don Manuel de Borda but had eventually agreed to legitimate his sons if he paid the "considerable sum . . . of forty thousand pesos."[38] Such a huge amount (600,000 reales) was presumably consistent with the view that the sexual immorality of priests and the legitimation of *sacrílegos* could be justified only by evidence of great merit or the expenditure of substantial sums of money.

Perhaps even more extraordinary was the fact that Dr. Don Manuel de Borda agreed to pay this minor fortune—the highest sum ever collected for a *gracias al sacar*, and 49 percent of all the money collected for legitimations in the eighteenth century (see Table 16 in Chapter 11). Royal officials may have placed the figure at this prohibitive level because they knew that Don Manuel was among the few in the empire who could afford to pay it. Don Manuel was the sole heir to one of Mexico's notable silver-mining families. His father, Don José de la Borda, once bragged that he had "mined more silver than they have minted in the best year of the Casa de Moneda."[39] One Mexican witness described his priest-son as "one of those miners whose wealth in land and goods could now be worth five hundred thousand pesos."[40] Motivated by his desire to secure the future of the next generation, Don Manuel paid the exorbitant price so that his two sons might inherit his properties. The Borda decision proved the rare exception to the rule that monetary considerations were secondary to other Cámara agendas; officials could only have been swayed by his willingness to pay such a price.

Six years later, in 1791, the Cámara seemed unclear to what degree the Borda judgment should serve as precedent for the Bolivian offspring of the dean of the La Plata cathedral.[41] Citing the Laws of Castile, the crown attorney noted that the offspring of clerics usually had limited inheritance rights from their fathers. He harshly criticized clerics who indulged in "punishable and damnable intercourse," and he was particularly critical of women who "prostitute themselves with priests with the hope that their children would inherit their possessions." He added that church law barred the offspring of priests from holding ecclesiastical offices, in order not to "foment vice." The attorney's censure of priestly sexuality and its inevitable by-products led him to the conclusion that there were very good reasons not to accept the petition.

Even though the lawyer seemed inclined to favor dismissal, he also understood the importance of precedent. He admitted that the Borda decision still served as a precedent, and so he recommended—perhaps facetiously— that if the Bolivians paid "the same quantities" of money he could have "no objection" if the Cámara approved their petition. The prejudice against the legitimation of *sacrílegos* had become so great that the attorney raised the issue of price even before the Cámara had made any decision on the merits of the case. Since the proposed sum was so large, he supported the use of exorbitant cost as yet another deterrent to legitimation of the offspring of clerics. Cámara officials seemed more sympathetic than the *fiscal*, reducing the requested amount from 40,000 to 8,000 pesos (120,000 reales). Perhaps this Bolivian family's influence and service to the state worked in its favor, for Don Melchor's and Don Agustín's immediate relatives included a *visitador*, a governor, the president of an *audiencia*, and an archbishop. The Cámara often took into account such nonmonetary services when they made decisions.

Although the crown attorney and the Cámara had now reached consensus on the Bolivian petition, the case still needed what was usually a pro forma approval from the Ministry of Justice and the king. This proved to be one of those rare instances in which the Cámara was overruled, for its decision was marked with the formulaic "I do not agree to concede this dispensation." The *Camaristas* acquiesced: "We obey that which his majesty commands." Whether Charles IV personally intervened on this occasion, or whether it was someone on the Junta del Estado, or whether the secretary of justice, Antonio Porlier, made the objection, is unclear. The last possibility is intriguing, given that Porlier had served in Bolivia in the *audiencia* of Charcas and would almost certainly have known this powerful family.[42] Whoever made the decision, this rebuke by imperial policy-makers signaled their anticlericalism as well as their approval of the more moralistic tendencies in the Cámara.

The official prejudice against *adulterinos* and *sacrílegos* in the 1770s, '80s, and '90s did not extend to *hijos naturales*; the Cámara approved 87 percent of their petitions. Even though applications multiplied more than fivefold during those years, officials never remarked on such increases but rather continued to focus their discussions on a case-by-case basis. Yet internal comments reveal that *Camaristas* began to discuss why some *hijos naturales* were more worthy than others. Although such preferences did not affect the outcome of cases, these remarks signal the continuing evolution of bureaucratic judgment. Significantly prior to 1795, when the crown published the imperial price list for *gracias al sacar*, officials had already arrived at a clearly defined profile of the ideal candidate for civil legitimation.

The comments of a bureaucrat in a 1785 case from Guatemala show that officials were reading legitimation petitions in ever more nuanced ways. Instead of simply demanding proof of natal status, bureaucrats were now concerned with morality and showed a heightened preoccupation with intent. This official explained that *hijos naturales* should be favored for legitimation because they were "the product of the fragility of young unmarried [persons] who covered their passion with hopes that were generally frustrated."[43] He did not extend consideration for the tribulations of love to other sexual liaisons, which he saw in a more sinister light. He railed against the "premeditated malice" with which married persons or priests became the parents of *adulterinos* and *sacrílegos*. Theirs was not the "weakness" shown by unmarried lovers but rather "malicious and offensive slips" not worthy of royal clemency.

Embedded within official description of the sexual liaisons that produced *hijos naturales* was the development of another bureaucratic agenda concerning *gracias al sacar*. The consideration of variables such as "passion" or of "malicious slips" hinted that bureaucrats were no longer content solely to identify the natal status of petitioners. Rather, officials began to focus on specific circumstances that made some cases of *hijos naturales* more worthy than others.

This continued redefinition of the most acceptable group of candidates led royal officials to contemplate their most bizarre role: that of imperial matchmakers. As bureaucrats reviewed a series of cases from Cuba in the 1790s, they continued to ponder whether legitimations ever served the best interests of the state. Royal officials began to hint that it might be better to encourage unwed parents to marry and automatically legitimate their *hijos naturales* than to rely on civil intervention. Such sentiment reflected their concern that easy legitimation might encourage promiscuity because single lovers could refuse to marry, confident that they could readily purchase dispensation for their illegitimate offspring. Although Cámara officials never went so far as to order estranged couples to reunite, even their tentative musings reflected their understanding that elite marriages underpinned the core of the colonial hierarchy and were to be encouraged in every way. It also signaled, yet again, that money-making was not their first priority.

The first intimation that officials were contemplating a matchmaker role surfaced in a 1790 case from Havana, in which Don Félix Palacios petitioned that the Cámara legitimate his natural daughter, Antonia.[44] Although Don Félix admitted that he had promised matrimony, he now steadfastly refused to marry, and so as part of a settlement he had agreed to support his estranged lover and pay for the legitimation of their daughter. Although confronted with clear proof of paternity, and that Doña Antonia was an *hija natural*, the Cámara legitimated her only reluctantly. The official who reviewed the documents pointed out that both parents were unwed and could still marry and thus provide an automatic legitimation. He declared that marriage was to be "much recommended," and that "in all manners and in all occasions it ought to be encouraged." However, he eventually came to the conclusion that the couple must not have been compatible, and he admitted the necessity of "mutual consent." "Truthfully," he concluded, "one cannot expect good results when the [marriage] ceremony proceeds as the result of pressure and censure."

That same year the Cámara took an even more rigid stance when Captain Don Juan Joseph Díaz of Havana requested legitimation of his sixteen-year-old son, Don Joseph Ramón.[45] The captain, who remained a bachelor, still protected the name of his lover, whom he described only as a "white woman" whose family was "of merit and distinction in Havana." He also admitted that she "was and still is an unmarried woman, able and ready to celebrate matrimony."

The official who reviewed the case expressed his perplexity that the couple had not resolved their dilemma through matrimony, "for the father and mother are unwed, and remain so; they are persons of *limpieza* and honor, and they do not have any impediment to be able to marry." He went on to enumerate plausible reasons why such lovers might not unite. His list included the death of one of the parties, the subsequent marriage of one or the other, or instances of "grave disequality." Since none of these seemed to apply in this case, he wondered "what cause or reason would prevent them from achieving . . . legitimation . . . with a subsequent marriage, which is in their power." He feared that a favorable ruling would only "serve as an inducement to some to commit equal disorder, secure that it would not be difficult to legitimate any offspring that [might] result."

The Cámara agreed, and, consistent with the bureaucratic activism of the time, asked the governor of Havana to investigate and to inform it of what "inconveniences could result from such a matrimony, given that both are unmarried." At this point the case took a dramatic turn, for the Cámara received more than an earful when the governor responded. Royal officials had uncovered perjury and fraud. The captain had lied about the race and status of his lover, who turned out to be the daughter of a slave, and he had falsified the baptismal certificate. The Cámara wrathfully proceeded against him and those who had provided false testimony. What is relevant here is the *fiscal*'s original comments and the Cámara's first judgment. Royal officials had agreed to deny legitimation to an *hijo natural* in the hope that they might force his parents to marry. Such attitudes foreshadowed even more serious attempts by Cámara officials to became matchmakers.

On the surface royal policy toward *expósitos* and those of unknown parentage was inconsistent during the 1780s and early 1790s. Cámara officials denied legitimation to some, granted it to others, and issued alternative decrees guaranteeing *expósito* rights to yet others. Yet underlying such disparities were equally discernible continuities. Officials continued to insist that petitioners not blend private and public information. The heightened moral agenda usually led them to deny the benefit of doubt to *expósitos* who sought *cédulas*, although they might receive the consolation decrees that confirmed their *expósito* status.

During these years royal officials even more openly began to pierce between the private and public information contained in *expósito* petitions and
to insist that one or the other be used as the basis for judgment. When Don
Antonio Morejón applied to legitimate his two daughters in 1793, he had
blended information on their private and public status.[46] He first confessed
that he was their father and that their mother had been a married women,
and he then added that his daughters had been officially entered at the Havana *casa de expósitos.*

The lawyer who reviewed his case noted that as *expósitos* his daughters
ought "to enjoy the concept and reputation as legitimate for those favorable
effects" and to be treated as "adopted daughters of his majesty." The official
questioned, however, whether the girls should enjoy this status in view of the
fact that "the own author of their disgraced luck confesses that they are the
product of adultery on the part of the mother." In this case Cámara officials
decided that the girls' natal status should be the guide. Ironically, Don Antonio's daughters benefited from his disclosure, for it was far better to be legitimated by *gracias al sacar* than to enjoy the dubious privileges granted to
expósitos.[47]

This period saw two telling exceptions to the trend that *expósitos* or those
of unknown parentage not be legitimated without firm information regarding their natal status. Officials granted a *gracias al sacar* to Habanera Doña
Rita Josepha Gonzáles, perhaps because she was a widow and mother who
wrote movingly of her concern for the future of her eight children if she
lacked honor.[48] Doña Josepha's story has appeared elsewhere; her 1785 petition claimed that she learned of the irregularities surrounding her birth only
when her father failed to leave her the usual portions in his will. Although
one bureaucrat ruminated that her petition "offers some doubts concerning
the truth," she nonetheless received a full legitimation.

Fifteen-year-old Doña María Jordánes of Mexico benefited from a similar decision the next year.[49] In this instance officials may have been influenced by the enthusiastic testimony of her adopted family, who attested to
her "frequent [attendance at] the sacraments," her "acts of virtue and religion," and her "valiant spirit in command and management of the household." The assurance by witnesses that she had "white skin" and was obviously free from the "infectious blood of mulatto or other vicious castes" may
also have worked in her favor, as racial considerations were becoming a more
obvious component of *expósito* issues. Although the favoritism demonstrated

in these cases from 1785 and 1786 predated the 1791 decision in which royal officials explicitly discussed the gendered consequences of legitimation, it suggests that officials may have been acting on such distinctions even earlier.

By the 1790s bureaucrats had arrived at a clear picture of those who met the documentary as well as the moral prerequisites for legitimation. The 1791 petition of Don Manuel Antonio Ponce de León met the test, for the official who analyzed it found it to be "most laudable."[50] Not only was Don Manual Antonio's birth status that of "*hijo natural*" but in addition his parents had engaged in a sexual relationship under the promise of matrimony. His parents had had "the intention and hope of making him legitimate." The marriage "could not be carried out" because Don Manuel Antonio's father, a soldier, had perished on an expedition in service to the king. Since the petitioner was an "only child," his father was dead, and his mother was of an "advanced age," Cámara officials could be positive that no one would be injured, especially inasmuch as he had asked to be legitimated only "for the honorific."

Don Manuel Antonio's application, as well as that of Doña María Antonia, which introduced this chapter, fulfilled the overriding concerns of the Cámara. Neither rewarded immorality, since these illegitimacies had resulted from sexual intimacy between engaged, unwed parents who planned to marry. Nor did legitimation threaten the property or status of third parties. Furthermore, the parties could document every salient aspect.

The Cámara remained less consistent about what prices should be charged. Between 1776 and 1793 there were fifty cases in which price could be determined, thirty-three from the viceroyalty of New Spain and seventeen from the viceroyalty of Peru. These demonstrate a continuing irregularity, for an illegitimate who was an *hijo natural* might pay the same as someone who was of adulterous birth (3,000 reales), and even more than a petitioner whose birth status was unknown (1,500 reales). Even though there seemed as many exceptions as rules, certain outlines also emerge. First, pricing continued to differ by viceroyalty. Second, the distinction between *hijos naturales* and bastards widened, as officials wielded cost as a weapon to discourage applications from the latter. Third, applicants showed an even greater willingness to bargain over price. Overall, the Cámara collected 793,849 reales in legitimations during this period, although 600,000 of this had been paid by the affluent Bordas (see Table 16 in Chapter 11).

The price differential between viceroyalties was a natural result of the bureaucratic evaluation process, for each viceroyalty had a crown attorney who searched his respective archive for precedents. Among *hijos naturales*, who received the greatest number of legitimations, petitioners from the kingdoms of Peru tended to pay less than those from New Spain (Mexico and the Caribbean). The price range for the legitimation of *hijos naturales* ranged from a low of 750 reales in both viceroyalties to highs of 4,500 reales in Peru and 7,500 in New Spain. The most consistent charge was in the viceroyalty of New Spain, where eight of the sixteen *hijos naturales* each paid 3,000 reales. However, even here there was no movement toward price consistency, given that some *hijos naturales* paid this sum at the beginning (1780) and others at the end (1792) of the period. On average *hijos naturales* from New Spain paid 2,602 reales for legitimation, while those from Peru paid 2,340 reales.

There was even greater inconsistency in the prices paid by bastards from New Spain and Peru. *Adulterinos* from Peru paid less than those from New Spain, while *incestuosos* and those of "unknown parentage" from New Spain paid less than those from Peru. On average those of adulterous birth paid more than *hijos naturales* (an average of 3,500 reales versus an average of 2,471 reales). The only *sacrílegos* to be legitimated during this period were the two Borda sons, whose 300,000 reales apiece dwarfed the sums paid by other illegitimates and composed almost half (49 percent) of the total amount collected for legitimations between 1717 and 1820. This charge demonstrated the use of price by royal officials to deter, for it was prohibitive by almost any measure. Given the rarity of subsequent applications by priests, it may well have conveyed the Cámara's attitude. *Camaristas* decided to reduce the price in cases of technical incest, however, since the subjects afterward married.

Several related cases just prior to the 1795 fixed price list introduced another factor: petitioner attempts to negotiate to reduce cost. Just as officials and colonists daily bargained for produce or cloth, some engaged in similar haggling over the price of legitimation. Three cases between 1790 and 1793 provide examples and may even be connected. Perhaps an especially savvy legal representative bargained for several applicants, or the petitioners themselves may have decided that such dickering might be effective.

In 1790 Don Domingo Antonio Zapiola of Buenos Aires complained about the price of 500 pesos (7,500 reales) for his *cédula* set by the Cámara.[51] His father had promised to pay for his legitimation but had since died. Because Don Domingo had inherited only a fifth of the estate, he argued that this sum was "extremely onerous," and officials eventually halved his cost. Two years later yet another Buenos Aires resident, Don Joseph Francisco de Larrachea, also negotiated a discount, pleading that he had "no other goods for his maintenance . . . [other] than the savings from the salary paid by his employer."[52] Royal officials gave him a discount to 200 pesos (3,000 reales).

The next year the ubiquitous Don Gabriel Muñoz from Medellín also protested the cost of his legitimation, which had been set at 500 pesos.[53] He noted his "growing number of children" as well as the cost of assembling his application, and rather disingenuously wondered whether "some inadvertent error of copying" might have produced the request for 500, rather than 50, pesos. More to the point was his citation of the Larrachea discount as a precedent for what turned out to be the reduction in the cost of his own legitimation to 50 pesos (750 reales). Such bargaining was about to end, however, for a royal decree in 1795 introduced "fixed prices" for *gracias al sacar*. As the next chapter will demonstrate, this was perhaps the only uncontroversial aspect of that decree, which, along with the 1794 legitimation of *expósitos*, expressed the most radical phase of Bourbon social reform.

ELEVEN

Reform and Retreat: Bourbon Social Policies After 1794

I order . . . that all the *expósitos* of both sexes, present and future . . . that do not have known parents . . . be held as legitimated by my royal authority and legitimated for all civil effects generally and without exception.[1]

Royal decree. Declaring that expositos *be held as legitimate offspring. January 5, 1794.*

For the legitimation of a son to inherit and enjoy or a daughter, when the parents had him [her] when . . . both were unmarried . . . 4,000 [reales]

. . . for extraordinary legitimations to inherit and enjoy . . . to the sons of professed knights of military orders . . . and married . . . and clergy . . . 24,200 [reales]

. . . for other legitimations of the similar class as the above to offspring of unmarried mothers when the fathers are married . . . 19,800 [reales]

. . . for the dispensation of the quality of *Pardo* . . . 500 [reales]. For the dispensation of the quality of *Quinterón* . . . 800 [reales].[2]

Royal Cédula . . . *of the pecuniary charges of the* gracias al sacar, *February 10, 1795.*

A royal decree and a royal *cédula*—one in 1794 and the other in 1795— marked breathtaking alterations in traditional policies toward the illegiti-mate. The 1794 measure officially granted the status of legitimates to *expósi-tos*; a 1795 price list (*arancel*) for *gracias al sacar* permitted *adulterinos* and *sacrílegos* to purchase legitimations and implied that all petitioners could inherit as if they were legitimate. Instead of the existing Cámara policy, which had denied legitimations to *expósitos* who applied for them, the 1794 decree granted a blanket legitimation to everyone of unknown parentage. In place of the Cámara's refusal to legitimate bastards, the 1795 decree encouraged them to purchase *cédulas*. Instead of rarely permitting illegitimates to inherit equally from their parents, it sanctioned such generational transfers. And as if that were not sufficient reform, an addition to the 1795 *gracias al sacar* made it possible for *pardos* and *quinterones* to purchase whiteness.

Both the 1794 and the 1795 decrees seem to have been written by officials who were not members of the Cámara of the Indies, who did not understand its informal policies, and who may have been ignorant of the radical implications of these revisions. The dearth of research on bureaucratic processes at the highest level of Spanish Bourbon reform makes it difficult to pinpoint policy-makers, or to comprehend what imperial agendas produced these alterations. Yet the timing and the preface to the legislation provide some tantalizing clues.

Revenue-enhancement must have been a priority of Bourbon reformers. Generally, the French revolutionary wars were putting excessive demands on the treasury in the 1790s and may have encouraged the search for new sources of income. More specifically, the preface to the 1795 *gracias al sacar* suggested that ministers felt that royal favor was sold too inexpensively. Besides legitimation, one of the other privileges that might be purchased was citizenship, giving foreigners the right to live and trade in the Indies. It was apparently when the price charged in one case was "not proportionate to [its] importance" that the re-evaluation of *gracias al sacar* prices and policies began.[3] Possibly supervising this review was Eugenio de Llaguno, secretary for Gracias y Justicia, who took office in 1794 with little experience with the Indies or "prior involvement" in legitimation policy.[4] He may have supplied the novel direction for the new decrees, even though the introduction to the 1795 *arancel* insisted that its authors had consulted the 1773 written price list "formed by the Cámara of Castile" and considered the "practice observed by [the Cámara] of the Indies."[5]

The resulting charges for legitimations were set at 4,000 reales for *hijos naturales,* 19,800 reales for those of adulterous birth (when the mother was unmarried), and 24,200 reales for worse cases of adultery and for the children of clerics.[6] In 1801 an *arancel* increased these amounts by approximately a fourth (the price for *hijos naturales* rose to 5,500, for *adulterinos* to 25,800, and for *sacrílegos* to 33,000.)[7] To the extent that increased income was a primary goal, the 1795 *gracias al sacar* was consistent with most Bourbon reform. Such was not the case with the *expósito* decree, which had no money-making potential but seems to have been prompted by a sincere concern to improve the state of abandoned infants.

A comparison between these decrees and the day-to-day policies forged during decades of Cámara decisions reveals striking disparity between the letter of the new legislation and previous policy. Officials had to decide how the newly issued decrees should be implemented. Their eventual reliance on precedent, rather than their active enforcement of the new legislation, provides unusual insight into the conflicts within the Spanish bureaucracy over Bourbon social policy. It highlights how upper- and mid-level administrators altered the impact of the law, and, in this case, put the brakes on the more radical of the Bourbon social reforms. The primary focus of this chapter is *gracias al sacar* policy: The first section explores the controversy surrounding the 1795 *arancel*, the next considers the even more revolutionary 1794 policy on *expósitos*. The final two sections first compare key Bourbon social measures and then place them within the wider panorama of eighteenth-century reforms.

THE PRIMACY OF PRECEDENT: CÁMARA RESPONSES TO THE 1795 'GRACIAS AL SACAR'

The royal *cédula* of 1795 was a benchmark in the history of *gracias al sacar*. It introduced new categories such as the purchase of whiteness, which had never before been institutionalized on an imperial level. It redefined which illegitimates might purchase decrees, altered the effects of legitimations in terms of honor and property, and regularized the prices to be charged. Yet when royal officials dealt with individual petitions, the precedents of previous years weighed more heavily than the changes incorporated in the 1795 legislation.

Post-1795 approvals and rejections show that officials continued to favor petitions according to their earlier priorities. They almost invariably endorsed the legitimation of *hijos naturales*, only reluctantly legitimating *adulterinos, sacrílegos,* and those of unknown natal status (see Table 15). Internal comments reveal that Cámara officials relying on precedent deliberately re-

TABLE 15
Legitimations from 1794 to 1820

Natal Status	Cédulas Only	Cases with Petition and Decision				N. Cases
		Yes	No	% Yes	% No	
Hijo natural	24	25	2	92.6	7.4	51
Adulterino	5	2	1	66.6	33.3	8
Sacrílego	0	1	1	50.0	50.0	2
Incestuoso	1	0	0	0.0	0.0	1
Unknown	9	3	3	50.0	50.0	15
Total	39	31	7	81.6	18.4	77

SOURCE: DB 2-216.

jected significant aspects of the 1795 legislation. Even if the king and ministers had wanted to open the gate wider and to encourage greater social and racial mobility, the officials of the Cámara effectively slammed the door on potential entrants.

As Cámara officials began to implement the 1795 decree, major conflicts emerged. Since the Cámara had increasingly discriminated against *sacrílegos* and *adulterinos*, officials had to resolve the disparity between precedent and a *gracias al sacar* that implicitly permitted them to purchase "extraordinary" legitimations.[8] They had to balance their concern that decrees might promote promiscuity against the revenue-making potential of the increased price list. It was unclear to *Camaristas* if the new legislation "really" enhanced an illegitimate's property rights, or whether existing law and practice radically limiting property transmission to the civilly legitimated still prevailed. The resolution of these issues dominated the last decades of the bureaucratic agenda concerning *gracias al sacar*.

It is striking that Cámara bureaucrats who commented on the 1795 *gracias al sacar* manifested ignorance, and even some surprise, concerning its contents. Their discussion of a 1799 case is particularly revealing in this regard, as it involved resolving the disparity between their precedents and the implications of the new legislation. The beginning of this dilemma stretched back to previous decades and the Cámara's growing concern that the legitimation of *hijos naturales* might encourage promiscuity. Although officials had debated whether they should prod unwed parents to marry and automatically legitimate their offspring, they had never actually proposed such a solution to unmarried parents or denied a legitimation decree on those grounds.

In 1799 the Cámara seemed ready to take a more activist role, and to send a strong message that unwed parents should unite. The crown attorney and the Cámara agreed to deny the request of the commanding general of the Algeçiras squadron, Don Bruno Heceta, that they legitimate his eleven-year-old son, Joseph Francisco.[9] Reviewing the particulars of the case, the consulting lawyer noted that the boy's parents were "able to legitimate their offspring with a subsequent marriage, since both remain[ed] unmarried." Nor were there any problems of inequality; Don Bruno's lover, Doña María Laureana Cenea, of Havana, was of "distinguished birth." He recommended that the Cámara "ought not concede the privilege solicited," since it would "prejudice the increase of [legitimate] population." He did leave an escape clause, however, for he concluded that, if the parties had "some insuperable impediment," the Cámara ought to legitimate the boy, who should not be "prejudiced without any fault of his own."

These recommendations never reached the concerned parties in Algeçiras and Havana. Instead, after the king and his ministers had reviewed this decision, they rejected it, issuing a counterorder to "concede the legitimation in the ordinary way" ("*forma ordinaria*"). This rare reversal signaled Cámara members that they had gone too far, and they summarily ended any further inclination on their part to consider the role of Cupid. Even more substantively it may have discouraged them from giving in to future temptations to forward Cámara agendas by taking an activist stance.

The monarchical dictum that the young Joseph Francisco's legitimation be granted in the "ordinary way" precipitated a revealing debate as the Cámara tried to determine what that phrase actually meant. The ensuing interplay revealed that Cámara officials were not familiar with the 1795 *gracias al sacar*, for they had to consult it to see what "ordinary" meant. One official wondered "if the expression of the resolution of his majesty 'in the ordinary way' means only for civil and honorific effects and in no way to inherit?"

When in doubt, the Cámara followed its usual procedure and searched for historical precedent. Officials agreed that the original "distinction" had been that some legitimations were "conceded for honors" while others "include[d] the right to inherit the goods of the father, equaling entirely the legitimated offspring with the legitimate [ones]." They found that the 1795 *cédula* explicitly redefined such guidelines. A *Camarista* commented that "one does not find this distinction, and only that made between ordinary and extraordinary legitimation." Instead of referring to the traditional dichotomy between honors and inheritance, the 1795 decree differentiated instead between the "ordinary" legitimation of *hijos naturales* and the "extraordinary" legitimation of bastards.

The new legislation flip-flopped the potential grounds and effects of *gracias al sacar*. Before 1795 an ordinary legitimation meant that petitioners were legitimated for honors and inheritance according to the law; after 1795 an ordinary legitimation meant that the petitioners were *hijos naturales* and could inherit from their parents in spite of the law. Before 1795 an extraordinary legitimation meant that illegitimates of all categories might inherit, even if the law prohibited it; after 1795, an extraordinary legitimation meant that the petitioners were bastards and could inherit in spite of law. Before 1795, "ordinary" and "extraordinary" defined inheritance potential; after 1795 they described natal status.

The implications for illegitimate inheritance were stunning. One Cámara official wondered if the 1795 *cédula* introduced potential for radical change, given that "all legitimation[s] were to *inherit and enjoy*" (his emphasis). Officials now had to decide if they should abide by the letter of the new law, particularly if those legitimated after 1795 could inherit equally with legitimate brothers and sisters. Or were petitioners still bound by the traditional proportions—the one-fifth if there were legitimate heirs—established by Spanish law?

Such post-1795 confusion as to what was ordinary and what was not, and what was heritable and what was not, prompted the Cámara to authorize an extensive brief that reviewed existing Spanish inheritance laws and cited commentaries by legal experts such as Covarrubios and Antonio Gómez. The Cámara finally agreed—the wording of the 1795 *cédula* notwithstanding—that it would maintain the procedure and customs of previous decades. The property rights of illegitimates were not to be changed by the 1795 wording. Instead, inheritance "in the ordinary form" should remain according to what "is disposed and permitted by the law." Such a judgment leads to the unmistakable conclusion that the bureaucratic interpretation of the 1795 decree had more policy impact than the wording of the document itself.

A similar process of review reshaped another aspect of the 1795 *cédula*: the insinuation that if bastards were willing to pay steep charges they might be legitimated. Prior to 1795 royal officials had escalated their discrimination against *sacrílegos* and *adulterinos*. Yet the appearance of a price list published throughout the Indies could only encourage them to apply, expect to pay, and be legitimated. Cámara officials confronted such an instance in 1799 when Havana priest Don Joseph Miguel Vianes de Sales petitioned that his twenty-one-year-old son be legitimated to inherit his property.[10] The priest referred to the 1795 *cédula*, particularly to that section entitled "extraordinary [*gracias*] for inheritance." Although he first offered to pay one hundred pesos (fifteen hundred reales), he admitted his willingness to provide "the established price for this type of *gracias*." The cleric gave no information on the marital status of his lover, although she must not have been white, since their son was baptized under the heading of "mulattos and blacks."

Although royal officials did not comment negatively on the racial category of the priest's son, they had much to criticize concerning his natal status. The reviewing lawyer reiterated the rationale that had developed over previous decades concerning the proper use of legitimations. He argued that their primary objective was to provide "comfort" to *hijos naturales* who needed legitimation "because of death or other impediment[s]." Petitions from "those of damnable and punishable couplings" were "odious." These needed "other special laudable circumstances" before being approved. Even though the official conceded that there was a "price list" that provided for the legitimation of "sons of clerics . . . this exists when there is merit for the concession of the *gracias* and it is convenient to grant it."

The crown attorney severely critiqued the application, but he neither approved nor rejected it, suggesting instead that the Cámara should "do what it will." This hesitation most likely occurred because he recognized an equivocal policy issue that the Cámara itself needed to resolve. There was now an ambiguity between the Cámara's reluctance to legitimate *sacrílegos* and the 1795 price list, which suggested that such applicants need only petition and pay. The Cámara showed no such ambivalence. It rejected the cleric's petition, and, when he reapplied, turned him down yet again.

The Cámara showed its moral stance even more clearly in a case from Bogotá in which sacrilege was not even technically an issue, for Don Mateo de Contreras had had the affair that produced Juan Nepomuceno before he was ordained.[11] His son, who was now twenty, applied for legitimation and expressed his desire to enter the priesthood. When the crown attorney reviewed the application, he conceded that *hijos naturales* should be favored for the "*gracia*." However he expressed concern that "if such are approved without just cause and with facility . . . it would open the door to dissolution and licentiousness, and place in ecclesiastical and secular positions persons who owe their existence to a sin." The Cámara approved the petition but with special limits: If the son did become a priest he could not hold higher church positions, such as that of a prebendary, but must remain a curate, and that never "in the town of his origin." Officials also demanded six thousand reales, rather than the usual four thousand reales fixed price for *hijos naturales*.[12] The Cámara's concern that the legitimation of priestly offspring might send the wrong message to local communities took priority over the letter of the law.

Although Cámara officials adamantly discriminated against those of sacrilegious birth, illegitimates who were *adulterinos* benefited from the 1795 decree. While the Cámara had never explicitly distinguished between *adulterinos* produced by married fathers and those born of married mothers, the new decree recognized the more common pattern of male promiscuity, even providing a discount if the mother were unmarried. Unfortunately the majority of such decisions appear only as final decrees, so it is impossible to determine if the Cámara accepted this distinction when it granted approvals (see Table 15). However, it is intriguing that four of the seven successful petitions arrived from Cuba after the 1808 Napoleonic invasion of the Spanish peninsula. At this point the Cámara might have been especially eager to grant approvals, collect legitimation fees, and appease colonials.[13] Yet when the Cámara denied an *adulterino* it continued to cite moral priorities, suggesting that "vicious origin" was the reason for rejecting the request.[14]

Although Cámara officials chose to reinterpret the 1795 *cédula* according to their previously established guidelines, they enthusiastically accepted the innovation of fixed prices. The 1795 and 1801 price lists streamlined the bureaucratic process and brought uniformity of fees and consistency throughout viceregal jurisdictions.[15] Scribblings on legitimation documents show that bureaucrats quickly adopted fixed prices. Prior to 1795 each successful petition had included a review of precedents to determine the price to be charged; after 1795 such investigations ceased. Sometimes officials mentioned a specific charge, sometimes they simply noted that the petitioner should pay the "*arancel.*" From 1795 to 1819 only four of the twenty-six legitimations from New Spain, and six of the twenty-three from Peru, did not pay fixed prices.

These exceptions to the price list were understandable. Both royal officials and colonists inhabited a Hispanic world in which few costs were ever "fixed," and it was not surprising that there was still some haggling over sums. Colonists tried to bargain and bureaucrats reserved the right to deviate from established prices. Officials generally defended the concept of fixed prices against colonists' attempts to negotiate discounts. When Chilean Don Joseph Briceño pleaded poverty in 1796 and asked for a reduction, the response was negative: "If one opened the door with this pretext . . . it would be difficult to collect the fee established in the price list, for it would be easy to have cases similar to that of Briceño."[16]

Yet when Cámara officials felt moved they might initiate price reductions. In 1797 the heartrending situation of Venezuelan Don Joseph Luciano Gutíerrez y Díaz led to such a decrease.[17] Don Joseph had spent his early years working to support himself, his younger brother, and his mother, who had gone mad when her lover, a soldier, sailed off to Spain and never returned to marry her. The official who reviewed his petition approved it, provided that Don Joseph could pay the established price. The Cámara peremptorily overruled this judgment, slashing the cost in half because of his "poverty." Cámara bureaucrats reserved substantial flexibility to themselves in their interpretation of both the substance and the details of the 1795 royal decree.

The traditional view that legitimations served primarily as a money-making mechanism for the crown is not borne out by a century of Cámara decisions. While Bourbon ministers at the highest levels may have had that object in mind when they revised the 1795 *gracias al sacar*, it was not the highest priority of the Cámara officials who administered the decree. When offered additional money to speed up a decision, or extra payment for a decision that contradicted their policy, *Camaristas* rejected the money in favor of due consideration and adherence to their policies. A hundred years of legitimation fees yielded 1,228,199 reales, or 81,879 pesos, for the royal coffers from the Americas (see Table 16). When the extra bounty from the Borda decision (600,000 reales) is subtracted, legitimations brought in 439,635 reales, or 29,309 pesos. Although such sums were no doubt welcome, they did not constitute a substantial source of income.

Bureaucrats of the Cámara operated as gatekeepers who used *gracias al sacar* policy to admit some and to exclude others according to priorities evolved throughout the century. Through legitimation of *hijos naturales* they incorporated blood relatives and strengthened local families and local elites; through rejection of *sacrílegos* and *adulterinos* they discouraged sexual promiscuity. Their interpretation of the 1795 *gracias al sacar* maintained these

TABLE 16

Sums Collected for Legitimations (Reales de Pesos)

| Viceroyalty New Spain | | | | | |
Audiencias	1720–1760	1761–1775	1776–1793	1793–1820	Total
Mexico	25,725		616,500*	26,200	668,425*
Mexico			(16,500)		(68,425)
Santo Domingo (Cuba)	23,625	23,000	97,300	176,450	320,375
Panama	2,200		3,000	4,500	9,700
Guatemala			26,625	14,200	40,825
Subtotal	51,550	23,000	743,425*	221,350	1,039,325*
			(143,425)		(439,635)
Viceroyalties Peru, Charcas, New Granada					
Audiencias					
Caracas			4,625	2,000	6,625
Santa Fe		2,000	6,750	10,000	18,750
Quito				12,000	12,000
Lima		2,250	17,250	46,700	66,200
Chile			3,750	12,000	15,750
Buenos Aires		9,000	15,750	14,500	39,250
Charcas			2,299	28,000	30,299
Subtotal		13,250	50,424	125,200	188,874
Total		36,250	793,849*	346,550	1,228,199*
			(193,840)		(628,199)

SOURCE: DB 2-216.
*Includes 600,000 reales paid by Bordas.
( )Excludes Borda payments.

goals in the face of legislation that encouraged expansion of the pool of the legitimated and the promise of greater revenue. The reluctance of Cámara officials to carry out the more radical Bourbon agenda would be tested even more severely as they confronted the explosive social implications implicit in the 1794 royal decree legitimating *expósitos*.

CÁMARA POLICY AND THE 1794 'CÉDULA' ON 'EXPÓSITOS'

Just as there seems to have been a significant difference in outlook between policy-makers who wrote the 1795 *gracias al sacar* legislation and Cámara bureaucrats who enforced it, so the 1794 decree legitimating *expósitos* reveals even wider disparities. The 1794 decree marked a historic shift in royal policy toward *expósitos*. Both in scope as well as in ultimate effect, it contradicted policies forged by decades of Cámara decisions. Consideration of imperial and local ordinances concerning *expósitos* provides the background against which to measure the later decisions of Cámara officials.

Although a papal bull of Gregory XIV had assigned a presumption of legitimacy and pure blood to foundlings in the Rome orphanage as early as 1591, Spanish legislation took longer to provide *expósitos* with such tolerance.[18] The *Novísima Recopilación* collected five laws concerning orphans between 1623 and 1796, legislation that discriminated against them in the seventeenth century but protected them in the eighteenth. For example, a 1623 pragmatic ordered administrators of orphanages to train their charges in crafts or to encourage them to become sailors, rather than to learn to read and write.[19] Some forty years later, in 1677, an edict ordered that *expósitos* be gathered from the provinces of Andalusia and Granada and sent to Cádiz to be trained as sailors, gunners, and pilots. Female *expósitos* were totally ignored in these earlier decrees, which for 165 years were the only relevant imperial proclamations.

By the late eighteenth century, when the crown once again legislated about *expósitos*, the tenor and tone of state policy had shifted dramatically. Children now had value as future citizens, and the state actively established institutions to care for them. *Expósitos* were no longer to be limited in education or channeled into the navy but were to be protected and eventually adopted by the Spanish king. The first intimation of this radically altered attitude emerged in a 1788 royal proclamation ordering administrators of orphanages to educate *expósitos* and release them only to those with proper credentials.[20] This order was apparently occasioned by an incident in San Lúcar de Barrameda, where a group of local reformers belonging to the Sociedad Económica de Amigos del País intervened to rescue two orphans who had been adopted by a group of traveling acrobats.[21] The performers had obtained their presumably unwilling charges from a Valencia *casa de expósitos*. Word of this unacceptable adoption reached royal officials, who proclaimed that training in "violent contortions of [the] body" was not considered to be a satisfactory education for orphans.

An even more laudable concern for bettering the lot of *expósitos* prompted the revolutionary decree of 1794, in which Charles IV mandated that "*ex-*

pósitos of both sexes . . . be held as legitimated by my royal authority." The decree described the "miserable situation" wherein thousands of *expósitos* died because of the distance between the place of their birth and the institutions that existed to accept them. Even when infants did arrive at the turning doors of the orphanages, they were still at the mercy of their wet nurses, who sometimes had to be coerced to suckle them along with their own infants. Such situations could only produce "continuous infanticides." Even if *expósitos* were able to overcome these hazards, they faced prejudice as adults, for they "have been and are treated with the greatest contempt and held as bastards, *espúreos* [*sacrílegos*], *incestuosos*, and *adulterinos*."

The 1794 decree challenged the popular conception that *expósitos* were illegitimate, and suggested that many such babies were legitimates who had been exposed by their parents "when they [saw] no other way of preserving their life."[22] The new legislation demanded that *expósitos* henceforth receive the benefit of the doubt:

> All *expósitos* of both sexes, present and future, both those that have been exposed in the *inclusas* or houses of charity [and] those that have been or were in any other site, and who do not have known parents, [are] to be held as legitimated by my royal authority and legitimated for all the general civil effects.

Royal officials in Spain and the Indies were to fine anyone who denigrated *expósitos* or who called them "illegitimate, bastard, *espúreo*, *incestuoso*, or *adulterino*."

The 1794 legislation both mandated the presumption of natal innocence and granted legitimacy. *Expósitos* were to enjoy the "same honors . . . [and] offices without difference from other honored vassals of the same class." This edict benefited *expósitos* of both genders: female orphans would be eligible for dowries from charitable bequests; orphan boys could enter *colegios*; and adult men could anticipate the possibility of political, economic, and social mobility. The *expósito* decree did include one major caveat: *Expósitos* were still not eligible for positions that had written guidelines demanding proof that the applicant was "legitimate" or "conceived in . . . true marriage." A 1796 ordinance concluded imperial attempts to better the plight of *expósitos* with the establishment of a network of orphanages throughout Spain and the Americas for nurturing and educating the king's adopted children.[23]

To what extent was the 1794 decree a radical departure from previous guidelines? Although nothing existed on the level of imperial legislation to equal it, this measure confirmed a myriad of individual cases and local ordinances that forbade discrimination against *expósitos*. Such measures ranged over the years from a 1762 decision by the Council of Castile that an *expósito* named Angela Fernández should not be presumed illegitimate, to a 1779 decree ordering that *expósitos* receive equal treatment in Segovia schools, to rulings by the Council of the Indies that *expósitos* of Havana (1772) and Cartagena (1791) should enjoy the privileges of legitimates.[24] Even Cámara officials confirmed such practices, for although they eventually excluded *expósitos* from the pool of acceptable applicants for *gracias al sacar*, they had issued individual decrees in the 1750s and 1760s that foreshadowed the 1794 legislation. These verified that a designated *expósito* was to be considered legitimate for most purposes and eligible for positions of honor.

Even though the 1794 *expósito* decree simply appeared to widen the scope of previous practice to the level of the empire, in reality it posed an extreme challenge to the social and racial status quo. Although the measure benefited all *expósitos*, its radical implications can be traced through the petitions of *expósitos* on the edge of acceptance by local elites, for these continued to be sent to the Cámara. Early in the century these *expósitos* might have been legitimated by *gracias al sacar*, or in midcentury they might have received a personal decree confirming their rights. Now they fell into the blanket category of those legitimated by the 1794 decree. Understanding why these *expósitos* continued to appeal, and how Cámara officials responded to their claims, illuminates why and how bureaucrats brought this most radical of Bourbon social measures to a decisive halt.

It should be no surprise that *expósitos* from Cuba were the most likely to seek additional support, given the ferocity of local discrimination against them. A 1796 petition from Don Juan Luis Marqueti, an officer (*mayordomo de propios*) of the Havana cabildo, sought official intervention to confirm the status of his wife, Doña Manuela Valdés, who, as an *expósita*, had taken the traditional surname of those deposited at the local *casa*.[25] Don Juan complained that, even though his wife had been abandoned, she was not given the benefit of the doubt, being instead "looked upon by many as born of a coupling damnable and punishable by the laws." He included a copy of the 1794 decree and asked for intervention, inasmuch as local attitudes violated "the pious royal resolutions . . . issued with the goal of avoiding such excesses." Don Juan's letter crystallized two of the profound faults of the *ex-*

pósito legislation. It revealed that local elites were unlikely to presume innocence, when they customarily presupposed guilt. Nor were elites willing to
acquiesce to state intervention and surrender their customary prerogatives to
accept or reject illegitimates through the individual and informal process of
passing.

Cámara officials had to decide the extent to which they would enforce the
1794 decree. Again, just as in the case of the 1795 *gracias al sacar*, they were
apparently not involved in drafting the order and seemed perplexed how to
enforce it. The Cámara debated how to evaluate the complaints of this
Cuban petitioner—should it proceed as in *gracias al sacar* and demand documentation? One official wondered if Doña Manuela should have provided
a document proving that she had been exposed at the Havana *casa de expósitos*. Others seemed unclear about the effect of the 1794 decree, and one
even consulted the 1795 *gracias al sacar* to determine if it somehow applied.

Finally, *Camaristas* decided that they need not seek any additional information, that they would simply "concede the legitimation" according to the
1794 decree. In this first case officials issued an individualized decree that resembled those they had granted in previous decades in favor of *expósitos*. Yet
bureaucrats had also implicitly responded to a petitioner's complaint that
the sweeping concessions of legitimacy embodied in the 1794 decree would
not be sufficient in and of themselves to change local attitudes. By the next
year *Camaristas* would beat a retreat from even this minimal activism in favor of *expósitos*.

The disinclination of Cámara officials to enforce the 1794 decree became
manifest as they confronted the shocking, if totally engaging, application of
Cuban matron Doña María Jardines.[26] Her 1797 petition encapsulated
many of the inherent contradictions of the new *expósito* policy, for only in
colonial Latin America might a mother apply so that her offspring would enjoy orphans' benefits! Doña María wrote a chatty and confiding letter that
provided telling details of her life, a letter that must have horrified *Camaristas* who had worked for decades to use legitimations to discourage promiscuity, and who now saw their efforts threatened by the new legislation.

Doña María began her letter with a short description of her own difficult
early years, for she had been baptized as an *expósito* and given to an adopted
mother who had left her at a hacienda in the countryside. It was there that
the "human fragility which so combats the strongest spirits" had overcome
her, and she "had the disgrace to lose her virginity with a certain man who,

even though distinguished, had an impediment to marry me." Doña María never clarified if her lover was a relation, married, or a priest, but the relationship was long lasting, given that she gave birth to "twelve children . . . including seven sons." All twelve had been baptized as *expósitos* and raised by their mother with the "greatest decency," so that they were of "good inclinations, pacific, fearful of God and of justice, [and] obedient to all superiors." Doña María assured royal officials of her own superior status; she was "white" and possessed "some fortune," including "houses, slaves, animals, and ten haciendas."

Her problem was that even though the *expósito* decree of 1794 had given her and her offspring "innumerable privileges," she was not convinced that these would be sufficient to ensure their future. There were too many "abuses [and] contrary interpretations" concerning the law, and "vulgar [and] indiscreet perturbations of peace and of civil and political society." She therefore offered to cede one of her best haciendas to the crown in exchange for a decree threatening the "most severe and restrictive penalties" to anyone daring to challenge the qualifications of her sons to enter the church or the military. Doña María's request no doubt reinforced the Cámara's growing perception that the 1794 decree would not be sufficient by itself to overcome prejudice against *expósitos*.

Besides the vibrant personality that shines through her letter to the Cámara, Doña María's petition revealed a significant shift in the strategy of *expósitos*. She no longer appealed to officials to guarantee her personal rights as an *expósito*, as that was presumably ensured by the 1794 legislation. Nor did she simply ask for a royal decree specifically confirming both her and her children's right to enjoy the benefits of royal legislation. Instead, she asked Cámara officials to join her in a preemptive strike—to issue a decree anticipating that the 1794 legislation would not eliminate the prejudice against her offspring.

What Doña María could not realize is that her request highlighted striking contradictions between previous Cámara policy and the implications of the 1794 *expósito* legislation. When royal officials considered her request, they continued their usual practice of distinguishing between the private reality and public status of petitioners. While the specific natal status of Doña María's children is unknown, it seems likely that they were some form of bastard. Given the length of her relationship and the number of her children, no doubt many of her neighbors were aware of her illicit relationship.

Yet the baptismal certificates of her twelve children nevertheless gave them the public status of *expósitos*, and thus the 1794 decree made them legitimate. Doña María's offspring had the natal status of bastards, an informal public status as bastards, and a potential official status as *expósitos* recently legitimated by the king.

The Cámara lawyer who reviewed her letter went to the heart of the matter and questioned how Doña María's children could be orphans when she admitted that she was their mother. Noting that the 1794 decree specified that the parents of *expósitos* had to be unknown, he decided "that it is not so that the referred are *expósitos*, nor can it be believed that they do not have known parents." Consequently he refused to recommend that the Cámara support the mobility of Doña María's offspring. However the official also recognized that baptismal certificates could establish *expósito* status, so he left Doña María a dubious opening. He suggested that if someone discriminated against her children and called them "illegitimate for some civil effect," that she might "use her right as it applies, with the corresponding justification of the quality of *expósitos*." The Cámara agreed.

The ultimate effect of this somewhat cryptic decision was that the Cámara withdrew from any active enforcement of the 1794 decree and left petitioners to resolve their own fates. Bureaucrats essentially told Doña María that if her offspring were prejudiced, she first had to convince those who discriminated that her children were *expósitos*. If she was successful, she might then resort to the 1794 decree to ensure their privileges, although the Cámara would not directly intervene to guarantee their rights. In effect the Cámara ceded to local elites the choice of whether to recognize informal or official public status—in this case, whether Doña Maria's offspring were bastards or *expósitos*—and then judge how to proceed.

The Cámara maintained this stance the next year when the adopted father of an *expósito* begged officials to preclude discrimination, so that "it would not happen to him as to others of his birth" that his son would be "vexed with false and calumnious objections" that would deprive him of those "honors and privileges that your majesty has conceded."[27] The father asked officials to issue a "declaration that he can obtain the employments corresponding to his birth, and that they make no inquiry [concerning] his parents." The crown attorney rejected the petition as "impetuous and not in accord with the royal *cédula* of . . . 1794." He added that since no one had challenged these rights, "there is no need for a new declaration."

By 1801 royal officials were expressing their doubts about the *expósito* legislation even more forcefully. When the royal treasurer from San Luis Potosí asked their permission to marry an *expósita*, who, he assured them, was a virgin and also white, they agreed.[28] However, they also noted that such petitions could bring "inconveniences," given the "frequency of such exposures in private houses, and the ease of justifying that there are unknown parents, even though they have them, and they are of damnable and punishable couplings." Such comments underline that even Cámara officials were unable to accord *expósitos* the presumption of innocence demanded by the 1794 legislation.

Given the reluctance with which the Cámara enforced the *expósito* legislation for whites, it should come as no surprise that it was even less willing to support *expósitos* who were racially mixed. A generation before the 1794 decree, bureaucrats were on record that "neither in Spain nor in the Indies have [*expósitos*] enjoyed nor ought they enjoy all the qualities of the truly legitimate" (1772). Rather, officials suggested that it would "poison the Republic to classify them as noble and of pure birth, in equality with those who are certain of their true parents." They had added a special stricture about American *expósitos*, given the "mixture of negroes, mulattos, and other castes that are accustomed to spring from such bad disposition."[29] When an *expósito* applied to be admitted to the bar in 1805, one official wrote disapprovingly of the "multitude of castes" in his Guadalajara district, given that parents were accustomed "to expose at the doors of an individual those of dark quality and tainted origin, thus achieving by this means . . . exemption from tribute . . . with grave prejudice to the State and the Royal Treasury."[30] Even though the monarch might have ordered that *expósitos* be given the benefit of doubt as to their birth, *Camaristas* shared the popular prejudice against those of unknown origin and possible racial mixture.

Why did the Cámara retreat and subvert the *expósito* decree through passivity? One practical answer might be that *Camaristas* rejected the extra work, for if some *expósitos* received special decrees others might make similar requests that would have to be processed. Yet a deeper understanding of the implications of their withdrawal suggests more substantive reasons and provides fundamental insight into why *expósito* legitimations could never be as effective as their *gracias al sacar* counterparts.

The 1794 *expósito* decree foundered because it contradicted essential Hispanic precepts of how social and racial mobility should operate. The conceptions of private and public spheres created the potential for individuals to pass and project superior persona in the public sphere, in spite of their private "defects." Elites in Spain and the Americas were participants in this process when they made informal and personal exceptions to accept such passing. This mode of social mobility was paralleled at the governmental level, for the essence of *gracias al sacar* derived from the prerogative of the monarch to confirm individual exceptions to law and to alter public birth, race, or ethnic status.

At its heart the *expósito* legislation posed a radical challenge to such traditional modes of mobility. It could not be popularly accepted, even by Cámara officials, because it challenged prevailing beliefs as to how evidence was to be assessed. It violated the predominant Hispanic presumption of guilt, that missing information hid the negative—in this case that *expósitos* were bastards or racially mixed.[31] Nor was there any particular consensus in Spain, much less in the Americas, that *expósitos* deserved passing and merited legitimation.[32] The even more radical aspect of the decree was its universal coverage. This directly contradicted the historical Hispanic process whereby mobility—whether given informally by local elites who sanctioned passing, or formally by the state through individual decrees—was awarded on a person-by-person, rather than a category-by-category, basis.

The refusal of Cámara officials to intervene in behalf of *expósitos* threw the decision-making process back to informal but traditional pathways. The Cámara yielded the ground to local elites, who could decide in the usual person-by-person manner whether they chose to recognize someone as an *expósito*, and if so, what benefits that might or might not bring. Such a reversion dampened the extremely explosive issue of race, as it limited significant mobility to *expósitos* who had personally passed local scrutiny. Given the rising prejudice of the late eighteenth century, elite judgments concerning *expósitos* were more likely to be negative.

BOURBON SOCIAL POLICIES COMPARED

Ironically, it is only by understanding the congruency between popular and official modes of passing, and the disparity between the letter and the enforcement of policy, that the Bourbon social reforms achieve coherence. Stating such a conclusion is much simpler than explaining it. On the surface the social reforms had contradictory goals: the Pragmatic Sanction on Marriages (1778) discouraged racial and social mobility; yet legitimations, whitening, and the *expósito* decree officially promoted passing. Assessing these measures according to themes of "precedent," "variable peninsular-American impact," "transformation over time," and "process" shows they were fundamentally consistent and essentially conservative.

The Bourbons were not innovators. The Pragmatic Sanction on Marriages, *gracias al sacar*, and the *expósito* decree had been tested over time, or in localities, or on individuals before they became imperial policy. Previous chapters have traced the centuries of legitimations that preceded the 1795 *arancel* and shown that both king and Cámara had conceded legitimacy or its equivalent to individual *expósitos* and to those in *casas de expósitos* long before the 1794 universal decree.

A similar process of testing occurred with the 1795 *gracias al sacar* price list, which sanctioned the purchase of "whiteness." For more than a century royal officials had issued decrees giving designated individuals the privileges of whites, even though the law generally discriminated against *pardos* and *morenos*. For example, Vicente Méndez, a *moreno*, was permitted in 1687 to hold the office of governor of a province in Panama because he had congregated the local Indians; in 1760 the sons of Commander Antonio Flores, a *pardo*, were awarded the prerogatives of whites to study medicine; in 1763 the crown ordered that a Havana *pardo* be permitted to qualify as a surgeon.[33]

The 1776–1778 Pragmatic Sanction on Marriages, which permitted parents to appeal to civil officials to prohibit religious ceremonies if the contracting parties were unequal, probably had the least historical precedent. However it was consistent with a tradition of pedagogical and theological advice that encouraged state intervention in spousal choice and family formation. For centuries fathers with entails (*mayorazgos*) had been able to include clauses that disinherited offspring who married unequally, while there were isolated cases in which clerics had exerted similar vetoes over what they viewed as inappropriate couplings.[34]

A second theme linking late-eighteenth-century reforms is that legislation originating from peninsular preoccupations often became transformed when applied to the Americas. This was particularly true of measures that affected

issues of birth or race, given the distinctions between the more homogeneous peninsula and the varied, complex, and increasingly tense milieu of
the colonies.

Unfortunately, any comparison between *gracias al sacar* legitimation policies in the peninsula and the Americas must await further research.[35] The expression of monarchical concern for abandoned infants on the peninsula—
who, even if they were bastards, or poor, were also white—had a profoundly
different impact in the Indies. There, both Cámara officials and local elites
feared that racially mixed parents might deliberately abandon their infants
as *expósitos* so that they might enjoy both the presumption of legitimacy and
of whiteness.

It is certainly possible, although it cannot be proved, that another peninsular preoccupation—providing increased funds to the treasury—might
have led to the *gracias al sacar* that "whitened." It is interesting that Cámara
officials were not familiar with the 1795 *gracias al sacar* until they had to enforce it. If those in the know did not participate, how did the compilers of
the 1795 price list decide what measures should be included? Given their almost word-for-word congruity, it seems likely that a first model was the *gracias al sacar* that had been formulated in 1773 for the Council and Cámara of
Castile.[36] Yet the compilers of the 1795 price list must have also consulted the
Indies archives for precedents, for they added some distinctive American
gracias to the 1795 decree, including one for whitening.

Both the location of the whitening clauses within the 1795 *arancel* and the
prices charged support the hypothesis that the drafters added these provisions more for administrative completeness and revenue enhancement than
for racial reform. In the 1795 decree, of the fifty-five *gracias* that might be
purchased the two whitening provisions were numbered fifty-four and fifty-
five—in effect, they were tacked on at the end. Furthermore, the cost of
whitening was disproportionately low compared with its benefits. An *hijo
natural* had to pay 4,000 reales and an *adulterino* 24,200 reales to be legitimated. Yet *pardos* paid only 500 reales to be whitened, while *quinterones*
(who were presumably more white than *pardos*) inexplicably paid more—
800 reales. Such disparities and inconsistencies suggest that drafters simply
included these provisions because they had found precedents in which
equivalent prices had been paid, and they failed to consider the impact of
the publication of such a revolutionary option in the Americas.

The Pragmatic Sanction on Marriages, originally part of the general Bourbon effort to wrest control of certain issues from the papacy and place them within the realm of the state, also affected Spain and the Americas differently.[37] The particular object of Bourbon discontent was the encyclical of Pope Benedict XIV of November 17, 1741, which permitted priests to perform marriages of conscience, or secret ceremonies without public banns, when couples had privately exchanged a promise to wed. In an advisory (*consulta*) to Charles III in 1775, his ministers condemned what they considered to be such excessive ecclesiastical intervention in civil matters. They noted:

> Other Catholic nations, without insult of the piety and veneration due to the Church . . . distinguish and separate that belonging to the Sacrament and its spiritual effects, with that corresponding to contract and its temporal effects.[38]

Officials feared that marriages that were "unworthy, contracted with the lowest and most infamous . . . against the will . . . of the parents of the family" would still be "valid according to the sacrament," and therefore produce "all the dependent effects of the contract." The next year the Royal Pragmatic on Marriages (1776) provided for parental intervention when such inequalities were present: Mothers and fathers could appeal to officials to prohibit the religious ceremony and the eventual transmission of family property to the "unworthy."

The mandate of the Royal Pragmatic altered significantly when it was applied in 1778 to the Americas, for the Spanish inequalities that had originally precipitated the legislation paled when compared with the social and racial complexities of the Indies. In Spain when a father opposed the marriage of a son or daughter, it was usually because he objected to Jewish or Moorish ancestry, illegitimate birth, or the social or economic inequality of the prospective spouse.[39] In the Americas opposition was customarily occasioned by racial inequalities.[40] It is telling that, even though the American version of the Royal Pragmatic omitted mention of mulattos and *pardos*, American parents from the start used the legislation to prohibit such marriages. Finally, in 1803, opposition to the racially mixed was formally sanctioned by the legislation.[41]

Peninsular and American objections to marital unions differed not only on the issue of race but also on that of class. In Spain, dissent over marital inequality tended to be concentrated in the upper social strata. In America the Pragmatic was used both by elites and lower-status whites who contested marriages with those who were racially mixed and upwardly mobile. Thus a measure initially prompted by the Gallicanist, antipapal tendencies of Bourbon reformers produced one effect on the peninsula and another in the Indies.

Bourbon social reform measures changed over time. There were two distinct reform periods. The first, from the 1770s through the mid-1790s, contained the more radical social agenda; the second, after 1795, saw royal officials in a pronounced conservative retreat. This chapter has already traced how *Camaristas* rejected the radical potentials of the 1795 *gracias al sacar* and refused to intervene to enforce the 1794 *expósito* legislation. Both the measures that whitened, as well as the Royal Pragmatic on Marriages, produced similar defensive pullbacks by administrators.

The effects of the 1795 *gracias al sacar* on whitening have been vastly overestimated. It was a dead letter almost from the moment of its appearance. One statistic is sufficient: Only thirteen *pardos* were whitened after 1795.[42] While a detailed study of the whitening decree still needs to be done, Santos Rodulfo Cortés has extensively documented the howls of protest from Venezuelan elites who overwhelmed Cámara officials with predictions of the dire consequences if *pardos* could purchase whiteness.[43] Feelings ran so high that the governor of Maracaibo issued an *obedezco pero no cumplo* ("I obey, but I do not comply"), the traditional temporary veto of an imperial action deemed too dangerous to implement.[44]

Given the American experience of the *Camaristas*, they needed no further warning to back off. By 1806 the Council of the Indies had conceded that "individuals of the vicious castes [continue] with notable inferiority and difference from legitimate whites and mestizos . . . that the dispensation of quality (*calidad*) that are conceded to those [whitened] are rare."[45] Although the whitening legislation was radical it was stillborn, and the least important of the Bourbon social reforms.

Just as the 1790s saw conservative interpretations of policies of legitimation and whitening, so the Royal Pragmatic on Marriages was weakened between the first and the second period of Bourbon reform. Particularly affected were clauses that disinherited sons and daughters who defied their parents and civil officials by marrying unequal spouses. After 1793 such parental disallowance was not automatic; fathers now had to make specific provisions to disinherit disobedient offspring, and were given the option of skipping a generation and leaving property to grandchildren.[46] The state's original insistence that church officials not perform weddings in disputed cases broke down, and clerics were again conceded much of the discretion they had enjoyed before the Pragmatic was enacted. Daisy Rípodas Ardanaz has pointed out that royal officials in the 1770s and 1780s tended to support the provisions of the Pragmatic; those after the 1790s tended to be lukewarm or in opposition.[47]

The last attribute shared by the Bourbon social reforms was process, for although there was significant disparity between the letter of the law and administrative enforcement, at their core all four reforms functioned similarly. Every measure empowered either Cámara officials or local elites to act as gatekeepers to preserve the social and racial hierarchy by deciding which few would be let in, thereby keeping out the many. Officials and elites decided on a person-by-person basis who might pass, sanctioning such mobility either through formal state intervention or informal local action. *Camaristas* supported illegitimates whose parents might have married but refused *cédulas* to those of sacrilegious and adulterous birth; they permitted a few exceptional *pardos* to purchase whiteness but discouraged the majority. The Royal Pragmatic empowered fathers to become gatekeepers, for they could judge if a questionable daughter or son-in-law had passed sufficiently to be admitted into the family. If the answer was no, they could rely on the state to support them.[48] Local elites were gatekeepers for local *expósitos*; the Cámara gave them the option of deciding who might, and who might not, benefit from the 1794 legislation.

The Bourbon social reforms worked at the level of the individual. As such, they were compatible with tradition and with popular and official attitudes concerning how racial and social mobility were to be rewarded. While the letter of these Bourbon measures suggests they had contradictory goals, the process rendered them congruent and conservative.

BOURBON REFORMS: A COMPARISON

When historians evaluate the era of Bourbon Reform (1759–1808), they often ignore the social measures, perhaps because these have appeared contradictory, or because they have not been much studied, or because their primary policy objectives were not in the social arena.[49] Bourbon priorities were to strengthen national defense, to raise new taxes, to increase governmental efficiency, to eliminate the Jesuits, and generally to enhance state power. Yet integration of the social reforms into the wider perspective is essential for any comprehensive understanding of late colonial-peninsular relationships.

Previous chapters have suggested some of the obvious ways that other Bourbon reforms affected Cámara bureaucrats and their policies. Bourbon administrative reorganizations decreased the jurisdiction of the Council of the Indies but notably increased its effectiveness. The steady arrival of *Camaristas* with American experience led to more sophisticated evaluations of depositions from the Indies, as well as increased sensitivity to the impact of governmental actions on local communities. While bureaucrats generally chose to follow their own policy rather than monetary goals, the decision in favor of the Bordas and the publication of the 1795 and 1801 price lists were consistent with measures to increase revenue. At least some of the impetus behind the Pragmatic Sanction on Marriages was Bourbon determination to enhance the power of the state over that of the church. Digging a bit deeper and comparing Bourbon reforms from the "inside out" suggests even more subtle contrasts and congruencies.

The social reforms were among the few reforms that were truly imperial, for many of the other Bourbon measures were not. The Pragmatic Sanction on Matrimony, the 1794 *expósito* decree, and *gracias al sacar* were applicable to all the Indies immediately upon their promulgation. Bourbon reformers were more cautious in other arenas: Some measures were extended to some *audiencias* but not to others, or were implemented by stages in the Americas. The governmental reorganization of the *intendente* system was introduced incrementally to Cuba, South America, and then Mexico but was never applied to New Granada or Quito. Free commerce also arrived sequentially, first in the Caribbean and finally in Mexico.[50] Allan Kuethe's observation that the Spanish government "rarely legislated for the empire as a whole" applies to most reforms but not to eighteenth-century social measures.[51]

Why might this be so? One answer may be that—with the signal exception of the *expósito* decree, which was blocked precisely for that reason—reformers conceptualized social policy as a process affecting relatively few individuals. Contrasted to governmental reorganization or revenue enhancement, the Bourbon social reforms did not employ the power of the absolutist state to effect widespread change.

While the Bourbon social reforms were distinctive because of their impe-

rial scope and their individual focus, they—along with the other measures—affected American locales differently and changed over time. On
balance, some regions benefited more than others from Bourbon activism.
Legislation that opened ports to trade, permitted the importation of slaves,
and energized the sugar economy meant that Cuba greatly prospered as a result of Bourbon reform.[52] At the same time, the new viceroyalty of La Plata
deprived Upper Peru of jurisdictions, of captive markets, and of the silver-
rich mine of Potosí, with the result that its fortunes sank.[53] Social reforms
promoted some and hindered others: Illegitimates from the Caribbean
flocked to the *gracias al sacar* remedy; Venezuelan elites reacted with horror
to the whitening option. The most intense years of the Bourbon reforms coincided with the tenure of Secretary of the Indies José de Gálvez (1776–1787)
and paralleled those decades (1770s, 1780s) when legitimation policies were
crystallized. The 1790s marked a retreat on most reformist fronts.[54]

Most historians agree that the Bourbon reforms in the Americas prepared
the way, even if they did not precipitate, the final break from Spain. David
Brading summarized the consensus when he suggested that "the price of reform was the alienation of the creole elite."[55] Yet as Jacques Barbier reminds
us, this was not the total picture, for in certain regions the "interests of the
elite . . . were more often furthered than harmed by the reformers."[56] Unlike
the abhorred tax measures, the despised monopolies on tobacco and alcohol,
and the discrimination against Creole office-holders, the Bourbon social reforms—not always on paper, but usually in practice—favored the personal
agendas and prejudices of local elites. Since their properties were rarely affected by legitimations, *gracias al sacar* pleased locals who applauded when
"defective" blood relatives became honored members of the family. Elite
mothers and fathers were able to erase their guilt, as well as the consequences
of their out-of-wedlock sexual encounters, as they passed honor to the next
generation. The Pragmatic Sanction enabled fathers to protect the social and
racial exclusivity of their family for posterity. When lack of elite support for
whitening or for *expósito* mobility became manifest, the social reformers re-
treated. Even as the Bourbon state appropriated new powers in other
spheres, its social policy placated local elites and empowered them to be
gatekeepers at the very moment when they felt most threatened.

For those illegitimates who applied for relief throughout the eighteenth
century, the intricacies of Bourbon policy were probably less important than
what eventually happened at home. For successful applicants the arrival of a

royal decree was not the goal but only the next step in the process; an official document marked with the royal seal was just paper. It could be effective only if local elites chose to validate the Cámara's judgment and to accept the successful petitioners as honored peers. The next chapter considers how *cédula* recipients tested the ways in which civil legitimation might or might not change their lives after they received the coveted *gracias al sacar*.

PART FOUR

Aftermaths

TWELVE

The Legitimated: Life After *Gracias al Sacar*

Around 9:30 P.M. one August evening in 1779 someone tossed a note though an open window of the home of Don Francisco Antonio Escalada, a prominent Buenos Aires merchant.[1] Don Francisco was not alone when this message landed on his floor; it was his customary practice to invite close friends in to play cards most evenings. What is arresting is the response of this table of five card players to the sudden appearance of this innocent-looking paper. Their testimony several weeks later serves as a persuasive reminder that elites who possessed honor—whether from birth or by the favor of the king— considered themselves vulnerable, for they might be called upon at any time to defend it. Their actions provide insight into how male friends might co-operate to protect each other when issues of honor were at stake.

The reactions of Don Francisco's guests suggest that anonymous challenges to honor were not rare; on the basis of previous experience his friends advised him how to cope with the threatening note. After the paper landed, Don Antonio del Moral, a merchant, remembered that he rose, picked it up, looked outside, and then told Don Francisco: "If I were you, I would burn it or throw it into the latrine, for letters or papers of this type are not usually a good thing." Don Eusebio Joseph de Boiso, a public notary, agreed with this advice, and added that "papers that come with such secrecy are generally with dirty insides . . . with consequences that might stain the honor of the master of the house." Don Joseph Vicente Carranzio, a Spanish lawyer, commented on "the bad consequences that these papers bring, for they are not directed to a good end, and usually bring discord to the house and especially to the marriage." Anonymous notes seem to have been a customary vehicle for conveying challenges to the honor of someone within a private circle of family and friends.[2]

Although none of Don Francisco's guests directly brought it up, they must have known that he had particular reason to worry about an attack on his honor. It had been only eight years earlier that he and his brother, Don Antonio José, both *hijos naturales*, had purchased their legitimations.[3] Yet although Don Francisco did not dismiss the concerns of his friends, he did not seem to feel especially vulnerable. Rather, he raised another matter for the group's consideration. He wondered, inasmuch as he was a merchant with business interests, if the note "could be some advice . . . that might be important." And so the card players had to weigh the consequences of opening a note that might damage the honor of Don Francisco, or one of their number, against the equally plausible possibility that the paper contained valuable information.

The group considered several solutions. Don Eusebio Joseph de Boiso remembered that when he had not wanted to read the contents of such a note he had "verified [its contents] through means of a confessor." But Don Eusebio realized that Don Francisco's "inclination was to open the note." Don Joseph Vicente Carranzio agreed and intervened to "avoid the threatening blow of the aforesaid paper." He asked Don Francisco to give him the paper; he then put it into his pocket, and the card game continued without further incident until the men left for home around eleven o'clock.

The next morning Don Francisco's card-playing friends learned the perhaps anticlimactic but nonetheless comforting news that their reputations were intact. Don Bonifacio Amarburu recalled that he had visited Don Francisco Antonio's shop around eleven, and "after a little bit . . . asked him if he had any news concerning the note that had been thrown the night before." The merchant responded that Don Joseph Vicente had sent a message advising him to "have no worry whatever concerning that paper, for it contained nothing of substance, and it was only inviting the *tertulia* to enjoy a laugh." Don Francisco told Don Antonio del Moral "that the letter thrown the night before contained nothing against the honor and estimation of his house, nor of anyone of the *tertulia*."

As it turned out the note had contained a *pasquín*, or satirical verse, which made fun of royal officials, military officers, and others of prominence in Buenos Aires society. That night Don Joseph Vicente brought it back to Don Francisco's house and the group enjoyed a laugh at the contents. Don Francisco then passed it on to his brother, Don Antonio José, who circulated it yet further. Royal officials were not amused that this scurrilous lampoon received wide distribution, and they later prosecuted some of the card players, which is how this incident entered the historical record.

The image of five men frozen with concern that the contents of an unknown letter might threaten their honor is compelling. Inasmuch as the note arrived at the house of Don Francisco, and in view of the fact that he had been illegitimate, he presumably had the greatest cause for concern. Yet because the group convened regularly at his house, everyone seemed to fear damage to his own, or to his family's, honor. One of the card players acknowledged this vulnerability when he noted that "even in the most distinguished [houses]" anonymous notes may "introduce harm, discord, and disgust, sometimes because of vengeance or other ends, as experience has shown."

If even those with impeccable credentials and virtuous houses might fear challenges to their honor, how much more vulnerable were those legitimated through *gracias al sacar*? What happened to the Escaladas and to the other successful petitioners after the Cámara of the Indies approved their legitimations? Did legitimation provide upward mobility and enhance public status? How might civil legitimation change the day-to-day experiences of those who received it?

The answer to these questions is deceptively simple: civil legitimation proved effective to the extent that it altered the balance in the negotiation of honor. The difficult part is defining the kinds of topics that were under negotiation, and who was contesting them. Discrimination might be totally, variably, or never resolved, depending upon the particular issue. Exploration of the status of petitioners after their legitimations provides insight into those underlying processes by which historical, official, and popular modes of discrimination might be superseded by state intervention. Since Don Francisco Escalada and his brother Don Antonio José were among the affected, let us continue with them.

Don Francisco's confidence that his own and his family's honor was un-questionable proved justified, not only in 1779 but beyond. At the time of the lampoon, his fellow card players attested to the "notorious" virtue of his household. As the years passed the merchant added those honors that demonstrated that he was fully accepted by elite Buenos Aires society. He served on the city council, was active in the merchant guild, and later par-ticipated in the independence movement.[4] His brother met with equal suc-cess: Don Antonio José held city council office and served in the merchant guild, the militia, and in *audiencia* offices; he also supported independence.[5] By every indicator both brothers overcame the initial obstacles of their birth.

The question still remains: Would the lives of the Escaladas have been different if they had not been legitimated? Might they have passed to achieve such positions in spite of their birth? Previous chapters have provided nu-merous examples of illegitimates who were informally accepted as persons of honor in the public sphere, their birth notwithstanding. Analysis of the lives of the legitimated cannot usually provide a direct cause-and-effect relation-ship between legitimation and achievement of honorable status, although at least one instance exists in which the legitimated literally waved his *gracias al sacar* documents in the faces of those who challenged his honor. The more usual effects of legitimation were not so directly attributable.

The contrast between the reasons petitioners gave for their applications (the discriminations levied against them) and their subsequent histories can be informative. It reveals that *gracias al sacar* proved most successful in end-ing the official status attached to illegitimacy. It was effective in countering written discriminatory guidelines but was much less consistent in combat-ing more popular forms of prejudice.

OFFICIAL STATUS AND THE LEGITIMATED

One of the most easily measurable ways that *gracias al sacar* changed the lives of illegitimates was obvious: Illegitimates became legitimate in official documents. Imperial, viceregal, provincial, and local archives provide nu-merous instances of individuals who had previously been identified as *hijos naturales*, or as of "unknown parentage," who were referred to after the decree as legitimate—or sometimes by the more technically correct term *le-gitimado* (legitimated). Even though such a transformation might be self-evident, it should not be underestimated. To the newly legitimated it meant that their birth was no longer a matter of shame when the critical documents in life—marriage certificates, parental wills, and their own testaments—were written. The official disappearance of illegitimacy was also of historical significance for the family, for defective natal status no longer marred testaments and genealogies, and honor might be passed securely on to succeeding generations.

It must have been some consolation to parents whose sexual relationships introduced illegitimacy into their families that they could erase their indiscretion so that their children could appear in documents as legitimate. The family documents of Don Pedro Dulces de Herrera, a seventeenth-century Antioqueño miner, illustrate this transformation.[6] Don Pedro applied for the legitimation of his son and daughter, Don Domingo and Doña Francisca, both of whom were *adulterinos*, in 1660. When he wrote his final testament in Cartagena fifteen years later, he did not refer to his daughter, who may have died, but he noted that Don Domingo was his "legitimate son."

Illegitimates themselves often obliterated their previous status in testaments written after successful applications. Don Joseph Gavino Morán y Carillo had petitioned to be legitimated in 1797 so that he might enter the priesthood.[7] In a succession of four wills written from 1828 to his last at age seventy-four in 1856, he referred to himself as a "legitimate son" and once—inaccurately—as a "legitimate son of a legitimate marriage" (1838). Similar changes can be traced in the testaments of Doña Rosa Pro, Don Gregorio Pro, and Don Joaquín de Luna Victoria of Peru and Doña María Rosa Aguilar of Chile.[8] Although the extent to which legitimation might affect the day-to-day lives of petitioners varied widely, from the date of their decree they could at least appear legitimate to their family, to their notaries, and to their posterity as honored ancestors.

WRITTEN DISCRIMINATION AND THE LEGITIMATED

Civil legitimation proved efficacious when wielded against written forms of discrimination that barred illegitimates from selected professions. In every case in which personal histories can be traced, the newly legitimated had but to present their *gracias al sacar* to achieve acceptance, be it to practice as a notary or to enter a chosen guild, the university, or the priesthood. Yet legitimation also had limits. While the newly legitimated might be permitted to step over previously forbidden thresholds, that might be only the first step into a competitive arena in which a multitude of other variables—competence, personal contacts, or luck—also determined the outcome.

Behind the simple presentation of a legitimation decree and ready admission to a profession could lie decades of preparation. The later history of Don Manuel Tames de la Vega of La Plata, Bolivia, demonstrates how *gracias al sacar* might effectively change the balance so that years of enterprise might culminate in occupational mobility.[9] It also reminds us that *gracias al sacar* could but open the door to certain careers; it could not guarantee success.

Don Manuel's early years were difficult, for his father, a student, had absconded over the mountains to Cochambamba, leaving his unmarried mother to raise him on her own. He had to shoulder responsibilities early; he remembered that "from his tender years" he had worked in the offices of the *audiencia*. The notary of the La Plata cabildo recalled that when he had arrived in town in 1769 Don Manuel was just eighteen years old but already was at work with "honor, impartiality, and loyalty." In 1783 he began taking testimony for his application to be a notary. Even though his baptismal certificate listed him as of "unknown father," he was able to produce witnesses to identify his father and to show that he had the requisite *limpieza de sangre* on both paternal and maternal sides.

Don Manuel's character and his ability were never in question. A chain of impressive witnesses testified in his favor. In 1789 a judge recalled that "the said Tames has been involved in the laborious work and heavy labor of dispatch . . . without salary or any compensation whatsoever." The royal official found this to be particularly laudable, given that Don Manuel collected only "some small sums . . . to maintain his poor wife and family" and added that "months, weeks and days pass without [his receiving] a *maravedí*, which seems to me very regrettable." Not only royal officials but also his potential colleagues in the notary office (with the exception of one "enemy") supported him.

Yet when his completed application reached the *audiencia* in July 1790, the judges refused to permit him to take the qualifying examination. Even though they praised his "aptitude, practice," and "good conduct," he was lacking in "legitimate birth." They encouraged him to "implore from your majesty the [necessary] indulgence," and to "give informed testimony of his qualities and good name, and the scarcity in this place of notaries." The next month Don Manuel, hoping that the *audiencia* would reconsider their rejection, reapplied and asked yet again to be admitted to the examination. The *audiencia* again refused, because "his illegitimacy does not permit it to be done."

Don Manuel applied and paid for his legitimation decree in May 1791, took the examination for notary in November, and was subsequently sworn into office. Although he achieved his goal, it is unclear the extent to which the decree changed his life. The La Plata notarial collections show that he practiced as a notary only during the last month of 1791, so it is unclear whether he entered the profession only to then give it up, or if he moved elsewhere, or died.[10] The record of others who sought to become notaries is clearer. The notarial practice of Don Manuel Núñez de Arco of Peru, legitimated in 1797, fills twenty volumes from 1800 through 1839 in the Trujillo archive.[11]

The pattern of written discrimination against illegitimates being overcome by a *gracias al sacar* is repeated in the case of Don Joseph Manuel Ignacio Martínez de Lejarzar. His story has been considered previously, for this *hijo natural* had been trained as an assayer by his father and half brother, who held such positions in Guanajuato, Mexico. But Don Joseph Manuel found his employment as an assayer blocked by the Mexico City Guild, a group that increasingly discriminated against those of irregular birth. Only after Don Joseph Manuel received his legitimation in 1795 did the guild permit him to take the qualifying examination, which he passed in 1796.

Yet even though Don Joseph was legitimated and a guild member, it is uncertain if he ever achieved his ultimate goal—an actual position as an assayer. The competition for such positions became so intense in late-colonial Mexico that by 1797 even Don Joseph's legitimate half brother, Don Pedro, could not turn his interim occupancy of his late father's Guanajuato post into a permanent position. Instead, this experienced assayer found himself shipped off to a position in Chihuahua. The newly legitimated Don Joseph Manuel seems to have fared even worse, for he never appears in relevant documents as holding a position as a smelter.[12]

In other cases, legitimation may have helped petitioners to fulfill their occupational goals. When Don Joseph Miño of Quito successfully sought a *gracias al sacar* in 1795, he specifically mentioned that he had an interest in "military employment."[13] Four years later Quito documents list him as an officer in an infantry regiment. Don Domingo Soriano y Lombana, a Bogotá merchant, legitimated his wife so that her absence of honor would not impede the graduation of their son, Don Ignacio, from the *colegio* of San Bartolomé in Bogotá.[14] Six years later Don Domingo's will proudly noted that his son had become a priest, with the title of "doctor."

Civil legitimation also smoothed the path for those who sought clerical careers. Such was the aspiration of the twenty-five-year-old Peruvian Don Vicente Camborda, who sought legitimation in 1795 and confessed that his ambition was to enter the priesthood.[15] In 1827 he wrote a testament that not only revealed that he had fulfilled this goal—he was the curate of Santo Domingo de Guasi—but that identified him as a deputy to the "congress of this capital." Similar benefits accrued to Don Juan Francisco Avellafuerte of Irapuato, Michoacán, who had been adopted by a childless couple and was eventually sent to study for the priesthood in Mexico City.[16] In 1766, Don Juan Francisco's adopted father died and reserved four thousand pesos to create a *capellanía* for Don Juan if he became ordained. The chaplaincy must have been established, for records some twenty years later show that Dr. Don Juan Francisco was not only a priest but also a partner with a fellow cleric in the cattle business in Irapuato.[17]

PUBLIC OFFICES AND LEGITIMATION

Gracias al sacar proved a more eclectic enhancer of status when written ordinances did not pose an obvious obstacle to be overcome. In such hazier arenas, negotiations of honor had less certain outcomes; imperial, regional, or local elites could weigh the worth of a *cédula* and decide whether it was sufficient to overcome their prejudice. Levels of discrimination varied widely from locality to locality, from the extreme prejudice of the Caribbean to the lesser discrimination of the Andes or Central America. Each attempt to pass—whether informally or whether officially through *gracias al sacar*—rested on a myriad of particular and individual variables including the goals of the upwardly mobile, the intensity of competition, personal competence, and family connections.

Although the Spanish state endorsed selected upward mobility for illegitimates, there were limits even for those with the official sanction of a *gracias al sacar*. The failure of Don Joaquín Cabrejo of Panama to achieve his dream in spite of his successful application provides an illuminating example of the limits of upward mobility in an instance in which royal officials had control. Don Joaquín Cabrejo has appeared previously as one of the more notable examples of informal passing. Even though an *hijo natural*, he had become a lawyer, had served brilliantly as judge advocate and lieutenant governor of Panama, and had received accolades and recommendations for promotion from his superiors. He failed in his petition to be appointed a high court judge when the governor of the Council of the Indies, José de Gálvez, rejected his promotion because of his "birth and birthplace."[18] Don Joaquín then purchased a *gracias al sacar* to resolve the issue of his illegitimacy. But he apparently failed to overcome Gálvez's well-known prejudice against the appointment of the American-born to colonial posts, another hallmark of Bourbon administrative reform.

Why could *gracias al sacar* not tip the balance in Don Joaquín's favor? One answer must be that the position of *oidor* was one of the most coveted and competitive of colonial posts. Even the most qualified aspirants might never be called to serve. Yet evidence suggests that Don Joaquín must have been a very competitive candidate, for the Cámara of the Indies not only seriously discussed his application but also felt that it had to justify its rejection to the viceroy in Bogotá.

It is instructive to compare the qualifications of the successful candidates for the Quito judgeship that Don Joaquín coveted. Between 1776 and 1779 there was an important turnover in the Quito high court as the Cámara of the Indies appointed four judges in just three years.[19] Three of the four were peninsulars, favored as part of the Bourbon administrative reforms—Don Joaquín was a Creole. The ages of the appointees ranged from the midthirties to the late forties—in 1779 Don Joaquín was forty-eight. While the résumés of two of the peninsular appointees were academic, the experiences of the other successful candidates were comparable to that of Don Joaquín. They had served, as was common in the Bourbon reform era, in a succession of posts.[20] One peninsular had held precisely the same level of positions for the same number of years as Don Joaquín, serving in Puerto Rico as judge advocate and lieutenant governor and in the same posts in Caracas.

The last Quito appointee was the only Creole appointed. Like Don Joaquín he had also started his career as a judge advocate, but after seven years, in 1771, he had achieved the rank of judge on the Santo Domingo high court. Although he lacked the advantage of peninsular birth, he did have two other factors in his favor. He was already a high court judge, so the move to Quito was as much lateral as upward. He had been in Spain prior to the Quito appointments, and his presence may have helped his successful lobbying effort.

Such comparisons suggest that there was some validity to Don Joaquín's continual complaints to his superiors that he had served for too many years at qualifying posts that made him eligible to be a judge. However, given the competition for high court positions, as well as the conscious discrimination against illegitimates and against Creoles, a colonial had to have more than just an "adequate" resumé and connections to achieve such prestigious offices. Susan Socolow's observation that Creoles who "combined education, connections, luck and ambition" might still reap the "eventual reward" of judgeship did not characterize Don Joaquín's case; legitimation did not prove sufficient to overcome the obstacles against him.[21]

Nor could *gracias al sacar* accomplish the admittedly ambitious program of Doña Francisca de Risco y Agorreta of La Plata, Bolivia.[22] Born in adultery to a prominent local couple, Doña Francisca had passed to marry Don Vicente Tardío Guzmán, a wealthy silver miner who on his death spoke of the "great love" they had for each other and left her pieces of worked silver, gold jewelry, diamonds, and pearls. As a widow Doña Francisca raised their young children and managed the family's mines, native laborers, and assorted haciendas on her own. After her successful application for legitimation in 1796, she continued to enhance her social position and undertook expensive renovations to her house that reflected her high status. She then applied to the Cámara of the Indies for a title of nobility. The dream of this La Plata matron of becoming the Condesa de Ensenada Alegre ended, however, when royal officials denied her request. They declared that such "Titles of Castile" were awarded only to supplicants who could prove their service to the monarchy and demonstrate sufficient wealth to maintain the position. Doña Francisca, they concluded, met neither criterion.

While legitimations proved less effective in tipping the balance in favor of *gracias al sacar* recipients who sought office or honors at the imperial level, the newly legitimated experienced greater success in negotiations of honor in their local communities, particularly in holding political office. The Escalada brothers, whose story introduced this chapter, both eventually held city council office in Buenos Aires. Don Joaquín de Luna Victoria of Peru also experienced upward mobility. Don Joaquín has appeared previously as the eleven-year-old boy who hid from his father and uncle, the bishop, rather than leave Panama for Peru. Even before his legitimation, Don Joaquín had flourished in the more tolerant atmosphere of Trujillo, where he married well and served as *procurador* on the cabildo and as sergeant in the local militia. Five years after his 1797 legitimation he appeared as a colonel in the militia. In a petition that referred to the "luster" of "his house and family," he applied to succeed his father-in-law in the even more prestigious post of *alguacil mayor*.[23] Of course not all cases ended so well. Even though his mother was legitimated, Don Mariano de las Casas never served on the Havana city council.

DAY-TO-DAY HONOR AND 'GRACIAS AL SACAR'

Historical documents rarely provide details of the substantive yet nuanced ways in which legitimations may have affected the day-to-day lives of petitioners. There is no evidence that women were able to marry husbands of higher status, nor is there evidence that successful applicants were more likely to be accepted as social peers by local elites. However, several incidents suggest that *gracias al sacar* might have meaningfully tipped the balance and provided security to the legitimated if they needed to defend their honor. A first intimation of such a likelihood has already appeared, in the incident of the Buenos Aires card players; the legitimated Don Francisco Escalada seemed to have been no more insecure than his guests at the potential threat of the anonymous note. In a colonial world in which confrontation was constant and traditionally led to insult, *gracias al sacar* provided the legitimated with the basis on which to insist that they, too, be treated as persons of honor in the public sphere.

Such direct linkage between legitimation and defense of one's honor occurred in Paraguay, where Don Pedro Nolasco Domec, a merchant, metaphorically and probably literally waved his legitimation decree at royal officials, insisting that they defend his honor.[24] Don Pedro, the son of the unwed mother Doña X of Buenos Aires, has appeared throughout this work. Raised by his possessive wet nurse, he was trained as a merchant by his father and legitimated in 1785. As an adult Don Pedro eventually settled in Asunción, where he continued his commercial enterprises, married well, and established a family. He was fifty years old, and had been legitimated for eighteen years, when his name became embroiled in a dispute concerning honor.

In October 1803 one of the relatives of Don Pedro's wife pressed charges of rape against a Don Felipe Díaz Colodrero. Don Felipe counterattacked, and in classic colonial fashion tried to smear the honor of his accuser as well as that of her immediate and extended family. He included in his list of charges the accusation that Don Pedro was a "bastard." Presumably Don Felipe was implying that since Don Pedro lacked honor, the reputation of his wife and her relatives was questionable as well, as might be the charge of rape.

Although Don Pedro was out of town when the charges were made, his family lawyer did not delay. He immediately sent for Don Pedro's legitimation decree, which had been preserved in the books of the Buenos Aires city council. When Don Pedro returned to Asunción the next month, he initiated a separate lawsuit against the "libel" perpetrated against his "person and birth." Don Pedro's defense included a classic litany of evidence that proved beyond doubt that he had been treated in public as a person of honor; he had served not only as a captain in the militia but also as an *alcalde* and *regidor* of the Asunción city council.

Don Pedro did not justify his status solely on the basis that he had held public office; he suggested that his achievements had contributed to his honor. He maintained that he was innocent of any defects attributed to his person: "If by the disposition of the most high I suffer some defect (for which I am not guilty) it was to be considered erased with the distinctions that I have merited through my conduct." Don Pedro also refuted Don Felipe's charge of bastardy, noting that his parents had been unwed and able to marry. A half-century after his birth he still protected the identity of the mysterious Doña X (a "Spanish women of distinguished circumstances") but admitted that he had been born an *hijo natural.*

At this point Don Pedro played his trump card. Brandishing his *gracias al sacar,* he informed officials how "your majesty, in use of your supreme authority, legitimated and restored me to all the corresponding honors of those offspring born of legitimate matrimony." He insisted that royal officials erase any references to his illegitimacy from documents concerning the case and "take out . . . such expression[s] . . . from the process." Additionally he demanded that they levy a fine against the infamous Don Felipe, because he had tried "to injure me with the note of bastardy." Don Pedro concluded that only royal intervention would be able "to repair the dishonor and discredit that I have suffered." He also asked the officials to "return the original" of his legitimation decree, which accompanied his petition, given that "the royal letter of legitimation is extremely necessary to guard my rights."

Local officials were not immediately responsive to Don Pedro's requests, for they suggested that the expressions of the accused rapist "in no way could offend the honor and the good name of . . . Domec." However Don Pedro did not see the issue the same way. He wrote officials: You "declare that it is true that such expressions do not serve in any way to offend my honor and good name; but what use is this explanation . . . if Colodrero remains with a safe conduct always to return to injure me when he feels like it?"

Embedded in Don Pedro's argument was the usually unexpressed paradox underlying such negotiations: Repeated public defense of one's honor served only to undermine it. As he explained to royal officials: "Each step that I have to [make to] contest . . . this case . . . has no other effect than [that of] an insufficient declaration . . . to erase the defect . . . [even though] his majesty has had the goodness to declare me undamaged." Although officials refused to expunge the references to Don Pedro's birth from official documents, they eventually demanded that Don Felipe appear before them. They threatened that if he did not "moderate" his actions they would "impose the fines [that] were appropriate."

While the case of Don Pedro Domec is the only conspicuous use of a *gracias al sacar* document in a lawsuit, other *cédula* recipients found themselves in similar situations in which their status was challenged. Even if the legitimated did not directly flourish their decrees, the possession of such a document must have provided the confidence that, like Don Pedro Domec, they could defend themselves if necessary.

Don Cayetano de la Vega of La Paz, Bolivia, demonstrated such assurance when he confronted the Catholic Church over the disposition of the properties of his deceased father, the cleric Dr. Don Dámaso.[25] When Don Cayetano had successfully petitioned for legitimation in 1796 he had explained that, even though his father was a priest, he had been unmarried when he had engaged in the sexual relationship that had led to Don Cayetano's birth. Five years later his father's testament named Don Cayetano the executor of his estate. Church officials contested this appointment by raising the irregularity surrounding his birth. One questioned whether Don Cayetano was "an *hijo natural* or a *sacrílego*," and the bishop finally decided that "he was not natural, but a *sacrílego*."

The real concern of church officials was that Don Cayetano had "de-

praved ideas to rob the parish church of Laxa of its own goods." They originally withheld the documents necessary for the probate of his father's estate,
but he sued before the *audiencia* in 1801 and won access to parish property
so as to take inventory. Fourteen months later Don Cayetano was obviously
procrastinating, for he had still not completed this task. The denunciation
of one priest that Don Cayetano's goal was to "consume the goods from the
testament of the mentioned cleric" may well have been accurate. Yet it seems
unlikely that Don Cayetano would have successfully defended himself
against church charges surrounding his birth or have won a favorable verdict
in the *audiencia* if he had not been able to document his legitimacy.

In some cases the absence of challenge served as a probable indication
that legitimation *cédulas* had enhanced status and provided their recipients
with honor. Given his situation it is significant, for example, that the birth
of Don Juan Francisco de la Cruz Sarabia of Mexico went unquestioned.[26]
Don Juan Francisco was the son of a priest. Applying in midcentury, when
the Cámara looked more leniently on such applications, he was legitimated
in 1748. He must not have come from a wealthy family, for his wife remembered that when they married "he absolutely lacked any fortune." However
Don Juan Francisco eventually achieved the position of *regidor* in the town
of Salamanca.

Although political mobility after legitimation was not remarkable, it is
notable that Don Juan Francisco held office in an atmosphere of vicious in-
fighting. The reputation of the quarrelsome Salamanca cabildo seems to
have been notorious in Mexico. Even royal officials called in to mediate
among the locals noted the continual "troublesome and bloody litigation,"
exacerbated by both "ancient and actual anxieties" that afflicted both
"townspeople and the city officers."[27] Yet even though Mexican documents
chronicle much name-calling and discord, in which Don Juan Francisco
played his part, there is no indication that his origins or his previous illegitimacy ever became an issue.

Nor did questions concerning birth arise in the later career of Don Eusebio Gómez, who was already serving as the *teniente asesor* of the governor
and *intendente* of Cochambamba when his legitimation arrived in 1785.[28]
Don Eusebio seems to have been a most unsavory character who aroused the
justifiable wrath of the Cochambamba locals: He alienated the bishop; appointed men of low birth to serve under him; demanded special privileges
not due his rank, including a cushion at church; threw a member of the city

council into jail; and severely beat a woman. Yet for all the hundreds of pages of charges and complaints against him, no one ever questioned his legitimacy or his birth. Usually for better, but sometimes for ill, a *gracias al sacar* could lift the shadows of the past. It provided successful petitioners with a critical advantage in that constant negotiation of honor that concerned all members of the colonial hierarchy.

As the eighteenth century moved to the next, and as the colonial era gave way to that of independent republics, issues of honor remained, even if their context and effect changed. Although deficiencies in birth might still return to haunt the legitimated, republican institutions and attitudes began to influence the expressions and remedies attached to issues of honor. One illustration of such changing mentality was the greater status awarded to those who practiced essential skills such as medicine. While colonial doctors, and especially surgeons, did not have the high status they attained later in the nineteenth century, evidence suggests that local society as well as royal officials were willing to make allowances for those with increasingly valued qualifications.

This kind of transition affected Don Joseph Domingo Díaz of Caracas, who had applied for but never received a *gracias al sacar*.[29] He had been sixteen and studying medicine at the University of Caracas when he directed his petition to the Cámara in 1788. Since the statutes of the university prohibited the graduation of those who could not document their parentage, he asked for the necessary dispensation to become a medical practitioner. Although the crown turned him down, Don Joseph Domingo must have graduated in spite of his illegitimacy, for he certainly went on to practice medicine. Venezuelan documents record that at the turn of the century the city of Caracas searched abroad for a doctor to coordinate a public health program. When that effort failed they turned to a Dr. Don Joseph Domingo Díaz and appointed him, at an annual salary of seven hundred pesos, to be the "city doctor" with the charge of assisting the poor and combating contagious diseases and epidemics.[30] In this instance, local need seems to have overcome rejection from the Cámara of the Indies.

Royal officials responded more positively to the 1806 application of Limeño José Manuel Valdés, who sought to be both legitimated and whitened so that he might take the examination and qualify as a medical doctor.[31] His testament, written in 1831, suggests that he had a distinguished career, for he became a professor of medicine at the Universidad Pontífica de

San Marcos. Both local societies and imperial officials seemed willing to encourage formal and informal passing by doctors so that they might exercise their profession.

A postcolonial challenge to honor is particularly revealing of continuities between earlier constructions of status and evidences of a new society in formation. The challenged was Don Juan Nepomuceno de Contreras, some of whose story has appeared earlier, for this twenty-year-old had begun his quest for honor in 1795.[32] Don Juan had confessed to the Cámara that he was the son of a priest who had engaged in a sexual relationship before his ordination; he also admitted that he hoped to follow his father into the priesthood. Although bureaucrats had reluctantly granted his application— he was an *hijo natural,* and these usually were approved—they had taken the rare step of qualifying their dispensation so that he could neither hold higher church offices nor serve as a cleric in the town in which his father was a priest.

It is unclear if these strictures were the cause, but Don Juan never entered the priesthood. Documents in 1806 show him mortgaging some of his father's property in a commercial venture.[33] He had been a merchant for many years and was forty-six when his reputation was threatened in 1821 on the plaza in Bogotá.

As with many challenges to honor, the underlying cause was competition, although the precipitating incident in this case revealed only superficial aspects of the contretemps. Don Juan had been gambling with a group of comrades in the Bogotá plaza when luck seems to have favored him; it failed Lieutenant Colonel Pedro Mires and his army officer friends, however.[34] Tensions must have been high, because the lieutenant colonel became violent and began cursing and threatening Don Juan.

Don Juan remembered that the officer had first called him a "robber" and then a "mulatto rogue," and he then challenged Don Juan to a duel in which he "promised to shed [his] blood, to take out [his] eyes, [his] tongue, and . . . cut [him] into pieces." Although defended by his friends, Don Juan declared that he could not underestimate the "gravity of [such] a public offense," especially since he had been called a "coward." However, the merchant added that he had refused to duel because he "respected the laws." Don Juan and his friends complained to the lieutenant colonel's superiors, and the officer was imprisoned to await judgment.

Although Don Juan's account of this incident is fascinating in its own right, it is even more so given the testimony of other witnesses. These spectators added details that Don Juan left out, details revealing that not only the traditional colonial preoccupations with race and birth but also clashes over republican politics could now become intermeshed in the negotiation of honor. The army officers at first had belittled Don Juan with the customary epithets, including that he was of "low birth," a "badly born, indecent robber," and "the son of a *mulata* whore." The lieutenant colonel then went on to add political insult to the equation. He declared that "when he was putting his breast to the bullets, Contreras was occupied in praising the *godos* [Colombian conservatives] in order to preserve his interests." He charged that the merchant "only lacks a lance to go out onto the roads to steal, for he is the greatest robber." The army officer considered himself, on the other hand, to be a "liberator."

Time in jail seems to have quelled some of the lieutenant colonel's passion. He wrote Don Juan that it made no sense "to want to sustain . . . such an involuntary offense." He admitted that he had "forgotten [his] education," and that "having regained [his] calm," he recognized that he had been "wrong" to utter such insults. He hoped that the "present letter" would serve as "sufficient satisfaction." The lieutenant colonel realized that public retribution was necessary to erase the insult. He assured Don Juan that he "would have no embarrassment in agreeing that [Don Juan] could show [the letter] to all the world, so that they could know that I am a man subject to error, my soul is sufficiently elevated to be able to confess its faults."

Don Juan responded generously to what seems to have been a less than humbly offered apology. He wrote the army officer: "I do not require any further satisfaction from you than that which you have condescended to give me through your letter. I consider it sufficient." He hoped that the insults against him were "erase[d] from the memory of those that heard them, and they have disappeared from my own." He suggested that the lieutenant colonel now "send to the commanding general your original letter, and this my answer, so that these documents might bring the most favorable effects." An obviously relieved general was happy to see the men reconciled, and he decided to punish his officer no longer.

This incident illustrates how the traditions of the colony could blend into those of the republic; negotiations over honor would be redefined and eventually replaced by other expressions and concepts.[35] What is relevant here is that Don Juan felt no need to brandish his civil legitimation, yet he still felt secure enough to act with a certain understanding and even grace when his reputation was impugned in public. His story, as well as those of others who were legitimated, reveals that *gracias al sacar* met its ultimate challenge when it provided personal security, enabling those who received it to interact confidently with their peers.

THIRTEEN

Conclusion

In 1801 an *expósito* returned to the *casa de expósitos* in Havana to seek his roots.[1] He asked an accommodating cleric to look up the date and time that he had been placed in the revolving door and left as abandoned. The incident became of historical significance when the anonymous priest added a comment to the original entry: He noted that there was a disparity between the race of the orphan as an infant and as an adult. As was customary in many orphanages that gave *expósitos* the racial benefit of the doubt, the abandoned baby had been listed as "apparently white." However the cleric observed that "the [person] listed in this entry presented himself to ask me for it, and he turned out to be a *pardo*, as he himself confessed."

Around the same time as the Havana incident, colonists in Yucatán complained that the "frequent mix" of "Spaniards, Indians, and mulattos" meant that it was increasingly difficult to divide the population for tax purposes, given that "the signs of color, skin, and appearance are very fallible."[2] In Sopetrán and Tunja in colonial Colombia, Indians and whites were so intermixed that settlers could distinguish the first only by their "census-listing, given the mixture and ties that have occurred."[3] In Cumaná, Venezuelan colonists charged that a "fatal mixture" of Europeans, Indians, and blacks had led to racial confusion; some had "written their baptismal certificates in the book [reserved for] Spaniards and erased the note [of race] of their ancestors through forbidden means."[4] In Caracas, colonists demanded that priests "justify quality" and keep different baptismal registers for "white legitimate Spaniards" so as not to "confuse families and to give occasion to lawsuits."[5]

In the last quarter of the eighteenth century local elites looked around them and did not like what they saw. These examples from the circum-Caribbean, where the process was most advanced, provide striking evidence that elites had become much more self-conscious about the ambiguous barriers of race and birth that had previously established their precedence and that were now under challenge. Their response was heightened discrimination, which, since it reduced opportunities for informal passing, encouraged their illegitimate sons and daughters to resort to *gracias al sacar.*

The collective biographies of those who sought civil redress form only the tip of a very large iceberg, but not the one described by Edward Shorter in the introductory chapter. His metaphoric ice floe characterized a "traditional society" that was "frozen by the command of custom."[6] The ice began to break up as couples either chose sexual intimacy out of affection or found their lives wrenched by the dislocations that would bring Europe and Anglo-America into the industrial age. Across the Atlantic in the Hispanic world, neither a sexual nor an industrial revolution had much changed the ways in which men and women courted, made love, chose to marry (or to live together without marrying), or formed families. Yet as the eighteenth century drew to a close, issues surrounding sexuality and illegitimacy still served as flawless markers of a society on the edge of metamorphosis.

After almost three colonial centuries during which natal and racial markers that legitimized hierarchy became increasingly ambiguous, Spanish America approached—if not a breakup—the beginning of a meltdown. The lives of the men and women who figure in the *gracias al sacar* depositions illuminate the attitudes and practices of a late-colonial world increasingly under challenge but that would still establish the core ethos for much of the century to follow.

A final weaving of the strands of this work reveals fundamental patterns that appear and reappear in the collective biographies of those whose lives are chronicled here. Since *cédula* petitioners were at the permeable boundary of the social hierarchy, their efforts to be included expose fundamental processes in how colonial society worked. Personal relationships were fundamental, for they coded what was private and what was public and determined who would pass and who would not. Even though a hierarchical culture demanded whiteness and legitimacy as prerequisites for honor, everything was subject to negotiation. Patriarchy promoted dual standards and unequal relationships between men and women, but it permitted unexpected flexibilities and demanded unanticipated prices. Colonial expressions of the private and the public, hierarchy, and gender form the warp and weft that reveal the larger social patterns of which *cédula* mothers, fathers, and illegitimates were but a part.

Eighteenth-century elites lived in dual worlds distinguished by personal connections. They inhabited a private world of family, kin, and intimate friends, as well a public world that included social peers and everyone else. Language distinguished between what was private and intimate and what was public and "notorious." This duality permitted the construction of public reputations that differed from private persona. Women might be privately pregnant and publicly virgins; parents might recognize illegitimate children in private but not in public; families nurtured illegitimate children privately, before their illegitimacy occasioned public insult; parents might leave illegitimate offspring possessions in private, in contradiction to public inheritance law; illegitimates or mulattos might construct public reputations as legitimates or whites. Royal officials found it necessary to probe both the private and public status of petitioners.

Passing was essential in a hierarchical society that explicitly accorded worth and power only to those who acted according to traditional norms and who met the ascribed characteristics of birth and race. Rather than succeeding in spite of "defects," individuals changed their birth or race to pass, and therefore to conform, at least in public. Passing succeeded when elites or the state made individual exceptions and informally or officially accepted the disparity between a private reality and a constructed public persona. The dynamic that underlay passing explains both the success and the ultimate failure of the Bourbon social reforms. An intervention such as *gracias al sacar*, which provided mobility to an individual, might be successful; universal legislation could not.

Honor was the reason that eighteenth-century Latin Americans wanted to pass, for it was the matrix through which Hispanic canons of birth and *limpieza de sangre*, which defined hierarchy, were made evident. To lack honor was simply to be disqualified from most positions of political, economic, and social prestige. Honor was a public phenomenon and constantly subject to challenge, for it could be threatened, lost, gained, and regained. Elite parents, their illegitimate offspring, royal officials, and prominent townspeople figured as protagonists in honor negotiations when traditional norms were violated.

Elite women had to maintain public reputations as persons of honor in order to marry well and pass honor on to the next generation. Although any other outcome was problematic, honor could still be in negotiation at many points along this continuum. Women put their honor in danger when they engaged in sexual intercourse with their lovers; they risked their reputation if pregnancy ensued, although the cost varied depending on whether the pregnancy remained private or became public knowledge. The status of unwed mothers remained in limbo as they waited for extended engagements to end, either successfully in marriage or unsuccessfully in rejection or abandonment. Women might reconstruct a challenged reputation with years of proper conduct, or fully restore it with marriage. Even women who, through sexual relationships with priests or married men, forfeited the potential to pass on honor might ease their own loss of honor with the purchase of civil legitimation for their offspring.

Inasmuch as the public persona of elite men was much more expansive than that of women, negotiations of honor were correspondingly different. Men bargained for status not only when they negotiated marriage and passed honor to their children but also when they held public office or practiced elite occupations. Both patriarchy and biology gave men much more latitude when certain issues of honor were at stake. Public knowledge of sexual relationships or broken promises to wed did not ultimately damage male honor. Yet negotiations might still occur as men struggled with their own consciences when they broke promises or failed to support lovers and offspring. Some fathers ultimately realized that certain issues of honor could not be negotiated, for their refusal to wed precluded the passage of honor to their illegitimate sons and daughters. Only an appeal for royal intervention might then ameliorate the situation.

Linked in blood but not in honor with their elite parents, illegitimates both were negotiated about and themselves negotiated the issue of honor. If unwed parents fulfilled their promises to marry, the automatic legitimation that followed fully restored honor to the next generation. If they did not marry, illegitimates might still informally pass as persons of honor. Applications for *gracias al sacar* initiated further give and take as petitioners provided and withheld information that would further their case. The newly legitimated continued the process of negotiation, for, just like everyone else, they still had to defend their honor against slander and challenge.

Royal officials negotiated honor when as agents of the king they balanced the effects of the royal power to dispense *gracias* against their own objectives as imperial gatekeepers. As the century passed, they debated the benefits of providing honor to the illegitimate offspring of colonial elites against the risks of condoning promiscuity. The solution of Bourbon reformers was first to demand a greater quantity of information. Reformers then opened the channel so that the natural children of unmarried parents might relatively easily acquire honor, pass it to the next generation, strengthen elite families, and maintain hierarchy. Yet the *Camaristas* steadfastly refused to promote Bourbon measures that indiscriminately bargained honor for cash or that opened the gate to the *adulterino*, the *sacrílego*, or the *expósito*.

The ultimate negotiators of honor were local elites, for they had the last word. Only they could decide on a day-to-day basis whether to accept public constructions that differed from private reality—for that was the arena in which the vast majority of honor negotiations took place. Their tolerance depended on a multitude of variables that affected passing, including the degree and obviousness of the defect, the manifest worth of the aspirant, and the efficacy of the private circle's promotion of an alternative persona. Elites who felt challenged proved less open to negotiation than their peers in other regions of the empire. As the century closed elites everywhere proved increasingly reluctant to make exceptions on issues of honor, facing, as they did, heightened pressures from below.

Given the depth of the patriarchal overlay on every aspect of social relations, there were few arenas in which gender did not make a difference. Elite women had public persona, but only as mates and mothers who could pass on honor; men enjoyed the full complement of public honors, responsibilities, and power. Female honor demanded public virginity although promises of matrimony, private pregnancies, and extended engagements might provide room for maneuver; men could be honorable and promiscuous. Mothers of illegitimates more commonly lacked access to material resources for themselves and their offspring; fathers of illegitimates were not prejudiced in their potential for political or economic success or in their marriageability. It was easier for illegitimate women informally to pass and enjoy honorable status than for illegitimate men. Royal officials considered the civil legitimation of women to be less a challenge to the status quo than that of men.

Ultimately the passage of years positioned men and women differently at distinctive points in their life courses. It was essential for younger elite women to maintain public reputations as virgins and women of honor so they might be eligible for matrimony. As these women grew older, issues that had been critical during their late teens or twenties were resolved by matrimony, precluded by public pregnancies or affairs, or became less pressing as the possibility of marriage declined. When illegitimate girls became adults they faced additional challenges as they tried to pass, first as marriageable women of honor and later, when they became mothers, to secure honor for the next generation.

The reputation of elite men throughout their life course was not much affected by public knowledge of their sexual activity. Younger eligible men were more likely to use the promise of matrimony as a lure to honorable female peers to engage in clandestine sexual liaisons. As they grew older bachelors commonly engaged in public and long-term and sometimes serial relationships; widowers often had affairs after or between wives. Illegitimate men lacked honorable public reputations, suffered severe discrimination, and were twice as likely as women to seek official legitimation. In their early adult lives illegitimate men applied to further their political and economic mobility; later they sought honor to pass it securely to their children.

The ways in which Spanish Americans constructed their private and public worlds, passed, legitimized hierarchy, and dealt across the gender divide would change as the eighteenth century flowed into the next. Much would also endure. Many of those whose lives appear here would participate in these transformations, or it would be their children or grandchildren who would confront, maintain, or alter the colonial legacy. Included among these was Don Gabriel Muñoz.

More than two hundred years ago Don Gabriel Muñoz failed to receive a proper hello on a street in Medellín, Colombia, and began his search for honor. In the process, he, and hundreds of others who shared his situation, provided extraordinary glimpses into some usually hidden aspects of the Hispanic colonial world. Because Don Gabriel started not only his own quest but also eventually my own, it seems appropriate to end with him.

After his legitimation in 1793 Don Gabriel was elected to the Medellín city council, a post that had never before been held by an illegitimate. His marriage to Doña María Castrillón Hernández resulted in five children—all of whom enjoyed that title of "Don" and "Doña" that had been so important to their father.[7] His youngest daughter, Doña Pascuala, married into a prominent Rionegro family and had five children of her own.[8] One of her sons, José María Córdoba, became one of Bolívar's best generals and a hero of Colombian independence. He commanded armies that fought from Boyacá to Ayacucho as the colonial world of his grandfather broke apart, and a new Latin America struggled to be born.

Reference Material

Sources, Data Bases, Monetary Usages, José, and *Audiencias*

THE MYSTERY HUNT FOR THE 'GRACIAS AL SACAR'

The heart of this study is the applications, responses by royal officials, and the resulting decrees of the *gracias al sacar*. When I began this research I was not sure if these existed or, if they did, how they might be found. I found mentions of *gracias al sacar* in the Medellín documents concerning Don Gabriel Muñoz, references in Magnus Mörner, a reprint of one case in the *Hispanic American Historical Review*, and the Konetzke collection included several examples.[1] These were the only clues I had to their existence. If a sufficient mass of such documents remained, they were likely to be in the collections of the Archive of the Indies in Seville, but exactly where was the question.

A one-month exploratory trip to Seville and a study of available indexes there yielded two important *legajos* (loose cartons with hundreds of pages) that referred directly to legitimation materials.[2] These included copies of some of the original legitimation decrees issued to petitioners in the Americas. However, these decrees were largely formulaic, containing only a personalized paragraph or two about the recipients: where they lived, whether their parents were known, and sometimes their natal status. That was a start, but the in-depth information supplied by the petitioners to the Council and Cámara of the Indies was still missing. Although there were tens of thousands of archival *legajos*, no available indexes led directly to this information.

When I returned for six months of Fulbright research in Seville, my goal was to find the more lengthy application depositions. The key to the puzzle proved to be the several legitimation cases published by Konetzke. When I used Konetzke's citations to consult the original documents, I found that they contained much more extensive information than he had published. The original documents included the letter from the petitioner, baptismal certificates, pages of depositions from witnesses, as well as commentaries by royal officials and their decision.

When I searched the Konetzke reprints of selected legitimation petitions for patterns, I discovered that his selections had originated from the earlier *legajos* in each of the thirteen *audiencia* divisions of the archive (Santo Domingo, Mexico, Guadalajara, Panama, Guatemala, Santa Fe, Quito, Lima, Charcas, Cuzco, Chile, Buenos Aires, and Caracas). Eventually I realized that the section described as *Cartas y Expedientes*, literally "Letters and Papers," seemed usually to include legitimation applications. The problem was that this general description was the only guide to that section, and that each of the thirteen divisions had such a section, which in turn was divided by year; each year contained usually two or three *legajos*. In other words, to look for eighteenth-century legitimation documents for just one *audiencia*, say Buenos Aires, I would need to review at least three hundred volumes with hundreds of pages in each volume; to cover all of the Spanish Americas I would have to search through more than three thousand *legajos*, each with hundreds of pages!

Back to the drawing board. I next began to look for an index to the section of *Cartas y Expedientes*. Susan Socolow was then working at the archive and knew the Buenos Aires *audiencia* well; I picked that jurisdiction so that I might consult with her. The beginning of the Buenos Aires *audiencia* catalogue contains lists of undescribed volumes entitled "Indices." I began to consult those to find a possible guide to the *Cartas y Expedientes* section. Eventually I discovered that in the nineteenth century someone had compiled a handwritten book indexing every document that had arrived and had been preserved in the Buenos Aires section of *Cartas y Expedientes*. Instead of calling up three hundred *legajos*, I could read a two-hundred-page index for this section of the Buenos Aires *audiencia*. The index was organized by year, so if, for example, sixty documents had arrived in 1784, they would be listed in order of arrival.

This handwritten index did not correlate directly with the current Archive of the Indies catalogue, which listed the number of *legajos* for each year in the section of *Cartas y Expedientes* for Buenos Aires. However, it was possible to look in the current index and discover, for example, that there were three *legajos* for 1784 for *Cartas y Expedientes*, as well as their present archival locations. If the nineteenth-century list for the year 1784 noted that an application for legitimation had arrived as document 3, the chances were that the document would be in the first volume of the three *legajos* for 1784, and so I could correlate this information with the current archival catalogue. There was therefore a close, if not always exact, correlation between the nineteenth-century handwritten index and the modern archival listings.

The *gracias al sacar* could now be found. Similar nineteenth-century handwritten indexes existed for the *Cartas y Expedientes* section in each *audiencia*.[3] Using these twelve nineteenth-century handwritten indexes, I was able to compile a master list of all legitimation petitions that had arrived in the eighteenth century, and then to consult and microfilm documents throughout the archive. In the course of this work I discovered that the handwritten indexes extended to 1820, but the actual documents stopped in 1799 (except for Santo Domingo). Although the reward of a dinner in the best restaurant in Seville was offered to anyone who could find the missing documents, they remain lost. I also searched for discussions in the Cámara over policy and petitions, which yielded a few more cases.

Therefore the data bases that make up this study proceed from a systematic sweep of relevant documents in all *audiencia* divisions of *Cartas y Expedientes*, combined with the two *legajos* of issued legitimation decrees. I am confident that this approach yielded the large majority of legitimation cases. This belief is confirmed by comments within documents in which royal officials refer to other cases; in only one instance do they refer to a case that is not included in this data base. As analysis proceeded, it became clear that the basic information could best be understood if divided into other data bases, which are explained below. In data base citations the first number indicates the particular data base, the second number the total number of cases.

EXISTING DATA BASES

Data Base 1-244 (DB 1-244)

This data base includes every possible reference to legitimation cases and is used to provide completeness concerning time and geographical sweep. The 244 cases used in the fullest data base include 101 cases with full petition and *cédula*; 41 with full petition (incomplete cases or those denied); 69 cases of *cédula* only; and 5 cases from Cámara testimony. The 28 remaining cases are "lost," inasmuch as they derive from index references to cases from 1799 to 1820 that appear in the nineteenth-century handwritten indexes to each *audiencia* that, with the exception of Santo Domingo, cannot be located in the archive.

Data Base 2-216 (DB 2-216)

This data base includes everything in DB 1-244 except the 28 missing cases. This data base incorporates the greatest number of documents with the most complete information.

Data Base 3-142 (DB 3-142)

This data base includes cases in which the legitimation can be traced from the original application to approval or disapproval by the Cámara. This data base measures the success rates of petitioners.

Data Base 4-187 (DB 4-187)

This data base selects for parents. Because some mothers and fathers had more than one illegitimate child, this data base counts such men and women only once.

Data Base 5-67 (DB 5-67)

This data base selects for cases from DB 2-216 that meet the criteria for private pregnancy.

Data Base 6-139 (DB 6-139)

This data base includes cases in which the year on the baptismal certificates of illegitimates can be determined. It analyzes information at the time of the sexual relationship rather than the time (usually decades later) of the application for legitimation.

Data Base 7-54 (DB 7-54)

This data base selects for private pregnancy from DB 6-139.

NOTES ON MONEY

Usually in references to payment for *gracias al sacar*, I have referred to the monetary denomination used in the document. However since petitioners paid for *gracias al sacar* in several different denominations, I have also had to convert disparate currencies into one to be able to compare prices over time and to total the amounts received. I have kept the following rules: pesos fuertes and duros sencillos were counted as equaling fifteen reales vellón. If the designation was just "pesos" I multiplied by fifteen reales vellón. A peso of silver (plata) was considered to be the equivalent of eight reales, which was multiplied by 2.5 to equal the number of reales vellón (one silver peso equaled twenty reales vellón). One peso equals sixteen quartos, or eight reales; where colonists used quartos I assumed it was a silver peso and multiplied by twenty for reales vellón.[4]

ON JOSÉ AND 'AUDIENCIA' NAMES

José, or the Latin American propensity to name men and women according to variations on the theme, proved to be a problem, as spelling even within documents could be erratic. Sometimes men would be called José, sometimes Josef, sometimes

Joseph. I decided to leave José when used but to convert the rest to Joseph and, if a woman, to Josepha.

I also eased geographical specificity for readers unfamiliar with New Spain (Mexico), New Granada (Colombia and Venezuela), Charcas (Argentina, Uruguay, and parts of Bolivia), Santa Fe de Bogotá (Bogotá), sometimes using the more familiar contemporary designations.

Supporting Tables

APPENDIX TABLE I

Percent of Private Pregnancies by Decade

Decade	Private Pregnancy		Other		Total
	N	%	N	%	N
Pre-1700	0	0.0	2	100.0	2
1710–19	5	71.4	2	28.6	7
1720–29	1	11.1	8	88.9	9
1730–39	5	50.0	5	50.0	10
1740–49	4	26.7	11	73.3	15
1750–59	8	38.1	13	61.9	21
1760–69	9	42.9	12	57.1	21
1770–79	15	48.4	16	51.6	31
1780–89	5	35.7	9	64.3	14
1790–99	1	14.3	6	85.7	7
1800–10	1	50.0	1	50.0	2
Total	54	38.8	85	61.2	139

SOURCE: DB 7-54.

Changing Nature of Sexual Relationships That Led to Private Pregnancies

| | Private Pregnancy | Promise of Matrimony | | | | | |
| | | Yes | | No | | Unknown | |
Decade	N	N	%	N	%	N	%
Pre-1700	0						
1710–19	5	1	20.0	2	40.0	2	40.0
1720–29	1	0	0.0	0	0.0	1	100.0
1730–39	5	2	40.0	0	0.0	3	60.0
1740–49	4	2	50.0	1	25.0	1	25.0
1750–59	8	4	50.0	2	25.0	2	25.0
1760–69	9	2	22.0	4	44.5	3	33.3
1770–79	15	4	26.7	6	40.0	5	33.3
1780–89	5	2	40.0	1	20.0	2	40.0
1790–99	1	0	0.0	0	0.0	1	100.0
1800–10	1	0	0.0	0	0.0	1	100.0
Total	5	17	31.5	16	29.6	21	38.9

SOURCE: DB 7-54.

Potential Marital "State" of Those Who Arranged Private Pregnancies

| | Single | | Married | | Religious | | Incestuous | | Unknown | | Total |
Decade	N	%	N	%	N	%	N	%	N	%	N
Pre-1700											0
1710–19	1	20.0	0	0.0	1	20.0	0	0.0	3	60.0	5
1720–29	0	0.0	0	0.0	0	0.0	0	0.0	1	100.0	1
1730–39	3	60.0	0	0.0	0	0.0	0	0.0	2	40.0	5
1740–49	2	50.0	1	25.0	0	0.0	0	0.0	1	25.0	4
1750–59	4	50.0	2	25.0	0	0.0	0	0.0	2	25.0	8
1760–69	5	55.6	1	11.1	1	11.1	0	0.0	2	22.2	9
1770–79	8	53.3	3	20.0	1	6.7	0	0.0	3	20.0	15
1780–89	2	40.0	0	0.0	0	0.0	1	20.0	2	40.0	5
1790–99	1	100.0	0	0.0	0	0.0	0	0.0	0	0.0	1
1800–10	1	100.0	0	0.0	0	0.0	0	0.0	0	0.0	1
Total											54

SOURCE: DB 7-54.

APPENDIX TABLE 4

Eighteenth-Century Promises of Matrimony by Decade

| Decade | Promise of Matrimony | | | | | | Total |
| | Yes | | No | | Unknown | | |
	N	%	N	%	N	%	N
Pre-1700	0	0.0	0	0.0	2	100.0	2
1710–19	1	14.2	3	42.9	3	42.9	7
1720–29	2	22.2	4	44.5	3	33.3	9
1730–39	2	20.0	3	30.0	5	50.0	10
1740–49	4	26.7	2	13.3	9	60.0	15
1750–59	6	28.6	8	38.1	7	33.3	21
1760–69	5	23.8	6	28.6	10	47.6	21
1770–79	8	25.8	8	25.8	15	48.4	31
1780–89	4	28.6	5	35.7	5	35.7	14
1790–99	0	0.0	3	42.9	4	57.1	7
1800–10	1	50.0	0	0.0	1	5.0	2
Total	33	23.7	42	30.1	64	46.1	139

SOURCE: DB 6-139.

APPENDIX TABLE 5

Marital State of Fathers at Birth of
Illegitimate Child

	N	%
Single	100	53.5
Priest	12	6.4
Widower	4	2.1
Married	19	10.2
Unknown	52	27.8
Total	187	100.0

SOURCE: DB 4-187.

APPENDIX TABLE 6
When Did Private Pregnancy Become Public?

	N	%
Still secret at time of petition	39	58.2
Public at death of mother	1	1.5
Public at time of petition	5	7.4
Public before petition	16	23.9
Unknown	6	9.0
Total	67	100.0

SOURCE: DB 5-67.

APPENDIX TABLE 7
Why Did Private Pregnancy Become Public?

	N	%
Never public	39	58.2
Mother acknowledged child	6	9.0
Mother publicly lived with father	2	3.0
Result of lawsuit	3	4.5
At time of petition	5	7.5
At time parents recognized child	3	4.5
At time parents married	1	1.4
At time scandal arose	1	1.4
Unknown	7	10.5
Total	67	100.0

SOURCE: DB 5-67.

APPENDIX TABLE 8

Reasons Given by Fathers of Illegitimates for Not Marrying

	N	%
Previous vows		
Already married	21	
Priest	11	
Subtotal	32	17.2
Need for Permission		
Relative	6	
Soldier	3	
Bureaucrat	2	
Subtotal	11	5.9
Other reasons		
Father:		
Wanted to marry another	5	
Rejected mother	4	
Mother a *parda*	3	
Father away during birth	2	
Needed money to marry	2	
Father died	1	
Wanted to be a priest	1	
Subtotal	18	9.6
Mother:		
Mother died	8	
Mother already married	4	
Subtotal	12	6.4
Unknown	114	60.9
Total	187	100.0

SOURCE: DB 4-187.

APPENDIX TABLE 9

Occupations of Father

	N	%
Military	27	14.4
Political	18	9.6
Religious	14	7.5
Commerce	13	7.0
Subtotal	72	38.5
Other	19	10.2
Unknown	96	51.3
Total	187	100.0

SOURCE: DB 4-187.

APPENDIX TABLE 10

Applications Involving Race and 'Gracias al Sacar'

Audiencia	N. Race	Total N. Audiencia	Race as % Audiencia	% Race Total	Audiencia as % Total
Panama	2	4	50.0	12.5	1.9
Buenos Aires	3	17	17.6	18.7	7.9
Mexico	3	30	10.0	18.7	13.9
Santa Fe	3	11	9.1	18.7	5.0
Santo Domingo	4	84	4.9	25.0	38.9
Lima	1	25	4.0	6.4	11.6
Other Audiencias*	0	45	0.0	0.0	20.8
Totals	16	216	7.4	100.0	100.0

SOURCE: DB 2-216.
*Audiencias with no petitions involving race include Charcas, Caracas, Quito, Guatemala, Guadalajara.

TABLE II

Comparison of Natal and Baptismal Status of Infants

	Baptismal Listing				Natal Status			
	Hijo natural	Padres no conocidos	Unknown	Total	Hijo natural	Bastard	Unknown	Total
Before 1749	18	20	5	43	27	6	10	43
After 1749	34	39	23	96	61	20	15	96
Totals	52	59	28	139	88	26	25	139

SOURCE: DB 6-139.

APPENDIX TABLE 12

Goal of 'Gracias al Sacar'

Reason given	N	%
Honor and property	98	45.4
Honor	86	39.8
Property	13	6.0
Other	19	8.8
Total	216	100.0

SOURCE: DB 2-216.

Passing and Political Office by Region

Region and *Audiencias*	Offices Held			
	Municipal Council	Royal Officials	Other	Total Offices
Caribbean and northern South America				
Santo Domingo	0	0	0	0
Caracas	0	0	0	0
Santa Fe	0	0	1*	1
Mexico				
Central Mexico	0	0	0	0
Guadalajara	0	0	0	0
South America				
Quito	0	0	0	0
Lima	2	0	0	2
Charcas	1	0	1**	2
Buenos Aires	1	0	0	1
Chile	0	0	0	0
Central America				
Guatemala	1	1	0	2
Panama	0	0	2	2
Total	5	3	2	10

SOURCE: DB 2-216.
* *alcalde juez pedáneo*
** *protector de naturales*

Male/Female Applications by Decade

	N. Male	N. Female	Ratio Male-Female
17th Century			
1630–39	2	2	1-1
1640–49	1	0	1-0
1650–59	3	1	3-1
Subtotal	6	3	2-1
18th Century: Decades of *Gracias al Sacar* Policy Formation			
1720–29	4	3	1.3-1
1730–39	1	1	1-1
1740–49	9	1	9-1
1750–59	5	0	5-0
1760–69	10	2	5-1
1770–79	6	4	1.5-1
Subtotal	35	11	3.2-1
18th Century: Decades of Greatest Increase in Applications			
1780–89	30	26	1.2-1
1790–99	49	19	2.6-1
Subtotal	79	45	1.8-1
19th Century			
1800–09	9	5	1.8-1
1810–19	14	9	1.6-1
Subtotal	23	14	1.6-1
Total	143	73	2-1

SOURCE: DB 2-216.

Glossary

ab intestato	Intestate succession without a written testament.
adulterino,(a)	Illegitimate son or daughter, when one or both of the parents is married.
aguardiente	Anise-flavored alcoholic drink.
alcalde juez pedáneo	Neighborhood (*barrio*) official.
alcalde ordinario	Annually elected city council (cabildo) official.
alguacil mayor	Constable of the district governor.
apoderado	Legal representative with power of attorney.
arancel	Price list.
audiencia	High court whose jurisdiction also defined territorial divisions in Spanish America. See Map 1.
barraganía	Medieval and early modern period legal contract between unwed lovers; concubinage.
calidad	Social standing defined primarily by birth and race but also by occupation, wealth, and kinship.
Cámara, Cámara de	Subcouncil of the Council of the Indies Gracias y Justicia that, among other duties, dispensed *gracias al sacar*.
capellanía	Religious trust, often supporting priests who celebrated masses for those who endowed them.
casas de expósitos	Depository for abandoned infants; orphanage.
casta	A general term designating the racially mixed; someone who is not white or Indian.
cédula	Royal decree.

colegio	Secondary school.
consulta	Advisory, written opinion.
contador	Auditor, treasury officer.
converso(a)	Convert to Catholicism, usually Jewish.
corregidor	Magistrate and chief judicial officer for a provincial jurisdiction.
Council of the Indies	The supreme administrative council that governed colonial Spanish America.
crianza	The upbringing and education of children.
encomienda	A grant to a colonist of the tribute (usually in goods or cash, sometimes in the early colony in labor) originating from a designated number of Indians. The recipient of an *encomienda* (*encomendero*) was obliged in turn to defend and Christianize his tribute-payers.
Español(a)	Spaniard born in Spain and the Americas; someone who is white.
esponsales	Engagement.
espúreo,(a)	Child born as a result of adultery or whose father was a cleric.
expósito(a)	Someone "exposed," or abandoned, as a child; designation on a baptismal certificate that signified unknown parentage.
fiscal	Crown attorney.
forced heirs	Relatives in a legally defined hierarchy of succession; the order of succession in an intestate succession.
fuero	Distinctive legal status attached to clergy, military, and Indians.
habilitación	Exemption from ecclesiastical discrimination against illegitimates seeking to become religious; did not eliminate civil prejudice.
hijo(a) natural	Illegitimate child whose parents were unmarried but not related by prohibited degrees of kinship.
hijosdalgo	"Men of importance"; an untitled noble.

incestuoso(a)	Illegitimate whose unmarried parents were related according to Catholic degrees of kinship.
legajo	Carton or book containing archival documents.
legítima	The four-fifths of an estate reserved for forced heirs, divided equally except for the *mejora*.
limpieza de sangre	Purity of blood, esp. absence of Moorish, Jewish, heretical, or, in the Americas, African ancestry.
machismo	The mentality that promoted male promiscuity.
mala raza	"Bad race"; racial mixture.
mala vida	"Bad life"; usually spousal abuse.
maravedí	Monetary unit, one thirty-fourth of a *real*.
marianismo	Female mentality reactive to *machismo* that emphasizes devotion to the Virgin Mary and female superiority.
mayorazgo	Entailed estate.
mayordomo de propios	Chief steward of civic property.
mejora	The one-third portion of the *legítima* that might be given to a favored forced heir.
mestizo(a)	Offspring of Spanish and Indian ancestry.
montepío	Benevolent society that aided the sick and aged, often established by guilds.
moreno(a)	Person who is racially mixed, nonwhite; mulatto.
morisco(a)	Person who is racially mixed, often with African and Indian ancestry.
mulato(a)	Person of mixed European and African ancestry.
Obedezco pero no cumplo	"I obey, but I do not comply"; the temporary local veto of a royal order deemed too disruptive to implement.
oidor	Judge on an *audiencia*.
padres no conocidos	"Unknown parents"; baptismal designation given to infants (usually illegitimates) not recognized by their parents.
padrino	Godfather at baptism.

palabra de casamiento	Promise of matrimony.
pardo(a)	Dark-skinned person.
pasquín	Satirical verse.
patria potestad	Patriarchal rights over offspring.
peninsular	Person born in Spain.
pragmática	Royal ordinance.
procurador general	City attorney.
quinteron(a)	Someone considered one-fifth racially mixed.
regidor	City council officer, usually a permanent official who purchased his position for life.
sacrílego(a)	Illegitimate son or daughter of a priest or nun.
sello	Royal seal, placed on documents to authenticate them.
tertulia	Social gathering.
vellón	Small coin.
visitador	Royal official sent (often unexpectedly) to judge the conduct of officials or to initiate reforms.

Notes

Chapter 1. Antecedents

I have established the following expedited procedure for citation of *gracias al sacar* cases. In the text, I will provide the reference on first mention in an analysis and will not cite it again if there are immediate following quotations. I will repeat the reference, however, if there is an intervening footnote with a different citation. In the notes, I will cite the archive only at the beginning if a series of documents all come from the same location.

1. ACM-Medellín, vol. 38, n. 7, 1787. See also Twinam, *Miners*, pp. 118–23; Dueñas-Vargas, pp. 138–39, has interesting comments on the use of "Doña."

2. Such popular usage of "Don" among elite peers was common, although not technically accurate, given that they were not *hijosdalgo*. Konetzke, 3:1, n. 251, 1779, reproduces a *consulta* of the Cámara of the Indies about this time in which an official complains of such "vulgar usage" and suggests that colonists be charged for the privilege. However the Council of the Indies decided that doing so would lead to "pernicious consequences." Konetzke, 3:2, n. 279, 1785, provides documentation of an even more interesting example, in which Don Pedro Marti y Romeu from Cuba petitioned the Council of the Indies to make him a noble in exchange for his many services to the crown, and instead they sent him back permission to use the title of "Don." He made the telling comment that "far from favoring him, this was prejudicial, given that the custom in America was to give this address to all the Spanish who lived [there] and had means." Since he was already a "Don," he refused the honor and the payment of the requisite tax! The title of Don was eventually included for purchase in the 1795 price list for *gracias al sacar* but remained a source of local controversy. Konetzke, 3:2, n. 348, 1796.

3. ACM-Medellín, vol. 38, n. 7, 1787.

4. Twinam, *Miners*, p. 122. My own research supported his proposition and also confirmed that Gabriel Muñoz had been such a host and had held office, albeit the lowest of neighborhood posts.

5. Twinam, *Miners*, pp. 118–29.

6. In the eighteenth century decisions were made by the Cámara de Gracias y Justicia, which was composed of royal officials from the Council of the Indies.

7. Twinam, *Miners*, p. 122.

8. Shorter, "Illegitimacy," p. 251; Crenshaw, p. 178.

9. Newman, p. 142; Rogers, pp. 368–69; Mitchison and Leneman, p. 231; Depauw, p. 189; Meyer, p. 252; Segalen, p. 131; Knodel and Hochstadt, p. 284; Lee, p. 422; Watt, p. 142; Kertzner, "Gender Ideology," p. 7; Rothman, p. 414; Smith, p. 370; Wells, pp. 354–55; Gieysztor, p. 431; Palli, p. 474.

10. Post, p. 29; Laslett, "Introduction," p. 26.

11. Shorter, "Illegitimacy," pp. 252–53.

12. Shorter, "Bastardy," p. 459.

13. Stone, "Comment," p. 509.

14. Tilly, Scott, and Cohen, p. 464.

15. Ibid., p. 469.

16. Mitchison and Leneman, p. 236.

17. Rogers, pp. 368–69; Segalen, p. 131; Levin and Wrightson, p. 175; Flandrin, p. 37; Fairchilds, p. 651; Lee, pp. 410, 419; Meteyard, "Comment," p. 512. Although European and U.S. scholars debate causation, there is much consensus as well. All agree that local custom strikingly influenced patterns of sexual relationships so that illegitimacy rates can vary widely within small areas—or, as Peter Laslett has suggested—by microlocalities. Examples include: Laslett, "Introduction," p. 59; Meyer, p. 250; Depauw, p. 162; Mitchison and Leneman, p. 231; Anderson, p. 21; Stern explores this issue for Mexico, pp. 286–94.

18. Fairchilds, p. 627; Tilly, Scott, Cohen, p. 464; Wells, p. 355.

19. Fairchilds is an important exception.

20. Solórzano y Pereyra, lib. 2, cap. 30, n. 21, notes that even though mestizos and mulattos could technically hold office, their birth excluded them, given that most were born "of adulterous or other illicit and punishable couplings because there are few Spaniards with honor who marry with Indian or black [women]." Konetzke, 3:2, n. 370, 1786, reprints a *consulta* that reviews the history of royal policy toward the racially mixed and that continually equated illegitimacy with miscegenation. See also Dueñas-Vargas, pp. 56, and Nazzari, "Concubinage." This is not to say that all mestizos were always illegitimate, for as Asunción Lavrin pointed out (personal communication to Ann Twinam, November 15, 1997), some mestizos married mestizos, especially later on.

21. White illegitimates in Spanish America existed in a different racial and social matrix than their counterparts in Europe or the United States. Even though related by kinship and blood to local elites, they also shared the pervasive colonial stigma of illegitimacy, even if not the totality of discrimination directed against the majority, racially mixed population. Mannarelli, p. 175, concludes that "the significance of illegitimacy is [differently] related with the criteria of separation and differentiation of the social groups."

22. Shorter, "Illegitimacy," pp. 265–72. For purposes of comparison I have used

only those thirty-three charts that show data between 1700 and 1800 and have calculated rates only for the eighteenth century. Illegitimacy continued to rise in many localities in the nineteenth century.

23. Wells, p. 354, estimates that there were between thirteen and eighteen bastards (presumably this is the Anglo definition) per thousand births. Smith, p. 370, described a much higher rate of prebridal pregnancy (not illegitimacy) starting at around 6.7 percent at the start of the century, with a midcentury high of around 16.7 percent. See also Nash, p. 954.

24. Examples include Laslett, "Introduction," p. 59; Meyer, p. 250; Depauw, p. 162; Mitchison and Leneman, p. 231; Anderson, p. 21; Stern, pp. 286–94.

25. Socolow, "Acceptable," p. 232, discovered that white illegitimacy increased from around 19 percent before 1778 to 32 percent in the Buenos Aires cathedral baptismal registry. Dueñas-Vargas, pp. 372–79, concluded that white illegitimacy rates in the Bogotá parish of La Catedral moved from around 30 percent midcentury to 15 percent by the 1780s, reaching a low of 6 percent at the end of the century. Illegitimacies among the white population of the poorer parish of Las Nieves went up from 30 percent midcentury to 50 percent at the end.

26. Dueñas-Vargas, pp. 375–76, traces a rise in the mestizo population of La Catedral and Las Nieves parishes from around 64 percent at midcentury to approximately 75 percent at the end.

27. Other demographers provide other bits and pieces of the picture. For Mexico, Aranda Romera and Grajales Porras, p. 3, estimate that white illegitimacy in the center of Puebla fluctuated between 27 and 33 percent—much like that of Mexico City—although they found illegitimate births to be lower (12 percent) among whites on the other side of the river. Rabell, "Matrimonio," p. 32, cites decreases in eighteenth-century illegitimacy in Zamora, Michoacán, and Tlaxcala. Figueroa, pp. 344–45, notes that mid-twentieth-century rates of illegitimacy in Mexico ranged between 17 and 27 percent. See also Castillo Palma.

Demographic figures for the rest of Spanish America are spotty and cannot approach the Mexican coverage. Pérez Brignoli, pp. 482, 485, estimated illegitimacy in the Costa Rican capital between 1770 and 1880 to have been around 30 percent, although he judged white illegitimacy to have been lower. The Dueñas-Vargas study (p. 209) of the parishes of La Catedral and Las Nieves reveals white illegitimacy at 20.2 percent and 39.1 percent, respectively, while comparable mestizo illegitimacy was 69.7 and 58.7 percent. For Brazil, Pinto Venacio, p. 11, estimates in the colonial Río de Janeiro parish of São José that one-quarter were natural children, although he provides no measure by ethnicity. Kuznesof, "Ilegitimidade," p. 166, estimates the Vila Rica illegitimacy rate to have varied between 5.5 and 65 percent from 1760 and 1800. Nizza da Silva, "O problema," p. 148, notes that *expósito* (usually illegitimate) births in São Paulo varied between 10 and 25 percent between 1741 and 1822. Marcilia, pp. 159, 188–91, sees an eighteenth-century increase in illegitimacy in São Paulo when the 1741–1755 rate almost doubled from 10.24 percent to 18.28 percent (1756–1770), and then rose to 31.49 percent (1831–1834).

28. Konetzke, 3:2, n. 300, 1788, reprints a typical white expression of the problem of *pardo* mobility that surfaced as part of the Royal Pragmatic of 1776. The classic position is Mörner. See also Cicerchia, p. 43; Rípodas Ardanaz, pp. 34, 45; Twinam, *Miners*, p. 93; Saguier, pp. 185–86; Stern, pp. 23, 28, 35, 185, 289; Dueñas-Vargas, pp. 29–31, 133–35. Rodríguez Jiménez, *Sentimientos*, p. 176, links social and racial mobility in colonial Colombia, for "to leave being a poor person was to "become white."

29. Mörner, p. 67. For example, Pescador C., *Bautizados*, pp. 167–69, documents that eighteenth-century endogamy rates among *españoles* in Santa Vera Cruz parish in Mexico City increased from 86 and 77 percent for women and men, respectively, (1749–1751) to 85 and 95 percent by 1810. Trends do vary by parish: *Español* endogamy in Mexico City's el Sagrario stabilized early in the eighteenth century at around 79 percent.

30. Rípodas Ardanaz, p. 314.

31. DB 2-216. Of the 216 petitions for legitimation for which race can be determined, 16, or 7.4 percent, involved either *pardos* or mestizos. For information on data bases and abbreviations, see Appendix 1.

32. The standard treatment of the Bourbons can be found in Brading, *The First* and "Bourbon." Other sources that contributed to this synthesis include Kuethe, *Cuba,* "Early"; McFarlane; Fisher et al.; Barbier, *Reform,* "Commercial," and "Culmination"; O'Phelan Godoy; and Herr.

33. Konetzke, 3:1, n. 247, 1778, reprints the American version.

34. Pérez y López, pp. 155–73; Zamora y Lazonado, pp. 389–94, reprints legitimation legislation.

35. *NR,* lib. 7, tit. 37, ley 4. Such an edict benefited female *expósitos* who would be eligible for dowries from charitable bequests and thus for more acceptable marriage partners, as well as their male counterparts who might enter *colegios,* previously barred professions, and perhaps political office. The decree did include one caveat: *Expósitos* were still not eligible for the many positions that had written guidelines insisting that candidates be "legitimate" or "conceived in . . . true marriage." Still, the potential effects of this legislation in the Americas cannot be overstated, for it empowered *expósitos* not only to be partially legitimated but also sometimes whitened.

36. Appendix 1 presents the details.

37. Stern, p. 54, is an exception, inasmuch as his study is clearly confined to poorer, racially mixed groups.

38. Ibid., pp. 219–21, on regional studies.

39. Louise Tilly, p. 306.   40. Charles Tilly, p. 323.

41. Cohen and Cohen, p. 55.   42. Hareven, p. x.

43. Charles Tilly, p. 323.

44. Hareven, p. xii. Charles Tilly, p. 321, comments on "reconstitution and emic analysis" and "connection and etic analysis."

45. Clifford Geertz, quoted in Kertzer, "Anthropology," p. 204.

46. For a recent treatment of Anglo "racial binary thinking," see Nash, p. 954.

47. Rípodas Ardanaz, pp. 27–35, provides an excellent discussion.

48. A classic statement is from eighteenth-century Spanish travelers Jorge Juan and Antonio Ulloa: "They come forth from one and the other castes as time goes by so that they become totally white, with the result that in the mixture of Spaniards and Indians, in the second generation they cannot be distinguished from the Spaniards by color; however they are not called Spaniards until the fourth generation." Quoted in Dueñas-Vargas, p. 123.

49. Brundage, p. 544. See also Brydall, p. 45. Teichman, p. 34, notes that English bastards could be legitimated only by an act of king and Parliament until the time of more modern legislation.

50. Macfarlane, p. 73, points out the lack of "fine language" in English to distinguish forms of bastardy.

51. Even though it is common in English to use the term "illegitimate" to cover all categories of offspring conceived out of wedlock, this can lead to an ahistorical and inaccurate use of terminology. Linda Lewin's comments ("Natural," p. 361) on the problems created when historians of Brazil fail to distinguish between natural children born to unmarried parents and bastards holds true for Spanish America as well: "A single linguistic stroke thus obliterates both a clear legal distinction in heirship and a subtle boundary in the family's socially constructed nexus." Yet to be exactly accurate without wordy circumlocutions can be difficult in English, so the reader is forewarned that whenever distinctions make a substantive difference, I will pointedly differentiate between *hijos naturales* and bastards (*adulterinos, sacrílegos, incestuosos*). However I will be less precise than eighteenth-century Spanish Americans, who seldom used the term "*ilegítimo*," and will employ the English "illegitimate" in general references to out-of-wedlock birth.

52. Rípodas Ardanaz, p. 28, quotes testimony from Caracas that expresses such attitudes toward long-term whitening. The witness noted that races could change over generations, given that individuals do not

> remain in the same being and state as their father, which does not happen here
> because since [the] mother . . . was a third more white than black, it follows
> that Juan Baptista Arias, her son, has to enjoy something of this quality and to
> be lighter than his father and by this we see, that in place of being the same, he
> advances more toward the class of whites.

53. See Habermas. Wahrman, p. 398, also provides an illuminating discussion of conceptual problems with the private-public dichotomy.

54. Davidoff, pp. 227–30, provides the discussion from which subsequent quotations are derived.

55. For example, even though Habermas, p. 1, starts with the admission that historical formulations of private and public blend into a "clouded amalgam," he then proceeds in a most etic fashion to pull together multiple meanings from multiple

cultures, from ancient Greece to modern times. He concludes that the "line between state and society . . . divided the public sphere from the private realm"
(p.30). Certain of his formulations, such as the idea of public as a "status attribute"
(p. 7), or of the core of the private sphere as an "intimate sphere" (p. 55, 152)—the
choice of words is most interesting, given colonial Spanish-American commentaries—suggest potential congruencies with historical Hispanic conceptualizations.
Yet even though his descriptions of contemporary private and public formulations
strike familiar chords, the lack of attention to the multiple historical and cultural
meanings of private and public and the tracing of their discrete transformations
into more recent conceptualizations of the private-public leaves the historical treatment unconvincing.

56. Cicerchia, p. 95.

57. Mannarelli, p. 125. Stern, pp. 9, 109, 142–43, in contrast, seems to accept
more traditional divisions of private and public, although he raises many topics that
use some notion of private-public separation. See Nizza da Silva, "Filhos," p. 123, in
which the private-public dichotomy is invoked in Brazil; Patiño Millán, p. 207, and
Rodríguez Jiménez, "Casa," p. 124, and Garrido, pp. 135–39, for Colombia; Cook
and David, p. 97, for Peru.

58. Private happenings such as conversations among the private circle could occur in public spaces, although they were more likely to take place within the home.

59. O'Hara, pp. 10–11.

60. Examples are in order: AGI, Santo Domingo, n. 1, 1723; Santo Domingo
1467, n. 1, 1782; Guadajalara 372, n. 1, 1780; Santo Domingo 1498, n. 30, 1799; Mexico 1771, n. 6, 1785.

61. Rodríguez Jiménez, "Casa," p. 125, provides excellent examples for colonial
Colombia.

62. Stern, p. 60, notes that kin and fictive kin could also be abusive.

63. See examples in Rabell, "Matrimonio," p. 33; Martínez Alier, "El honor,"
p. 56; Martínez Alier, *Marriage*, pp. 49, 71–76, 163; Patiño Millán, p. 204–5.
Mörner, p. 84, uses the word. Stern's discussion, p. 16, of "social race" reflects the effects of passing. A fascinating exploration of other kinds of passing, for example
from mulatto to mestizo, is explored in Castillo Palma, pp. 141–43.

64. Martínez Alier, pp. 71–76, 132–33, has brilliantly explored the issue of racial
passing. See Dueñas-Vargas, pp. 106–30, for an excellent discussion with examples
from colonial Bogotá. On the popular use of "Don," see note 2, above.

65. Passing was clearly easier for some than for others. Without doubt the invis-
ibility of the stigma of illegitimacy and the comparatively lesser prejudice against
those of "defective" birth made it easier for illegitimates than for the racially mixed
to be upwardly mobile.

66. Laslett, *Family*, p. 102.

67. Laslett, "Introduction," p. 3.

68. Examples include Pitt-Rivers, Campbell, Peristiany, Schneider, Jiménez
Asenjo, Kirshner, Guillamón Alvarez, Collier, Kertzer, and Brettell. Particular re-

search on honor in Latin America includes Gutiérrez, "Honor;" *When*; Seed, "Marriage," *To Love*; Rodrígues Jiménez, "Elección"; Twinam, "Honor, Sexuality"; Ruggiero; Findlay; Mannarelli; Stern. A version of these comments on honor will appear as "The Negotiation" in Johnson and Lipsett-Rivera.

69. Sponsler, p. 433.

70. Ots Capdequi, p. 149.

71. Seed, *To Love*, pp. 9, 62, 240.

72. Among the many problems of Seed's interpretation, p. 225, is a mistaken temporal frame. Variables she assigns as of primary significance in seventeenth-century manifestations of honor as virtue, such as the protection of feminine reputation, are equally viable indicators in the eighteenth century; while issues she sees as key in the eighteenth century for honor as status, such as economic standing, "freedom from the necessity of manual labor," and race were important earlier. Stern, pp. 162, 168, and 171, also makes assumptions concerning honor, yet it is unclear what the men and women in his study themselves stated concerning honor.

73. For example, see Boyer, "Honor."

74. Cohen, p. 599–600. She argues that historians need to be aware that those they study express their differences through their vocabulary and practices: Words such as "honor," "reputation," "respect," "dishonor," and "shame" can vary substantially depending on the context.

75. Ibid.

76. Stern, pp. 15–16, divides honor up, but without much evidence from his sources to justify his divisions. Nor does he suggest that the elite definition of honor was exclusive.

77. Garrido, pp. 135–39, has an excellent discussion of the *"ser público"* (p. 135).

78. For example, see Van der Valk. Stern, p. 18, seems to imply an overarching "honor/shame" complex. However before any discussion of such an overarching mentality can be conclusive, it must also integrate the assumption that elites rejected the presence of honor in others. Martin, pp. 141–48, provides an interesting discussion of how nonelites absorbed and incorporated notions of honor into their own ethos, and how this challenged elite exclusivity. She notes: "Those in positions of authority were . . . caught in a trap of their own making. . . . They could hardly protest when mestizos, mulattos and others presented evidence that they had in fact tried to conform to these dictates of church and state" (p. 143).

79. Cohen, p. 617, provides a similar observation for early modern Rome: "In honor culture a person's sense of worth lies not in internal virtue—as manifested in good intentions or a guiltless soul—but in the external of bearing and deed, and in society's appreciation of them. Public respect certifies honor; public ridicule induces shame. Virtue and vice thus exist only when visible to onlookers." Maravall, p. 59, also suggests that honor could be less a "personal quality . . . than a social condition." Rodríguez Jiménez, *Sentimientos*, describes family honor in colonial Colombia as public. On the other hand, Seed, "Marriage Promises," p. 254, considers honor to embody moral integrity.

Chapter 2. Precedents: Sexuality and Illegitimacy, Discrimination, Civil Legitimation

1. Villalón, p. 282, reproduces the legitimation for García Fernández Manrique granted in 1453. The formula for this typical medieval legitimation reads: "Given that the pope can legitimate for the spiritual so kings have the power to legitimate for the temporal for those that are not born of legitimate marriage." More than three hundred years later, the Cámara de Gracia y Justicia formulated: "Given that our holy father has the power to legitimate and habilitate in the spiritual, so kings have [the power] to legitimate and habilitate in the temporal those not procreated and born of legitimate marriage"; AGI, Lima 910, n. 53, 1785. The major difference between the two is that the 1453 formula gave the count's son explicit rights of inheritance: "to hold and to inherit all and whatever villas and places and castles and vassals." In contrast, a typical eighteenth-century legitimation permitted petitioners "to have and to be admitted in our kingdoms of the Indies to all the corresponding honors as much and fully as those children born of legitimate matrimony."

2. Venezuelan Don Joseph Antonio Betancourt wrote of the "natural goodness that your majesty is always ready to dispense to his loved vassals . . . to make less heavy the burdens of human life"; AGI, Caracas 299, n. 22, 1788. Cuban Don Joseph Mariano de Casas reminded the king that "neither the laws nor our sovereign . . . desires that his honored vassals" suffer from shame; Santo Domingo 1483, n. 38, 1792. Doña María Josepha Basco wrote the monarch of her hope that her three young sons would be "useful vassals to you and to the state"; Santo Domingo 147, n. 28, 1789. The similar idea that legitimation proceeded from a monarch-vassal relationship can also be found in England, where Brydall, p. 37, noted that legitimations occurred "for the most part, in such cases only where either the father of the child, or the child himself offered himself to be attendant on the Court or Prince."

3. Quoted in Quaife, p. 235. Dillard, p. 57, notes similar customs in twelfth- to fourteenth-century Spain: "It seems plain that sexual intercourse itself was not condemned, unexpected or even unusual between betrothed couples, but only the groom's repudiation of his bride after it happened."

4. Lavrin, "*Lo fémenino*," p. 115, notes that in Mexico a distinction existed between "*doncella*," which referred to a virgin, and "*soltera*," where virginity was not assumed. See also Castañeda, *Violación*, pp. 80–81.

5. See Brundage, pp. 551–67, for an overview of Trent reforms concerning marriage. See Donoso for canon law.

6. Gacto Fernández, "El grupo," pp. 38–39; Córdoba de la Llave, pp. 577–79. Women who engaged in sexual relationships with priests were called *mancebas* and not looked upon favorably, even if such liaisons were common; ibid., p. 578. Dillard, pp. 20, 36–67, 128–35, provides an excellent discussion of twelfth- to fourteenth-century peninsula practices.

7. Córdoba de la Llave, p. 608, concludes that society was "more tolerant in these questions than the modern mentality is many times disposed to admit."

8. García Gonzáles, pp. 632–34; also Dillard, pp. 38–40. On canon law, see Cavalario, vol. 2, pp. 459–63.

9. Segalen, p. 109; García Gonzáles, p. 636; Dillard, pp. 46–47, 56–57.

10. Flandrin, p. 34.

11. McCaa, "Tratos," p. 35, notes that the promise of future marriage (*matrimonio con palabras de futuro*) was prohibited in Valencia only in 1687, more than one hundred years after Trent, and lasted even longer in the Basque country.

12. Gacto Fernández, "El grupo," p. 39, suggests that this definition of *barragania* as a category inferior to matrimony was originally linked to the creation of the in-between category of *hijos naturales*.

13. For the Roman and Visigothic roots of the *palabra de casamiento*, see García Gonzáles, pp. 611–64.

14. Historians of colonial Mexico, including Lavrin, "Sexuality in Colonial Mexico," p. 61; McCaa, "Gustos," p. 597; Seed, "Marriage," p. 257; and Penyak, p. 50, pp. 85–86, note that the exchange of a gift, or *prenda*, was customary when couples exchanged the *palabra de casamiento*. My own research suggests that this may not have been as common outside of Mexico, nor were written promises of marriage usual. I found just two.

15. The time frame regarding state reluctance to jail men who reneged on promises of matrimony is still unclear. Seed, *To Love*, p. 100, implies that recalcitrant men were less likely to be jailed by the end of the seventeenth century. However McCaa, "Tratos," notes that it was not until 1796 in Spain that jail sentences were ended for those who had seduced women and broke promises of matrimony. Whatever the law, it was difficult for women to force men to the altar. McCaa, "Gustos," p. 601, found in eighteenth-century Parral that, of the forty-two women who initiated lawsuits after their fiancés refused to fulfill promises of matrimony, 43 percent remained abandoned and unmarried, and few received compensation.

16. García Gonzáles, pp. 638–39. McCaa, "Tratos," pp. 23, 52–53, suggests that in the long run this 1803 decree was more important than the Pragmatic Sanction, given that it was later incorporated into republican Mexican law and diminished women's potential to petition for redress. Instead, "the scales of justice were totally recalibrated in favor of the seducer" (p. 39). The potential effects of this decree cannot be traced in the *gracias al sacar* legitimations, for, with the notable exception of Cuba, those end in the years between 1810 and 1830 with independence—somewhat before illegitimates who might have been the product of changes in courtship patterns would have become adults and petitioned. Further local research is needed to evaluate the decree's ultimate effects.

17. In this I differ from Seed, "Marriage"; see comments by Dueñas-Vargas, pp. 212–14, on the significance of engagement in Bogotá. The *palabra de casamiento* proves to be one of those places where sex was, as suggested by Foucault, "put into discourse" (p. 11), for witnesses commonly spoke about it.

18. Margadant, p. 29, suggests that the *palabra de casamiento* was less formal than *esponsales*, which were regulated by the *Siete Partidas* and the Royal Pragmatic

of 1776. One Cuban expressed the "impossibility" that one woman would have had a sexual relationship with a suitor without a promise of matrimony, given her "retirement, honest way of living . . . and because she is a woman of honor"; AGI, Santo Domingo 1483, n. 38, 1792. Another insisted on the "honesty and honor" with which one woman had lived "in the states of virgin, wife, and widow," so that she "never would have engaged in intercourse with the indicated gentlemen . . . unless she had received a contract of marriage"; Santo Domingo 1488, n. 15, 1796. See also Lavrin, "*Lo féminino*," p. 160–61.

19. AGI, Mexico 1778, n. 6, 1793.

20. AGN-Lima, Notaríal. Escribano Ignacio Ayllon Salazar, December 13, 1799, f. 1037, n. 92.

21. Examples include Caviéres F. and Salinas M., p. 91; Penyak, p. 50; Seed, *To Love*, p. 68; Kuznesof, "Raza," p. 382; Castañeda, *Violación*, p. 84; Boyer, *Lives*, p. 95. For Europe and Anglo-America, see Quaife, p. 235. Evidence from European customs also suggests that virginity might also be socially constructed. Watt's discussion, p. 133, of marriage-contract disputes in Neuchatel between 1547 and 1806 notes that there was a formula for determining virginity that did not necessarily involve any physical qualifications: "[A] girl will be considered a virgin if she had good morals and a good reputation without any suspicion, and if she does not give in to the will of a young man unless he has first promised her the faith of marriage in the presence of at least two honorable men."

22. Gacto Fernández, *Filiación*, p. 96. See also Brundage; Teichman; Brydall; and Croke.

23. For legal guidelines, see Nichols, pp. 84–85, and Cavalario, vol. 2, 178–96. (I thank Professor Asunción Lavrin for this reference.) Most of the Spanish ordinances concerning illegitimacy appear in the thirteenth-century *Siete Partidas*.

24. Croke, p. 103.

25. Brydall, p. 38. Legitimation in England necessitated an act of Parliament. Teichman, pp. 35–36, notes that the stringent category of bastard was eased somewhat in 1926 with the creation of the status of "special bastard." If parents eventually married and they had openly raised their eldest son, he could inherit.

26. Mitchison and Leneman, p. 79, note the post hoc option in Scotland.

27. Tilly, Scott, and Cohen, p. 469, on European customs.

28. Historians have also noted such post hoc legitimations in various parts of the Americas. See Caviéres F. and Salinas M., p. 105, for Chile; Arnaud Rabinal et al., p. 102, for Florida; Ramos, p. 156, and Lewin, "Natural," p. 381, for Brazil.

29. AGN-Mexico, Bienes Nacionales 1016, exp. 12.

30. AGN-Mexico, Bienes Nacionales 960, exp. 18.

31. Herr, p. 96, outlines the distinctions between the Grandes de España, those who held Títulos de Castilla, and *hidalgos*, who had few privileges. The latter could not be arrested for debts or forced to quarter soldiers, and they were addressed as "Don." It was this address that was later democratized, even though the American "Dons" did not technically meet the requirements. See Lynch, pp. 130–37; Mariéjol,

pp. 262–77; and, on the Americas, Konetzke 3:2, n. 279, 1785. See also Chapter 1, note 2.

32. Sicroff, p. 343, traces the concept that the king was the ultimate or the "only source of political and civil nobility" to the *Siete Partidas* (part. 2, lib. 6, tit. 17), for the king "can bestow the honor of nobility to those that are not so by lineage."

33. Maravall quotes Vélez de Guevara, p. 84.

34. Sicroff, p. 268.

35. See Fernández Pérez for Spanish examples that surfaced concerning heresy and Jewish ancestry with the enforcement of the Royal Pragmatic of 1776.

36. Ibid., p. 218. The award was granted because the rabbi, who had become a Catholic and later the bishop of Burgos, had supposedly converted forty thousand Jews with his preaching.

37. Domínguez Ortíz, *Judeoconversos*, p. 242, notes that Ferdinand granted similar dispensations.

38. For early practices, see Brundage, pp. 103, 223, 543–44. For Spain, Ortíz de Montalván, pp. xi–xii.

39. Also entail (*mayorazgo*). For copies of *gracias al sacar* legislation, see Pérez y López, pp. 155–73; Zamora y Lazonado, pp. 389–94. Lanning and King examined one example, while Rodulfo Cortés explores Venezuelan cases, particularly regarding race, and prints key documents. Nizza da Silva, "Filhos," p. 121, provides some Brazilian examples of the legitimation equivalent that was administered by the *Desembargo do Paço*. See also Lewin, "Surprise Heirs."

40. AGI, Santo Domingo 1474, n. 11, 1789, contains a traditional American rendering. Those with *limpieza de sangre* "have always been known, held, and commonly reputed to be white persons, Old Christians of the nobility clean of all bad blood and without any mixture of commoner, Jew, Moor, mulatto or converso in any degree, no matter how remote." At least legally, racial mixture with Indians did not violate the *limpieza de sangre* statutes. In 1790 a Mexico City colonist sent a document to the crown in which he commented on his purity of blood, including the absence of any Indian ancestry. The Council of the Indies reprimanded him and noted that Indian mixture should not be counted as constituting a "stain." Konetzke, 3:2, n. 321, 1790.

41. *NR*, lib. 11, tit. 27, ley 4 (1492); *NR*, lib. 11, tit. 27, ley 11 (1528); *NR*, lib. 11, tit. 27, ley 23 (1638).

42. Sicroff, p. 121.

43. Maravall, pp. 96–109, notes that the Order of Calatrava in 1568 and the Order of Montesa in 1589 originally limited proven *limpieza* to parents and grandparents. Alcántara asked for proofs through the fourth generation. The Order of Santiago asked for proof of parental *limpieza* in 1603 and extended this to grandparents in 1653. Sicroff, pp. 295–96, 252, adds that Santiago eventually required four generations of proof of *limpieza*, although some investigations went back seven generations. One reformer tried to limit proofs to one hundred years.

44. Ibid., p. 238.

45. AHN, Consejos lib. 1489e, n. 34, cites the *limpieza* requirements for the *colegio* mayor of San Bartolomé in the University of Salamanca, on which many of the constitutions of the American institutions are based. To receive a scholarship a student had to have five witnesses testify that he was legitimate and that his parents and grandparents on both sides were Old Christians.

46. AGI, Buenos Aires 280, n. 14, 1796; Santa Fe 1068, n. 6, 1789.

47. Sicroff, p. 293, quotes from Fray Gerónimo de la Cruz, who wrote a 1637 treatise on the problems of proofs of nobility and *limpieza*. A similar idea appears in Kirshner's description, p. 6, of fifteenth-century Italy, where a "life without honor" was considered a "living death."

48. *SP*, part. 7, tit. 6, ley 2.

49. *SP*, part. 7, tit. 6, ley 1.

50. *SP*, part. 7, tit. 6, ley 7.

51. Chauchadis, p. 8, comments that the first modern Spanish dictionary by Covarrubias noted that honor was "the same" as *honra*.

52. Although historians debate the extent to which this reference to "clean blood" marks a benchmark in rising prejudice against *conversos*, the conceptual link between illegitimacy and *limpieza* seems established; Sicroff, pp. 117–18. Both Sicroff and Domínguez Ortíz imply that this was too early to be a *limpieza de sangre* statute against *conversos*, but that it discriminated solely against illegitimates. Yet if early fifteenth-century Spaniards wanted to exclude illegitimates from the university, they need only have prohibited those without *fama* from entering, for that would have excluded all illegitimates. It seems more logical that the addition of the *limpieza* requirement was to disqualify additional candidates, such as *conversos*. The *Siete Partidas* did not exclude *conversos* from public offices but empowered them: "If some Jews become Christians, that all in our kingdom should honor them . . . that they can hold all the offices and honors as other Christians." *SP*, part. 7, tit. 24, ley 6.

53. Muñoz, p. 72. I thank Professor John Brackett of the University of Cincinnati for help in the translation.

54. Sicroff, p. 189.

55. Ibid.

56. Quoted in Ibid., pp. 53–56.

57. *NR*, lib. 7, tit. 15, ley 6.

58. Muñoz, p. 72. Offices specifically excluded were councilors, *oidores*, chancellors, secretaries, *alcaldes, alguaciles, mayordomos, contadores mayores, contadores menores*, treasurers, *pagadores, contadores de cuentas, escribanos de cámara, escribanos de rentas, chancillerías, registradores, relatores, abogados, fiscales*, "nor any other public office." Also noted were *corregidores*, judges, *alcaldes, alguaciles, merinos, vienticuatros, regidores, fiel executores*, public notaries, surgeons, and pharmacists, who could not "hold any other public office in the cities, villas and places of our kingdoms."

59. In the mid-seventeenth century, Solórzano y Pereyra, lib. 3, cap. 6, commented that many illegitimates had been successful in obtaining political office: "There is no law that gives them the note of infamy nor excludes them from dignities nor magistrates but only that in equality of merits they ought to be placed be-

hind [those who are] legitimate." Apparently the *Partida* dictate that illegitimates lacked *fama*, or reputation, did not necessarily mean that they possessed the quality of infamy that would presumably deprive them of access to offices.

60. *Recopilación*, lib. 5, tit. 3, ley 4. Konetzke, 1, n. 98, 1536, reprints a 1536 royal decree that notes that *alcaldes* in Santiago de Cuba should not only know how to read and write but also be "honradas."

61. Konetzke, 1:1, n. 151, 1544.

62. Ibid., n. 167, 1549. Even in this early example birth and race were given, for "no mulatto nor mestizo nor man that is not legitimate" could hold public office (Kontezke, 1:1, n. 473, 1591).

63. Konetzke, 2:1, n. 349, 1663.

64. Maravall, p. 128, discusses this "condition to receive honor" in terms of *limpieza*.

65. Ibid., pp. 131–32. Maravall quotes Caro Baroja, who portrays *pureza de sangre* as "a social institution that serves to regularize the path of honors, the *cursus honorum* of an entire society."

66. Ibid., p. 59.

67. Sicroff, pp. 119–20, notes that *conversos* might enter but could not graduate from the Universities of Salamanca, Valladolid, and Toledo.

68. Konetzke, 3:1, n. 205, 1768, reprints a royal order that required that those enrolled in *colegios* and universities prove their *limpieza de sangre* and legitimacy before graduation. This ordinance is especially interesting because it was clearly directed against "those of vile birth [such as] *zambos*, mulattos, and other worse castes," but the requirement for legitimacy presumably affected white illegitimates as well.

69. *Recopilación*, lib. 1, tit. 23, ley 4 for seminarians and lib. 4, tit. 13, ley 8 for lawyers.

70. See Solórzano y Pereyra, lib. 4, cap. 10, on prohibitions on the ordination of illegitimates, and lib. 4, cap. 12, on *habilitaciones*.

71. Konetzke, 3:2, n. 311, 1789.

72. Konetzke, 3:1, n. 202, 1768, reprints an example of a *habilitación* for a priest who was the son of a priest in Durango. From the sixteenth through the eighteenth centuries, royal officials constantly confronted petitions from illegitimates who had been ordained and who sought *habilitaciones*. Even though they usually granted them, officials continued to order that illegitimates not be ordained. Konetzke reprints a number of these: Konetzke, 2:1, n. 5, 1594; Konetzke, 2:1, n. 159, 1621; Konetzke, 2:1, n. 231, 1636; Konetzke, 2:2, n. 439, 1676; Konetzke, 2:2, n. 526, 1685. In 1789 the Cámara of the Indies remarked that "these petitions are so frequent as to prove the abandonment of customs on this point," and suggested that fathers were encouraging their illegitimate sons to enter the priesthood even if they lacked a vocation. Councilors ended with the usual fruitless order "not to admit with ease to holy orders those that are not legitimate offspring of legitimate marriage"; Konetzke, 3:3, n. 305, 1789. Even when illegitimates were ordained, upward mobility was limited without *habilitaciones*, and even when the Cámara of the Indies agreed to

these, it began to limit the potential for promotion as the eighteenth century drew to a close.

73. AGI, Indiferente General 16, July 24, 1782, contains the petition of Mexican curate Don Alonso Moreno y Castro, who had been habilitated to hold church offices in 1769 but who then applied for civil legitimation to be able to enjoy the "honors, exemptions, and privileges" of a legitimate offspring.

74. DB 2-216.

75. Sicroff, p. 295, comments on the fourth generation requirement.

76. Domínguez Ortíz, *Judeoconversos*, pp. 247–48. The actual phrase is "*de paso.*"

77. This debate is discussed in Domínguez Ortíz, *Los conversos*, pp. 193–94.

78. For earlier practices, see Brundage, pp. 103, 223, 543–44.

79. Ortíz de Montalván, pp. xi–xii.

80. The Simancas numbers come from my counts from Ortíz de Montalván's *Registro General de Sello* and AGS, Cámara, Libros de Relación, 1475–1697. The Madrid numbers from my research in the Consejos section of the Archivo Histórico Nacional. I have gathered cases from both archives for a comparative work in progress on sexuality in Spain and the Americas. For comments on the collection of legitimations in the Archive of the Indies, see Appendix 1.

81. Córdoba de la Llave, pp. 612–13. My percentages differ slightly from those cited in his work because I combined some categories. These are the totals: *sacrílegos* (N. 139, 54.7 percent); *hijos naturales* (N. 48, 18.9 percent); *adulterinos* (N. 37, 14.6 percent); unknown (N. 29, 11.4 percent); *incestuosos* (N. 1, 0.4 percent); total (N. 254, 100.0 percent).

82. Escudero, *Secretarios*, traces these developments in detail.

83. Much of the following relies on the introduction in Burkholder, *Biographical*, pp. xi–xxxv; and Barbier, "Culmination."

84. Calvo, "Warmth," p. 299. The legislation is reprinted in Konetzke, 1, n. 473, 1591.

85. Margadant, p. 50.

86. Konetzke, 2:1, n. 213, 1631.

87. ANH-Quito, Cedulários, caja 2, 1660, contains a reference to the 1654 *cédula* and its annulment in 1660. The reference from the legitimation petition is in AGI, Indiferente General 1535, December 31, 1663.

88. AGI, Indiferente General 1535, September 22, 1662 (Quito); Indiferente General 1535, December 31, 1663 (Quito); Indiferente General 1535, June 26, 1609 (two offspring, Santa Fé); Indiferente General 16, December 25, 1635 (three offspring, Mexico); Indiferente General 1535 October 14, 1633 (Guatemala). Konetzke prints several earlier legitimations (although none after 1700) not included in my data base. For example, see 2:1, n. 16, 1596. See also Dueñas-Vargas, pp. 59–60, on Colombian legitimations.

89. Burkholder, *Biographical*, pp. xii–xiii.

90. Barbier, "Culmination," pp. 56–57. Barbier notes that the Ministry of the Indies was interposed between the Council of the Indies and the monarch, since de-

cisions that needed to be signed by the king—including legitimations—had to go to the minister first. Although such a chain of command was "codified" in 1754, he sees precedents in practice as early as 1717. In 1787 Charles III divided the Ministry of the Indies into two portfolios: one for Grace and Justice under Antonio Porlier, which included the Council of the Indies and the Cámara, and the other for war, finance, and commerce. In 1790 Porlier combined the Justice functions for both Spain and the colony.

91. Ibid., pp. xiv, xv.

92. Venezuela moved between the two viceregal jurisdictions. It was under the control of the Santo Domingo *audiencia* until 1717, then was switched to New Granada until 1726, then switched back to Santo Domingo, and finally again to New Granada in 1739. Ferry, pp. 113, 142, 303.

93. Burkholder, *Biographical*, pp. xi–xxxv, esp. xxv, xxvi. The numbers were six of twenty (1717–1739), eleven of twenty-one (1740–1773), and thirty-one of thirty-nine (1773–1808). See also Haring, pp. 108–9.

94. Burkholder, *Biographical*, pp. xiv, xv. The numbers were thirteen of seventeen appointments after 1773.

95. Ibid., p. xv. He is speaking here primarily of appointments, while I would apply it to even more substantive issues.

Chapter 3. Mothers: Pregnant Virgins and Abandoned Women— the Private and Public Price of Sexuality

1. An earlier, shorter version of this chapter has appeared in Twinam, "Honor, Sexuality."

2. AGI, Mexico 1770, n. 35, 1780. Two of her brothers were priests. In 1596 one of Doña Margarita's ancestors had participated in the "pacification and population of the Californias."

3. Stevens has the classic statement. See also Aramoni, Collier, Pescatello, Reyes Nevares, and Rodríguez Baños.

4. AGI, Mexico 1770, n. 35, 1780.

5. His father spoke of the "love and affection" that Don Miguel had shown toward Joseph Antonio, who was left money in his father's will. Don Antonio himself mentioned that he "looked on him with the affection of a son." It was not uncommon in such private pregnancies for fathers to raise their illegitimate children.

6. Mothers were more likely to come forward when their chances for matrimony declined. In AGI, Santo Domingo 1497, n. 24, 1799, a mother appeared twenty-five years after the birth; in Santo Domingo 1498, n. 30, 1799, she did so after ten. In yet another case a mother explained that "because of the honor appropriate to her sex she had deferred it for so many years"; Ultramar 166, 1813. Pescador C., "Nupcialidad," p. 144, notes that most Spanish women had married in Mexico City (1700–1850) by age twenty-eight. Presumably after that time the potential for marriage was lessened.

7. AGI, Santo Domingo 1492, n. 42, 1797.

8. AGI, Caracas 299, n. 22, 1788.

9. AGI, Mexico 1771, n. 6, 1785.

10. Mannarelli, p. 227, quotes an example from Peru; Dueñas-Vargas, p. 250, from Bogotá. Castañeda, p. 92; Seed, *To Love*, pp. 99, 276; Boyer, *Lives*, p. 140; and Penyak, p. 131, provide Mexican examples of the fragility excuse. Nizza da Silva, "Filhos," p. 124, makes similar comments for eighteenth-century Brazil.

11. AGI, Mexico 1770, n. 35, 1780. A priest who had known the couple since they were children noted that their illegitimate son was "merely an *hijo natural*," rather than a child produced in adultery, incest, or sacrilege and therefore "of damnable and punishable intercourse."

12. This is not to say that the collective surveillance of neighbors' sexual relations as noted by scholars of Europe and the United States did not occur in Spanish America. Toth, p. 46; Cott, p. 43. The difference was whether knowledge that intimate relations occurred ever became publicly linked to the couple's reputation.

13. AGI, Chile 295, n. 4, 1795.

14. AGI, Santo Domingo 1474, n. 28, 1789.

15. AGI, Indiferente 1535, January 24, 1811.

16. AGI, Guatemala 609, n. 2, 1798.

17. AGI, Caracas 299, n. 22, 1788.

18. AGI, Mexico 1770, n. 35, 1780. Nazzari, "Urgent," p. 16, provides examples from Brazil.

19. AGI, Caracas 299, n. 22, 1788.

20. Caviéres F. and Salinas M., p. 53.

21. Rothman describes similar leniency given to courting couples in the late eighteenth- and nineteenth-century United States.

22. AGI, Santo Domingo 421, n. 1, 1723.

23. AGI, Santa Fe 717, n. 8, 1793.

24. AGI, Mexico 1779, n. 2, 1795; Chile 297, n. 21, 1796.

25. See Gottlieb for the Middle Ages. Socolow, "Acceptable," p. 226, makes the comment for colonial Spanish America.

26. Kertzer, "Gender Ideology," p. 13, refers to clandestine pregnancy in eighteenth- and nineteenth-century Italy; Brettell and Feijo, p. 221, for Portugal. Mannarelli, p. 231, describes cases in seventeenth-century Lima that correspond to the private pregnancy pattern; Pedraja, pp. 207–8, details secret arrangements in Colombia; Nazzari, "Urgent," pp. 1, 16, for Brazil.

27. Twinam, "Honor, Sexuality."

28. AGI, Mexico 1770, n. 35, 1780.

29. AGI, Charcas 560, n. 15, 1795.

30. Solórzano y Pereyra, vol. 1, lib. 5v, cap. 9, 26. Those included in this prohibition were viceroys, presidents, *oidores, alcaldes fiscales,* governors, and *corregidores,* as well as their sons and daughters. Margadant, pp. 36–37, cites these 1578 restrictions, as well as a 1764 ordinance that threatens loss of office if such marriage took

place. Chandler, p. 41, notes an increased enforcement of such marriage prohibitions in the 1780s. Don José may well have been right; a precipitate marriage might have hurt his as well as Don Ramón's career.

31. AGI, Charcas 560, n. 15, 1795.   32. AGI, Mexico 1771, n. 6, 1785.

33. AGI, Charcas 560, n. 15, 1795.   34. AGI, Mexico 1771, n. 6, 1785.

35. AGI, Buenos Aires 183, n. 4, 1771, and Guatemala 609, n. 2, 1790, contain such private wills, which were fairly common in notary records.

36. AGI, Lima 910, n. 53, 1785.

37. AGI, Buenos Aires 250, n. 14, 1785.

38. AGI, Chile 290, n. 9, 1792.

39. AN-Santiago, Real Audiencia, vol. 824, 2a, 1776, casts some doubt concerning his choice. His eventual bride, Doña Rosa Rojas, seems to have badly mistreated the slaves of the household, one of whom sued for redress.

40. AGI, Santo Domingo 1484, n. 14, 1793.

41. AGI, Caracas 200, n. 22, 1788.

42. The names of married men and priests were also protected on baptismal certificates to avoid scandal.

43. The only noticeable fluctuations were in the 1760s and the 1770s, during which more couples seem to have initiated sexual relationships without marriage promises. However the numbers are so small and the trend so inconclusive as to merit a comment rather than any conclusion.

44. Caviéres F. and Salinas M., p. 94, provide descriptions of such arrangements, although they do not characterize them as extended engagements.

45. AGI, Santo Domingo 425, n. 2. 1741.

46. Seed, *To Love*, p. 100; McCaa, "Gustos," p. 601.

47. AGI, Santa Fe 717, n. 8, 1793.

48. Her many transactions appear in AHA-Medellín, Notarios, Cajas 12–17, 1754–1770.

49. AHA-Medellín, Notarios, Caja 14, f. 7, 1760.

50. AGI, Santa Fe 720, n. 26, 1796.

51. In only 4 of the 216 cases are children referred to without any notice of illegitimacy, but simply called "niño" or "niña."

52. AGI, Santa Fe 720, n. 26, 1796.

53. AGI, Santa Fe 677, n. 19, 1766.

54. AGI, Santo Domingo 1483, n. 38, 1792.

55. See Cook, p. 72, for similar official expressions in another case of bigamy.

56. Pescador C., *Bautizados*, pp. 205–8, explores this point for Mexico.

57. Yet the introduction of a baby with unknown antecedents could raise questions concerning the morality of the household. One pair of Buenos Aires women refused to take an illegitimate relative into their home because it might lead to "prejudice," and they feared that others "could suspect their honor and exemplary living." AGI, Buenos Aires 161, n. 2, 1762.

58. AGI, Chile 297, n. 21, 1796.

59. Caviéres F. and Salinas M., p. 59.

60. AGI, Chile 297, n. 21, 1796.

61. AN-Santiago, Real Audiencia 2896, pz. 1a, 1776, contains a lawsuit between his mother and wife over the property.

62. AGI, Santo Domingo 1467, n. 1., 1782. Don Joseph was *comisario* of the Plaza in 1763 when the English took Havana; he later served as *intendente*, and died in 1776. Rosain, p. 145.

63. Tuirán Gutiérrez, p. 300; Rabell, "Estructuras," p. 275. The high proportion of unmarried women was not confined to Spanish America. Kertzer and Brettell, p. 103, note that in seventeenth-century Italy approximately half of the men and three-fourths of the women over fifty never married.

64. It was not uncommon for local notables to testify in favor of an illegitimate's petition, and to note that they had played together and gone to the same schools.

65. There is a final group of twenty women (45.5 percent) who can be classified as having had public pregnancies, but the exact circumstances (extended engagement, forms of concubinage) are unknown.

66. Calvo, "Concubinato," p. 209; Mannarelli, p. 107.

67. Caviéres F. and Salinas M., p. 78.

68. Kuznesof, "Raza," p. 387. Stern, pp. 271–72, makes an even stronger case for the poorer, mixed-blood population.

69. AGI, Santo Domingo 1456, n. 5, 1761.

70. Boyer, *Lives*, p. 90, quotes a Mexican case in which one party spoke of an "illicit friendship" to describe a sexual relationship where he did not plan to marry; as does Dueñas-Vargas, p. 211.

71. AGI, Charcas 554, n. 25, 1791.

72. Her daughters married a lawyer, a high court judge, and a *regidor*. One son became a priest and another a lawyer.

73. AGI, Charcas 562, n. 22, 1796. It may be that this relationship fits the "adulterous concubinage" model proposed by Guiomar Dueñas-Vargas, pp. 230–42, for eighteenth-century Bogotá. In such liaisons, adult married men might form long-term relationships with other women where "adultery was a second marriage without a legal separation from the first."

74. Córdoba de la Llave, p. 585, also notes that husbands were more likely to be absent in instances in which married women committed adultery.

75. For an essay on the *mala vida*, see Boyer, "Women," and *Lives*, pp. 128–40.

76. AGI, Buenos Aires 280, n. 14, 1796.

77. Eventually Olmedo petitioned to become white. AGI, Buenos Aires 282, n. 24, 1797. He had been married twice, and had seven children.

78. AGI, Buenos Aires 280, n. 14, 1796.

79. Of course there was a long tradition of husbands murdering erring wives. For examples from medieval Spain, see Córdoba de la Llave, pp. 589, 591, who notes that even if men murdered wives and failed to receive a royal pardon, the sentence

of death against such murderers was usually not carried out. Mannarelli, p. 144, notes, for seventeenth-century Lima, that relationships in which wives had extramarital affairs were "frankly scarce." Nazzari, "Urgent," p. 4, quotes Brazilian ecclesiastical law codes that expressed explicit concern for the physical safety of women who committed adultery.

80. Ibid., p. 234, notes that long-term consensual unions did not necessarily mean that "white women" could not enter the "matrimonial market," although she provides little evidence to bolster this point. See also Boyer, *Lives*, pp. 147–48.

81. At least among the colonial elites there did not appear to be a group of women who could be classified as a subsociety of bastard-bearers. This possibility was originally raised by Laslett, *Family*, p. 107. It has subsequently been challenged; see Stewart, p. 139.

Chapter 4. Fathers: Life Course and Sexuality

1. AGI, Santo Domingo 421, n. 1, 1723. An abbreviated version of this chapter appears in Twinam, "Honor."

2. AN-Santiago, Real Audiencia, vol. 1226, n. 2a, 1778. Information on the birth of his son is in AGI, 295, n. 4, 1795.

3. Of course men might pay prices that do not enter easily into the historical record. The family of the abandoned woman might have spoken negatively of him, or exerted pressure so that he was not elected to the city council.

4. Seed's, *To Love*, p. 99, also pp. 60–74. She argues that men go back on their "word of honor" (p. 96) but provides no examples in which colonists explicitly linked the two concepts of "word" and "honor." This is in no way to deny that colonial men had integrity, but it does suggest that they expressed it differently, and that the link between word and honor is not as direct as Seed's mostly literary allusions imply. Kertzer, "Gender Ideology," p. 16, notes that nineteenth-century Italian illegitimacy cases contain "nary a mention of men's honor."

5. AGI, Guadalajara 368, n. 6, 1761.

6. AGI, Lima 910, n. 53, 1785.

7. AGI, Santo Domingo 425, n. 2, 1741.

8. AGI, Santa Fe 677, n. 19, 1766.

9. AGI, Santa Fe 720, n. 26, 1796.

10. Chandler, p. 44. Konetzke, 3:1, n. 233, 1775, prints a decree that preceded the Royal Pragmatic on Marriages in which officials also note that secret marriages were "popularly called of conscience," suggesting the private, rather than the public nature of the commitment.

11. Darrow, p. 266.   12. AGI, Guatemala 609, n. 2, 1798.

13. Lavrin, "Lo fémenino," p. 161–62.   14. Mannarelli, p. 229.

15. AGI, Indiferente General, September 12, 1818, provides another example.

16. Nero da Costa, p. 204, also notes that eighteenth- and nineteenth-century

Brazilian men did not boast about their seduction of women because "public opinion" worked to "inhibit this type of masculine attitude."

17. AGI, Caracas 299, n. 22, 1787.

18. AGI, Guadalajara 368, n. 6, 1761.

19. AGI, Guatemala 609, n. 2, 1798.

20. DB 5-67. The identities of sixteen (23.9 percent) of the sixty-seven private pregnancy mothers were revealed, while thirty-nine (58.2 percent) remain unknown.

21. Chandler, pp. 34–53; Konetzke, 3:1, n. 179, 1760.

22. See Caviéres F. and Salinas M., p. 93, for Chile; Fuentes Bajo, p. 52, for Venezuela; Ramos, p. 154, for Brazil. There is insufficient data to determine the extent to which the men rejected women for emotional reasons, because lovers usually gave more pragmatic reasons; see Stone, "Family," p. 73. A few *gracias al sacar* cases hint at hidden depths. One father noted that the marriage did not take place because of "some jealousy" (AGI, Santa Fe 717, n. 9, 1793); another father suggested that "because of various accidental reasons" the couple had not married (Buenos Aires, n. 14, 1771.) My interpretation challenges Seed, *To Love*, p. 112, who suggests that women were as likely as men to break engagements in the eighteenth century, although she does not provide any statistics. Of course since the sexual intimacies of *cédula* mothers resulted in pregnancy, they may have been less willing to use "vain pretexts" (Seed, *To Love*, p. 122) to end engagements.

23. Margadant, pp. 27–56, summarizes changing legislation concerning marriages of military and civil officials. See also AHN-Madrid, Osuna, leg. 3117, n. 18, 1742, and Solórzano y Pereyra, lib. 5, cap. 9, pp. 138–57.

24. AGI, Caracas 348, n. 22, 1797.

25. AGI, Santa Fe 720, n. 36, 1795.

26. AGI, Guatemala 411, n. 11, 1784. It also affected bureaucrats; Chapter 3 discussed the problems of *Oidor* Don Ramón de Rivera and Doña María del Carmen López. Charcas 560, n. 15, 1795.

27. AGI, Charcas 553, n. 9, 1791.

28. AGI, Santa Fe 1201, n. 9, 1803.

29. Lavrin, "Sexuality in Colonial Mexico," p. 64, also confirms the lack of violent response. Calvo, "The Warmth," p. 297, suggests that violence might have been more common in cases of adultery, and in the country than the city.

30. Boyer, *Lives*, p. 93, provides evidence of local communities that forced already married courtiers to wed yet again to save female reputations.

31. DB 4-187. Where determined, the mother's family was more likely to have been one or two generations in the area: Creole (N. 52, 27.8 percent); not from area (N. 10, 5.3 percent). Fathers were more evenly divided; roughly half were established in the area: Creole (N. 34, 18.2 percent); from Spain or from other colonial locations (N. 33, 17.6 percent). Caviéres F. and Salinas M., p. 52, document that men were approximately 25 to 30 percent more mobile in the colonial Chilean towns of Illapel and San Felipe. Mannarelli, p. 69, quotes a seventeenth-century commentator on Peru (Pedro de León Portocarrero) who noted that "there are always double [the

number of] women because they do not travel by sea nor land, nor do they go to war, and so they maintain [themselves] better and live longer."

32. AGI, Mexico 1770, n. 35, 1780, provides a case of multigeneration illegitimacy, for the father of an illegitimate had a father who was also illegitimate.

33. The legitimation petition for son Santiago is in AGI, Lima 893, n. 42, 1778–1793. AGN-Lima, Notarial. Gaspar Urquízu Ibáñez, Escribano Pedro José Angulo, February 27, 1783, t. 1, f. 567v, contains the will of the *Oidor*. AGN-Lima, Notarial. Escribano Baltasar Núñez del Prado, October 8, 1837, leg. 456, f. 565v, contains the will of María del Carmen Urquízu.

34. AGN-Lima, Notarial. Escribano Ignacio Ayllon Salazar, June 11, 1811, leg. 15, f. 722, contains Don Santiago's will and his mention of his brother's and his own illegitimate offspring. Only Don Santiago ever appeared in *gracias al sacar* petitions.

35. His letters to his half brother appear in AGN-Lima, Real Audiencia, Causas Civiles, leg. 286, 1790.

36. His will is in ADA-Arequipa, Notarial. Bernardo Gutiérrez, Protocolo 352, f. 661. 1764.

37. Laslett, "Illegitimate," p. 461, suggests that the "procreative career" should be considered as a continuous process—before marriage, during marriage, between marriages, and after the death of a spouse.

38. AGI, Guatemala 602, n. 4, 1785.

39. DB 4-187. The case evidence is vague as to how many men exchanged a *palabra de casamiento*, for the intentions of the majority (N. 98, 52.4 percent) were unknown. Of the rest, as many men promised (N. 43, 23.0 percent) as failed to promise (N. 46, 24.6 percent) matrimony.

40. The division was as follows: multiple courtiers of women, four; church, one; private pregnancy, fifteen; total, twenty. The number of private pregnancies is not equal to the total in DB 5-67 because some of these fathers were married rather than unmarried, and therefore fit into other categories.

41. AGI, Indiferente General 1535, June 5, 1785.

42. AGI, Santo Domingo 1484, n. 17, 1793.

43. AGI, Indiferente General, September 18, 1810. Another double courtship can be found in Lima 963, n. 21, 1797.

44. AGI, Ultramar 166, no n., 1813.

45. AGI, Chile 290, n. 3, 1792; Buenos Aires 250, n. 14, 1785.

46. Also in AGI, Santo Domingo 1497, n. 24, 1799, an unwed father left his possessions to a sister and brother rather than to his lover and illegitimate child.

47. ADA-Arequipa, Notarial. Bernardo Gutiérrez, Protocolo 352, f. 661. 1764.

48. ADA-Arequipa, Notarial. Bernardo Gutiérrez, Protocolo 349, f. 263, 1759, contains the will of his mother, Doña Melchora de Esquibel.

49. ADA-Arequipa, Notarial. Escribano Pedro de Figueroa, Protocolo 310, f. 758, 1781, contains the will of Doña Marcelina's mother, Doña Juana de Dios Murillo y Hidalgo, who shared a house with her two sisters and was worth approximately nine hundred pesos. She left everything to her daughter.

50. In 1790 a Don Rafael Calatayúd also began a lawsuit charging that Don Antonio was his father. His case was unconvincing, given that the merchant was said to have signed some documents in Lima even though he had by then been away from Peru for years. This suit does include several more letters by Don Antonio. AGN-Lima, Real Audiencia, Causas Civiles, leg. 286, cuad. 2534, 1790; Causas Civiles, leg. 315, cuad. 2864, 1793.

51. AGI, Lima 910, n. 53, 1785.

52. AGI, Lima 910, n. 53, 1785.

53. ADA-Arequipa, Notarial. Bernardo Gutiérrez, Protocolo 352, f. 661, 1764.

54. These were included in the legitimation case, AGI, Lima 910, n. 53, 1785, to prove paternity.

55. The colorful details in these letters to Doña Marcelina contrast to the more matter of fact tone of his business letters to his half brother, found in AGN-Lima, Real Audiencia, Causas Civiles, leg. 286.

56. AGI, Lima 910, n. 53, 1785.

57. His will is located in AGN-Lima, Real Audiencia, Causas Civiles, leg. 286, cuad. 2534, 1790.

58. The date of Don Antonio León's death appears in ADA-Arequipa, Causas Civiles, leg. 14, 1779. The comment on the Order of Santiago is contained in his sons' combined legitimation petition, AGI, Lima 910, n. 53, 1785.

59. Pescador C., *Bautizados*, p. 77, comments that monthly patterns of rise and fall in the number of illegitimate births paralleled that of legitimate ones, in that both fell as a result of Lenten sexual abstinence. It is suggestive of the normalcy of irregular liaisons that lovers still kept Lenten restrictions even though they chose to live together in sin.

60. AGI, Lima 954, n. 41, 1795.

61. ADA-Arequipa, Notarial. Escribano Rafael Hurtado, no n., ff. 43–143, 1795.

62. These charges and the details of the case appear in ADA-Arequipa, Intendencia-Administrativa, 1792–1794. The documents suggest that Don Anselmo Camborda paid a four thousand peso surety to the interim governor Don José Menendes, who was later transferred to Huamanga. When Don Anselmo Camborda asked for the money back and apparently even confessed that it "was from the royal treasury," the governor responded that he could "go to the devil" before he would repay him.

63. ADA-Arequipa, Notarial. Escribano Rafael Hurtado, no n., ff. 43–143, 1795.

64. AGN-Lima, Notarial. Unk. escribano, f. 295, n. 551, July 6, 1816; AGN-Lima, Notarial. Escribano Gaspar de Salas, Don Anselmo Antonio Camborda, f. 185, n. 669, October 24, 1822.

65. AGI, Lima 942, n. 59, 1792.

66. AGN-Lima, Notarial. Escribano Gaspar de Salas, Don Anselmo Antonio Camborda, f. 185, n. 669, October 24, 1822.

67. Chandler, p. 45, describes a pattern in Mexico whereby bureaucrats in their sixties might marry young women, promising them a lifetime pension following

their death. After 1789 this practice was prohibited in Mexico. It is unclear if similar motivation might have applied in this Peruvian instance.

68. AGN-Lima, Notarial. Escribano José Mendoza y Santa Cruz, leg. 402, f. 152v, July 21, 1820.

69. AGN-Lima, Notarial. Escribano Gaspar de Salas, Don Anselmo Antonio Camborda, f. 185, n. 669, October 24, 1822.

70. AGN-Lima, Notarial. Unk. escribano, f. 295, n. 551, July 6, 1816. Royal officials customarily supervised the distribution of mercury, used for refining silver.

71. AGN-Lima, Notarial. Escribano Gaspar de Salas, Don Anselmo Antonio Camborda, f. 185, n. 669, October 24, 1822.

72. Although Pescador C., "Nupcialidad," p. 140, suggests that the "custom to maintain oneself at the margin of ecclesiastical marriage was not that common" in colonial Mexico, he also noted that "many of the consensual unions in time were changed into sanctified marriages," either to legitimate children or to avoid church authorities and jail.

73. AGI, Guadalajara 372, n. 1, 1780.

74. AGI, Santo Domingo 1469, n. 7, 1785.

75. AGI, Santo Domingo 1471, n. 6, 1787.

76. AGI, Mexico 1779, n. 2, 1795, contains the legitimation petition of Don Joseph Manuel Ignacio Martínez de Lejarzar. Relevant information on his father can be found in AHG-Guanajuato, Bienes Difuntos, leg. 2, exp. 2, 1766; Cabildo, ff. 219–227, 1766; Presos, ff. 85–93, 1773. Notice of his father's death appears in Testamento Protocolo de Presos, f. 222, 1774.

77. AGI, Mexico 1779, n. 2, 1795. It is unclear whether this affair occurred before or after her relationship with Don Ignacio.

78. AGI, Santa Fe 1068, n. 6, 1789.

79. There may have been a difference in the propensity to marry, depending on whether Spanish men or women crossed the racial divide. For example, Rabell, "Matrimonio," p. 21, notes that in Guanajuato, Spanish women were more likely to marry mestizo men than were Spanish men to marry mestiza women. Spanish women may have made different calculations regarding the eventual social "damage" that might accrue to them, because marriage to a racially mixed partner might be less damaging than the countervailing stigma attached to female sexual intimacy outside of matrimony.

80. AGI, Buenos Aires 280, n. 6, 1792. In this case, petitioner Don Joseph Ramón de Olmedo noted: "If a mestizo marries with a Spaniard it produces a *cuarteron*, if this [latter] also marries with a Spaniard it leads to a *puchuelo*, and if this [latter] marries with a Spaniard it creates a pure Spaniard in the common understanding of the people and of those authors that deal with this material." See also Buenos Aires 258, n. 17, 1792, for another popular expression of the one-eighth dividing line.

81. AGI, Santa Fe 1068, n. 6, 1789.

82. She was baptized on June 6, 1747, and classified under the racial designation of *"pardos and morenos."*

83. Martínez Alier (Stolcke), *Marriage*, p. 129. See also Rodríguez Jiménez, "Elección," p. 38, concerning such interracial mobility.

84. Pescador C., "La Nupcialidad," p. 144.

85. Arnaud Rabinal, p. 112, notes that women were able to remarry faster than men in Florida (1600–1763), given their scarcity. McCaa, "La Viuda," p. 303, similarly comments that scarcity favored female remarriage in California, Sonora, and Vera Cruz, but not in Guadalajara. Pescador C., *Bautizados*, pp. 147–49, correlates varying illegitimacy rates with "excess" female population in Mexico City parishes. Dueñas-Vargas, p. 351, notes that 59 percent of Bogotá's population in 1779 was female.

86. Mannarelli, p. 126.

87. See Waldron; see also Taylor, pp. 185–90.

88. Ibid., p. 188.

89. Brading, *First*, p. 472.

90. Only two priests initiated legitimation petitions for their children. Dr. Don Manuel Borda paid the exorbitant sum of forty thousand pesos, AGI, Indiferente General 1535, December 17, 1787. Don Vianes Sales was the second, Santo Domingo 1497, n. 22, 1799.

91. AGI, Santo Domingo 1470, n. 33, 1786.

92. AGI, Mexico 684, n. 11, 1757.

93. AGN-Mexico, Tierras, leg. 2427, exp. 10, 1794.

94. AGI, Charcas 854, n. 25, 1791. Similar comments concerning discretion occur in cases concerning priestly sexuality in Brazil. Nizza da Silva, "Filhos," p. 123.

95. See Taylor. Ots Capdequi, pp. 150–51, notes the unsuccessful attempts by civil and ecclesiastical authorities to promote priestly celibacy.

96. The legitimations of their offspring can be found in AGI, Indiferente General 16, September 15, 1748, Don José Antonio Cayetano; Santo Domingo 425, n. 17, 1739, Doña María Thomasa de Florencia; Santo Domingo 1469, n. 6, 1785, Don Mariano Ayllon; Indiferente General 16, April 4, 1816, Doña María de la Concepción Castellanos; Indiferente General 16, July 26, 1816, Doña María de los Dolores Toledo y Maldonado.

97. These cases can be found, respectively, in AGI, Caracas 279, n. 18, 1784; Guatemala 411, n. 11, 1784; Indiferente General 16, October 19, 1799, Don Pablo Joseph María de la Guardia; Santo Domingo 420, n. 5, 1720; Charcas 562, n. 22, 1796.

98. Mannarelli, p. 143, also notes how geographic mobility created propitious conditions for adulterous relationships in seventeenth-century Peru.

99. *SP*, part. 4, tit. 19, ley 1.

100. *SP*, part. 4, tit. 19.

101. *SP*, part. 4, tit. 19, ley 5.

102. Gacto Fernández, *Filiación*, pp. 139–41.

103. Caviéres F. and Salinas M., p. 75, comment on the lack of affection between fathers and illegitimate offspring in colonial Chile; Penyak, p. 90, suggests that lower-class fathers were less responsible when it came to paying for the support of their children in late colonial Mexico.

104. AGI, Lima 910, n. 53, 1785. Details concerning this lawsuit were included in the combined legitimation petition for the merchant's two sons.

105. DB 2-216. Primary support provided by mother (N. 14, 6.5 percent), father (N. 107, 49.5 percent), others (N. 22, 10.2 percent), unknown (N. 73, 33.8 percent), total (N. 216, 100 percent). In ten cases listed under "father," mothers also provided support. It seems logical to presume that, in any "real pool" of illegitimates of varying classes and races, *cédula* illegitimates were more likely to receive maintenance.

106. DB 4-187. Fathers with no legitimate offspring (N. 59, 31.6 percent), with legitimate offspring (N. 20, 10.6 percent), unknown (N. 108, 57.8 percent). Mannarelli, p. 191, noted that, when men married and fathered legitimate offspring in seventeenth-century Lima, they were less likely to recognize their natural children.

107. AGI, Mexico 684, n. 8, 1754.

108. AGI, Indiferente General 16, November 17, 1814, Don Manuel Joaquín Gómez de Lizana.

109. AGI, Lima 893, n. 42, 1778–1793. Although he eventually married Don Santiago's mother and legitimated all his sons, Don Gaspar never legitimated their half sister, who remained an *hija natural* throughout her life. AHN-Lima, Notarial. Escribano Baltasar Núñez del Prado, n. 456, f. 5654, August 10, 1837, contains her last testament.

110. AGI, Santa Fe 720, n. 26, 1796.

111. AGN-Bogotá, Testamentaria-Bolívar, t. 43, ff. 900–912, October 14, 1799.

112. Ibid. This appears as an additional notation dated August 21, 1800, on the testament.

113. Mothers, it goes without saying, did not experience such crises of conscience, for their honor had also been compromised by their lover's inability or failure to wed. Presumably most would have married if they could, not only to save their honor but also to legitimate their children.

114. AGI, Santo Domingo 1471, n. 6, 1787.

115. AGI, Lima 893, n. 42, 1778.

116. AGI, Santo Domingo 1484, n. 14, 1793.

117. AGI, Santo Domingo 1488, n. 15, 1795.

118. AGI, Guatemala 609, n. 2, 1798.

119. AGI, Santo Domingo 1468, n. 6, 1786.

120. AGI, Santo Domingo 1497, n. 22, 1799.

121. AGI, Santo Domingo 1479, n. 50, 1790.

Chapter 5. Babies and Illegitimacy: The Politics of Recognition from the Font to the Grave

1. AGI, Santo Domingo 1429, n. 4, 1785.

2. *NR*, ley 9, tit. 8, lib. 5. The critical standard for *hijos naturales* was that at the time of their conception or birth "their fathers be able to marry with their moth-

ers . . . without dispensation." See Puig Peña, "Hijos naturales." After illegitimates received civil legitimations they sometimes referred to themselves as "legitimated" and at other times as "legitimate," although the first was more technically accurate.

3. *SP*, Quarta Partida, Título 15, ley 1.

4. Puig Peña, "Hijos incestuosos." For canon law, see Cavalario, vol. 2, pp. 481–87. Segalen, p. 122, notes that the church prohibition of marriage within the fourth degree extended up to and included the children of first cousins. Rodríguez Jiménez, "Matrimonio," p. 53, finds that only 5 percent of incestuous marriages in eighteenth-century Medellín, Colombia (1700–1810), were between first cousins; the majority were between relatives of third and fourth degrees of kinship. See also Rípodas Ardanaz, pp. 169–93, who notes that the monarchy and Spanish-American archbishops and bishops were continually frustrated by the papacy's reluctance to give them full authority to dispose of such impediments rather than permit them to issue a certain number within a designated time period. The issue was resolved in 1770 with a general dispensation. This may explain why royal officials so readily legitimated *incestuosos*, since their defect was technical and partially caused by papal recalcitrance. *Incestuosos* accounted for 6, or 2.7 percent, of the 216 total, DB 2-216.

5. Puig Peña, "Hijos adulterinos." *Adulterinos* accounted for thirty-four applicants (15.7 percent), while there were twelve *sacrílegos* (5.6 percent), DB 2-216. I have avoided use of the term *espúreo*, because the meaning varied. Some colonists used it to refer to both *adulterinos* and *sacrílegos*, while others used it exclusively in reference to the offspring of clerics.

6. AGI, Lima 893, n. 42, 1778. Konetzke, 3:1, n. 141, reprints a petition from the recently appointed *Oidor* Don Gaspar Urquízu for license to keep some family property in the jurisdiction.

7. Burkholder and Chandler, *Biographical*, pp. 334–35, cite the license grant in 1742 but mistakenly imply that he married her around that time.

8. AGI, Lima 893, n. 42, 1778.

9. In 1793 a Cámara minister added a note to the original petition to the effect that the request for further data had never been answered.

10. AGN-Lima. Jacoba Sánchez de Alba. Escribano Pedro José de Angulo, May 12, 1782, f. 306, leg. 48.

11. AGN-Lima. Gaspar Urquízu Ibañez. Escribano Pedro José de Angulo, February 27, 1783, f. 567, leg. 48.

12. AGN-Lima. Santiago Urquízu. Escribano Pedro José Angulo, July 13, 1785, f. 577, leg. 49.

13. AGN-Lima. Santiago Urquízu. Escribano Ignacio Ayllón Salazar, July 11, 1811, f. 722, leg. 15.

14. Lewin, "Natural," p. 381, notes similar confusion in Brazil, where there was some "limited acceptance" that not only *incestuosos* but even *adulterinos* might be legitimated through subsequent matrimony.

15. Gacto Fernández, *Filiación*, p. 104. Royal officials tended to grant such legitimations.

16. Morín, p. 392, comments that baptismal registers were critical in "a society where the written testimony has more valor than the oral and where legitimacy—and the possibility to prove it—controls inheritance, succession, and social ascent."

17. Merzario, p. 534.

18. Bossy, p. 57, mentions the three-day requirement. Aranda Romera and Grajales Porras, p. 11, estimate that there was a three- to three-and-a-half-day interval in Puebla between birth and baptism. Morín, p. 396, notes a five-day interval in Zacatelco, Acatzingo, and Yahuquemehcan and suggests that three-fourths of infants were baptized within a week. Of course in emergencies baptism would occur immediately. In private pregnancies baptisms might be delayed as part of strategies of concealment. One Guatemalan said that his parents had delayed his baptism for nine months, AGI, Guatemala 609, n. 2, 1798.

19. *Sínodo* discusses the Cuban regulations. The 1684 rules divided baptismal listings between only Spanish and slaves, pp. 24, 29–30.

20. Martínez Alier, *Marriage*, pp. 71–76, 132, provides a classic description of the process. One Venezuelan document suggests that the *padrinos* as well as the priest played a role in identifying the racial classification of illegitimates. The godparents mistakenly told the priest to register an illegitimate baby under the category of *pardos*, even though the parents were white. Later the baby's father and grandfather—both of whom were Dons—successfully appealed that the listing be changed so that the child would be listed as an *hijo natural* and as white. AGN-Caracas, Diversos, t. 59, f. 68, 1784. Dueñas-Vargas, pp. 123–25, discusses the issue of race and baptismal certificates. Castillo Palma, p. 142–43, 148, 153, discusses how priests might determine racial categories in Mexico. See also Lavrin, "*Lo fémenino.*"

21. DB 2-216. Race appears as a factor in sixteen (7.4 percent) cases. However, some of these mentions occur as part of successful colonist arguments that they were not of mixed blood, but were to be classified as white.

22. Mannarelli, p. 200.

23. DB 2-216.

24. AGI, Santo Domingo 1498, n. 30, 1799.

25. AGI, Buenos Aires 250, n. 14, 1785.

26. Twinam, "Honor," pp. 142–46.

27. AGI, Chile 297, n. 21, 1796.

28. AGI, Santo Domingo 1483, n. 39, 1792.

29. Of the fifty-five certificates that designated *hijos naturales*, only mothers identified themselves in ten (18.2 percent), only fathers in twelve (21.8 percent), and both parents in twenty-one (38.2 percent). There was no certificate in twelve (21.8 percent).

30. Baby boys were more likely (70.0 percent *hijos naturales*, 66.2 percent total) to be recognized as *hijos naturales* than were infant girls (29.1 percent *hijos naturales*, 33.8 percent total).

31. The status of *hijos naturales* has been portrayed as interchangeable with that of bastards or *expósitos*, while babies christened as *expósitos* were generally considered

to be abandoned. For example Calvo, "Concubinato," p. 203, suggests that the difference between an *expósito* even if legitimate and an *hijo natural* would not be great. However, *expósitos* could never officially use the family name, which meant that they could never prove legitimacy. Arnaud Rabinal et al., p. 102, and Cramaussel, p. 426, imply that most *expósitos* were really abandoned. McCaa, "Introduction," p. 212, mistakenly suggests that *hijo natural* was a "euphemism for bastards."

32. Boswell, pp. 15–17, reviews literature on child abandonment in Europe; Tilly et al., "Child," provides a critique. The debate is the extent to which abandoned children were taken in by strangers, or whether abandonment approached infanticide.

33. Aranda Romera and Grajales Porras, p. 12. Spanish-American orphanages may have accepted a substantially greater percentage of illegitimates in the nineteenth century. See Salinas Meza. *Recopilación*, lib. 1, tit. 1, ley 17, contains provisions for the 1624 foundation of a *casa* for mestizas in Mexico City. Dueñas-Vargas, pp. 261–72, provides data on colonial orphans in Bogotá.

34. Ramos, p. 161.

35. Rodríguez Jiménez, *Sentimientos*, p. 107.

36. Mannarelli, p. 168. She also notes, p. 172, the greater propensity for whites to hide evidence of illegitimacy. Evidence from San Marcelo in Lima shows that whites were more than twice as likely to baptize illegitimates as "unknown" (54 percent) as were the mixed population (21 percent). Whites were far less likely to identify the mother (13 percent) than were *castas* (45 percent). Fathers were identified 9 percent of the time for whites and 25 percent of the time for *castas*.

37. Avila Espinosa, pp. 307–9, suggests that white Mexico City *expósitos* were also more likely to be abandoned; Nazzari, "Urgent," p. 12, finds a similar pattern in the rural parish of Santo Amaro in São Paulo. Yet the situation could be even more dire for the poor and nonwhite. Malvido correlated rates of infant abandonment with periods of hardship among the indigenous population of Tula. She concluded that abandoned indigenous infants became another form of tribute, given that they were expropriated by the better-off to be used as laborers.

38. DB 2-216. Where available, the breakdown of baptismal listings of *expósitos* to *padres no conocidos* by *audiencia* was Charcas 3-0, Santa Fé 4-1, Mexico 10-3; Santo Domingo 9-19, Guatemala 1-6. Other *audiencias*: Guadalajara 2-1, Caracas 2-1, Buenos Aires 1-0, Panama 0-1, Lima 0-1. Quito and Chile none. Some of these ratios may have been affected by time as well, given the 1770s shift from the use of *padres no conocidos* to *expósitos* as noted in this chapter.

39. DB 6-139. There was a ratio of twenty-five *padres no conocidos* to fourteen *expósitos* from 1700 to 1769, and a ratio of eight to seven from 1770 to 1799. The smaller number of applications of *expósitos* and *padres no conocidos* after 1770 was likely due to the lessening possibility that royal officials would approve legitimation.

40. AGI, Santo Domingo 1471, n. 6, 1787.

41. AGI, Santo Domingo 1470, n. 14, 1786.

42. AGI, Mexico 1772, n. 2, 1795.

43. Unmarried parents had the option either to identify themselves and swear

that their infants met the conditions for being baptized as *hijos naturales*, or to refuse to admit their sexual relationship, with their baby then receiving an unclear listing. One way to gauge change over time is to compare the natal and baptismal status of infants. Such analysis reveals that parents were somewhat more likely to admit their sexuality and list their babies as *hijos naturales* in the first rather than in the second half of the eighteenth century. Before 1750 there were twenty-seven babies whose parents were unwed and who could have chosen to list their offspring as *hijos naturales*. Two-thirds (N. 18, 66.6 percent) actually did so. In the last half of the century there were sixty-one babies whose parents had the same choice, but fewer, slightly more than half (N. 34, 55.7 percent), made this decision. See Appendix 2, Table 11.

44. AGI, Charcas 554, n. 25, 1791.

45. Mannarelli, p. 169, notes that of 1,493 babies classified as illegitimate only 18 (1.2 percent) were later recognized by parents. Of those, 11 were legitimated (it is unknown whether by *gracias al sacar* or subsequent matrimony) and 7 were recognized as *hijos naturales*. Aranda Romera and Grajales Porras, p. 17, noted two such recognitions in Puebla. Castañeda, "La formación," p. 84, suggests that in New Galicia illegitimate sons were more likely to be recognized by both parents than were girls. Such comments suggest that the *gracias al sacar* illegitimates were substantially more likely to be recognized by parents than the norm.

46. DB 2-216. Of these the mother returned to acknowledge her offspring in two instances, the father in eleven, and both parents in six.

47. AGI, Charcas 652, n. 30, 1796.

48. AGI, Santo Domingo 1471, n. 6, 1787.

49. AGI, Santo Domingo 1488, n. 15, 1796.

50. AGI, Santo Domingo 1497, n. 24, 1799.

51. AGI, Santo Domingo 1474, n. 11, 1789. The more usual tactic for illegitimates classified as *expósitos* or as having unknown parents was to avoid presenting any documents that linked them with parents of lesser status or mixed blood, and to hope for royal clemency given the absence of such "incriminating" information. It was the public and official recognition in a testament as well as the extreme prejudice against illegitimacy in Cuba that precipitated this petition.

52. AA-Habana. Casa de Beneficiencia y Maternidad, lib. 1, no. 155, 1735. When a baby was brought to the *casa*, the sex, time of entry, and description of any clothing or accompanying notes were entered in the register. Sometimes parents provided names or stated if the baby had already been baptized. Later entries might note whether the parents ever returned to acknowledge the infant, or if the baby had died. Zenea, pp. 26–27, provides a vivid history of the Havana institution, which he describes as a "tomb for infants" located in "a few badly ventilated rooms." He envisions the resident nurse "with breasts exhausted at the time with three or four babies and pregnant, perhaps with spoiled milk." The problem was less finances than bad management, since the institution had an endowment of some ninety-five thousand pesos by the 1780s.

53. It was customary for all Havana *expósitos* to take the surname of Valdés, in

honor of the orphanage's founder. AA-Habana, leg. 36, exped. 46, 1874; AGI, Santo Domingo 1474, n. 11, 1789. Mannarelli, p. 299, remarks on a similar custom in Lima, where *expósitos* took the name Atocha.

54. AGI, Santo Domingo 1474, n. 11, 1789.

55. *NR*, lib. 7, tit. 27 ley 4. The crown tried to enhance the status of *expósitos* and establish the principle that colonists should give them the benefit of the doubt as to any questionable natal or racial status.

56. AGI, Santo Domingo 1474, n. 11, 1789. *SP*, part. 4, tit. 20, ley 4 supported his claim, for it stated that parents who abandoned children or took them to churches or hospitals could not reclaim them, but "lose the power that they have over them." Alvarez Santalo, p. 103, found that 5.4 percent of parents returned for a baby left in the Sevilla *casa de expósitos* in the seventeenth century, 4.1 percent in the eighteenth century, and 2.6 percent in the nineteenth century. Mannarelli, p. 290, recounts an example in which a mother reclaimed an infant in the Lima *casa de expósitos*.

57. Other examples include a Mexican case that stressed the duality of the recognition that one legitimate brother accorded his illegitimate half brother, for the acknowledgment was "in public and in secret." AGI, Mexico, 1779, no. 2, 1795. Although the sisters Echevarría of Havana had received official recognition only in their father's will, this document also admitted that the relationship was "public and notorious," the conventional description of such informal acknowledgments; Santo Domingo 1488, no. 15, 1796. Nizza da Silva, "Filhos," p. 124, provides a similar example from Brazil in which the father recognized in the "public" and in the "particular" and also fed and educated his sons.

58. Gacto Fernández, *Filiación*, pp. 80–83.

59. Mannarelli, p. 277.

60. AGI, Santo Domingo 1470, n. 14, 1786.

61. Castillo Palma, p. 160, makes a similar observation for racial classifications, for an individual might appear differently depending on the document.

62. AGI, Mexico 684, n. 8, 1754.

63. AGI, Mexico 1779, n. 2, 1795.

64. Gacto Fernández, *Filiación*, pp. 129–30, notes that Spanish law provided no guidelines about when family names might or might not be used.

65. AGI, Mexico 1770, n. 35, 1780.

66. AGI, Santo Domingo 1467, n. 1, 1782.

67. AGI, Quito 355, n. 38, 1795.

68. Gacto Fernández, *Filiación*, p. 92.

69. For example, in the private recognition case from Peru witnesses noted that the parents "knew her in secret as their *hija natural*." AGI, Lima 826, n. 57, 1788.

70. AGI, Santo Domingo 1492, n. 43, 1797.

71. AGI, Mexico 1771, n. 6, 1785.

72. Although the alterations in Doña Justa's birth and racial status were striking, they were not uncommon. Changes in female racial status were more usual when

white women married men of lower caste and assumed the inferior "quality" of their Indian, *pardo*, or mulatto husbands. See McCaa, "Gustos," p. 607, for Parral; Rabell, "Matrimonio," p. 4, for Guanajuato; Socolow, "Acceptable," p. 231, for Argentina; Rípodas Ardanaz, p. 30, for Venezuela.

73. AGI, Santo Domingo 1429, n. 4, 1785.

74. Castañeda, *Violación*, pp. 76–77, notes that prior to marriage couples had to provide information on their race, marital state, legitimacy, age, and residence, among other qualifications.

75. AGI, Santo Domingo 1429, n. 4, 1785.

76. AGI, Santo Domingo 1483, n. 38, 1792. When illegitimate Doña Antonia de Rey Blanco married Don Juan Andrés de las Casas, he was described as "from this city, legitimate son of Don Damián de la Casa and Doña Juana Jacinta Pedraza," while Doña Antonia was listed as "white, from this city," with no mention of her parents.

77. AGI, Mexico 684, n. 11, 1757.

78. AGI, Mexico 684, n. 11, 1757.

79. AGI, Guadalajara 368, n. 6, 1761.

80. Nazzari, "Urgent," p. 17, however, documented cases in which parents served in that capacity in Brazil.

81. AGI, Guadalajara 368, n. 6, 1761.

82. There were 125 cases in which natal and baptismal status could be compared. Of the three clear cases of deliberate falsification, one concerned race; AGI, Santo Domingo 1479, n. 50, 1790. Another concerned adulterous birth; AGI, Caracas 279, n. 18, 1784. In the last instance, a lawyer knew that his infant was an *incestuoso* but listed her as legitimate; AGI, Indiferente General 16, March 5, 1803.

83. AGI, Caracas 279, n. 18, 1784.

84. For an analysis of bigamy in colonial Mexico, see Boyer.

85. AGI, Caracas 279, n. 18, 1784.

86. They did, however, suggest that he might continue his suit to recover property in local courts.

Chapter 6. Children: Growing Up Illegitimate

1. AGN-Lima, Superior Gobierno, leg. 28, cuad. 894, 1802, contains the story.

2. ADL-Trujillo, leg. 69, n. 1162, describes his possessions, worth approximately 34,710 pesos; leg. 65, Escribano 114, Carlos Flores, 1803, contains his testament. He married the daughter of a *regidor* and *alguacil mayor* (Doña María Theresa de Zurita y Plaza), served as a *procurador general* and *alcalde ordinario*, and owned the haciendas of Santa Clara del Sol and San José de Buena Vista in the Valley of Chicama.

3. AGI, Lima 963, n. 22, 1791.

4. See Lavrin, "Mexico," for an introduction.

5. Boswell, p. 345, summarizes Spanish laws. For comments on twelfth- to

fourteenth-century customs, see Dillard, p. 156. For definitions of *crianza* and the duties of fathers and mothers, see *SP*, part. 4, tit. 19 ley 1–5; *SP*, part. 4, tit. 20, ley 2. Nizza da Silva, "Divorce," p. 335, notes a similar three-year dividing line for Portugal and Brazil.

6. AGI, Lima 921, n. 71, 1786.   7. AGI, Lima 934, n. 46, 1790.

8. AGI, Buenos Aires 183, n. 4, 1771.   9. AGI, Mexico 1779, n. 2, 1795.

10. See Sussman, *Selling*, pp. 3–7, 20–25, on European customs and on the wet nurse establishment in Paris. Also Lindemann.

11. Calvo, "Warmth," p. 261.

12. Laslett, *Family*, p. 122, notes that in Seville the best wet nurses were more likely to be installed in private homes. Lindemann, p. 385, notes that eighteenth-century German elites customarily brought wet nurses into the home, and that many of these women stayed on to become dry nurses and nannies.

13. AA-Habana. For analysis of the Havana *casa de expósitos*, see Chapter 5, pages 138–39. Other research on such institutions includes Quesada for Buenos Aires, and Nizza da Silva, "O problema," for São Paulo.

14. AA-Habana. Casa de Beneficiencia y Maternidad, lib. 1, 1711–1740. The twenty-seven and twenty-four babies entered in 1717 and 1718 do not figure in this total because deaths were not registered in those years. Dueñas-Vargas, p. 268, notes a 41 percent mortality rate for babies deposited in the Bogotá *casa de expósitos* in 1810.

15. Avila Espinosa, p. 302.

16. Alvarez Santalo, pp. 43–44, 193, estimates that approximately 10 percent of annual births in Seville were deposited in the *casa de expósitos*.

17. Potash, p. 13; Mannarelli, p. 283.

18. Tilly et al., "Child," p. 12; Kertzer, "Gender Ideology," pp. 8–10.

19. Sussman "Parisian," p. 639, notes the difficulties of calculating infant mortality rates. Higginbotham, p. 260, estimated that illegitimates had "at least" double the crude death rate of legitimate babies in Victorian London; Kertzer, "Gender Ideology," pp. 8–10, suggested that illegitimate mortality in nineteenth-century Italy was double to triple that of legitimates. Such calculations are complicated by the unknown number of infant deaths that occurred before babies were brought to institutions, as well as the lack of subsequent record-keeping after the first months or years of life.

20. One of the most well known comments concerning the relationship between wet nurses and their charges is attributed to Simón Bolívar, who, during the independence wars, received notice that Hipólita, his black nurse, was in difficulty. He wrote back to his sister in Caracas: "See that she gets whatever she asks for. . . . Hipólita gave me the milk that nourished me as a child, she was, to this orphan, both father and mother. Let her want for nothing." Lansing, p. 210.

21. AGI, Indiferente General 16, February 24, 1812.

22. AGI, Ultramar 166, 1813.

23. AGI, Lima 926, n. 57, 1789. Cramaussel, p. 435, notes similar intimate links between elite families and their servants.

24. Brettell and Rui Feijo, p. 223, note that in nineteenth-century Portugal women might be paid to be wet nurses for abandoned infants for two years, and then continue as dry nurses until the child reached the age of seven.

25. AGI, Caracas 299, n. 22, 1787.

26. Mannarelli, p. 285, also provides examples from seventeenth-century Peru of wet nurses who developed emotional ties with their charges and did not want to give them up.

27. AGI, Buenos Aires 250, n. 14, 1785.

28. AGI, Santo Domingo 1470, n. 14, 1786.

29. Waldron provides typical examples.

30. AGI, Santo Domingo 1456, n. 5, 1761.

31. Calvo, "Warmth," p. 306.

32. DB 4-187. Petitioners supplied little information as to whether mothers or fathers bequeathed property to illegitimates (unknown N. 169, mothers; N. 130, fathers), although fathers seemed almost four times more likely to do so than mothers (fathers, N. 46; mothers, N. 12). The remainder (mothers, N. 6; fathers, N. 11) clearly left no property.

33. AGI, Mexico 684, n. 1, 1727.

34. AHG-Guanajuato, Bienes Difuntos. Ramo Protocolos. Cabildo t. 1699, f. 9.

35. AGI, Mexico 684, n. 1, 1727.

36. AGI, Quito 359, n. 38, 1795; AGI, Indiferente General, August 15, 1810; and Indiferente General, December 8, 1815, provide other examples of wives raising their husband's illegitimate offspring. See also Calvo, "Warmth," p. 301, for a similar pattern.

37. Lewin, "Natural," p. 386.

38. AGI, Buenos Aires 250, n. 14, 1785.

39. AGI, Santo Domingo 1469, n. 6, 1786.

40. AGI, Buenos Aires 259, n. 29, 1790.

41. AGI, Santo Domingo 1498, n. 30, 1799.

42. AGI, Lima 954, n. 41, 1795.

43. AGI, Guatemala 609, n. 2, 1798.

44. Ramos, p. 160, finds that unwed mothers had smaller houses and fewer servants in Ouro Preto, Brazil (1754–1838). Such a conclusion makes sense for both Portuguese and Spanish America, although the demographic data are lacking.

45. DB 4-187. Fifty-two women had no other illegitimate children, 26 had another child by the same lover, 3 by another lover, while information is lacking on 106.

46. AGI, Santo Domingo 1498, n. 19, 1790.

47. Whether such estrangement occurred in the case of Doña Antonia is unknown. The only information that emerges is that her father did not fulfill his promise to legitimate her when she was a baby, waiting until she was seventeen before he sought a *gracias al sacar*. Whether such belated intervention promised his support or lack of it in subsequent years is difficult to say.

48. AGI, Quito 359, n. 38, 1795.

49. AGI, Santo Domingo 1456, n. 5, 1761.

50. AGI, Chile 290, n. 9, 1792.

51. AN-Santiago, vol. 134, Real Audiencia, ff. 1–271, and Escribanos, vol. 878, José Rubio, ff. 169–74, 199–201, 1776–77, contains his testament; Escribanos, vol. 781, Antonio Zenteno, ff. 43–55, 1789, the entail.

52. AN-Santiago, vol. 134, Real Audiencia, ff. 1–271.

53. AGI, Santo Domingo 1467, n. 7, 1781.

54. AGI, Charcas 506, n. 5, 1776.

55. AGI, Mexico 1778, n. 6, 1793.

56. AGI, Buenos Aires 274, n. 32, 1793.

57. AGI, Mexico 1776, n. 6, 1789.

58. Literature on this topic from the sixteenth through nineteenth centuries questions when adolescence appears as a discernible life stage. See Stone, "Family." Morel, p. 323, summarizes recent scholarship that suggests that the years from ten to twelve marked a turning point in children's lives as they became apprentices or began full-time work. Laslett, *Family*, p. 171, notes that children often left home at ten to become servants. Cramaussel, p. 428, comments that seventeenth-century Mexican baptismal records used the age of ten as the dividing line between "children" and "adults."

59. For example, the statutes of the *colegio* of San Carlos in Cartagena established that entrants had to be at least twelve years old, "legitimate," and free of all "bad race"; Kontezke, 3:2, n. 298, 1786. In Arequipa students between eleven and fourteen years of age had to present their parents' marriage lines and their own baptismal certificates; Konetzke, 3:2, n. 356, 1802. The entrance requirements to the Colegio de Nobles Americanos in Granada were even higher; Konetzke, 3:2, n. 328, 1792.

60. AGI, Chile 295, n. 4, 1795.

61. AGI, Indiferente General 16, March 9, 1804.

62. DB 6-139. The breakdown by decade of age of illegitimates who sought *gracias al sacar* was 1–9 (N. 9), 10–20 (N. 29), 20s (N. 33), 30s (N. 33), 40s (N. 22), 50s (N. 8), 60s (N. 1), 70s (N. 4).

Chapter 7. Adults: Passing, Turning-point Moments, and the Quest for Honor

1. AGI, Panama 291, no n., 1798. He was also a *pardo*, which complicated his case. Royal officials seemed more ready to legitimate than to "whiten" him.

2. AGI, Santo Domingo 1467, n. 7, 1781.

3. DB 2-216. N. 186 (86.1 percent) were addressed as Don or Doña; N. 9 (4.2 percent) were not; N. 21 (9.7 percent) were sometimes addressed that way and sometimes not. For popular customs on the use of "Don," see Chapter 1, note 2.

4. See the comments concerning Don Pedro Minjares in AGI, Guadalajara 368, n. 6, 1761.

5. AGI, Buenos Aires 280, n. 14, 1796.

6. One merchant stated that his illegitimacy was "a continuous cause which afflicted him and bothered his business," since those who wished him harm "when they could not find any personal vice with which to judge him" resorted to the "infamy occasioned by his birth"; AGI, Santo Domingo 1467, n. 12, 1781. See also a case cited by Patiño Millán, p. 207, on the importance of reputation to the ability to "make contracts."

7. AGI, Lima 898, n. 32, 1780.

8. DB 2-216. Men N. 143 (66.2 percent); women N. 73 (33.8 percent).

9. AGI, Panama 285, n. 9, 1784.

10. AHN-Bogotá, Milicias y marinas, t. 126, n. 837, ff. 605–14, 1767; AHN-Bogotá, Milicias y marinas, t. 42, n. 103, ff. 832–43, 1759.

11. He acted as *asesor general, auditor de guerra,* and served on the *juzgado de artillería,* the *asesoría of reales rentas,* and the *juzgado de bienes de difuntos.* AHN-Bogotá, Milicias y marinas, t. 90, n. 3810, ff. 797–99, 1792.

12. AHN-Bogotá, Milicias y marinas, t. 94, n. 4522, ff. 805–8, 1766.

13. AHN-Bogotá, Milicias y marinas, t. 126, n. 837, ff. 721–23, 1767.

14. AHN-Bogotá, Milicias y marinas, t. 77, n. 1598, ff. 903–7, 1777.

15. Burkholder, "From Creole," provides an excellent case study.

16. AHN-Bogotá, Milicias y marinas, t. 140, n. 2773, ff. 143–44, 1777. Burkholder, *Biographical,* pp. 45–46, provides a capsule biography of Gálvez.

17. AGI, Panama 285, n. 9, 1784.

18. AHN-Bogotá, Milicias y marinas, t. 147, n. 3936, ff. 1063–67, 1792.

19. AHN-Bogotá, Milicias y marinas, t. 90, n. 3810, ff. 797–99, 1795.

20. He does not appear as an *audiencia* minister in Burkholder and Chandler.

21. AGI, Caracas 299, n. 22, 1788.

22. Konetzke, 3:1, n. 215, reprints a 1770 *consulta* of the Council of the Indies that notes requirements. See also Konetzke, 3:1, n. 132, 1737, where locals wanted to require potential cabildo officers to submit baptismal certificates for themselves, their parents, and their grandparents. The Council of the Indies was not so strict, saying that only those with a "notorious defect" could be kept from office.

23. See Twinam, *Miners,* pp. 112–23; Rodríguez Jiménez, "Elección," p. 40.

24. Saguier, pp. 162–63, provides examples of passing in which Argentinians held cabildo office even though known as illegitimate.

25. AGI, Guatemala 605, n. 4, 1793.

26. Both *regidor* and *procurador general* had been offices forbidden in the Pragmatic Sanction of 1501.

27. AGI, Santo Domingo 1483, n. 38, 1792.

28. ACM-Habana, Actas Capitulares, January 1, 1786.

29. AGI, Santo Domingo 1483, n. 38, 1792.

30. ACM-Habana, Actas Capitulares, April 28, 1786.

31. AGI, Santo Domingo 1483, n. 38, 1792.

32. My examination of the Havana cabildo elections for the rest of the century does not show him as an officer.

33. For another example, see Don Joseph Cañete de Antequera in Paraguay, who held a series of local offices including *alcalde ordinario* and *regidor* before he applied for legitimation. AGI, Buenos Aires 228, n. 27, 1779.

34. Martínez Alier, "El honor," p. 36, also notes that illegitimate elite women had problems finding marital partners. Caviéres F. and Salinas M., p. 97, provide a similar example in which the unknown parentage of the mother hurt the marital possibilities of her child. This may have been especially common in smaller towns, where everyone knew each other.

35. AGI, Caracas 279, n. 18, 1784.   36. AGI, Charcas 560, n. 15, 1795.

37. AGI, Caracas 299, no n., 1788.   38. AGI, Chile 290, n. 9, 1792.

39. AGI, Santo Domingo 1474, n. 28, 1789.

40. Lanning, pp. 175–76.

41. AGI, Santa Fe 677, n. 19, 1766.

42. AHN-Bogotá, Testamentos de Cundinamarca, t. 41, ff. 1–180, 1771.

43. AGI, Santa Fe 677, n. 19, 1766.

44. AHN-Bogotá, Testamentos de Cundinamarca, t. 41, ff. 1–180, 1771. The couple's second son, Ignacio, took advantage of the ruling, for he became a priest and received special consideration in his father's will.

45. AGI, Santo Domingo 1470, n. 33, 1786.

46. AGI, Indiferente General 16, July 15, 1819.

47. Brading, "Bourbon," p. 147, uses the word. Classic works include Knight; and Martínez Alier, *Marriage.*

48. ACM-Medellín, vol. 38, n. 7, 1787.

49. Before they applied for *cédulas*, Chileans Don Nicolás de Pozo and Don Joseph Briceño had also enjoyed similar latitude; the former served as a royal official in the mail service, and the latter was a notary. Don Nicolás de Pozo's comments on his occupation and his proof of *limpieza* (but not legitimacy) is in AN-Santiago, Archivo Judicial de la Serena, leg. 81, 1761–1798, Pieza 16, 1789; his legitimation in AGI, Chile 295, n. 3, 1795. Chilean Don José Briceño had applied for legitimation (AGI, Chile 297, n. 21, 1796) but apparently never had the money to purchase it, for he declared himself as an *hijo natural* on his final testament. AN-Santiago, Notarios 927, José Briceño, ff. 270–75, 1797–1799.

50. I thank Professor Roger Daniels for the concept of cluster applications. AGI, Santo Domingo 421, n. 1, 1723. This was Doña María Catalina, the daughter of Havana captain Don Diego de Alarcón.

51. AGI, Lima 898, n. 32, 1789.

52. AGN-Lima, Notarial. Gregorio de Pro León, Escribano Gerónimo de Villa-fuerte, May 22, 1814, ff. 398, n. 1017.

53. AGN-Lima, Notarial. José Antonio Cobián, Escribano Faustino Olaya, Oc-

tober 16, 1849, f. 541. In Guatemala the legitimation of one family member may have encouraged another to apply. When Guatemalan Don Francisco Javier Paniagua asked for a decree in 1793, he identified his mother as a Doña Tecla de Medina of Comayagua. Two years later Don Joseph Mariano de Cáceres of Guatemala City sent documents to the Cámara that also named Doña Tecla Medina of Comayagua as his mother. Petitions are in AGI, Indiferente General 16, August 23, 1793; AGI, Guatemala 606, n. 4, 1795.

54. AGI, Charcas 560, n. 15, 1795.

55. Burkholder, *Biographical*, pp. 107–8 details his career; AGI, Charcas 854, n. 25, 1791, were his wife's cousins.

56. AGI, Buenos Aires 183, n. 4, 1771; AGN-Buenos Aires, IX, 40-8-2, Tribunales, leg. 5, exped. 8, 1784.

57. Evidence of their service together is in AGN-Buenos Aires, Reales Ordenes, ley 9, f. 190, 1779; Zapiola's legitimation petition is AGI, Buenos Aires 259, n. 20, 1790.

58. AGI, Santo Domingo 426, n. 1, 1741, Don Joseph Alemán y Salgado; AGI Santo Domingo 427, n. 5, 1746, Don Agustín Palomino y Sanabria.

59. AGI, Caracas 259, n. 4, 1779, Doña Rafaela Espinosa de los Monteros; AGI, Caracas 279, n. 18, 1784, Doña Margarita Theodora Gonzáles.

60. Circumstantial evidence also connects two petitions from Cumaná, Venezuela, both in 1788, and both from *adulterinos*. AGI, Caracas 299, n. 20, 1788, Doña Juana de Figueroa; Caracas 299, n. 22, 1788, Don Joseph Antonio Betancourt.

61. Boyer, *Lives*, makes this point throughout his work.

62. The breakdown is in Chapter 1, Table 1. The actual percentage is 75.6.

63. Some historians point to an increase in peer intermarriage, or endogamy, as an example. Rabell, "Matrimonio," pp. 10–11, notes the lesser tolerance for exogamous marriages in Guanajuato in the second half of the eighteenth century, a finding also confirmed by Pescador C., "Nupcialidad," pp. 157–59, for Mexico City parishes (1700–1850).

64. Schneider, p. 2.

65. Asunción Lavrin, however, also noted (personal communication to author, November 1997) that elite women at the end of the eighteenth century might have been "exercising a degree of agency that was very difficult before."

66. AGI, Mexico 1779, n. 2, 1795.   67. AGN-Mexico, Minería 43.

68. AGI, Mexico 1779, n. 2, 1795.   69. AGI, Mexico 684, n. 1, 1727.

70. AGI, Mexico 1770, n. 30, 1780.   71. AGI, Indiferente General 1535, 1814.

72. AGI, Panama 291, n. 6, 1798.

73. NL-Ayer, ff. 62, 731, n. 876 (May 2, 1789). *Habilitaciones* can also be found in the Cartas y Expedientes section of each *audiencia* in the Archive of the Indies.

74. AGI, Santo Domingo 1498, n. 49, 1799.

75. The regulation for the Cuba militia published in 1769 contained no requirement that entrants be legitimate, although their prospective wives had to prove their

honor and *limpieza de sangre*; Konetzke, 3:1, n. 209, 1769. Kuethe, *Cuba*, pp. 148, 65, describes the "striking degree of continuity" in Cuba militia units and mentions the Zayas as among the "prominent clans" in Puerto Príncipe.

76. AGI, Santo Domingo 1498, n. 49, 1799.

77. AGI, Mexico 1776, n. 6, 1789.

78. A similar lack of concern as to whether the illegitimate was living or dead characterized official reaction to the application of Don Joseph Valero of Lima. He petitioned to legitimate his dead wife so that her lack of honor would not prejudice their offspring. Royal officials rejected his request, not because his wife was dead but because of the scanty documentation that supported his case. AGI, Lima 925, n. 57, 1789.

79. AGI, Indiferente General 16, October 21, 1789.

Chapter 8. Adults: The Quest for Family Property

1. AGI, Mexico 684, no n., 1743.

2. See Couturier; also Arrom, "Changes," for background on colonial and republican laws.

3. This was different from Portuguese inheritance law and legitimation procedure, which distinguished between nobles and commoners; see Lewin, "Surprise Heirs." Of course, Spanish nobles, Dons, and even those who were not Dons might also purchase an entail (*mayorazgo*) through *gracias al sacar*, which bypassed these normal effects of law.

4. AGI, Guadalajara 368, n. 6, 1761.

5. AGI, Lima 898, n. 32, 1780. The father's wills are in AGN-Lima, Don Francisco Pro León y Colmenares, Escribano Valentín de Torres Preciado, December 15, 1761, t. 2, leg. 1057, f. 98; Escribano Valentín de Torres Preciado, March 1, 1762, t. 11, leg. 1058, f. 98.

6. Vázquez Richart, pp. 46–62, reviews the legal effects of illegitimacy in laws from *Fuero Juzgo* (681), *Fuero Real de España* (1255), *Siete Partidas* (1256–1265), *Fuero Viejo de Castilla* (1356), *Ordenamiento de Alcalá de Henares* (1386), *Ordenanzas Reales de Castilla* (1484), *Leyes de Toro* (1502), *Nueva Recopilación* (1567), and *Novísima Recopilación* (1805). See also Puente y Quijano, pp. 13–26; Gacto Fernández, "El grupo," pp. 56–64; and Covarrubias y Leyva, pp. 153–93.

7. *NR*, lib. 10, tit. 20, ley 3. See also Gómez, p. 25; *Testamentarías*, pp. 70–73; Gacto Fernández, "El grupo," pp. 52–53.

8. According to the *Fuero Real*, the party that received the third of the *mejora* could not also receive the fifth that was given freely. This was changed in the *Siete Partidas* so that a favored child might receive both, or the "*mejora de tercio y quinto*." See Gacto Fernández, ibid.

9. *SP*, Sexta Partida, tit. 13, ley 11, notes that "mothers always are certain of the children that they bear and for this reason all children should inherit the goods of the mother . . . be they legitimate or not."

10. *NR*, lib. 10, tit. 20, ley 5.

11. Lewin, "Natural," p. 361.

12. *NR*, lib. 10, tit. 20, ley 6.

13. Gacto Fernández, *Filiación*, pp. 139–43, 196.

14. On maintenance, see *NR*, lib. X, tit. 20, ley 6, 9. Comments on Don Manuel Joaquin de Zapiola's testament are in the legitimation petition. AGI, Buenos Aires 259, n. 20, 1790. It is notable that the disposition of goods is different in the Buenos Aires version of the testament, in which Don Manuel left only half of the fifth to his *hijo natural* and the other half to his sisters in Spain. According to the inventory of goods, his son was to receive 8,591 pesos. Don Manuel Joaquin said he has five rather than four legitimate offspring. Of course it may be that his sisters and one of his children had died in the intervening year. AGN-Buenos Aires, Sucesiones 8821, 1789.

15. *NR*, lib. 10, tit. 20, ley 6.

16. AGN-Lima, Don Francisco Pro León y Colmenares, Escribano Valentín de Torres Preciado, December 15, 1761, t. 2, leg. 1057, p. 98; Escribano Valentín de Torres Preciado, March 1, 1762, t. 11, leg. 1058, p. 98.

17. *NR*, lib. 10, tit. 20, ley 6.

18. *NR*, lib. 10, tit. 20, ley 14.

19. Although the Law of Soria does not mention nuns, the next clause specifically refers back to it and includes professed nuns under the same restrictions as priests. *NR*, lib. 10, tit. 20, ley 5.

20. Ibid. If a woman had both natural children and *adulterinos* or *incestuosos*, inheritance proceeded "by their order and grade either with or without a testament." There was one exception to this rule. If a mother produced a bastard as the result of "damnable and punishable intercourse," which was defined in the Laws of Toro as when the mother "incurred pain of death," the code forbade inheritance either through a written will or intestacy. However, even then the law conceded that the mother "could in life or death remit up to the fifth part of her goods but not more" to such offspring. The Laws of Toro are silent on which actions might lead to the death penalty, but the *Siete Partidas* prescribes burning when a married woman had sexual intercourse with a servant; part. 7, tit. 17, ley 15. In AGI, Santo Domingo 1458, n. 17, 1766, the crown attorney described *incestuosos* and *sacrílegos* with these adjectives.

21. Gómez, p. 45.

22. Lewin, "Natural," p. 358.

23. *Testamentarías*, pp. 70–81.

24. The law classified the bastards of mothers, but not those of fathers, as forced heirs. However Gacto Fernández, "La filiación ilegítima," pp. 940–41, concludes that offspring born to mothers of "damnable and punishable intercourse" could never receive more than a fifth of the maternal estate. He says that offspring of female and male religious could receive subsistence only from such parents, not to exceed the one-fifth. For the controversy over collateral succession, see ibid.

25. Puente y Quijano, p. 21.

26. Gacto Fernández, *Filiación*, p. 170. The Partidas also established a *legitima* of one-third that would go to ascendant heirs, but this was not followed in the later Laws of Toro.

27. Ibid., pp. 175, 179. It was not clarified until a 1868 legal decision that noted that the Partida designation of the sixth was still operative, given that the Laws of Toro were silent on the issue.

28. Ibid., p. 176.

29. Information from the testament is in AGN-Lima, Notaría. D. D. Antonio de Bedoya, Essno. Ignacio Ayllon Salazar, December 13, 1799, f. 1037, n. 92. The legitimation petition is AGI, Lima 942, n. 59, 1792.

30. *NR*, lib. 10, tit. 20, ley 7. The legitimate heirs could be either "born or legitimated by subsequent marriage."

31. AGI, Indiferente General 16, December 9, 1818.

32. There has been much confusion on this issue. For example Potthast-Jutkeit, p. 217, wrongly assumes that the mention of an illegitimate mestizo in a testament was "an act that equalled legitimization." Recognition of an illegitimate child was never the same as official, civil legitimation. However if the parent had no legitimate children, such recognition and specific bequests would permit the illegitimate to inherit as if he or she were a legitimate child. Seed, "Church," p. 287, also misinterprets the potential legal consequences when she states that offspring of parents who lived together would be "ineligible for the substantial inheritances that went to legitimate children of a marriage." If the unmarried parents had no legitimate children and wrote testaments that recognized their *hijos naturales*, they could leave property as if their offspring were legitimate.

33. AGI, Indiferente General 1535, November 4, 1640. Another case of inheritance by an *adulterino* from Mexico about the same time is AGI, Indiferente General 16, December 15, 1635.

34. AGI, Santo Domingo 1469, n. 6, 1785.

35. AGI, Santo Domingo 1484, n. 14, 1793.

36. Legitimation petition is AGI, Chile 290, n. 9, 1792; court case is AN-Santiago, Real Audiencia, vol. 134, ff. 1–271.

37. AGI, Santo Domingo 1456, n. 5, 1761.

38. AGI, Santo Domingo 1469, n. 5, 1785.

39. AGI, Santo Domingo, 1497, n. 24, 1799.

40. Lewin, "Natural," p. 356.

41. AHG-Guanajuato, Presos 1773, ff. 85–93, 240–48. In this instance the illegitimate received even less than a fifth, for in his petition he notes that he inherited four thousand pesos, or one-half of the fifth. His illegitimate sister received another half. AGI, Mexico 1779, n. 2, 1795.

42. AGI, Santo Domingo 1481, n. 23, 1791. Another such private will is located in AGI, Guatemala 609, n. 2, 1798.

43. AN-Santiago, Escribanos de Santiago de Antonio Zenteno, vol. 860, ff. 280–89, 1774–75.

44. Mannarelli, p. 196.

45. NL-Graff Collection, f. 9, n. 18. "Nuebas instrucciones para el juzgado de bienes de difuntos," May 29, 1802.

46. Gacto Fernández, "La filiación ilegítima," p. 941.

47. Cobián, pp. 53–55. Note how even in the twentieth century this author makes the qualification about "intimate" friend.

48. AGI, Santo Domingo 425, n. 17, 1739.

49. AGI, Santo Domingo 1458, n. 17, 1766.

50. AGI, Indiferente General 1535, May 10, 1805. See also Miller.

51. AGI, Caracas 259, n. 4, 1779.

52. AGI, Indiferente General 16, March 5, 1803; AGN-Mexico, Historia 120, exp. 17, 18, summarizes the father's career.

53. The original case is in AGI, Caracas 279, n. 18, 1784.

54. AGI, Guatemala 602, n. 5, 1784.

55. AGI, Guatemala 411, November 22, 1784.

56. Such legitimations were very common in the fifteenth and sixteenth centuries. See Ortíz de Montalván et al., which indexes these early legitimation petitions, found in the AGS.

57. AGI, Santo Domingo 1458, n. 17, 1766.

58. AGI, Mexico 684, n. 8, 1750.

59. AGI, Santo Domingo 1497, n. 22, 1799.

Chapter 9. Royal Officials: Prelude (1717–1760) and Early Policy Formation (1761–1775)

1. Brading, "Bourbon," p. 118.

2. See Barbier, "Culmination;" and Burkholder, *Biographical.*

3. Burkholder counts 172 men who served in the Council of the Indies from 1717 to 1808. Of these, 46 also served on the Cámara; pp. xiv, xi, xii.

4. AGI, Santo Domingo 467, n. 12, 1781.

5. AGI, Buenos Aires 259, n. 20, 1790. For background for this 1773 decree, see Rodulfo Cortés, pp. 120–21.

6. AHN-Madrid, Consejos lib. 1476, n. 17, f. 103.

7. AHN-Madrid, Bca 1902, 1722.   8. AGI, Mexico 684, n. 4, 1743.

9. AGI, Mexico 684, n. 7, 1748.   10. AGI, Mexico 684, n. 8, 1750.

11. AGI, Mexico 684, n. 11, 1757.   12. AGI, Mexico 684, n. 4, 1739.

13. In a 1723 Cuban case the father was apparently still alive, but he did not come forth to testify in behalf of his illegitimate daughter. His sister confirmed that the family accepted her as blood kin. AGI, Santo Domingo 421, n. 1, 1723.

14. Burkholder and Chandler, pp. 323–24, provide a biographical sketch of the father, Don Gerónimo de Soria Velásquez, 1660–1740. It is unclear whether the Marqués ever married; he may well have remained unwed, for he left no surviving

legitimate children inasmuch as his nephew succeeded to the title. He became the Vizconde de Ribera and Marqués de Villahermosa y Alfaro in 1711, the year his illegitimate son was born. He served as an *oidor* on the Mexico City *audiencia* from 1705 until his death in 1740.

15. AGI, Mexico 684, n. 4, 1739.

16. Even though *hijos naturales* usually paid less for legitimations than did bastards, the differential remained smaller in the Indies than on the peninsula. *Sacrílegos* in the Americas paid an average of 1.2 times more than *hijos naturales* to be legitimated, while in Spain the 1722 price list demanded 2.7 times as much for their legitimation.

17. A 1727 Mexican case shows how one Cámara decision might be linked to others on the issue of price. Since the Cámara did not demand detailed proof of natal status during these early years, it is unclear if petitioner Don Gonzalo de Leazgui was an *hijo natural* or an *adulterino*. Nor, significantly, did this consideration seem to figure in any assessment of the price to be paid. The royal lawyer searched the Cámara's New Spain archive and turned up a case from Mexico City (now lost) in which a petitioner paid 125 pesos; another case, from Tolula, revealed that three siblings had paid 250 pesos. At that point the petitioner's representative in Spain offered to pay 300 pesos (8 reales) for the legitimation, and the Cámara acquiesced; AGI, Mexico 684, n. 1, 1727. Twelve years later this Leagui case served as precedent when the Cámara approved the legitimation of Don Mariano Joseph de Soria; Mexico 684, n. 4, 1739. The crown attorney again consulted the archive, and, although not mentioning names, referred to the cases in which others had paid "125," "250," and "300" pesos. The petitioner's legal representative demurred and successfully argued that since this legitimation was "neither to succeed nor inherit" that 200 pesos should be acceptable. Although the natal status of Don Mariano was uncertain, his price seemed to set a standard for several succeeding cases in 1748, 1750, and 1757, when *sacrílegos* paid the same price. In 1754, when Don Joseph Francisco Dioniso de los Ríos in Zimapán sought legitimation, the attorney again cited the 1743 and 1748 cases; Mexico 684, n. 8, 1754. However, in this instance natal status figured in the calculation of price; the crown attorney acknowledged that the petitioner was an *hijo natural*, rather than a bastard, and so gave him a discount to 140 pesos. Such a concession was significant, for as the century progressed royal officials would show themselves increasingly ready to use cost as a weapon to discriminate against bastards and in favor of *hijos naturales*.

18. AGI, Santo Domingo 1458, n. 17, 1766. Those who referred to the Muñoz case were Caracas 299, n. 22, 1787, and Santo Domingo 1484, n. 14, 1793.

19. The three Muñozes paid 20,000 reales *vellón*, or 6,666 each.

20. AGI, Lima 860, n. 8, 1771.

21. AGI, Santo Domingo 1456, n. 5, 1761.

22. AGI, Guatemala 593, n. 4, 1761.   23. AGI, Guadalajara 368, n. 6, 1761.

24. AGI, Guadalajara 372, n. 1, 1764.   25. AGI, Buenos Aires 161, n. 2, 1762.

26. AGI, Panama 273, n. 11, 1761.

27. AHN-Madrid, Consejos, lib. 1487e, n. 15, 1773. There may have been some intermediary raises between 1722 and 1773, for the *arancel* noted that the *hijo natural* price had increased from 100 to 150 ducats; yet this first was a higher price than the 1722 quote.

28. *Adulterinos* now had to pay 6 (and *sacrílegos* 7.3) times more than *hijos naturales*. This new price more than doubled the penalty for the *sacrílegos*, for they had paid only 2.7 times more than *hijos naturales* in the 1722 *arancel*.

29. Barbier, "Culmination," pp. 55, 56.

30. AGI, Santo Domingo 1456, n. 4, 1762.

31. I could not find copies of the sixteenth-century legitimations. All of the eighteenth-century cases are included in the data base. From the viceroyalty of Peru, AGI, Buenos Aires 161, n. 2, 1762. From New Spain: Mexico 684, n. 11, 1757; Santo Domingo 426, n. 2, 1741; Santo Domingo 426, n. 1, 1741; Santo Domingo 427, n. 5, 1746; Indiferente General, September 15, 1748.

Chapter 10. Bourbon Reformers: The Activist Cámara, 1776–1793

1. AGI, Ultramar 166, May 13, 1793.

2. AGI, Indiferente General, April 4, 1789. Don Nicolás Mathias Fernández Méndez, the father of a natural daughter, notes that his lover was a "widow of an unequal marriage that she contracted before the publication of the pragmatic." Presumably this had nothing directly to do with the application of her daughter for legitimation, except implicitly to suggest that she was white.

3. Such an interpretation contradicts conclusions reached by Patricia Seed, who suggests that female honor was devalued in the eighteenth as compared to the seventeenth century. Seed, *To Love*, p. 188.

4. AGI, Buenos Aires 228, n. 27, 1779.

5. See Saeger, "Clerical," p. 95, for an account of his death. This article and "Institutional" detail the Antequera controversy.

6. AGI, Buenos Aires 228, n. 27, 1779.

7. Brading, *First*, p. 503.

8. AGI, Charcas 506, n. 5, 1776. He was the *asesor* of the cabildo, the *protector de naturales*, the *defensor Junta de Temporalidades*, and *asesor* of the *Real Caja*. Yet even though the royal official was impressed, someone with Don Diego's education and expertise might have been expected to hold even higher posts—for example, to be elected to the cabildo.

9. The next year the Council of the Indies, faced with the appointment of yet another illegitimate lawyer to a Bolivian post, ordered the *audiencia* to demand that lawyers prove their legitimacy before they were admitted to the bar. Konetzke, 3:2, n. 263, 1782.

10. AGI, Mexico 1771, n. 6, 1785.

11. AGI, Santo Domingo 1469, n. 5, 1785.

12. AGI, Lima 926, n. 57, 1789.

13. AGI, Santo Domingo 1467, n. 1, 1782.

14. Boyer, *Lives*, pp. 167–217, provides fascinating information on such flows of information. Note that royal officials wanted to find an "intimate" friend, presumably someone who would know of the family illegitimacies.

15. The Urquízus of Lima (1778) never reapplied but did marry. AGI, Lima 893, n. 42, 1778–1793. The Pérez Volcán *cédula* was granted in 1781. Santo Domingo 1467, n. 12, 1781. The Garro Zayas' petition was refused in 1779. Santo Domingo 1466, n. 3, 1779. Soto y Cevallos from Guadalajara applied in 1776 and received the *cédula* in 1780. Guadalajara 372, n. 1, 1780. The Domecs petitioned in 1783 and received the *cédula* in 1785. Buenos Aires 250, n. 14, 1785.

16. AGI, Lima 860, n. 9, 1771–1780.

17. AGI, Lima 901, n. 6, 1781.

18. AGI, Panama 285, n. 9, 1784.

19. AGI, Santo Domingo 1467, n. 7, 1781.

20. AGI, Santo Domingo 1470, n. 14, 1786.

21. AGI, Mexico 1770, n. 35, 1780.

22. AGI, Santo Domingo 1469, n. 6, 1785.

23. AGI, Lima 934, n. 46, 1790.

24. AGN-Lima, Notarial de Dr. D. Toribio de Bernuy, Essno. José de Aizcorbe, February 17, 1783, f. 955, ley 23.

25. ANH-Quito, Criminales, 15-XI-1768; 25-IX-1769; 16-II-1770, contains this extraordinary case. See also Twinam, "Ecuadorian."

26. ANH-Quito, Archivo Notarial de Philipe Santiago Navarrete, Años 1770–71, February 22, 1770.

27. AGI, Quito 362, n. 35, 1797.

28. AGI, Santo Domingo 1484, n. 17, 1793.

29. AGI, Caracas 299, n. 22, 1788.

30. AGI, Caracas 299, n. 20, 1788.

31. AGI, Santo Domingo 1469, n. 6, 1785. Such attitudes colored official remarks in the case of Don Mariano Ayllon of Havana, for his father, Don Tomás, had been married to someone else when he had an affair with Doña Juana María Ramona Hernández. Even though the couple married after Don Tomás's first wife died, the ceremony did not lessen the condemnation of royal officials.

32. AGI, Lima 860, n. 8, 1771.

33. AGI, Santo Domingo 1469, n. 6, 1785.

34. AGI, Santo Domingo 1481, n. 23, 1791.

35. AGI, Santo Domingo 1484, n. 14, 1793.

36. The statistics suggest 1 percent more in their favor after the comments that women should be supported. DB 3-142. Using the entire data base to calculate rates of success shows that men achieved legitimation 5.5 percent more often than women. From 1795 to 1820 men were 4.5 percent more successful than women. Total data base: seventy-six of ninety-five men (80 percent) were approved; thirty-five

of forty-seven females (74.5 percent) were approved (difference equals 5.5 percent). From 1795 to 1810, twenty-three of twenty-five men (92 percent) were approved, and seven of eight women (87.5 percent) (difference equals 4.5 percent).

37. AGI, Indiferente General 1535, December 17, 1787.

38. AGI, Charcas 854, n. 25, 1791.   39. AGN-Mexico, Minería 114.

40. AGN-Mexico, Minería 83.   41. AGI, Charcas 554, n. 25, 1791.

42. Special thanks to Professor Mark Burkholder, personal letter to Ann Twinam dated November 20, 1996, for suggesting this connection.

43. AGI, Guatemala 602, n. 4, 1785.

44. AGI, Santo Domingo 1498, n. 19, 1790. Seed, *To Love*, p. 120, argues that there was a "decreasing value and respect" for emotional attachments. Yet royal officials seemed to recognize the need for mutual affection.

45. AGI, Santo Domingo 1479, n. 50, 1790.

46. AGI, Santo Domingo 1484, n. 14, 1793.

47. In at least two instances from Cuba (Angulo Rizo, 1786; Sale y Valdez, 1789), petitioners effectively conceded that they could not supply this required information, and instead applied solely for confirmation of their rights as *expósitos*. AGI, Santo Domingo 1470, n. 33, 1786; Santo Domingo 1474, n. 11, 1789.

48. AGI, Santo Domingo 1429, n. 4, 1785.

49. AGI, Mexico 1772, n. 6, 1786.

50. AGI, Santo Domingo 1481, n. 31, 1791.

51. AGI, Buenos Aires 259, n. 20, 1790.

52. AGI, Buenos Aires 268, n. 17, 1792.

53. AGI, Santa Fe 717, n. 8, 1793.

Chapter 11. Reform and Retreat: Bourbon Social Policies After 1795

1. AHN-Madrid, Consejos lib. 1497, no. 33, 1794.

2. AHN-Madrid, Consejos lib. 1498, n. 4, 1795. The 1801 version, which increased costs, is reprinted in Konetzke, 3:2, n. 354, 1801.

3. AHN-Madrid, Consejos lib. 1498, n. 4, 1795.

4. I thank Professor Mark Burkholder for the suggestion about Llaguno, in his letter to me of November 20, 1996.

5. Rodulfo Cortés, t. 2, pp. 11–19, reprints the 1773 *arancel* of the Cámara of Castilla, which also makes the distinction concerning "extraordinary" legitimations and the *adulterinos* of unmarried mothers.

6. Ibid. This legislation also introduced the potential for "whitening."

7. AHN-Madrid, Consejos lib. 1500, n. 53, 1800.

8. *Incestuosos* were not mentioned in the *arancel.*

9. AGI, Santo Domingo 1498, n. 30, 1799.

10. AGI, Santo Domingo 1497, n. 22, 1799.

11. AGI, Santa Fe 720, n. 27, 1795.

12. Royal officials were more lenient on *adulterinos*. They issued five decrees (which do not contain any official commentary as to why they were approved) and approved two out of three cases in which full documentation was submitted.

13. AGI, Indiferente General 16, November 9, 1811; July 26, 1815; April 7, 1816; July 15, 1819.

14. AGI, Santo Domingo 1492, n. 43, 1797. This was the case of Don Manuel Gonzáles, whose father the marquess denied him recognition, which seems to have been another reason for the Cámara to reject him.

15. The 1795 *arancel* increased the cost of legitimation for *hijos naturales* and *adulterinos*, but not for *sacrílegos*. From 1776 to 1794 *hijos naturales* had paid an average of 2,471 reales to be legitimated. The new *arancel* almost doubled their cost to 4,000 reales and increased it yet again after 1800 to 5,500 reales. *Adulterinos* faced a quintupling of price, from an average just prior to 1795 of 3,500 reales to 19,800 reales and then 25,800. Ironically, *sacrílegos* fared the best with fixed prices, for just prior to 1795 the Cámara had legitimated the Bordas for the monumental sum of 300,000 reales each. The *arancel* for *sacrílegos* of 24,200 and then 33,000 reales proved a bargain—if Cámara officials could be persuaded to rule favorably. Considered from another perspective, the *arancel* confirmed the increased propensity of royal officials to discriminate against bastards. Even though both *hijos naturales* and *adulterinos* paid more with fixed prices, the latter paid much more. Before 1795 *adulterinos* had paid 1.4 times more than *hijos naturales* (average for *adulterinos*, 3,500; *hijos naturales*, 2,471). Fixed-price legitimation proved three-and-a-half times more costly to *adulterinos*. Of course a set price was no guarantee, particularly for *sacrílegos*, that royal officials would approve their petition.

16. AGI, Chile 297, n. 21, 1796.   17. AGI, Caracas 348, n. 22, 1797.

18. Martínez Alier, *Marriage*, p. 168.   19. *NR*, lib. 7, tit. 27, ley 1–2.

20. The eighteenth-century laws are *NR*, lib. 7, tit. 37, ley 3–5.

21. Herr, p. 156, notes that one of the mandates of these Bourbon-inspired societies was to supervise vocational training, which may be why they became involved in this case.

22. *NR*, lib. 7, tit. 37, ley 4.

23. *NR*, lib. 7, tit. 37, ley 5.

24. Konetzke, 3:2, n. 295, 1786, on the 1762 case; AHN-Madrid, Consejos lib. 1490, n. 78, 1779, concerned the *expósitos* in Segovia; AGN-Madrid, Consejos lib. 1497, n. 33, 1794, mentions the privileges of the Cartagena *expósitos*. See Margadant, p. 51, for a 1772 decree that gave the presumption of innocence to *expósitos* although its consequences were not as extensive in the Indies, because so many *expósitos* were racially mixed. Konetzke, 3:1 n. 224, reprints a 1772 royal decree that orders that *expósitos* of the Havana *casa* be treated as legitimates. In a 1786 case, royal officials noted that *expósitos* not only enjoyed the "state of legitimates" but also that they were eligible for "offices of honor that require clean blood"—even though the laws demanded that candidates prove their "quality" and "purity," which orphans clearly could not; Konetzke, 3:2, n. 295, 1786.

25. AGI, Santo Domingo, 1488, n. 20, 1796.

26. AGI, Santo Domingo 1492, n. 42, 1797.

27. AGI, Santo Domingo 1490, n. 8, 1797.

28. Konetzke, 3:2, n. 357, 1802.

29. Konetzke, 3:1, n. 225, 1772.

30. Konetzke, 3:2, n. 368, 1805.

31. Royal officials declared that when there was doubt concerning someone's "quality" that "one ought to presume the most favorable," but documents make clear that this was not the popular attitude; Konetzke, 3:2, n. 296, 1786. In Konetzke, 3:1, n. 225, 1772, officials commented that "neither in Spain nor in the Indies [have *expósitos*] enjoyed nor ought they enjoy all the qualities of the truly legitimate." The 1794 decree also pointed out that *expósitos* were treated with the "greatest contempt and held as bastards." Konetzke, 3:2, n. 338, 1794. This attitude contrasts with the elite willingness to presume the best concerning peers when honor was at stake.

32. Even the 1794 decree (*NR*, lib. 7, tit. 37, ley 4) conceded that orphans were more often discriminated against because of their uncertain birth and race.

33. Konetzke, 2:2, n. 546, 1687; Konetzke, 3:1, n. 177, 1760; ibid., n. 189, 1763.

34. See Lavrin, "Introduction," p. 17; and Rípodas Ardanaz, pp. 64, 307, for pre–Pragmatic Sanction ecclesiastical measures that involved parental opposition. The latter, pp. 216–66, provides an excellent review of the controversy between parents, church, and the state over free marriage choice.

35. I am presently analyzing the Spanish legitimations for a monograph entitled "Sex in the Old World and the New." One goal will be to identify the reformers behind the 1794 *expósito* decree.

36. AHN-Madrid, Consejos Libros 1487, n. 15, 1773; Consejos Libros 1498, n. 4, 1795.

37. Herr, p. 17.

38. Konetzke, 3:1, n. 233, 1775. Historians have debated the extent to which the Pragmatic Sanction originated as an anticlerical measure, or as a bolster to patriarchal power. These do not seem mutually contradictory. For examples of the debate, see Cicerchia, pp. 93, 96, 109; Arrom, "Perspectivas," p. 399; McCaa, "Gustos," p. 586.

39. See Fernández Pérez, pp. 17–20, who notes that fifty cases of opposition to marriage in Spanish Granada included only four cases of racial inequality; they were more likely to involve Jewish or Moorish ancestry, illegitimate birth, or socioeconomic inequality. Officials in the Americas were unclear regarding the potential impact of the Pragmatic, for one remarked that "we continue daily looking for the meaning of the laws." Quoted in Rípodas Ardanaz, p. 270.

40. Historians have debated the extent to which the Pragmatic was aimed at the elimination of social or racial equality. For example, Rípodas Ardanaz, p. 268, argues that the "intention" was "social before racial," while Seed, *To Love*, p. 205, proclaims that "differences . . . such as status, wealth or political power did not constitute in-

equality under the terms of the Pragmatic." It seems to me that the interpretation of Rípodas Ardanaz makes sense for Spain, and, contrary to Seed, also applied to potential marriages between white elites in the Americas. However, Seed is also correct that race and status were inextricably intermingled in the colonies, and that opposition also occurred to liaisons between lower-status whites and the racially mixed. Socolow, "Acceptable," p. 234, best describes this dual function of the Pragmatic. See also Rodrígues Jiménez, "Elección," p. 28; Rípodas Ardanaz, p. 306; Martínez Alier, *Marriage*, p. 26.

41. Socolow, "Acceptable," p. 219.

42. This assumes that the applications were successful. I plan to analyze the *pardo* applications for an article under preparation. I found only twenty whitenings: seven prior to the 1795 decree, and thirteen afterward. The *audiencia* breakdowns were these: Santo Domingo, 4; Panama, 3; Caracas, 11; Santa Fe, 1; and Mexico, 1.

43. Rodulfo Cortés reprints thirty-five key documents in vol. 2.

44. Ibid., p. 67.

45. Konetzke, 3:2, n. 370, 1806.

46. Konetzke, 3:2, n. 333, 1793; Konetzke, 3:2, n. 350, 1798.

47. Rípodas Ardanaz, p. 288. Examples of the misgivings of later bureaucrats concerning the Pragmatic are also expressed in Konetzke, 3:2, n. 350, 1798. Of course if the couple married without parental approval, the civil penalties might apply. See also Martínez Alier, *Marriage*, p. 44.

48. At least this was the theory. More regional studies need to explore how the Royal Pragmatic on Marriages functioned in practice, particularly the social dynamics between state officials, church officials, parents, and children.

49. For example, see works by Herr; Brading; Kuethe; MacFarlane; Barbier; Fisher; and Martin.

50. Brading, "Bourbon," pp. 128–29, 136.

51. Kuethe, "The Early," p. 28.

52. Brading, "Bourbon," p. 147.

53. O'Phelan Godoy, p. 166.

54. Kuethe, "The Early," p. 32; Brading, "Bourbon," p. 129, 157–59; MacFarlane, p. 250.

55. Brading, "Bourbon," p. 132.

56. Barbier, "Reform," p. 190.

Chapter 12. The Legitimated: Life After 'Gracias al Sacar'

1. AGN-Buenos Aires, IX-32-2-4, Criminales, leg. 15, exped. 20, 1779. Socolow, *Merchants*, p. 86, refers to this incident in a different context.

2. Rodrígues Jiménez, *Sentimientos*, p. 235, provides similar challenges to the honor of the house in New Granada.

3. AGI, Buenos Aires 183, n. 4, 1771, contains their legitimations; the *pasquín* incident is in AGN-Buenos Aires, IX-32-4, Criminales, leg. 15, exped. 20, 1779.

4. Socolow, *Merchants*, pp. 20, 57, 100, 123, 135, 154, contains further information on the business and political activities of the Escalada brothers.

5. Further information on Don Antonio José Escalada is in AGN-Buenos Aires, IX-32-4-8, Criminales, leg. 36, exped. 12, 1791. He sued a Manuel Antonio Warner for *injurias* and detailed his "distinguished quality, honor, and probity."

6. The legitimation degree is in AGI, Indiferente General 1535, July 28, 1660, Don Domingo Dulces Herrera y Doña Francisca Dulces Herrera. The testament is in AHN-Bogotá, Testamentarias Bolivar, t. 43, Pedro Dulces de Herrera, 1675.

7. The legitimation petition is in AGI, Indiferente General 1535, August 26, 1811, Don Alonso Gavino Morán y Carillo. His testaments are in AGN-Lima in the following *escribanías*: Esso Juan de Dios Moreno, November 4, 1828, f. 101v, leg. 444 ("*hijo legítimo*"); Esso José Simeon Ayllon Salazar, August 9, 1838, f. 222v, leg. 64 ("*hijo legítimo y de legítimo matrimonio*"); Esso Lucas de Lama, 1846, f. 425 ("*hijo legítimo*"); Esso Felipe Orellana, September 27, 1856, f. 462v, leg. 487 ("*hijo legítimo*").

8. Doña Rosa Pro's testament is in AGN-Lima, Esso José María de la Rosa, February 15, 1814, f. 126v, leg. 630; Don Gregorio Pro is in AGN-Lima, Essno Gerónimo de Villafuerta, May 22, 1814, f. 398, leg. 1017; ADL-Trujillo, leg. 69, n. 1162, 1806. Doña Rosa Aguilar in ANC-Santiago, Notaries, vol. 875, Antonio Centeño, ff. 55–58v, 102–10, 1797–1799. In only one instance did a successful petitioner—Don Manuel Núñez de Arco, from Trujillo, Peru—continue to refer to himself as an *hijo natural* in a later testament (1839). The legitimation decree is AGI, Lima 963, n. 21, 1797; his testament is ADL-Trujillo, Notarial Protocolos, 555, f. 108, Essno Juan de la Cruz Ortega, March 21, 1839.

9. ANB-Sucre, exp. 1791, n. 30, 1791, contains local testimony concerning his expertise. The legitimation decree is in AGI, Charcas 553, n. 9, 1791.

10. ANB-Sucre, exp. 1791, n. 387, is the only book containing his production as an *escribano*.

11. ADL-Trujillo, Essno Manuel Nuñez del Arco, 20 vols., 1800–1839.

12. AGN-Mexico, Minería 43, 1797, notes Don Pedro Lexarjar's move to Chihuahua. Although the section Minería contains many references to this clan, I could not find any mention that Don Joseph Manuel ever held a post. His legitimation is in AGI, Mexico 1779, n. 2, 1795.

13. His legitimation decree is AGI, Quito 335, n. 38, 1795. The list of Quito officers is in ANH-Quito, Hojas sueltos, "Razón del . . . circunstancias de nacimiento, fortuna, estado y costumbres de las oficiales que fueron del regimento de infantería de milicias de esta ciudad," August 31, 1799.

14. The legitimation decree is AGI, Santa Fe 677, no. 19, 1766. AHN-Bogotá, Testamentos, Cundinamacara, t. 41, ff. 1–180, 1772, contains his will and a special bequest to Dr. Don Ignacio.

15. AGI, Lima 954, n. 41, 1795, contains his legitimation; AGN-Lima, Notarial,

José Prospero del Castillo y Munive, "DD Vicente Camborda," August 23, 1827, f. 110, leg. 142.

16. AGI, Indiferente General 14, June 4, 1766, contains his legitimation; AGN-Mexico, Ayuntamientos 201, exp. 3, 1766, his father's will.

17. AHG-Guanajuato, Tierras Irapuato, exp. 26, 1789.

18. AHN-Bogotá, Milicias y Marinas, t. 140, n. 2773, ff. 143–44, 1777. See Brading, "Bourbon," p. 126, on Gálvez.

19. Burkholder and Chandler, pp. 36–47, detail the qualifications of the appointments.

20. Brading, "Bourbon," p. 127, comments that Bourbon administrative reform was characterized by the "revived insistence on promotion between and within *audiencias*. . . . It became the rule for judges to start as *alcaldes del crimen* or as *oidores* in lesser courts . . . and then to transfer to the viceregal courts."

21. Socolow, *Bureaucrats*, p. 81. See also pp. 82, 109–53.

22. The Sucre archives contain many documents concerning her wealth (ANB-Sucre, Expedientes 1785, n. 76), mining (Minas 131), and house-building activities (EC, n. 164.), as well as the inventory of the property (EC, n. 86) she inherited from her husband, Don Vicente Tardío de Guzmán.

23. AGN-Lima, Superior Gobierno, leg. 28, c. 894, f. 30, 1802.

24. The suit is contained in AGN-Buenos Aires, Tribunales, leg. 134, exp. 2, 1803.

25. ANB-Sucre, Expedientes 1803, n. 115, f. 30, 1803, contains the lawsuit over his father's property. His legitimation is AGI, Charcas 652, n. 30, 1796.

26. Fights over his property can be found in AGN-Mexico, Civil 263, exp. 4, 1766. His legitimation is in AGI, Mexico 684, n. 7, 1748.

27. Details of local conflicts appear in AGN-Mexico, Civil 294, exp. 10.

28. His legitimation decree is AGI, Indiferente General 1535, July 16, 1785. The investigation of his conduct is AGN-Buenos Aires, IX-31-4-4, Justicia, leg. 15, exped. 30, 1789.

29. The failed petition is in AGI, Caracas 2998, n. 17, 1788.

30. AGN-Caracas, Empleadas de la Colonia, t. 37, n. 19, 1802. Further information on his medical career is in Empleadas de la Colonia, t. 31, n. 14, 1797–98. Since he was an *expósito*, he may have benefited from the 1794 legislation.

31. His testament is in AGN-Lima, Notarial. Esso José Joaquín Luque, March 26, 1831, n. 379, f. 856. His whitening and legitimation are in AGI, Indiferente General 1535, June 11, 1806.

32. His petition is in AGI, Santa Fe, 1720, n. 27, 1795.

33. AHN-Bogotá, Notario Santa Fe, September 24, 1806.

34. This incident is recounted in AHN-Bogotá, Criminales de la República, t. 76, ff. 383–403, 1821.

35. Ruggiero, for example, provides evidence that conceptualizations of honor changed substantially by the late nineteenth century.

Chapter 13. Conclusion

1. AA-Habana, Casa de Beneficiencia y Maternidad, lib. 6, 1801.

2. Konetzke, 3:2, n. 358, 1802.

3. AHA-Medellín, Estadísticas y Censos, vol. 343, n. 6539, 1808, provides the quote concerning Sopetrán; Rípodas Ardanaz, p. 45.

4. Konetzke, 3:2, n. 300, 1788.

5. AGN-Caracas, Limpieza de Sangre, t. 35, ff. 208–54, 1809. Castillo Palma comments, p. 157, that the response of mestizos and *afromestizos* to rising prejudice and elite endogamy was "*de obedecer pero no cumplir*" (to obey but not to comply).

6. Shorter, "Illegitimacy," p. 237.

7. Additional information on Muñoz can be found in Arango Mejía, who notes that his offspring used "Don" and "Doña"; t. 2, p. 114. See also Twinam, *Miners*, pp. 118–123.

8. Arango Mejía, t. 1, p. 227, has information on Doña Pascuala and her five children, who included Generals Salvador and José María Córdoba. For a capsule biography of the latter, see Duque Betancur, pp. 539–58, 611–29.

Appendix One

1. See Mörner, p. 44; King; Lanning; some examples from Konetzke include 3:2, n. 257, 1780; 3:2, n. 258, 1781; 3:2, n. 343, 1795; 3:2, n. 347, 1796.

2. AGI, Indiferente General 16 and 1535.

3. See "Pesos" and "Reales."

4. The indexes to the *Cartas y Expedientes* sections of the AGI can be found in Buenos Aires 300; Charcas 455; Chile 231; Cuzco 14; Guadalajara 367; Guatemala 592; Lima 982; Mexico 1687; Panama 298; Quito 277; Santa Fe 731, 985, and 1184; Santo Domingo 1347. A printed index, *Audiencia de Caracas*, provides access to the Venezuelan documents.

Abbreviations

The following are abbreviations to citations in the notes that include archival collections, libraries, published primary sources, and frequently cited journals.

AA-Habana   Archivo Arzobispal (Havana, Cuba) Casa de Beneficiencia y Maternidad (cited by libro).

ACM-Habana   Archivo del Consejo Municipal (Museo de la Habana, Havana, Cuba) (cited by date).

ACM-Medellín   Archivo del Consejo de Medellín (Medellín, Colombia) (cited by volume, number, year).

ADA-Arequipa   Archivo Departamental de Arequipa (Arequipa, Peru) (cited by section, number, folio, year).

ADL-Trujillo   Archivo Departamental de La Libertad (Trujillo, Peru) (cited by *legajo* and number).

AGI   Archivo General de Indies (Seville, Spain) (cited by *audiencia, tomo*, document number, and year).

AGN-Buenos Aires   Archivo General de la Nación (Buenos Aires, Argentina) (cited by section, *legajo, expediente*, year).

AGN-Caracas   Archivo General de la Nación (Caracas, Venezuela) (cited by section, *tomo*, number, year).

AGN-Lima   Archivo General de la Nación (Lima, Peru) (cited by section, year, folio, number).

AGN-Mexico   Archivo General de la Nación (Mexico City, Mexico) (cited by section, number, *expediente*).

AGS   Archivo General de Simancas (Simancas, Spain) (cited by section, *legajo*, year).

AHA-Medellín	Archivo Histórico de Antioquia (Medellín, Colombia) (cited by section, volume, year).
AHG-Guanajuato	Archivo Histórico de Guanajuato (Guanajuato, Mexico) (cited by section, folio, year).
AHN-Bogotá	Archivo Histórico Nacional (Bogotá, Colombia) (cited by section, *tomo*, folio, year).
AHN-Madrid	Archivo Histórico Nacional (Madrid, Spain) (cited by section, number, document number, and year).
AN-Santiago	Archivo Nacional (Santiago, Chile) (cited by section, volume, year).
ANB-Sucre	Archivo Nacional de Bolivia (Sucre, Bolivia) (cited by *expediente*, number, folio, year).
ANH-Quito	Archivo Nacional Histórico (Quito, Ecuador) (cited by section, *caja*, number, year).
CC	*Continuity and Change.*
HM	*Historia Mexicana.*
JFH	*Journal of Family History.*
JIDH	*Journal of Interdisciplinary History.*
JSH	*Journal of Social History.*
Konetzke	Richard Konetzke. *Colección de documentos para la historia de la formación social de hispanoamérica, 1493–1810.* 5 vols. Madrid: Consejo Superior de investigaciónes científicas, 1958–1962) (cited by volume, number of volume, document number, year).
NL	Newberry Library, Ayer Collection.
NR	*Novísima Recopilación de las leyes de España.* 6 vols. Madrid: Boletín Oficial del Estado, 1805.
SP	*Las Siete Partidas del sabio rey D. Alfonso el nono.* Madrid: Joseph Thomas Lucas, 1758.

Works Cited

Alvarez Santalo, León Carlos. *Marginación social y mentalidad en Andalucia occidental: expósitos en Sevilla (1613–1910)*. Seville: Grafitálica, 1980.

Anderson, Michael. *Approaches to the History of the Western Family, 1500–1914*. London: Macmillan Press, 1980.

Aramoni, Aniceto. "Machismo." *Psychology Today* (January 1972): 67–72.

Aranda Romera, José Luis, and Agustín Grajales Porras. "Niños expuestos y hijos naturales en la Puebla de los Angeles a mediados del siglo XVIII." Paper presented at the 47th Congreso Internacional de Americanistas, New Orleans, La., July 7–11, 1991.

Arango Mejía, Gabriel. *Genealogías de Antioquia y Caldas*. Medellín: Editorial Bedout, 1973.

Arnaud Rabinal, Juan Ignacio, Alberto Bernárdez Alvarez, Pedro Miguel Martín Escudero, and Felipe del Pozo Redondo. "Estructura de la población de una sociedad de frontera: La Florida española, 1600–1763." *Revista Computense de Historia de América* 17 (1991): 93–120.

Arrom, Silvia M. "Changes in Mexican Family Law in the Nineteenth Century: The Civil Codes of 1870 and 1884." *JFH* (Fall 1985): 305–17.

———. "Perspectivas sobre historia de la familia en México." In *Familias novohispanas siglo XVI al XIX*, edited by Pilar Gonzalbo Aizpuru, 389–99. Mexico City: El Colegio de México, 1991.

Avila Espinosa, Felipe Arturo. "Los niños abandonados de la casa de niños expósitos de la ciudad de México, 1767–1821." In *La familia en el mundo Iberoamericano*, edited by Pilar Gonzalbo Aizpuru and Cecilia Rabell, 265–310. México: Universidad Nacional Autónima de México, 1994.

Barbier, Jacques A. *Reform and Politics in Bourbon Chile 1755–1796*. Ottawa: University of Ottawa Press, 1980.

———. "Commercial Reform and *Comercio Neutral* in Cartagena de Indias, 1788–1808." In *Reform and Insurrection in Bourbon New Granada and Peru*, edited by John R. Fisher, Allan J. Kuethe, and Anthony McFarlane, 96–120. Baton Rouge: Louisiana State University Press, 1990.

———. "The Culmination of the Bourbon Reforms, 1787–1792." *Hispanic American Historical Review* 57, no. 1 (1977): 51–68.

Bellingham, Bruce. "The History of Childhood Since the 'Invention of Childhood': Some Issues in the Eighties." *JFH* 13 (1988): 347–58.

Bethell, Leslie, ed. *Colonial Spanish America.* Cambridge, Eng.: Cambridge University Press, 1987.

Bossy, John. "The Counter-reformation and the People of Catholic Europe." *Past and Present* 47 (1970): 51–70.

Boswell, John. *The Kindness of Strangers: The Abandonment of Children in Western Europe from Late Antiquity to the Renaissance.* New York: Pantheon, 1988.

Boyer, Richard. "Women, *La Mala Vida*, and the Politics of Marriage." In *Sexuality and Marriage in Colonial Latin America*, edited by Asunción Lavrin, 252–86. Lincoln: University of Nebraska Press, 1989.

———. *Lives of the Bigamists: Marriage, Family and Community in Colonial Mexico.* Albuquerque: University of New Mexico Press, 1995.

———. "Honor Among Plebians: Mala Sangre and Social Reputation." In *Sex, Shame, and Violence in Colonial Latin America*, edited by Lyman Johnson and Sonya Lipsett-Rivera. Albuquerque: New Mexico University Press, 1998.

Brading, David A. "Bourbon Spain and Its American Empire." In *Colonial Spanish America*, edited by Leslie Bethell, 112–62. Cambridge, Eng.: Cambridge University Press, 1987.

———. *The First America: The Spanish Monarchy, Creole Patriots, and the Liberal State, 1492–1867.* Cambridge, Eng.: Cambridge University Press, 1991.

Brettell, Caroline, and Rui Feijo. "The Roda of Viana do Castelo in the Nineteenth Century: Public Welfare and Family Strategies." *Cadernos Vianeses* (1989): 217–49.

Brumberg, Joan Jacobs. "'Ruined' Girls: Changing Community Responses to Illegitimacy in Upstate New York, 1890–1920." *JSH* (Winter 1984): 247–72.

Brundage, James A. *Law, Sex, and Christian Society in Medieval Europe.* Chicago: University of Chicago Press, 1987.

Brydall, John. "Lex Spuriorum, or the Law Relating to Bastardy [1703]." Facsimile ed. in *Classics of English Legal History in the Modern Era*, edited by David S. Berkowitz and Samuel E. Thorne. New York: Garland, 1978.

Burguiere, Andre. "The Formation of the Couple." *JFH* 12 (1987): 39–53.

Burkholder, Mark A. "From Creole to Peninsular: The Transformation of the *Audiencia* of Lima." *Hispanic American Historical Review* 52 (February 1972): 1–15.

————. *Biographical Dictionary of Councilors of the Indies: 1717–1808.* Westport, Conn.: Greenwood Press, 1986.

Burkholder, Mark A., and D. S. Chandler. *Biographical Dictionary of Audiencia Ministers in the Americas, 1687–1821.* Westport, Conn.: Greenwood Press, 1982.

Calvo, Thomas. "Concubinato y mestizaje en el medio urbano: el caso de Guadalajara en el siglo XVII." *Revista de Indias* 44, no. 173 (1984): 203–12.

————. "The Warmth of the Hearth: Seventeenth-Century Guadalajara Families." In *Sexuality and Marriage in Colonial Latin America,* edited by Asunción Lavrin, 287–312. Lincoln: University of Nebraska Press, 1989.

————. "Matrimonio, iglesia y sociedad en el occidente de México: Zamora (siglos xvii a xix)." In *Familias novohispanas siglo XVI al XIX,* edited by Pilar Gonzalbo Aizpuru, 101–8. Mexico City: El Colegio de México, 1991.

Campbell, J. K. *Honour, Family and Patronage: A Study of Institutions and Moral Values in a Greek Mountain Community.* Oxford: Clarendon Press, 1964.

Casey, James. *The Kingdom of Valencia in the Seventeenth Century.* Cambridge, Eng.: Cambridge University Press, 1979.

————. *The History of the Family.* Oxford: Basil Blackwell, 1989.

Castañeda, Carmen. "La formación de la pareja y el matrimonio." In *Familias novohispanas siglo XVI al XIX,* edited by Pilar Gonzalbo Aizpuru, 73–90. Mexico City: El Colegio de México, 1991.

————. *Violación, estupro y sexualidad: Nueva Galicia, 1790–1821.* Guadalajara: Editorial Hexágono, 1989.

Castillo Palma, Norma Angélica. "El estudio de la familia y del mestizaje a través de las fuentes eclesiásticas: el caso del archivo parroquial de San Pedro Cholula." In *Las fuentes eclesiásticas para la historia social de México,* edited by Brian F. Connaughton and Andrés Lira González, 133–64. Mexico City: Universidad Nacional Autónima de México, 1996.

Castro Carvajal, Beatriz, ed. *Historia de la vida cotidiana en Colombia.* Bogotá: Editorial Norma, 1996.

Cavalario, Domingo. *Institucióñes del Derecho Canónico.* 3 vols. 4th ed. Paris: Kubrerua de Salva, 1846.

Caviéres F., Eduardo, and René Salinas M. *Amor, sexo y matrimonio en Chile tradicional.* Serie monografías históricas n. 5. Valparaiso: Universidad Católica de Valparaiso, 1991.

Cevallos-Candau, Francisco Javier, et al., eds. *Coded Encounters: Writing, Gender, and Ethnicity in Colonial Latin America.* Amherst: University of Massachusetts Press, 1994.

Chandler, S. *Social Assistance and Bureaucratic Politics: The Montepíos of Colonial Mexico 1767–1821.* Albuquerque: University of New Mexico Press, 1991.

Chauchadis, Claude. *Honneur morale et societé dans L'Espagne de Philippe II.* Paris: CNRS, 1984.

Chena, Rodolfo R. "La población de una parroquia novohispana del siglo xviii: Santa María de la Presentación de Chilapa." *Estudios demográficos y urbanos* 7, no. 1 (1992): 169–92.

Cicerchia, Richard. "Via familiar y prácticas conyugales, clases populares en una ciudad colonial Buenos Aires: 1800–1810." *Boletín del Instituto de Historia Argentina y Americana.* "Dr. E. Ravigani" tercera serie, 2 (1990): 91–109.

Cobián, Victor. "Hijos sacrílegos." In *Nueva enciclopedia jurídica,* vol. 10, pp. 53–55. Barcelona: Francisco Seix, 1975.

Cohen, Elizabeth S. "Honor and Gender in the Streets of Early Modern Rome." *JIDH* 22 (spring 1992): 597–625.

Cohen, Elizabeth S., and Thomas V. Cohen. "'Camilla the Go-Between': The Politics of Gender in a Roman Household, 1559." *CC* 4 (1989): 53–77.

Collier, Jane F. "From Mary to Modern Woman: The Material Basis of Marianism and Its Transformation in a Spanish Village." *American Ethnologist* 13, no. 1 (1986): 100–107.

Connaughton, Brian F., and Andrés Lira González, eds. *Las fuentes eclesiásticas para la historia social de México.* Mexico City: Universidad Nacional Autónima de México, 1996.

Cook, Alexandra, and Noble David. *Good Faith and Truthful Ignorance: A Case of Transatlantic Bigamy.* Durham, N.C.: Duke University Press, 1991.

Córdoba de la Llave, Ricardo. "Las relaciones extraconyugales en la sociedad castellano bajomedieval." *Anuario de estudios medievales* 16 (1986): 571–619.

Cott, Nancy F. "Eighteenth-Century Family and Social Life Revealed in Massachusetts Divorce Records." *JSH* 10 (1976): 20–43.

Couturier, Edith. "Women and the Family in Eighteenth-Century Mexico: Law and Practice." *JFH* (fall 1985): 294–304.

Covarrubias y Leyva, Diego. *Textos jurídico-políticos.* Madrid: Diana, Artes Gráficas, 1957.

Covián, D. Victor. "Hijos sacrílegos." In *Nueva enciclopedia jurídica,* vol. 10, pp. 53–55. Barcelona: Francisco Seix, 1975.

Cramaussel, Chantal. "Ilegítimos y abandonados en la frontera norte: Parral y San Bartolomé en el siglo XVII." *Colonial Latin American History Review* 4 (1995): 405–38.

Crenshaw, Edward. "The Demographic Regime of Western Europe in the Early Modern Period: A Review of the Literature." *JFH* 14 (1989): 177–89.

Croke, Alexander. *A Report of the Case of Horner Against Liddiard with an Introductory Essay upon the Theory and the History of Laws Relating to Illegitimate*

Children and to the Encouragement of Marriage in General. London: A. Stahan, 1800.

Darrow, Margaret H. "Popular Concepts of Marital Choice in Eighteenth-Century France." *JSH* (winter 1985): 261–72.

Davidoff, Leonore. *Worlds Between: Historical Perspectives on Gender and Class.* New York: Routledge, 1995.

Depauw, Jacques. "Illicit Sexual Activity in Eighteenth-Century Nantes." In *Family and Society: Selections from the Annales,* edited by Robert Forester and Orest Ranum, 245–91. Baltimore: Johns Hopkins University Press, 1976.

Dillard, Heath. *Daughters of the Reconquest: Women in Castilian Town Society, 1100–1300.* Cambridge, Eng.: Cambridge University Press, 1984.

Domínguez Ortíz, Antonio. *Los conversos de origen judío después de la expulsión.* Madrid: Consejo Superior de Investigaciónes Científicas, 1955.

———. *Los judeoconversos en españa y américa.* Madrid: Ediciones Istmo, 1971.

Donoso, Dr. D. Justo. *Instituciónes de derecho canónico américo.* Valparaiso, Chile: Imprenta y Librería del Mercurio, 1849.

Douglas, William A. "Iberian Family History." *JFH* 13, no. 1 (1988): 1–12.

Dueñas-Vargas, Guiomar. "Gender, Race and Class: Illegitimacy and Family Life in Santafé Nuevo Reino de Granada, 1770–1810." Ph.D. diss., University of Texas-Austin, 1995.

Dupaquier, J., et al. *Marriage and Remarriage in Populations of the Past.* New York: Academic Press, 1981.

Duque Betancur, Francisco. *Historia del Departamento de Antioquia.* 2d ed. Medellín: Editorial Albon, 1968.

Enciclopedia universal ilustrada. Barcelona: Espasa-Calpe, 1921–23.

Escudero, José Antonio. *Los secretarios de estado y del despacho 1474–1721.* 4 vols. Madrid: Instituto de estudios administrativos, 1969.

———. *Los orígenes del Consejo de ministros en España: La Junta Suprema del Estado.* Madrid: Editoria Nacional, 1979.

Fairchilds, Cissie. "Female Sexual Attitudes and the Rise of Illegitimacy: A Case Study." *JIDH* 8, no. 4 (spring 1978): 627–67.

Fernández Pérez, Paloma. "Estado y familia en la transición a la España contemporánea: El impacto de las pragmáticas borbónicas sobre consentimiento paterno en el declinar de la familia corporativa, 1776–1814." Paper presented at the Congreso Internacional de Historia de la Familia. Murcia, December 14–16, 1994.

Ferry, Robert J. *The Colonial Elite of Early Caracas: Formation and Crisis, 1567–1767.* Berkeley: University of California Press, 1989.

Figueroa, Beatriz. "Relaciones del Registro tardío de nacimientos con la condición de legitimidad y el tipo de unión de los padres." *Demografía y economía* 18, no. 59 (1984): 334–77.

Findlay, Eileen J. "Gender, Generation, and Honor in Colonial Mexican History." *Radical History Review* 53 (1992): 81–89.

Fisher, John R., Allan J. Kuethe, and Anthony McFarlane, eds. *Reform and Insurrection in Bourbon New Granada and Peru.* Baton Rouge: Louisiana State University Press, 1990.

Flandrin, J. L. "Repression and Change in the Sexual Life of Young People in Medieval and Early Modern Times." In *Family and Society: Selections from the Annales,* edited by Robert Forester and Orest Ranum, 27–47. Baltimore: Johns Hopkins University Press, 1976.

Forester, Robert, and Orest Ranum, eds. *Family and Society: Selections from the Annales.* Baltimore: Johns Hopkins University Press, 1976.

Foucault, Michel. *The History of Sexuality.* New York: Pantheon, 1978.

Fuentes Bajo, María-Dolores. "Amor y desamor en la Venezuela hispánica: Caracas 1701–91." *Boletín de la Acádemia Nacional de la Historia* (Caracas) 75, no. 298 (1992): 49–62.

Fuero Real: Opúsculos Legales del Rey Don Alfonso el Sabio. 2 vols. Madrid: Imprenta Real, 1836.

Gacto Fernández, Enrique. *La filiación no legítima en el derecho histórico español.* Seville: Universidad de Sevilla, 1969.

———. "La filiación ilegítima en la historia del derecho español." *Anuario de Historia del Derecho Español* 16 (1971): 899–944.

———. "El grupo familiar de la edad moderna en los territorios del mediterráneo hispánico: Una visión jurídica." In *La familia en la España Mediterránea,* edited by Pierre Vilar, 36–64. Barcelona: Editorial Crítica, 1987.

García Gonzáles, Juan. "El incumplimiento de las promesas de matrimonio en la historia del derecho español." *Anuario de historia del derecho español* 23 (1953): 611–42.

Garrido, Margarita. "La vida cotidiana y pública en las ciudades coloniales." In *Historia de la vida cotidiana en Colombia,* edited by Beatriz Castro Carvajal, 131–58. Bogotá: Editorial Norma, 1996.

Garrigan, Kristine Ottensen, ed. *Victorian Scandals: Representations of Gender and Class.* Athens: Ohio University Press, 1992.

Gieysztor, I. "Les enfants illégitimes dans une paroisse de Pologne aux dix-septième et dix-huitième siècles." In *Marriage and Remarriage in Populations of the Past,* edited by J. Dupaquier et al., 429–36. New York: Academic Press, 1981.

Gómez, Antonio. *Compendio de las varias resoluciones de Antonio Gómez.* Madrid: Imprenta de Don Benito Cano, 1789.

Gonzalbo Aizpuru, Pilar, ed. *Familias Novohispanas siglo XVI al XIX.* Mexico City: El Colegio de México, 1991.

Gonzalbo Aizpuru, Pilar, and Cecilia Rabell Romero, eds. *La familia en el Mundo Iberamericano.* Mexico City: Universidad Autónoma de México, 1994.

———. *Familia y vida privada en la historia de iberoamérica.* Mexico City: El Colegio de México, 1996.

Gottlieb, Beatrice. "The Meaning of Clandestine Marriage." In *Family and Sexuality in French History,* edited by Robert Wheaton and Tamara K. Hareven, 49–83. Philadelphia: University of Pennsylvania Press, 1980.

Guillamón Alvarez, Javier. *Honor y honra en la España del siglo XVIII.* Madrid: Universidad Computense, 1981.

Gutiérrez, Ramón A. "Honor Ideology, Marriage Negotiation and Class-Gender Domination in New Mexico, 1690–1846." *Latin American Perspectives* 12 (winter 1985): 81–104.

———. *When Jesus Came, the Corn Mothers Went Away.* Stanford: Stanford University Press, 1991.

Habermas, Jürgen. *The Structural Transformation of the Public Sphere: An Inquiry into a Category of Bourgeois Society.* Translated by Thomas Burger. Cambridge: MIT Press, 1992.

Hanawalt, Barbara A. "Childrearing among the Lower Classes of Late Medieval England." *JIDH* 7 (summer 1977): 1–22.

Hareven, Tamara K. "Family History at the Crossroads." *JFH* 12 (1987): ix–xxiii.

Haring, C. H. *The Spanish Empire in America.* New York: Harcourt Brace, 1963.

Heredia Herrera, Antonio. "Organización y descripción de los fondos de la audiencia de Quito del Archivo General de Indias." *Historiografía y Bibliografía Americanista* 21 (1977): 139–65.

Herr, Richard. *The Eighteenth Century Revolution in Spain.* Princeton: Princeton University Press, 1958.

Higginbotham, Ann R. "'Sin of the Age': Infanticide and Illegitimacy in Victorian London." In *Victorian Scandals: Representations of Gender and Class,* edited by Kristine Ottensen Garrigan, 257–88. Athens: Ohio University Press, 1992.

Jiménez Asenjo, Enrique. "Delitos contra el honor." In *Nueva enciclopedia jurídica,* pp. 630–43. Barcelona: Francisco Seix, S.A., 1975.

Johnson, Lyman, and Sonya Lipsett-Rivera. *Sex, Shame, and Violence in Colonial Latin America.* Albuquerque: New Mexico University Press, 1998.

Kertzer, David I. "Anthropology and Family History." *JFH* 9 (fall 1984): 201–16.

———. "Gender Ideology and Infant Abandonment in Nineteenth-Century Italy." *JIDH* 22 (summer 1991): 1–25.

Kertzer, David I., and Caroline Brettell. "Advances in Italian and Iberian Family History." *JFH* 12 (1987): 87–120.

King, James F. "The Case of José Ponciano de Ayarza: A Document on *Gracias al Sacar.*" *Hispanic American Historical Review* (August 1944): 440–51.

Kirshner, Julius. *Pursuing Honor While Avoiding Sin: The Monte Delle Doti of Florence.* Milan: Dott A Giuffre Editore, 1978.

Knight, Franklin W. "Origins of Wealth and the Sugar Revolution in Cuba." *Hispanic American Historical Review* (May 1977): 232–53.

Knodel, John, and Steven Hochstadt. "Urban and Rural Illegitimacy in Imperial Germany." In *Bastardy and Its Comparative History,* edited by Peter Laslett, Karla Oosterveen, and Richard Smith, 284–312. Cambridge, Mass.: Cambridge University Press, 1980.

Konetzke, Richard, ed. *Colección de documentos para la historia de la formación social de hispanoamérica, 1493–1810.* 5 vols. Madrid: Consejo Superior de investigaciónes científicas, 1958–1962.

Kuethe, Allan J. *Cuba, 1753–1815, Crown, Military and Society.* Knoxville: University of Tennessee, 1986.

———. "The Early Reforms of Charles III in the Viceroyality of New Granada, 1759–1776." In *Reform and Insurrection in Bourbon New Granada and Peru,* edited by John R. Fisher, Allan J. Kuethe, and Anthony McFarlane, 19–40. Baton Rouge: Louisiana State University Press, 1990.

Kuznesof, Elizabeth Anne. "Ilegitimidade, raça e laços de familia no Brasil do século xix: Um análise da informacão de censos e de batismos para São Paulo e Rio de Janeiro." In *Historia e populacão: Estudos sobre a América Latina,* edited by Sérgio Odiolon Nadalin, María Luiza Marcílio, and Altiva Pillati Balhana, 164–74. São Paulo: Fundacão SEADE, 1990.

———. "Raza, clase y matrimonio en la Nueva España: Estado actual del debate." In *Familias novohispanas siglo XVI al XIX,* edited by Pilar Gonzalbo Aizpuru, 373–88. Mexico City: El Colegio de México, 1991.

———. "Sexual Politics, Race and Bastard-Bearing in Nineteenth-Century Brazil." *JFH* 16 (1991): 241–60.

Lanning, John Tate. "The Case of José Porsiano de Ayarza: A Document on the Negro in Higher Education." *Hispanic American Historical Review* 24 (August 1944): 432–41.

———. *The Royal Protomedicato: The Regulation of the Medical Professions in the Spanish Empire.* Edited by John Jay TePaske. Durham: Duke University Press, 1985.

Lansing, Marion. *Liberators and Heroes of South America.* Boston: L. C. Page, 1942.

Laslett, Peter. *Family Life and Illicit Love in Earlier Generations.* Cambridge, Mass.: Cambridge University Press, 1977.

———. "Introduction: Comparing Illegitimacy over Time and Between Cultures." In *Bastardy and Its Comparative History,* edited by Peter Laslett, Karla

Oosterveen, and Richard Smith, 1–70. Cambridge, Mass.: Cambridge University Press, 1980.

———. "Illegitimate Fertility and the Matrimonial Market." In *Marriage and Remarriage in Populations of the Past*, edited by J. Dupaquier et al., 461–71. New York: Academic Press, 1981.

———. "The Character of Familial History, Its Limitations and the Conditions for Its Proper Pursuit." *JFH* 12 (1987): 263–84.

Laslett, Peter, Karla Oosterveen, and Richard Smith, eds. *Bastardy and Its Comparative History*. Cambridge, Mass.: Cambridge University Press, 1980.

Las Siete Partidas del sabio rey D. Alfonso el nono. Madrid: Joseph Thomas Lucas, 1758.

Lavrin, Asunción, ed. *Sexuality and Marriage in Colonial Latin America*. Lincoln: University of Nebraska Press, 1989.

———. "Sexuality in Colonial Mexico: A Church Dilemma." In *Sexuality and Marriage in Colonial Latin America*, edited by Asunción Lavrin, 47–92. Lincoln: University of Nebraska Press, 1989.

———. "Introduction: The Scenario, the Actors, and the Issues." In *Sexuality and Marriage in Colonial Latin America*, edited by Asunción Lavrin, 1–43. Lincoln: University of Nebraska Press, 1989.

———. "Mexico." In *Children in Historical and Comparative Perspective*, edited by Joseph M. Hawes and N. Ray Hiner, 421–55. Westport, Conn.: Greenwood, 1991.

———. "*Lo fémenino*: Women in Colonial Historical Sources." In *Coded Encounters: Writing, Gender, and Ethnicity in Colonial Latin America*, edited by Francisco Javier Cevallos-Candau et al. eds., 153–76. Amherst: University of Massachusetts Press, 1994.

Lee, W. R. "Bastardy and the Socioeconomic Structure of South Germany." *JIDH* 7, no. 3 (winter 1977): 403–25.

Levin, David, and Keith Wrightson. "The Social Context of Illegitimacy in Early Modern England." In *Bastardy and Its Comparative History*, edited by Peter Laslett, Karla Oosterveen, and Richard Smith, 158–75. Cambridge: Cambridge University Press, 1980.

Lewin, Linda. "Natural and Spurious Children in Brazilian Inheritance Law from Colony to Empire: A Methodological Essay." *The Americas* 11 (January 1992): 351–96.

———. "'Surprise Heirs': The Changing Inheritance Rights of Illegitimate Offspring in Imperial Brazil, 1750–1850." Unpublished manuscript.

Lindemann, Mary. "Love for Hire: The Regulation of the Wet-Nursing Business in Eighteenth-Century Hamburg." *JFH* (winter 1981): 379–92.

Lutz, Chistopher H., et al. *Territorio y sociedad en Guatemala: Tres ensayos históricos.* Guatemala City: Universidad de San Carlos de Guatemala, 1991.

Lynch, John. *Spain Under the Hapsburgs: Spain and America 1598–1700.* Vol. 2. New York: Oxford University Press, 1969.

Macfarlane, Alan. "Illegitimacy and Illegitimates in English History." In *Bastardy and Its Comparative History,* edited by Peter Laslett, Karla Oosterveen, and Richard Smith, 71–85. Cambridge, Mass.: Cambridge University Press, 1980.

Malvido, Elsa. "El abandono de los hijos—una forma de control del tamaño de la familia y del trabajo indígena." *HM* 4, no. 116 (1980): 521–61.

Mannarelli, María Emma. *Pecados públicos: La ilegitimidad en Lima, siglo XVII.* Lima: Ediciones Flora Tristán, 1994.

Maravall, José Antonio. *Poder, honor, y élites en el siglo XVII.* Madrid: Siglo XXI, 1989.

Marcilia, María Luiza. *A cidade de São Paulo: Povoamento e populacão, 1750–1850.* São Paulo: Universidade de São Paulo, 1974.

Margadant, Guillermo F. "La familia en el derecho novohispano." In *Familias novohispanas siglo XVI al XIX,* edited by Pilar Gonzalbo Aizpuru, 27–56. Mexico City: El Colegio de México, 1991.

Mariéjol, Jean Hippólyte. *The Spain of Ferdinand and Isabella.* New Brunswick: Rutgers University Press, 1961.

Martin, Cheryl English. *Governance and Society in Colonial Mexico: Chihuahua in the Eighteenth Century.* Stanford: Stanford University Press, 1996.

Martínez Alier, Verena. "El honor de la mujer en Cuba en el siglo xix." *Revista de la Biblioteca Nacional José Martí* 13, no. 2 (1971): 29–61.

———. *Marriage, Class and Colour in Nineteenth-Century Cuba.* Oxford: Cambridge University Press, 1974.

McCaa, Robert. "Gustos de los padres, inclinaciones de los novios y reglas de una feria nupcial colonial: Parral 1770–1814." *HM* 40, no. 4 (1991): 579–614.

———. "Introduction." *JFH* 16, no. 3 (1991): 211–14.

———. "La viuda viva del México borbónico: Sus voces, variedades y vejaciones." In *Familias novohispanas siglo XVI al XIX,* edited by Pilar Gonzalbo Aizpuru, 299–324. Mexico City: El Colegio de México, 1991.

———. "Tratos nupciales: La constitución de uniones formales e informales en México y España, 1500–1900." In *Familia y vida privada en la historia de iberoamérica,* edited by Pilar Gonzalbo Aizpuru and Cecilia Rabell Romero, 21–57. Mexico: El Colegio de México, 1996.

McFarlane, Anthony. *Colombia Before Independence: Economy, Society, and Politics Under Bourbon Rule.* Cambridge, Eng.: Cambridge University Press, 1993.

Merzario, Raul. "Land, Kinship, and Consanguineous Marriage in Italy from the Seventeenth to the Nineteenth Centuries." *JFH* 15 (1990): 529–46.

Meteyard, Belinda. "Illegitimacy and Marriage in Eighteenth-Century England." *JIDH* 10, no. 3 (winter 1980): 479–89.

———. "Comment and Controversy: A Reply." *JIDH* 11, no. 3 (winter 1981): 511–14.

Meyer, Jean. "Illegitimates and Foundlings in Pre-industrial France." In *Bastardy and Its Comparative History*, edited by Peter Laslett, Karla Oosterveen, and Richard Smith, 249–63. Cambridge, Mass.: Cambridge University Press, 1980.

Miller, Gary. "Bourbon Social Engineering: Women and Conditions of Marriage in Eighteenth-Century Venezuela." *Americas* 46, no. 3 (January 1990): 261–90.

Mintz, Steven. "Regulating the American Family." *JFH* 14, no. 4 (1989): 387–408.

Mitchison, Rosalind, and Leah Leneman. *Sexuality and Social Control: Scotland 1660–1780.* Oxford: Basil Blackwell, 1989.

Morel, Marie-France. "Reflections on Some Recent French Literature on the History of Childhood." *CC* 4 (1989): 323–37.

Moreno Garbayo, Natividad. *Colección de reales cédulas del Archivo Histórico Nacional.* Madrid: Ministerio de Educación y Ciencia, 1977.

Morín, Claude. "Los libros parroquiales como fuente para la historia demográfica y social novohispana." *HM* 21, no. 3 (1972): 389–418.

Mörner, Magnus. *Race Mixture in the History of Latin America.* Boston: Little Brown, 1967.

Muñoz, D. Miguel Eugenio. *Recopilación de las leyes, pragmáticas, reales decretos y acuerdos de real protomedicato.* Valencia: Imprenta Viuda de Antonio Bordazar, 1751.

Nash, Gary B. "The Hidden History of Mestizo America." *Journal of American History* 82, no. 3 (December 1995): 941–62.

Nazzari, Muriel. "Concubinage in Colonial Brazil: The Inequalities of Race, Class, and Gender." *JFH* 21, no. 2 (April 1996): 107–24.

———. "An Urgent Need to Conceal: The System of Honor and Shame in Colonial Brazil." Unpublished paper.

Nero da Costa, Iraci del. "Vila Rica: Casamentos (1727–1826)." *Revista de historia* (São Paulo Brasil) 56, no. 111 (July–Sept. 1977): 195–208.

Newman, Anthea. "An Evaluation of Bastardy Recordings in an East Kent Parish." In *Bastardy and Its Comparative History*, edited by Peter Laslett, Karla Oosterveen, and Richard Smith, 141–57. Cambridge, Mass.: Cambridge University Press, 1980.

Nichols, Barry. *An Introduction to Roman Law.* Oxford: Clarendon, 1979.

Nizza da Silva, María Beatriz. "O problema dos expostos na capitania de São Paulo." *Anais do Museo Paulista* 30 (1980–81): 147–58.

———. "Divorce in Colonial Brazil: The Case of São Paulo." In *Sexuality and*

Marriage in Colonial Latin America, edited by Asunción Lavrin, 313–40. Lincoln: University of Nebraska Press, 1989.

———. "Filhos ilegítimos no brasil colonial." *Sociedade Brasileira de Pesquisa Histórica, Anais da XV Reunião* (1995): 121–24.

Novísima Recopilación de las leyes de España. 6 vols. Madrid: Boletín Oficial del Estado, 1805.

Odiolon Nadalin, Sérgio, María Luiza Marcílio, and Altiva Pillati Balhana, eds. *Historia e populacão: Estudos sobre a América Latina.* São Paulo: Fundacão SEADE, 1990.

O'Hara, Diana. "'Ruled by My Friends': Aspects of Marriage in the Diocese of Canterbury, 1540–1570." *CC* 6 (1991): 9–41.

O'Phelan Godoy, Scarlett. *Rebellions and Revolts in Eighteenth Century Peru and Upper Peru.* Köln: Böhlau Verlag, 1985.

Ortíz de Montalván, Gonzalo, et al. *Registro General de Sello.* Valladolid: Imprenta Librería Casa Martin, 1950.

Ortmayer, Norbert. "Matrimonio, estado y sociedad en Guatemala (siglo XIX y XX)." In *Territorio y sociedad en Guatemala: Tres ensayos históricos,* edited by Christopher H. Lutz and George Lovell, 58–118. Guatemala City: Universidad de San Carlos de Guatemala, 1991.

Ots Capdequi, José María. "Bosquejo histórico de los derechos de la mujer casada en la legislación de Indias." *Revista general de legislación y jurisprudencia* 137 (1917–20): 139–52, 162–82, 185–206.

Palli, H. "Illegitimacy and Remarriage in Estonia During the Eighteenth Century." In *Marriage and Remarriage in Populations of the Past,* edited by J. Dupaquier et al., 473–79. New York: Academic Press, 1981.

Patiño Millán, Beatriz. *Criminalidad, ley penal y estructura social en la Provincia de Antioquia: 1750–1820.* Medellín: Talleres Gráficos, 1994.

Pedraja, René de la. "La muger criolla y mestiza en la sociedad colonial, 1700–1830." *Desarrollo y Sociedad* 13 (January 1984): 199–229.

Penyak, Lee Michael. "Criminal Sexuality in Central Mexico 1750–1850." Ph.D. diss., University of Connecticut, 1993.

Pérez Brignoli, H. "Deux siècles d'illègitimitè au Costa Rica 1770–1970." In *Marriage and Remarriage in Populations of the Past,* edited by J. Dupaquier et al., 481–93. New York: Academic Press, 1981.

Pérez Herrero, Pedro. "Evolución demográfica y estructura familiar en México (1730–1850)." In *Familias novohispanas siglo XVI al XIX,* edited by Pilar Gonzalbo Aizpuru, 345–71. Mexico City: El Colegio de México, 1991.

Pérez y López, Antonio Javier. *Teatro de la legislación universal de España y Indias.* Madrid: M. Gonzáles, 1791–1798.

Peristiany, J. G. *Honor and Shame: The Values of the Mediterranean.* Chicago: University of Chicago Press, 1966.

Pescador C., Juan Javier. *De bautizados a fieles difuntos: Familia y mentalidades en una parroquia urbana: Santa Catarina de México, 1568–1820.* Mexico City: El Colegio de México, 1992.

———. "La nupcialidad urbana preindustrial y los límites del mestizaje: Características y evolución de los patrones de nupcialidad en la Ciudad de México, 1700–1850." *Estudios demográficos y urbanos* 7, no. 1 (1992): 137–68.

Pescatello, Ann. "Ladies and Whores in Colonial Brazil." *Caribbean Review* 5, no. 2 (1973): 26–30.

———, ed. *Female and Male in Latin America.* Pittsburgh: University of Pittsburgh Press, 1973.

"Peso." In *Enciclopedia universal ilustrada,* vol. 43, pp. 1423–25. Barcelona: Hijos de J. Espasa, 1928.

Pinto Venacio, Renato. *Ilegitimidade e concubinato no Brasil colonial: Rio de Janeiro e São Paulo.* São Paulo: CEDHAL, 1986.

Pitt-Rivers, Julian. *Mediterranean Countrymen: Essays in the Social Anthropology of the Mediterranean.* Paris: Mouton, 1963.

———. "Honor." In *International Encyclopedia of the Social Sciences,* vol. 6, pp. 503–11. New York: The Free Press, 1968.

———. *People of the Sierra.* 2d ed. Chicago: University of Chicago Press, 1971.

Post, John D. "The Morality Crises of the Early 1770s and European Demographic Trends." *JIDH* 22, no. 1 (summer 1990): 29–62.

Potash, Jane Ruth. "The Foundling Problem in France, 1800–1869: Child Abandonment in Lille and Lyon." Ph.D. diss., Yale University, 1979.

Potthast-Jutkeit, Barbara. "The Ass of a Mare and Other Scandals: Marriage and Extramarital Relations in Nineteenth-Century Paraguay." *JFH* 16 (1991): 215–39.

Puente y Quijano, José Manuel de la. *Estudio de los efectos del reconocimiento de un hijo natural produce según el código civil vigente.* Madrid: Librería de Don Victoriano Suarez, 1895.

Puig Peña, Fedérico. "Hijos adulterinos." *Nueva enciclopedia jurídica,* vol. 10, pp. 3–8. Barcelona: Francisco Seix, 1975.

———. "Hijos ilegítimos." *Nueva enciclopedia jurídica,* vol. 10, pp. 14–23. Barcelona: Francisco Seix, 1975.

———. "Hijos incestuosos." *Nueva enciclopedia jurídica,* vol. 10, pp. 14–25. Barcelona: Francisco Seix, 1975.

———. "Hijos de padres desconocidos." *Nueva enciclopedia jurídica,* vol. 10, pp. 8–14. Barcelona: Francisco Seix, 1975.

———. "Hijos naturales." *Nueve enciclopeda jurídica*, vol. 10, pp. 42–52. Barcelona: Francisco Seix, 1975.

Quaife, G. R. "The Consenting Spinster in a Peasant Society: Aspects of Premarital Sex in 'Puritan' Somerset 1645–1660." *JSH* 11, no. 2 (winter 1977): 228–44.

Quale, G. Robina. *Families in Context: A World History of Population.* Westport, Conn.: Greenwood, 1992.

Quesada, Vicente G. "Fundación de la casa de niños expósitos." *La revista de Buenos Aires* 1 (1863): 583–95.

Rabb, Theodore K., and Robert I. Rothberg, eds. *The Family in History: Interdisciplinary Essays.* New York: Harper & Row, 1971.

Rabell, Cecilia Andrea. *La población a la luz de los registros parroquiales.* Mexico City: Universidad Nacional Autónima de México, 1990.

———. "Estructuras de la población y características de los jefes de los grupos domésticos en la ciudad de Antequera (Oaxaca), 1777." In *Familias novohispanas siglo XVI al XIX,* edited by Pilar Gonzalbo Aizpuru, 273–98. Mexico City: El Colegio de México, 1991.

———. "Matrimonio y raza en una parroquia rural: San Luis de La Paz, Guanajuato 1715–1810." *HM* 47, no. 1 (1992): 3–44.

Ramos, Donald. "A mulher e a familia em Vila Rica do Ouro Preto: 1754–1838." In *Historia e populacão: Estudos sobre a América Latina,* edited by Sérgio Odiolon Nadalin, María Luiza Marcílio, and Altiva Pillati Balhana, 154–63. São Paulo: Fundacão SEADE, 1990.

"Real." *Encilopedia universal ilustrada,* vol. 49, pp. 1000–1009. Barcelona: Espasa-Calpe S.A., 1923.

Recopilación de leyes de los reynos de las Indias [1791]. Madrid: Gráficas Ultra, 1943.

Reyes Nevares, Salvador. "El Machismo en Mexico." *Mundo Nuevo* 46 (1970): 14–19.

Rípodas Ardanaz, Daisy. *El matrimonio en Indias: Realidad social y regulación jurídica.* Buenos Aires: Fundación para la Educación, la Ciencia y la Cultura, 1977.

Rodrígues Baños, Roberto, Patricia Trejo de Zepeda, and Edilberto Soto Angli. *Virginidad y machismo en México.* Mexico City: Posada, 1973.

Rodrígues Jiménez, Pablo. "Elección matrimonial y conflicto interétnico en Antioquia." *Revista ciencias humanas* (Medellín) 11 (1988): 25–46.

———. "Matrimonio incestuoso en el Medellín colonial 1700–1810." *Revista Extensión Cultural* 24–25 (1988): 52–58.

———. "Casa y orden cotidiano en el Nuevo Reino de Granada, s. XVIII." In *Historia de la vida cotidiana en Colombia,* edited by Beatriz Castro Carvajal, 103–30. Bogotá: Editorial Norma, 1996.

————. *Sentimientos y vida familiar en el Nuevo Reino de Granada.* Bogotá: Ariel, 1997.

Rodulfo Cortés, Santos. *El regimen de "las gracias al sacar" en Venezuela durante el periodo hispánico.* 2 vols. Caracas: Italgráfica, 1978.

Rogers, Nicholas. "Carnal Knowledge: Illegitimacy in Eighteenth-Century Westminster." *JSH* 23, no. 2 (winter 1989): 355–75.

Roper, Lyndal. "Will and Honor: Sex, Words and Power in Augsburg Criminal Trials." *Radical History Review* 45 (1989): 45–71.

Rosain, Domingo. *Necrópolis de La Havana: Historia de los cementerios de esta ciudad con multitud de noticias interestantes.* Havana: El Trabajo, 1875.

Rothman, Ellen K. "Sex and Self-Control: Middle-Class Courtship in America, 1770–1870." *JSH* (spring 1982): 409–26.

Ruggiero, Kristin. "Wives on 'Deposit': Internment and the Preservation of Husbands' Honor in Late Nineteenth-Century Buenos Aires." *JFH* 17 (1992): 253–70.

Saeger, James Schofield. "Clerical Politics in Eighteenth-Century Peru: The Trial of José de Antequera." *Journal of Church and State* 17, no. 1 (1975): 81–96.

————. "Institutional Rivalries, Jurisdictional Disputes, and Vested Interests in the Viceroyalty of Peru: José de Antequera and the Rebellion of Paraguay." *The Americas* 32, no. 1 (July 1975): 99–116.

Saguier, Eduardo R. "El combate contra la 'limpieza de sangre' en los orígenes de la emancipación argentina. El uso del estigma de la bastardía y del origen racial como mecanismos de defensa de las élites coloniales." *Revista de historia de América* 10 (July/December 1990): 155–98.

Salinas Meza, René. "Orphans and Family Disintegration in Chile: The Mortality of Abandoned Children, 1750–1930." *JFH* 16 (1991): 215–29.

Salman, Toni, ed. *The Legacy of the Disinherited, Popular Culture in Latin America: Modernity, Globalization, Hybridity and Authenticity.* Utrecht: CERES, 1995.

Schafer, Ernesto. *El Consejo Real y supremo de las Indias.* 2 vols. Sevilla: M. Carmona, 1900, 1983.

Schneider, Jane. "Of Vigilance and Virgins: Honor, Shame and Access to Resources in Mediterranean Societies." *Ethnology* 10 (June 1971): 1–23.

Seed, Patricia. "The Church and the Patriarchal Family: Marriage Conflicts in Sixteenth-Century New Spain." JFH (fall 1985): 284–93.

————. "Marriage Promises and the Value of a Woman's Testimony in Colonial Mexico." *Signs* 13 (1988): 253–76.

————. *To Love, Honor and Obey in Colonial Mexico: Conflicts over Marriage Choice, 1574–1821.* Stanford: Stanford University Press, 1988.

Segalen, Martine. *Historical Anthropology of the Family.* Cambridge, Eng.: Cambridge University Press, 1986.

Shorter, Edward. "Illegitimacy, Sexual Revolution, and Social Change in Modern Europe." *JIDH* 2, no. 2 (autumn 1971): 237–72.

———. "Bastardy in South Germany: A Comment." *JIDH* 8, no. 3 (winter 1978): 459–69.

Sicroff, Albert A. *Los estatuos de limpieza de sangre: Controversias entre los siglos XV y XVII.* Madrid: Taurus Ediciones, 1979, 1985.

Sínodo diocesana que de origen de SM celebro el ilustrísimo Señor Doctor Don Juan García de Palacios, Obispo de Cuba en Junio de 1684, reimpresa por orden del ilustrísimo Señor Doctor Don Juan José Diaz de Espanada y Landa, Segundo Obispo de La Habana. Havana: Oficina de Arazoza y Soler, Impresores del Gobierno y de la Real Sociedad Patriotica, 1814.

Smith, Daniel Scott. "The Long Cycle in American Illegitimacy and Prenuptial Pregnancy." In *Bastardy and Its Comparative History*, edited by Peter Laslett, Karla Oosterveen, and Richard Smith, 362–78. Cambridge, Mass.: Cambridge University Press, 1980.

Smout, Christopher. "Aspects of Sexual Behaviour in Nineteenth-century Scotland." In *Bastardy and Its Comparative History*, edited by Peter Laslett, Karla Oosterveen, and Richard Smith, 192–216. Cambridge, Mass.: Cambridge University Press, 1980.

Socolow, Susan. *The Merchants of Buenos Aires: 1778–1810.* Cambridge, Eng.: Cambridge University Press, 1978.

———. *The Bureaucrats of Buenos Aires, 1769–1810: Amor al Real Servicio.* Durham, N.C.: Duke University Press, 1987.

———. "Acceptable Partners: Marriage Choice in Colonial Argentina, 1778–1810." In *Sexuality and Marriage in Colonial Latin America*, edited by Asunción Lavrin, 209–46. Lincoln: University of Nebraska Press, 1989.

Solórzano y Pereyra, Juan de. *Política Indiana* [1647]. 5 vols. Madrid: Ibero-Americana, 1930.

Sponsler, Lucy A. "Women in Spain: Medieval Law Versus Epic Literature." *Revista de estudios hispánicos* 7 (October 1973): 427–48.

Stern, Steve J. *The Secret History of Gender.* Chapel Hill: University of North Carolina Press, 1995.

Stevens, Evelyn P. "Mexican Machismo: Politics and Value Orientations." *Western Political Quarterly* (December 1965): 848–57.

———. "Marianismo, the Other Face of Machismo in Latin America." In *Female and Male in Latin America*, edited by Ann M. Pescatello, 89–102. Pittsburgh: University of Pittsburgh Press, 1973.

Stewart, Susan. "Bastardy and the Family Reconstitution Studies of Banbury and Hartland." In *Bastardy and Its Comparative History*, edited by Peter Laslett,

Karla Oosterveen, and Richard Smith, 122–40. Cambridge, Mass.: Cambridge University Press, 1980.

Stolcke, Verena. See Martínez Alier, Verena.

Stone, Lawrence. "Comment and Controversy." *JIDH* 11, no. 3 (winter 1981): 507–9.

———. "Family History in the 1980s: Past Achievements and Future Trends." *JIDH* 12, no. 1 (summer 1981): 51–87.

Sussman, George D. "Parisian Infants and Norman Wet Nurses in the Early Nineteenth Century: A Statistical Study." *JIDH* 7 (spring 1977): 637–53.

———. *Selling Mothers' Milk: The Wet-Nursing Business in France, 1715–1914.* Urbana: University of Illinois Press, 1982.

Taylor, William B. *Magistrates of the Sacred: Priests and Parishioners in Eighteenth-Century Mexico.* Stanford: Stanford University Press, 1996.

Teichman, Jenny. *Illegitimacy: An Examination of Bastardy.* Ithaca, N.Y.: Cornell University Press, 1982.

Testamentarías y abintestatos: Manual que contiene toda la teoría relativo a succesiones. Madrid: Biblioteca económica de legislación y jurisprudencia, 1890.

Tilly, Charles. "Family History, Social History, and Social Change." *JFH* 12 (1987): 319–30.

Tilly, Louise A. "Women's History and Family History: Fruitful Collaboration or Missed Connection?" *JFH* 12 (1987): 305–15.

Tilly, Louise A., Rachael G. Fuchs, and David Kertzer. "Child Abandonment in European History: A Symposium." *JFH* 17 (1992): 1–23.

Tilly, Louise A., Joan W. Scott, and Miriam Cohen. "Women's Work and European Fertility Patterns." *JIDH* 6, no. 1 (winter 1976): 447–76.

Toth, Istvan Gyorgy. "Peasant Sexuality in Eighteenth-Century Hungary." *CC* 6 (1991): 43–58.

Tuirán Gutiérrez, Rodolfo. "Algunos hallagos recientes de la demografía histórica mexicana." *Estudios demográficos y urbanos* 7, no. 1 (1992): 273–312.

Twinam, Ann. *Miners, Merchants, and Farmers in Colonial Colombia.* Austin: University of Texas Press, 1982.

———. "Honor, paternidad e ilegitimidad: Los padres solteros en América Latina durante la colonia." *Estudios sociales* 3 (September 1988): 9–32.

———. "Honor, Sexuality and Illegitimacy in Colonial Spanish America." In *Sexuality and Marriage in Colonial Latin America*, edited by Asunción Lavrin, 118–55. Lincoln: University of Nebraska Press, 1989.

———. "An Ecuadorian Murder Mystery: Gender Wars, Drunkenness and Death on an Eighteenth-Century Hacienda." Paper presented at the Midwest

Association of Latinamericanists Conference, Baños, Ecuador. November 19–21, 1995.

————. "The Negotiation of Honor: Elites, Sexuality, and Illegitimacy in Eighteenth-Century Spanish America." In *Sex, Shame, and Violence in Colonial Latin America,* edited by Lyman Johnson and Sonya Lipsett-Rivera. Albuquerque: New Mexico University Press, 1998.

Van de Walle, Etienne. "Illegitimacy in France During the Nineteenth Century." In *Bastardy and Its Comparative History,* edited by Peter Laslett, Karla Oosterveen, and Richard Smith, 264–83. Cambridge, Mass.: Cambridge University Press, 1980.

Van der Woude, A. "Introduction to Part V." In *Marriage and Remarriage in Populations of the Past,* edited by J. Dupaquier et al., 413–19. New York: Academic Press, 1981.

Van der Valk, Juultje. "Chastity as Legal Empowerment, the Province of Tetepango, Mexico, 1750–1800." In *The Legacy of the Disinherited, Popular Culture in Latin America: Modernity, Globalization, Hybridity and Authenticity,* edited by Toni Salman, 93–111. Utrecht: Cáceres, 1995.

Vázquez Richart, José. *Situación y porvenir legal de los hijos ilegítimos y adoptados.* Madrid: Gráficas Orbe, 1971.

Vilaplana Jové, José. *Legislación eclesiástica, civil, militar, penal y procesal sobre esponsales, matrimonio, legitimaciones y divorcio.* Villanueva y Geltrú (Barcelona): Imprenta J. Soler, 1916.

Villalón, L. J. Andrew. "The Law's Delay: The Anatomy of an Aristocratic Property Dispute 1350–1577." Ph.D. diss., Yale University, 1984.

Wahrman, Dror. "'Middle Class' Domesticity Goes Public: Gender, Class, and Politics from Queen Caroline to Queen Victoria." *Journal of British Studies* 32 (October 1993): 396–432.

Waldron, Kathy. "The Sinners and the Bishop in Colonial Venezuela: The *Visita* of Bishop Mariano Martí, 1771–1784." In *Sexuality and Marriage in Colonial Latin America,* edited by Asunción Lavrin, 156–77. Lincoln: University of Nebraska Press, 1989.

Watt, Jeffrey R. "Marriage Contract Disputes in Early Modern Neuchatel, 1547–1806." *JSH* (fall 1988): 129–48.

Wells, Robert V. "Illegitimacy and Bridal Pregnancy in Colonial America." In *Bastardy and Its Comparative History,* edited by Peter Laslett, Karla Oosterveen, and Richard Smith, 349–61. Cambridge, Mass.: Cambridge University Press, 1980.

Wheaton, Robert. "Introduction: Recent Trends in the Historical Study of the French Family." In *Family and Sexuality in French History,* edited by Robert

Wheaton and Tamara K. Hareven, 3–25. Philadelphia: University of Pennsylvania Press, 1980.

Zamora y Lazonado, José María. *Biblioteca de legislación ultramarina.* 3 vols. Madrid: Alegria y Charlain, 1845.

Zenea, Evaristo. *Historia de la Real Casa de Maternidad de esta ciudad en la cual se comprende la antigua casa cuna, refiriendose sus fundaciones, delorable estado y felices progresos que después ha tenido hasta el presente.* Havana: D. Jose Severino Boloña, Impresos de la Real Marina, 1838.

Index

In this index, an "f" after a number indicates a separate reference on the next page, and an "ff" indicates separate references on the next two pages. A continuous discussion over two or more pages is indicated by a span of page numbers, e.g., "57–59." *passim* is used for a cluster of references in close but not consecutive sequence. Individuals who are cédula mothers (M), fathers (F), and illegitimates (I), are identified respectively. Modern designations are used for national identities, including areas of Spanish America now part of the United States.

Library of Congress Cataloging-in-Publication Data

Twinam, Ann
    Public lives, private secrets : gender, honor, sexuality, and illegitimacy
in colonial Spanish America / Ann Twinam.
      p.   cm.
    Includes bibliographical references and index.
    ISBN 0-8047-3147-0 (cloth : alk paper)
    1. Illegitimacy—Latin America—History.   2. Unmarried mothers—
Latin America—History.   3. Sex customs—Latin America—History.
4. Masculinity—Latin America—History.   5. Honor—Latin
America—History.   6. Social classes—Latin America—History.
I. Title.
HQ999.L29T89   1999
306.874—dc21   98-45252

♾   This book is printed on acid-free, recycled paper.

Original printing 1999
Last figure below indicates year of this printing:
07 06 05 04 03 02 01 00 99